THE STATE OF
BLACK AMERICA 1992

 Published by **National Urban League, Inc.**

January 1992

THE STATE OF BLACK AMERICA 1992

Editor

Billy J. Tidwell, Ph.D.

Copyright © National Urban League, Inc., 1992
Library of Congress Catalog Card Number 77-647469
ISBN 0-9632071-0-5

Price $24.95

The cover art, "No Place Like Home," is the creation of Louis Delsarte. "No Place Like Home" is the sixth in the "Great Artists" series of limited edition lithographs on African Americans commissioned for the National Urban League through a generous donation from the House of Seagram.

National Urban League, Inc.

The Equal Opportunity Building • 500 East 62nd Street • New York, New York 10021

Founded in 1910, the National Urban League is the premier social service and civil rights organization in America. The League is a nonprofit, community-based organization headquartered in New York City, with 114 affiliates in 34 states and the District of Columbia. The mission of the National Urban League is to assist African Americans in the achievement of social and economic equality. The League implements its mission through advocacy, research, program services, and bridge building.

Dedication

The seventeenth edition of *The State of Black America* is dedicated to the memory of **Whitney Moore Young, Jr.**, the fourth Executive Director of the National Urban League. He was the visionary who propounded a "Domestic Marshall Plan" for America as early as 1963. Mr. Young's concept--the foundation of the League's current "Marshall Plan for America" --called for a massive effort to close "the intolerable economic, social, and educational gap that separates the vast majority of us Negro citizens from other Americans." In 1969, President Lyndon Johnson awarded Mr. Young the Medal of Freedom, the nation's highest civilian honor. His civic activism and commitment thrust him into national and international spotlights. He was in Lagos, Nigeria, attending the annual African-American Dialogue when he drowned on March 11, 1971, at the age of 49.

TABLE OF CONTENTS

About the Authors

DR. ROBERT D. BULLARD
Professor of Sociology
University of California - Riverside

Dr. Robert D. Bullard is a professor of sociology at the University of California - Riverside. He has worked on and conducted research in the areas of urban land use, housing, community development, industrial facility siting, and environmental equity for more than a decade.

Professor Bullard's scholarship and activism have made him one of the leading experts on environmental racism in the nation. He is active on numerous boards and panels, including the Editorial Board of *Capitalism Nature Socialism* and a member of the Environmental Equity Committee (ad hoc) of the Internal Work Group, U.S. Environmental Protection Agency in Washington, DC.

Dr. Bullard has written more than three-dozen articles, monographs, and scholarly papers. The author of four books, he is currently working on a new one with B.H. Wright, *Environmental Justice and People of Color* (Boston: South End Press). His most recent book, *Dumping in Dixie: Race, Class, and Environmental Quality* (Boulder: Westview Press, 1990), has become a standard text in the field. He received the Gustavus Myers Award in 1990 for the Outstanding Book in 1989 on Human Rights in the United States for *In Search of the New South* (Tuscaloosa: University of Alabama Press, 1989).

Professor Bullard earned his B.S. degree in government from Alabama A&M University; his M.A. degree in sociology from Atlanta University; and his Ph.D. degree in sociology from Iowa State University.

DR. HENRY A. COLEMAN
Executive Director
U.S. Advisory Commission on Intergovernmental Relations

Dr. Henry A. Coleman serves as the Executive Director of Government Finance Research at the U.S. Advisory Commission on Intergovernmental Relations (ACIR) in Washington, DC.

Prior to assuming his current responsibilities, Dr. Coleman served as a policy adviser on fiscal, budget, and housing issues for New Jersey Governor James Florio.

Dr. Coleman has extensive experience in economics and intergovernmental relations, having held the positions of the Executive Director of the New Jersey State and Local Expenditure and Revenue Policy Commission (1985-88); the senior economist in the Office of the Chief Economist, U.S. General Accounting Office; and a Brookings Economic Policy Fellow and Visiting Scholar at the U.S. Department of Housing and Urban Development. He was also employed as the assistant director for operations and research in the New Jersey Department of Treasury, Office of State Planning.

Dr. Coleman taught in the Economics Department at Tufts University from 1975-1980.

Dr. Coleman earned his B.A. degree in economics from Morehouse College and his Ph.D. degree in economics from Princeton University.

DR. WILLIAM A. DARITY, JR.
Professor of Economics
University of North Carolina - Chapel Hill

Dr. William A. Darity, Jr. is the Cary C. Boshamer Professor of Economics at the University of North Carolina - Chapel Hill.

His research interests include the causes of inequality among nations, regions, and racial and ethnic groups; the history of economic thought; macroeconomics and monetary theory; and trade and development.

Professor Darity has published more than 80 scholarly articles and written or edited four books. Among the latter: *The Loan Pushers* (with Bobbie L. Horn, Cambridge: Ballinger Publishing, 1988), a study of the role of commercial banks in creating the international debt crisis, and *Race, Radicalism, and Reform* (New Brunswick: Transaction Publications, 1989), an edited volume of essays by Abram Harris, Jr., the first black academic economist in the United States.

Dr. Darity is active in numerous professional organizations; he chairs the board of editors of the *Review of Black Political Economy* and is a member of the editorial board of the *Eastern Economic Journal*. He also serves on the board of the Eastern Economic Association.

Professor Darity earned his B.A. degree, with honors, in economics and political science from Brown University. He did post-undergraduate study in economics at the London School of Economics and Political Science. He received his Ph.D. degree in economics from the Massachusetts Institute of Technology.

SANDRA T. GRAY
Vice President of Leadership and Management
INDEPENDENT SECTOR

Sandra Trice Gray is the Vice President of INDEPENDENT SECTOR, an alliance of 800 voluntary organizations, corporations, and foundations to encourage giving, volunteering, advocacy, and not-for-profit initiatives. She is currently responsible for the Leadership/Management Program and for examining INDEPENDENT SECTOR's possible role in the international arena.

Prior to joining INDEPENDENT SECTOR, Ms. Gray was Executive Director of the National School Volunteer Program. She has also served as Assistant Commissioner, U.S. Department of Education; the Assistant and Policy Advisor to the Undersecretary of Education; and HEW Fellow and Special Assistant to the Secretary of Health, Education and Welfare [now Health and Human Services].

After an extensive career in education at the federal, state, and local levels, Ms. Gray engaged in professional interests and issues related to volunteering; education, business, government, and community partnerships; responsible citizenship; as well as organized volunteer activities outside of the United States.

A recipient of numerous honors and recognitions, Ms. Gray was a member of the President's Committee on Education Partnerships; a delegation of American women leaders to the Soviet Union, sponsored by the Rockefeller Foundation; and was chosen as one of America's Top 100 Black Business and Professional Women.

Ms. Gray has served on several nonprofit boards and commissions. She has published numerous articles on such topics as community involvement, business and education partnerships, leadership and management, and giving and volunteering.

Ms. Gray earned her Bachelor of Arts degree from Philander Smith College (Little Rock, AR) and her Master of Education degree from the University of Massachusetts - Amherst. She is also a Certified Association Executive (CAE), awarded by the American Society of the Association of Executives, and has completed several leadership and management seminars and training programs.

DR. LENNEAL J. HENDERSON
Distinguished Professor of
Government and Public Administration
University of Baltimore

Dr. Lenneal J. Henderson is an expert on fiscal policy. In addition to his professorship, he is a Senior Fellow in the William Donald Schaefer Center for Public Policy and a Henry C. Welcome Fellow at the University of Baltimore. Before assuming his current positions, Dr. Henderson was Head and Professor of Political Science at the University of Tennessee - Knoxville, a senior faculty member at the Federal Institute in Charlottesville, VA, and a professor in the School of Business and Public Administration at Howard University.

Other academic accomplishments include his being a Ford Foundation - National Research Council Postdoctoral Fellow at the Johns Hopkins School of Advanced International Studies, a Kellogg National Fellow, and a Rockefeller Research Fellow.

Professor Henderson has lectured or consulted in sub-Saharan Africa, Egypt, Israel, India, Brazil, Peru, the Caribbean, the Soviet Union, and the People's Republic of China.

He has published or edited five books and numerous articles in many publications, including *The Urban League Review, The Review of Black Political Economy, The Annals, Policy Studies Journal, Howard Law Journal,* and *The Black Scholar.*

Dr. Henderson earned his B.A., M.A., and Ph.D. degrees from the University of California, Berkeley.

DR. ROBERT B. HILL
Director
Institute for Urban Research
Morgan State University

Dr. Robert B. Hill is currently the Director of the Institute for Urban Research at Morgan State University in Baltimore, MD. He is also an Adjunct Fellow at the National Center for Neighborhood Enterprise. Before assuming his present position, he was a research consultant (1986-1988); Senior Research Associate at the Bureau of Social Science Research, Inc. (1981-1986); and Director of Research, The National Urban League, Inc. (1972-1981).

Dr. Hill has taught on the adjunct faculty of the University of Pennsylvania, University of Maryland, Howard University, Morgan State University, Princeton University, New York University, and Fordham University. Dr. Hill has served on several distinguished panels: the U.S. Bureau of the Census Advisory Committee on the Black Population in the 1980 Census; the 1981 White House Conference on Aging; the 1980 White House Conference on Families; and the National Academy of Science's Committee on Child Development Research and Public Policy.

Dr. Hill is a member of the Association of Black Sociologists, the National Economic Association, and the American Statistical Association.

Dr. Hill's publications include "Critical Issues for Black Families by the Year 2000," "Structural Discrimination," "The Black Middle Class Defined," "The Polls and Ethnic Minorities," *Economic Policies and Black Progress, Discrimination and Minority Youth Employment, Informal Adoption Among Black Families, The Strengths of Black Families*, and various articles for the National Urban League's annual *The State of Black America*.

Dr. Hill received his B.A. degree in sociology from the City College of New York and his Ph.D. degree in sociology from Columbia University.

DR. JULIANNE M. MALVEAUX
Economist
Syndicated Columnist

Dr. Julianne M. Malveaux is an economist, a writer, and a syndicated columnist whose weekly column appears nationally in some 20 newspapers through the King Features Syndicate. She is also: a contributing writer for *Essence* magazine; a regular contributor to *Ms.* magazine and *USA Today*; and a weekly contributor to the *San Francisco Sun Reporter*. Her academic and popular writing appears in other magazines, newspapers, and journals. Further, she provides radio and television commentary on sociopolitical issues, especially for CNN's "Crier and Company" and is a talk show host on San Francisco's newstalk station KGO.

As a scholar, Dr. Malveaux has most recently been a member of the visiting faculty at the University of California - Berkeley, in the African American Studies Department. She has worked on the staff of the Council on Economic Advisors; she was a Visiting Research Fellow at the Rockefeller Foundation. She previously held the post of assistant professor of economics at the New School for Social Research and at San Francisco State University. Her research focuses on the labor market and public policy and the impact of such policy on women and minorities. She is co-editor of *Slipping Through the Cracks: The Status of Black Women* (with Margaret C. Simms, New Brunswick: Transaction Publications, 1986); she has also completed a manuscript on the status of black women in the labor market.

Dr. Malveaux is an activist whose community work in San Francisco includes the drafting of citizen initiatives on the divestment of public funds from South Africa. She has also served as the President of the local Black Leadership Forum and the San Francisco Business and Professional Women's Club as well as a board member of the San Francisco NAACP. Nationally, Dr. Malveaux is Vice President of the National Child Labor Committee and a board member of the Center for Policy Alternatives.

Dr. Malveaux's academic credentials include a B.A. degree in economics and urban affairs from Boston College (magna cum laude), an M.A. degree in economics from the same institution, and a Ph.D. degree in economics from the Massachusetts Institute of Technology, specializing in labor, urban, and fiscal economics.

DR. WALTER E. MASSEY
Director
National Science Foundation

Dr. Walter E. Massey, appointed by President George Bush as Director of the National Science Foundation, began his six-year term of office on March 4, 1991. As Director, he is responsible for an agency charged with strengthening the national scientific and engineering research potential and with improving science and engineering education at all levels. He oversees an annual budget exceeding $2.3 billion; he annually awards 13,000-15,000 grants for research in all fields of natural and social sciences and engineering.

Dr. Massey's research has been in the many-body theories of quantum liquids and solids. He has lectured and written on the physics of quantum liquids and solids, the teaching of science and mathematics, and the role of science and technology in a democratic society.

Before his presidential appointment, Dr. Massey was first Professor of Physics then Vice President for Research at the University of Chicago and Director of Argonne National Laboratory, where he formulated, represented, and implemented the university's research policies and relations with industry and federal agencies.

Dr. Massey has served as an associate and then full professor at Brown University and was named Dean of the College in 1975. While at Brown, he was the originator and Director of Inner City Teachers of Science (ICTOS) --a program to educate science teachers for urban schools.

Dr. Massey has been a member of the National Science Board and the board of Directors of the American Association for the Advancement of Science (AAAS); he was also on the Board of Trustees of the Rand Corporation and the MacArthur Foundation. He chaired the board of the Argonne National Laboratory/University of Chicago Development Corporation (ARCH) and served as a member of the boards of Amoco Corporation, First National Bank of Chicago, Tribune Company, Motorola, and Materials Corporation. He is a past trustee of Brown University and a past member of the Physics Department Visiting Committee of Massachusetts Institute of Technology (MIT). He was vice president of the American Physical Society, president of AAAS, and most recently served as a member of President Bush's Council of Advisers on Science and Technology.

The holder of numerous honorary degrees, Dr. Massey earned his B.S. degree in physics and mathematics from Morehouse College and his M.S. and Ph.D. degrees in physics from Washington University, St. Louis, Missouri.

DR. SHIRLEY M. McBAY
President
Quality Education for Minorities Network

Dr. Shirley M. McBay assumed the position of President of the Quality Education for Minorities (QEM) Network on July 1, 1990, following ten years as Dean for Student Affairs at the Massachusetts Institute of Technology (MIT) and three years as Director of the Quality Education for Minorities Project.

The QEM Network is a nonprofit organization established to help implement the recommendations contained in the QEM Project's action plan for providing quality education for minorities.

Prior to serving as a member of the MIT administration, Dr. McBay served as Program Manager/Director in the Science Education Directorate of the National Science Foundation and as a member of the Spelman College faculty in Atlanta, GA.

At the National Science Foundation, Dr. McBay directed two national programs aimed toward increasing the participation of minority students in science and engineering. The purpose of the first program, The Resource Centers in Science and Engineering--which she helped to launch with funding and support from the U.S. Congress and the National Science Foundation--was to establish regional resource centers based at universities to facilitate access to science and engineering by minority and low-income students.

While at Spelman, Dr. McBay held various academic positions, including Professor of Mathematics, Department Head, Division Chairman, and Associate Academic Dean.

Dr. McBay has been and is a member of several advisory boards to projects related to the education of women, minorities, and persons with disabilities. She has written and lectured extensively on issues specifically related to the participation of members of these groups in science and engineering.

Dr. McBay earned her B.A. degree--summa cum laude--from Paine College, at the age of 19; she earned her M.S. degrees in chemistry and mathematics from Atlanta University, and her Ph.D. degree in mathematics from the University of Georgia.

SYLVESTER MURRAY
Director
Public Management Program
The Urban Center
Cleveland State University

Sylvester Murray is the Director of the Public Management Program, The Urban Center, Cleveland State University. In this post, he is responsible for providing consulting, technical assistance, and management development training to government units and nonprofit organizations. His teaching and professional specialty is municipal finance.

Prior to his current duties, Mr. Murray was the Manager of Government Consulting for Coopers and Lybrand. He has held the post of City Manager for the cities of San Diego, Cincinnati, Ann Arbor, and Inkster (MI).

Mr. Murray is the Past President of the American Society for Public Administration and the International City Management Association. He is currently a Fellow of the National Academy of Public Administration.

Mr. Murray served on President Jimmy Carter's Committee on Balanced National Growth and the National Research Council's Urban Policy Committee. In 1985, he won the National Public Service Award.

Mr. Murray earned his B.A. degree in history from Lincoln University; he holds masters' degrees in governmental administration and economics from the Wharton School of the University of Pennsylvania and Eastern Michigan University, respectively. He is a graduate of the Federal Executive Institute.

DR. SAMUEL L. MYERS, JR.

Director, Afro-American Studies Program
Professor, Afro-American Studies and Economics
University of Maryland - College Park

Dr. Samuel L. Myers, Jr., is the Director of the Afro-American Studies Program at the University of Maryland - College Park. He is also Professor of Afro-American Studies and Economics on the same campus. In his present capacities, Dr. Myers is helping to train future policy analysts who can bring superior problem-solving skills to minority communities. The Afro-American Studies Program, which provides technical assistance and research support to state and local governments and community-based organizations, is one of the only academic programs in the nation combining technical training in public policy analysis with a comprehensive analysis of the problems of the black community.

Professor Myers is an economist specializing in the analysis of the impacts of social policies on the poor. He has pioneered in the use of applied econometric techniques: to examine racial disparities in the criminal justice system, to detect illegal discrimination in consumer credit markets, to assess the impacts of welfare on family stability, and to evaluate the effectiveness of government transfers in reducing poverty.

Dr. Myers has served as a Senior Staff Economist at the Federal Trade Commission; taught economics at the University of Texas - Austin, and at the Graduate School of Public and International Affairs, the University of Pittsburgh. He has been a research fellow at the Institute for Research on Poverty, the University of Wisconsin, the National Institute of Justice, and the DuBois Institute of Harvard University.

Professor Myers is the past president of the National Economics Association and a member of the editorial boards of the *Review of Black Political Economy, Social Science Quarterly*, and *Evaluation Review*.

Dr. Myers has been active in the attempts to translate academic research results into policies relevant to black communities.

Dr. Myers received his undergraduate training at Morgan State University, and earned his Ph.D. degree in economics from the Massachusetts Institute of Technology.

DR. DIANNE M. PINDERHUGHES

Professor of Political Science and Afro-American Studies
University of Illinois, Urbana-Champaign

Dr. Dianne M. Pinderhughes is Professor of Political Science and Afro-American Studies at the University of Illinois, Urbana-Champaign. Her current research focuses on the impact of civil rights interest groups on the development of voting rights policy.

A much-sought-after lecturer on the political history of blacks and women, Dr. Pinderhughes is the author of *Race and Ethnicity in Chicago Politics, A Re-examination of Pluralist Theory* (University of Illinois Press, 1987) and co-editor with Linda F. Williams of *Race, Class, and the New Urban Politics* (Chatham House, forthcoming). She has also published "The Case of African Americans in the Persian Gulf: The Intersection of American Foreign Policy and Military Policy with Domestic Employment Policy in the United States" in *The State of Black America 1991*; "The Articulation of Black Interests by Black, Civil Rights, Professional, and Religious Organizations in the Jackson Campaign" in *The Social and Political Implications of the Jesse Jackson Presidential Campaign*, edited by Lorenzo Morris; and numerous other articles and book reviews on racial issues, voting rights politics, and urban policy.

Dr. Pinderhughes has been named a University Scholar (1988-1991) by the University of Illinois. She is the Past President of the National Conference of Black Political Scientists.

Before assuming her current duties at the University of Illinois, Dr. Pinderhughes was Assistant Professor of Government at Dartmouth College, Visiting Assistant Professor at Howard University, Guest Scholar at the Brookings Institution, and a Postdoctoral Fellow at the Center for Afro-American Studies at the University of California at Los Angeles.

Dr. Pinderhughes earned her academic degrees in political science--her Ph.D. and M.A. degrees from the University of Chicago, and her B.A. degree from Albertus Magnus College in New Haven, CT.

DR. DAVID H. SWINTON
Dean of the School of Business
Professor of Economics
Jackson State University

Dr. David H. Swinton, Dean of the School of Business and Professor of Economics at Jackson State University, is a nationally known economist and education administrator. He is recognized as a leading expert on the economics of social policy and minority groups and is often invited to testify before the Congress and national commissions.

Dean Swinton has implemented a new quality assurance program at Jackson State to ensure that all graduates have the skills, competencies, and attitudes required for success in corporate America.

The former Director of Research for the Black Economic Research

Center in New York City, Dr. Swinton has also lectured at City University of New York; State University of New York - Stony Brook; and the Urban Institute in Washington, DC.

Dr. Swinton is also the former Director of the Southern Center for Studies in Public Policy and Professor of Economics at Clark College in Atlanta. While at the policy center, he was the principal fund-raiser and architect of the research program.

Dean Swinton has published several books, monographs, and major research reports, as well as scores of articles. He is active in the profession and has served on the board or has been an officer of numerous professional organizations and journals, including a stint as President of the National Economics Association.

Dr. Swinton earned his Ph.D. and M.A. degrees in economics from Harvard University, and his B.A. degree in economics--with honors, including Phi Beta Kappa--from New York University.

DR. BILLY J. TIDWELL
Director of Research
The National Urban League, Inc.

Dr. Billy J. Tidwell is the Director of Research for the National Urban League, Inc., a position he has held since 1985.

A practitioner of public policy research for almost 20 years, Dr. Tidwell was formerly a Senior Researcher with Mathematica Policy Research, a private consulting firm in Princeton, NJ. He also served in that capacity with the Gary Income Maintenance Experiment in Gary, IN, in association with Indiana University.

Dr. Tidwell has authored numerous reports on the socioeconomic conditions of African Americans, including *Beyond the Margin: Toward Economic Well-Being for African Americans; Stalling Out: The Relative Progress of African Americans*; and *The Price: A Study of the Costs of Racism in America*. The latter study includes an analysis of the impact of racism on the national economy. Dr. Tidwell also authored the League's recent report, *Playing to Win: A Marshall Plan for America*, which outlines a strategy for improving the nation's economic competitiveness.

Dr. Tidwell is Editor of *The State of Black America 1992* and is a frequent contributor to edited volumes, journals, and other publications.

Dr. Tidwell earned his B.A. and M.S.W. degrees from the University of California at Berkeley and his Ph.D. degree in social welfare from the University of Wisconsin at Madison.

DR. BERNARD C. WATSON
President and Chief Executive Officer
The William Penn Foundation

Dr. Bernard C. Watson is the President and Chief Executive Officer of The William Penn Foundation in Philadelphia, PA.

He assumed this position after a distinguished career as an educator--a career in which he served as a teacher and administrator in the public schools of Indiana; Deputy Superintendent of the Philadelphia public schools; and Professor of Urban Studies and Urban Education and Academic Vice President of Temple University.

President Lyndon Johnson appointed Dr. Watson to the National Council on Education Professions Development; he subsequently served as the Council's Vice Chairman.

President Jimmy Carter appointed Dr. Watson to the National Council on Educational Research. In addition, he has served on numerous boards and commissions, including the Philadelphia City Planning Commission, World Affairs Council, Council on Foreign Relations, Public Interest Law Center, and the National Urban Coalition.

Dr. Watson currently serves as Senior Vice Chairman of the Board of the National Urban League, Vice Chairman of the Pennsylvania Convention Center Authority, Vice Chairman of the Pennsylvania Council on the Arts, Secretary of the New Jersey Academy for Aquatic Sciences, and the boards of First Fidelity Bancorporation and Fidelity Bank, Comcast Corporation, and Comcast Cablevision.

Dr. Watson is the author of a book, *In Spite of the System*, 14 monographs, chapters in 14 books, 100 career folios, and more than 35 articles in professional journals. He is a member of the American Philosophical Society.

Among his many honors are a graduate seminar room furnished and named in his honor at Temple University and a cash award for the best social science dissertation in the College of Education. He is the recipient of more than 100 awards, including 13 honorary degrees.

Dr. Watson earned his bachelor's degree at Indiana University, his master's degree from the University of Illinois, and his Ph.D. degree from the University of Chicago; he has done postdoctoral work at Harvard University.

Black America, 1991: An Overview

John E. Jacob
President and Chief Executive Officer
National Urban League, Inc.

By any standards, 1991 will go down in history as a momentous year. The final, irrevocable end of the Cold War; the destruction of communism in the Soviet Union, indeed, the breakup of the Soviet Union itself; the Gulf War and the consequent dominance of U.S. power--all events our grandchildren will read about in their school history texts.

But the wave of triumphalism that engulfed the nation in the wake of those events was soured by the realization that the new world order of the future will be shaped by national economic and social strengths, and that the United States enters this new era with significant deficits in those areas.

Our international relations were often driven by activist policies implemented with decisiveness. But the domestic issues that will ultimately determine our place in the world were victims of deep neglect tempered by political opportunism. The stark contrast between our activist foreign policy and the lack of a cohesive domestic policy is a fault line exposing America's vulnerability.

The most significant aspect of 1991 is not what we *did* do, but what we did *not* do--develop a domestic policy adequate to the nation's critical needs. That terrible vacuum in domestic policy is perhaps the most salient aspect of an event-filled year, one that threatens to subvert our future.

Even as we celebrated international triumphs, critical issues such as the deepening recession, widespread poverty, mounting racial and ethnic tensions, substandard schools, deteriorating cities and a crumbling infrastructure, restricted access to health care, and many others were largely ignored by public policymakers. By year's end, the White House was coming under mounting criticism for its neglect of domestic policy, as a recession-wracked nation sought to determine just what went wrong and how to fix it.

It became apparent that the frenzied go-go years of the 1980s did not put the nation on the road toward permanent prosperity. Rather, a decade of deepened social divisions, growing inequality, private sector excesses, and government indifference weakened America's ability to compete in the global economy.

America retained its dubious distinction of being the industrial nation with the greatest amount of economic inequality. In the 1980s, the richest 1

1

percent of the population nearly doubled its income, while most families either made modest gains or lost ground. One study found that the top 1 percent of earners had almost as much after-tax income as the 100 million Americans in the bottom 40 percent of the income ladder.[1] And the Census Bureau says that, in constant dollars, the median family income in 1990 after Social Security taxes was *below* the median family income in 1973.[2]

But even such startling evidence of eroding living standards and growing inequality masks the deteriorating position of African Americans and the poor. Dr. David H. Swinton considers this issue in-depth in his essay, "The Economic Status of African Americans: Limited Ownership and Persistent Inequality." Drs. William A. Darity, Jr., and Samuel L. Myers, Jr., examine other aspects of this issue in "Racial Earnings Inequality into the 21st Century." Let me add to some of the salient points these distinguished authors propound.

The Census Bureau reported that 2.1 million more people became poor in 1990, and that figure may double when the 1991 figures are reported, thanks to a recession of deepening severity. Some 33.6 million Americans were living in poverty, driving the national poverty rate to 13.5 percent, from 12.8 percent in 1989. The black poverty rate, at 31.9 percent, was triple the white rate.[3]

More devastating, child poverty has become endemic. An estimated 50 percent of all black children under age six live in poverty. Nationwide, 5.1 million children of all races under age six live in families falling below the understated poverty line. Another 4.2 million children were in families just above the line, but still severely disadvantaged, as indicated by their eligibility for such social programs as supplemental food aid.[4]

Another neglected aspect of the growth in poverty is the explosion of what has been called "hyper-poverty"--the number of people who survive on incomes less than half of the official poverty level. It is estimated that over 12 million people fall into this "poorest of the poor" category, an increase of almost 50 percent since 1979. Again, while there are far more whites than blacks in this, as in other poverty categories, it is African Americans who are disproportionately affected, especially children. African American children living in families whose incomes ranged between 50 and 100 percent of the official poverty line fell by 10 percent between 1979 and 1989. But in that same period, there was a 52 percent rise in the number of black children in families surviving on incomes less than half the poverty line![5]

African American family income lagged far behind white income as well. Curiously, year-to-year figures showed a small gain in the ratio of African American family income to white family income, but that was the result of a decline in white incomes, not a rise in black incomes. That atypical phenomenon still left the typical black family with only 58 percent of the income of the typical white family. With the recession deepening and spreading, it is likely the black-white ratio widened further in 1991.

Certainly, the recession's effect on African American employment was becoming more apparent. Comparing the third quarter of 1991 to the same period in 1990, the official black unemployment rate jumped from 11.7 percent to 12.1 percent. In addition to the 1,666,000 African Americans who were officially unemployed, nearly one-and-a-quarter million more were classified by the Labor Department as "discouraged workers"; i.e., people not actively searching for jobs because they believe no work is available. Discouraged workers are not counted in the labor force or in the official unemployment statistics. The National Urban League's Hidden Unemployment Index, which adds involuntary part-time workers and discouraged workers to the official definition of the unemployed, stood at 22.2 percent for black workers at the end of the third quarter, while for white workers the figure was 11.3 percent.[6]

With traditional safety net programs shredded, many families were left in dire straits. Unemployment insurance covered fewer of the unemployed than in the past, and the abandonment of extended jobless aid for the long-term unemployed forced many families to the wall. The number of Americans receiving welfare aid and food stamps increased to record highs, even as many states cut their own human services programs and reduced staff available to process welfare and food stamp claims.[7]

Those severe cutbacks by state and city governments reflected one of the glaring lies of the Reagan era--the pretense that government was being cut. What actually happened was that federal government spending escalated, but it shifted to higher interest outlays for the mounting federal deficit and to drastically higher military spending. Meanwhile, responsibilities formerly assumed by the federal government were moved down the governmental ladder, to state and local governments, whose strained resources could not support them. As a result, most states enacted steep tax increases in 1991, and major urban centers, such as New York and Philadelphia, experienced fiscal crises.

Already hit hard by private sector layoffs, many cities are trimming their payrolls as well. In addition to having a negative effect on the quality of life in many cities, these cutbacks have serious implications for the black economy and for the fragile black middle class, since government employment has been a major source of jobs for African Americans, especially for workers in managerial and administrative positions.

This situation was compounded by the continuing crime wave of discrimination that limited opportunities for African Americans. Studies were released in 1991 documenting that black jobseekers were more likely than whites to be discriminated against; that blacks had less access to health care; that mortgage lenders routinely discriminated against black and His-

3

panic homebuyers; and that blacks and the disadvantaged were prime victims of home equity loan scams.

Such discrimination concentrated minority energies on passage of the Civil Rights Act, which would have reversed several U.S. Supreme Court decisions that encouraged employers to abandon minority hiring efforts and made it more difficult for victims of job discrimination to seek redress. The Administration had long labeled the Civil Rights Act a "quota" bill that would force employers to hire unqualified minorities and women in preference to white men. The naked political appeal of the quota charge drove much of the opposition to the civil rights bill. Finally, thanks to a bipartisan coalition spearheaded by Senators John Danforth (R-MO) and Edward Kennedy (D-MA), the Administration agreed to support a compromise bill that largely embodied proposals it had fought.

What caused this reversal? One theory holds that the White House owed a political favor to Senator Danforth and other moderate Republicans who led the fight to confirm Clarence Thomas as Associate Justice of the U.S. Supreme Court.

Whatever the role of the Thomas nomination struggle in the Administration's decision to accept a compromise civil rights bill, that decision may have also been spurred by fears that the Administration's actions were encouraging racism.

The Administration was still trying to explain away the 1988 Willie Horton ads that many condemned as racist. An overstated presidential attack on pro-Israel lobbyists generated masses of anti-semitic hate mail in support of the stance, surprising and alarming the White House. Political strategists suggested that continuing the anti-quota rhetoric would be seen by the public as pandering to racism, a politically dangerous perception at a time when the Administration and the Republican Party were trying to distance themselves from former Nazi and Klan leader, David Duke, who was running for governor of Louisiana as a Republican.

The rise of David Duke strips away the veil of American racism and exposes it to full view. Had Duke donned his Klan hood and waved *Mein Kampf* at election rallies, he would have been dismissed as a lunatic. But in his newly adopted guise of a populist conservative, he mouthed sentiments and code words made familiar through long usage by national leaders, making his sewer ideology appear respectably mainstream.

Because of the appeal of racially divisive campaigns and the continued prominence of the ambitious ex-Klan leader, the Duke phenomenon cannot be dismissed as a transient or localized exception to national norms. It is a wake-up call to Americans to reexamine our fundamental beliefs and principles and to reject appeals to the dark, vicious side of our history. It cannot be taken lightly by national leadership, which must clearly stamp Duke and his followers as outside the pale of legitimacy, and definitively reject their attempts to subvert a major political party and to dominate the democratic process.

It will not do to dismiss the clear and present danger racism poses to our nation or to explain the Duke vote away as "middle-class anger." While the economic squeeze on working people has sparked frustrations that find an outlet in anti-establishment candidates, it is dangerous to ignore the purely racial aspects of what is, after all, a barely hidden appeal to racism.

We should recall Lyndon Johnson's explanation of the interaction between race and class in American history and politics: "I'll tell you what's at the bottom of it. If you can convince the lowest white man that he's better than the best colored man, he won't notice you picking his pocket. Hell, give him somebody to look down on, and he'll empty his pockets for you."[8]

Duke exploited that deep vein of racism in our country--but his threat is domesticated by blaming it all on "middle-class anger." And anger about class-based policies does not necessarily translate into racism. Thus, a long-time supporter of civil rights, Senator Harris Wofford (D-PA), was elected because his liberal positions on economic recovery and national health insurance addressed major concerns of working people of all races. A major factor in his victory, neglected by the "experts," was the voters' rejection of his opponent, former Attorney General Dick Thornburgh, who was a leading opponent of the civil rights bill.

That suggests an important positive in the tangled relationship between race and politics: while a Duke can exploit widespread racist feelings, most Americans are repelled by racism in all its forms.

Therefore, candidates like Senator Wofford can mine the rich lode of votes available to political leaders calling for racial justice. It may be frayed and tattered from a decade of backward national policies, but there is still a mainstream consensus in favor of civil rights and social fairness.

From the black perspective, the "middle-class anger" theory for Duke's support rings false. We have been subjected to four centuries of slavery, oppression, discrimination, and inequality; our middle class has been subjected to tokenism and glass ceilings. Our resentments encompass not merely vague feelings of no longer being preferred over other races, but widespread discrimination and daily pinpricks of racially inspired slights and slurs. If the privileged white middle class is so burdened that it is driven to support an admirer of Hitler, to what extremes should the disadvantaged black middle class be driven?

In fact, the continued moderation of African Americans and their continued loyalty to American ideals and values suggest an important lesson for white America. Oppressed people have always been susceptible to extremist appeals, and African Americans have not been totally immune. Our history has included temporarily popular extremist movements and figures, right up to the present day, as demagogic leaders who reflect the anger and frustration of ghetto life surface in many communities. But the overwhelming majority of African Americans are solidly in the mainstream of American political thinking and reject righteous anger as an excuse for extremism.

If American politics are deformed by scapegoating minorities and the poor and by channeling anger at economic inequality into racial and economic hatred, then this nation is doomed. For we have become the world's most diverse society, a nation of many peoples and cultures that can prosper only if we learn to live in harmony with each other. Dr. Bernard C. Watson eloquently examines this issue in his essay, "The Demographic Revolution: Diversity in 21st Century America."

Just how difficult that is can be seen not only in the white-black confrontations, such as the revolting incident in which Los Angeles police officers wantonly beat a black motorist while joyfully shouting racist expletives, but also in local inter-ethnic feuding.

In 1991, there were serious incidents of friction in some cities between African Americans and Koreans, between Hispanics and blacks, between Arabs and blacks, between Hasidic Jews and blacks in New York's Crown Heights section. In Washington, DC, African Americans were in the extraordinary position of being seen as the dominant power structure. Black police and city officials moved swiftly to deal with complaints by South American immigrants about aggressive policing and cultural insensitivity, but the riot in the nation's capital last summer is an indication that the path to inter-ethnic harmony is a difficult one.

The African American community is challenged to find ways to resolve these culture clashes, which is a difficult burden on a community beleaguered by economic hardships and a host of social ills. There is an ever-present danger that the just resentment at a system that limits our opportunities and condemns so many of us to poverty will be channeled into feuding with other ethnic groups, many of whom suffer similar injustices. That cannot be allowed to happen, for the disadvantaged of all races and ethnic backgrounds have a common interest in joining together to help move our society to recognize its diversity and to provide equal opportunities for all in a growing economy.

The strengths of America's diversity were best seen in the Persian Gulf War. Almost half of the fighting forces massed in the desert were women, African Americans, and other minorities. They were led, and led magnificently, by a black man--General Colin Powell, Chairman of the Joint Chiefs of Staff. The war demonstrated to the nation that the armed forces is the most integrated institution in the nation, more integrated than the churches that preach brotherhood or the corporations that preach teamwork.

6

And the Gulf War also suggested to many Americans that if we applied the same will and resources to protect our domestic interests as we did to protect our foreign interests, we would move further along the road to a stronger, more equal, more competitive society and economy. Because Operation Desert Storm was not matched by an Operation Urban Storm--an all-out attack on the nation's social and economic problems--America is ill-prepared to meet the challenges of the future.

Our crumbling public infrastructure, failing schools, and deteriorating cities weaken our ability to compete against economic rivals who pour resources into developing an advanced infrastructure and into educating their young people for the skills needed in an Information Age. While they have been investing heavily in their futures, we have been disinvesting in ours. Sylvester Murray discusses the infrastructure investment issue in his article, "Clear and Present Danger: The Decay of America's Physical Infrastructure," while Dr. Robert D. Bullard examines some of the adverse consequences of neglected infrastructure on African Americans and their communities in "Urban Infrastructure: Social, Environmental, and Health Risks to African Americans."

Federal investment in developing the nation's human resources, its technology, and its physical capital amounted to 3 percent of the gross national product (GNP) in 1978, and only 1.8 percent in 1989. If those 1989 expenditures were increased by 1.2 percent of the GNP to match the 1978 ratio, we would have spent $65 billion more on investments in our future. Federal investments in education and training averaged about 0.9 percent of the GNP in the years 1976-1981 and slightly more than half of that since. Federal nondefense research and development investments are running at less than half of their share of the GNP in the late 1960s.[9]

As economist Robert Heilbroner has observed: "For something like twenty years the condition of our infrastructure . . . has been steadily deteriorating for lack of adequate investment."[10] That has had a devastating effect on productivity and on the health of the private sector.

The persistent disinvestment in activities essential to economic productivity and growth has placed the nation at a gross competitive disadvantage. Surely, it is a factor in the findings of a *New York Times*/CBS News poll taken in the fall of 1991 that found almost two-thirds of Americans saying that "things" in the country have "pretty seriously gotten off on the wrong track."[11]

The National Urban League's proposal for a Marshall Plan for America, which lays out the case for the United States to invest in our human and physical capital to become more productive, was published in 1991 and stimulated intense interest among citizens and policymakers. The author of that publication, Dr. Billy J. Tidwell, summarizes the elements of the plan in his incisive chapter, "Serving the National Interest: A Marshall Plan for

America." While this is a long-term national economic investment plan, it would result in an immediate economic boost to a recession-wracked economy and to increased employment opportunities through skills training opportunities and targeted jobs in infrastructure programs.[12]

The end of the Cold War brought with it the "peace dividend" of sharply reduced military outlays now available for long-term economic investments. Unfortunately, the bandwagon effect of the "middle-class anger" theory triumphed over common sense, and at year's end, lawmakers were rushing to support another round of tax cuts.

That would be a mistake. The United States is the least taxed of the major industrial nations. Our problem is not too much taxes but what we do with the tax revenues we do collect. Over the past decade, we poured over two trillion dollars into military expenditures while our economic rivals were spending their tax dollars to build their human and physical capacity to outproduce us. We spend more per day on a Stealth bomber than we do on Head Start; more on the savings-and-loan bailout than on grants to state and local governments; more on tax deductions for homeowners than on low-income housing.

Given such a gross misallocation of resources, it would be foolhardy to repeat the mistake of the early 1980s by starving government programs that strengthen the foundations for future economic growth. The peace dividend represents a major opportunity to divert resources away from unnecessary military spending to investments in our nation's competitiveness. Dr. Lenneal J. Henderson addresses this issue and suggests other investment options in his article, "Public Investment for Public Good: Needs, Benefits, and Financing Options."

The immediate prospects for such policies are questionable. Congress is concerned with currying favor by cutting taxes and appears unlikely to initiate major domestic programs, especially since it tied its own hands with a long-term budget deal that prevents switching resources from military to domestic needs. And the Administration has showed no interest in domestic policy, other than unveiling a national education policy that is long on rhetoric, short on resources, and backs sweeping school choice programs that could severely weaken the public schools. Read Dr. Shirley McBay's timely chapter, "The Condition of African American Education: Changes and Challenges," to discover some solutions to these problems.

Yet there is an urgent need for national leadership to develop policies that address America's critical needs. The continuing failure to do so places the nation in jeopardy. America's leaders must rise above short-term political considerations to develop visionary, effective national policies.

The "vision thing" is often derided, but all successful nations are driven by a vision of where they want to be and by policies designed to help get them there. Absent a public policy roadmap that helps to guide us to the desired destination of lasting economic strength and social cohesiveness, America is in danger of continuing her aimless drift into second-class status and intergroup divisiveness.

That is why the disastrous public policy vacuum must be filled in 1992 by vigorous debate that focuses on the appropriate policies required to meet our national goals. A national presidential election campaign is the proper forum for a debate on such vital issues as the Urban League's Marshall Plan for America, national health insurance, job creation, economic development, urban revitalization, and ending poverty, among many others. Several of our scholars--including Dr. Walter E. Massey, Dr. Robert B. Hill, Dr. Henry A. Coleman, Sandra T. Gray, and Dr. Dianne M. Pinderhughes--collectively offer a framework for this debate in their respective chapters.

But the social strains in our society also offer politicians the tempting alternative of stoking the fires of ideological and ethnic divisiveness. That irresponsible path must be fought by African Americans, minorities, and all concerned Americans.

In 1992, we must press the candidates to support policies that lead to racial parity, economic growth, and social peace. We must reject campaigns built around sound bites and code words. We must ask those who wish to lead us to tell us *where* they want to lead us--their vision of our future--and the public policies they will adopt to achieve that vision. For more on this directive, consider Dr. Julianne M. Malveaux's compelling essay, "The Parity Imperative: Civil Rights, Economic Justice, and the New American Dilemma."

The Urban League's Marshall Plan for America is a plan that candidates should turn to, for it addresses America's most urgent economic issues and supplies a vision of a competitive nation comfortable with diversity.

The state of Black America in 1992 mirrors the state of the nation as a whole in many ways--a nation caught in a tangle of recession and racial *dis*advantage, but poised for a real breakthrough if America's leadership rejects racial divisiveness and adopts policies, such as the Marshall Plan for America, that can revive our economy and create opportunities for all.

This seventeenth edition of *The State of Black America*, like previous ones, contributes to the nation's awareness of the reality of life within Black America and to the decision-making process in 1992. We express our gratitude to the authors.

Serving the National Interest:
A Marshall Plan for America

Billy J. Tidwell, Ph.D.

INTRODUCTION

Led by high rates of unemployment, business failure, and personal bankruptcy, the hardships occasioned by the most recent recession have been pronounced and widespread. At this writing, there continues to be great anxiety about the prospects for economic recovery, and, indeed, the outcome is highly uncertain. However, concern about the condition of the economy should not be limited to these immediate problems and adversities. Some longer-term developments may pose even more serious threats to the nation's economic well-being and the quality of life of the average American family.

The central issue is economic competitiveness. The central problem is that America in recent decades has lost her competitive position in the global economy. The central task before us is to reverse the decline.

There can be no doubt that our most vital national interests are at stake, and the threat to these interests mounts as world economic competition intensifies. Established industrialized nations, such as Japan and Germany, clearly are determined to press the competitive advances they have achieved, while other developing economies have signaled that they intend to become forces to be reckoned with in the global economic order of the 21st century. America must quickly and forthrightly respond to this rapidly changing environment.

How do we do it? How do we successfully meet the challenge of competitiveness and move the economy forward? Although the problem is complex, the key requirement is to increase economic productivity; that is, to raise the efficiency with which American workers produce goods and services. Realizing productivity objectives, in turn, requires that we improve our human resources and the physical infrastructure that supports economic activity. How well we produce as a nation is chiefly determined by the quality of the people and facilities the economy has at its disposal.

The National Urban League's Marshall Plan for America recognizes the imperatives by calling for a sustained program of strategic investment in the nation's human and physical capital.[1] While designed to benefit the nation as a whole, the program promises uncommon benefits to the African Ameri-

11

can community, inasmuch as it stresses a targeted investment strategy. The emphasis on targeting is based on several considerations:

- African Americans are comprising a growing share of the U.S. population and its work force. This demographic change means that they could be the critical human resources of the future.
- African Americans continue to experience exceptional disadvantages with respect to the human capital requirements of the changing economy.
- The urban centers in which African Americans remain heavily concentrated are also the areas in which their educational and skills deficits are most prevalent and pronounced.
- The urban centers having large African American populations are the areas that have seen the greatest degree of deterioration of our physical infrastructure.

Thus, in this instance, in the all-important matter of economic productivity and competitiveness, the nation's interests are tightly interwoven with the needs and interests of African Americans. This interdependence and related issues are discussed more fully below.

THE LOSS OF COMPETITIVENESS

Just how much of a competitiveness problem does America really have? After all, the U.S. economy generates about $5 trillion in goods and services per year, which easily translates into the largest gross national product (GNP) in the world. In 1990, our GNP was more than a third larger than Japan's, more than twice the size of Germany's, and almost quadruple the United Kingdom's GNP.[2] Likewise, we create more jobs than our chief international competitors. Between 1979 and 1988, the U.S. economy generated 16.1 million new jobs, posting a job creation rate--i.e., the percentage of new jobs relative to total employment--of 16.3 percent. The job creation rate for Japan during the same period was 9.8 percent; West Germany's was 4.9 percent; Italy's was 4.7 percent; and the United Kingdom attained a job creation rate of just 3.4 percent.[3]

It is also worth noting that the wages of U.S. workers, in terms of purchasing power, are the highest in the world. The same is true for per capita income. Between 1973 and 1988, our per capita income, adjusting for purchasing power, was 41 percent higher than Japan's, 31 percent higher than West Germany's, 42 percent higher than Italy's, 33 percent higher than the United Kingdom's, and 32 percent higher than per capita income in France.[4]

Add to these advantages the fact that the 1980s brought the longest sustained economic recovery in the nation's history, and it is understandable why some might view skeptically claims about low U.S. competitiveness and dire forecasts regarding our role in the changing global marketplace. Nonetheless, there are conditions that hamper present functioning of the economy and trends that portend serious problems in the future.

For one thing, the United States has amassed huge and chronic budget and trade deficits, which have impaired our financial strength and moved us from being the world's largest creditor to the largest debtor nation. The federal budget deficit for the 1990 fiscal year was $220.4 billion, and the Office of Management and Budget has projected a much larger deficit of $348 billion for 1991. Since 1980, the federal debt has tripled, and this does not include the estimated $250 billion in borrowing needed to finance the savings-and-loan bailout.[5]

The trade deficit in 1990 was $101 billion, in current dollars, while the projected figure for 1991 is still unacceptably high at $65 billion. Our inferior trading position did not emerge overnight. Thus, in 1951, the U.S. economy accounted for nearly a third of the world trade among the top 16 industrialized nations. By 1971, the U.S. share had dwindled to just 18 percent.[6] A decade ago, in 1980, the United States was a net lender to the rest of the world in the amount of $106 billion. By 1990, we were $500 billion in debt to other nations.[7]

Uppermost in this assessment is the fact that the U.S. economy has experienced a dramatic decline in the rate of productivity growth. America's productivity growth rate in the 1980s was 1.1 percent, sharply lower than the 3.1 percent average in the 1960s. As Table 1 shows, other nations have achieved substantial gains on this measure of economic performance. Over the extended period 1960-1988, the annual average productivity growth rate of our economy was surpassed by that of Japan, Italy, France, West Germany, and the United Kingdom. The success of Japan has been particularly remarkable. In 1960, Japan's productivity rate was just 29 percent that of the United States. This figure grew to 56 percent in 1970, 66 percent in 1980, and 75 percent in 1989.[8]

Table 1

Annual Productivity Growth Rates
for Selected Countries, 1960-1988

Country	Growth rate (percent)
Japan	5.2
Italy	3.8
France	3.1
West Germany	2.9
United Kingdom	2.1
United States	1.2

Source: Economic Policy Institute.

Although American wage rates still rank relatively high, the decline in productivity has significantly slowed real wage growth in this country (see Table 2). The average annual wage increase for American manufacturing workers between 1979 and 1988 was a mere 0.3 percent, as against 2.1 percent for their counterparts in Japan and France; 2.4 percent for those in West Germany; and 2.2 percent for workers in the United Kingdom. The only reason U.S. wages grew at all was because of extraordinary increases among certain categories of workers; viz., supervisors and managers. Production and nonsupervisory workers in manufacturing saw their wages drop by 0.4 percent per year during the decade. The United States was the only country in which production workers lost wages, while their counterparts elsewhere saw increases.[9] Thus, other countries have been closing the gap in buying power. In 1950, for example, a West German family averaged only 40 percent of the earnings of an American family. By 1986, the proportion had climbed to 84 percent.[10]

Table 2

Annual Wage Growth for Manufacturing Workers in Selected Countries, 1979-1988

Country	All workers	Wage Growth (percent) Production workers
Japan	2.1	0.9
France	2.1	2.2
West Germany	2.4	1.9
United Kingdom	2.2	1.9
United States	0.3	-0.4

Source: Economic Policy Institute.

Mirroring the sluggish growth in wages, family income in the United States has stagnated, increasing at an annual rate of just 0.3 percent between 1979 and 1988, compared to 0.9 percent between 1973 and 1979, and 2.7 percent in the 1967-1973 period. At the same time, however, income inequality has widened. Between 1977 and 1988, families in the upper fifth of the income distribution enjoyed a 34 percent gain in after-tax income and now account for about half of the national total. On the other hand, families in the lowest fifth of the distribution actually lost income during the period; they now have just a 5 percent share of total income.[11] Thus, the rich have gotten richer and the poor poorer. There is more income inequality in the United States than in any other industrial nation, and the condition is worsening.

The data confirm that our record on critical measures of economic performance has deteriorated, while other nations have progressed in the same areas. America is far from being the undisputed economic superpower it once was. Moreover, the prospects for the future are less than optimistic. This observation keys on the fact that the U.S. economy's expansion in recent decades has been propelled by the entry of new workers into the labor force. The civilian labor force grew by 16 percent in the 1960s, 26 percent in the 1970s, and 15 percent in the 1980s. The coming of age of baby boomers and a sharp rise in the labor supply of women were largely

15

responsible for these increases. By force of sheer numbers, the additional workers stimulated the production of goods and services. Real GNP growth averaged 4.0 percent per year in the 1960s, 2.8 percent in the 1970s, and 2.6 percent in the 1980s. The problem is that labor force growth has slowed. It is expected to average slightly more than 1 percent per year during the 1990s, well below historical rates.[12] Consequently, we no longer can rely on an expanding working population to have the economy growing and producing at competitive levels.

The most far-reaching implication of this analysis is that America's future economic growth and competitiveness is contingent upon achieving real productivity gains, measured in terms of output per worker. This means more investment in improving the skills of the available work force and more investment in the physical infrastructure that is the foundation of the economy.

THE INVESTMENT IMPERATIVE

If a society's workers are its heart, its infrastructure is the interlocking network of arteries through which economic energies, ideas, and products flow. Both must be kept in good repair and upgraded if a high level of economic well-being is to be sustained. However, present conditions in each of these areas act as constraints on the performance of the American economy and threaten our economic future.

Human Resources

There is justifiable concern about the extent to which the coming generation of American workers will be able to meet our human resource needs.[13] The concern is strongly linked to increasing job skills requirements. As Table 3 indicates, the fastest growing occupations require varying amounts of post-secondary education. For example, by the beginning of the next century, the number of paralegal, medical assistant, medical technician, and computer specialist positions is expected to double. At the same time, demands for reasoning, math, and language proficiency are escalating throughout the labor market. The majority of future new jobs, even those that do not involve advanced education, will require mastery of these basic academic skills.[14]

Table 3

Fastest Growing Occupations: 1988-2000

Occupation	Projected New Positions Number (000s)	Change (%)
Paralegals	62	75.0
Medical Assistants	104	70.0
Home Health Aides	160	68.0
Radiology Technicians	87	66.0
Data Processing Equipment Repairers	44	61.0
Medical Records Technicians	28	60.0
Medical Secretaries	120	58.0
Physical Therapists	39	57.0
Surgical Technologists	20	56.0
Operations Research Analysts	30	55.0
Securities & Financial Services Sales Workers	109	54.0
Travel Agents	77	54.0
Computer System Analysts	214	53.0

Source: Bureau of Labor Statistics.

The capability to give or receive directions and to think analytically in the workplace is becoming increasingly important. Moreover, as the U.S. labor market is progressively dominated by service-oriented jobs, good skills in interpersonal relations with clients, customers, and coworkers will be treated as essential attributes by a growing number of employers. In short, the U.S. economy of the 21st century will have few worthwhile employment opportunities for unskilled or poorly educated workers.

Numerous reports have lamented the academic achievement of American youth.[15] The dismay is fueled by international comparisons of performance on standardized achievement tests. The scores of American students consistently lag behind those of their counterparts in other industrialized countries. Further, the gaps are widest on measurements of math, science, and language skills--the most critical proficiencies in today's information-based, services-oriented economies.

Actually, the situation is even worse than international comparisons indicate. The added dimension involves inexorable changes in the composition of the U.S. work force. An expanding proportion of the work force is comprised of African Americans and other minorities who experience extraordinary educational disadvantages. By the year 2000, they will account for more than a quarter of all U.S. workers and one-third of all net new entrants into the labor force. However, these disadvantaged groups tend to concentrate in the bottom fifth of the score distribution on major standardized achievement tests. Thus, studies have found a 30-point gap between the average scores of African American and Hispanic youth and those of their white counterparts on the National Assessment of Educational Progress (NAEP) and a 200-point differential on the Scholastic Aptitude Test (SAT).[16] Moreover, drop-out rates range from 30 to 50 percent in poor, predominantly minority school districts, and rates approaching 80 percent are not uncommon in some inner-city schools.

So long as such deficits and disparities persist, we will be hard-pressed to realize productivity gains relative to our major competitors. They will persist if we do not increase our investment in human resource development, and they will worsen if we do not implement more effective targeted measures to address the education and training needs of disadvantaged youth.

Physical Infrastructure

The nation's physical infrastructure includes as its major components the transportation, utilities, and communications systems. A recent assessment by the National Council on Public Works Improvement concluded that "the quality of America's infrastructure is barely adequate to fulfill current requirements, and insufficient to meet the demands of future economic growth and development."[17] Conditions in the transportation area, the largest infrastructure component, give validity to this judgment.[18] For example:

- Almost two-thirds of the country's paved roads need repair, including 11 percent of the interstate highway system. Many of the roads built in the 1950s had reached the end of their useful lives by the early 1980s. Congestion in metropolitan areas could triple or quadruple over the next 15 years.
- More than 41 percent of our bridges are structurally unsound or functionally obsolete. Estimates indicate that nearly one in four bridges was structurally deficient in 1986.

• A growing number of airports are severely congested, perhaps reaching as many as 36 by 1995. The number of airports experiencing major congestion climbed from 10 in 1981 to 212 in 1990.

The deterioration of our transportation infrastructure has been costly to the economy. In 1985, for instance, vehicle highway delays totaled 722 million hours. Almost three billion gallons of gasoline, about 4 percent of the country's annual consumption, were wasted. Indeed, it is estimated that highway congestion costs interstate commerce more than $35 billion per year. Similarly, in 1986, air travel delays generated $1.8 billion in additional airline operating expenses and $3.2 billion in lost travel time. Flight delays at just 21 airports total 20,000 hours a year.

Concern about the nation's physical infrastructure extends well beyond the condition of our transportation system. Another problem area is water supply and treatment. Decayed, leaky pipes are causing significant reductions in water quality and pressure in the older cities of the East and Midwest, while rapid population growth in the newer cities of the West and South are taxing existing water systems. Although the number of persons served by wastewater facilities increased by 17 percent between 1976 and 1987, there is still a substantial share of the population being served by substandard treatment facilities.[19]

The nation also faces a serious crisis in solid-waste disposal. Approximately 95 percent of our solid waste, which averages almost half a million tons per day, is discarded in rapidly filling landfills, and new disposal sites are becoming harder to create. In addition, more than one out of two present landfills need upgrading--including liners, drainage systems, and pollution-control equipment.[20]

America's infrastructure problems are not all of the "bricks and mortar" type. Some of our most salient needs are in the area of telecommunications. Productive economic activity in the global economy is becoming increasingly dependent upon advanced information transmission and receiving systems. A modernized communications infrastructure could greatly boost our capacity to bring new products to domestic and international markets and to reduce the lead time involved in the production process. America is being outdistanced by other nations in this area.[21]

In summary, with regard to the development of both our human resources and physical infrastructure, the United States is largely unprepared to meet the contemporary challenge of competitiveness. The record shows that we have failed to make the investments necessary to keep pace with demands for sustained economic growth and competitiveness. It is instructive to review some of the shortfalls.

PATTERN OF NEGLECT

The neglect is clear when one compares our investment behavior in recent decades with that of our chief international competitors. America simply has not been very aggressive. In terms of human resources, current federal spending on education as a percentage of the GNP is significantly lower than it was in 1980. Further, based on comparative data for 1985, the United States spent less on preprimary-secondary education, relative to the GNP, than Japan, Sweden, the United Kingdom, and West Germany, among others (see Table 4). In real outlays, federal aid for elementary, secondary, and vocational education declined from $10.3 billion in fiscal year 1980 to $9.2 billion in 1989, a reduction of 11 percent for the decade. Curtailment of federal support for employment and training programs has been much more drastic, down 69 percent, in real terms, between 1980 and 1989.[22]

Table 4

Expenditures on
Preprimary-Secondary Education
for Selected Countries
as Percent of Gross Domestic Product, 1985

Country	Spending as Percent of GDP
Sweden	7.0
Austria	5.9
Switzerland	5.8
Norway	5.3
Japan	4.8
Canada	4.7
West Germany	4.6
France	4.6
United Kingdom	4.5
United States	4.1

Source: Economic Policy Institute.

In light of the issues surrounding improved economic productivity, international comparisons of special efforts to assist youth to enter and perform effectively in the labor market are particularly disturbing. Other nations have been significantly more progressive in delivering such services. In 1987, for example, the proportion of the United Kingdom's GNP devoted to special youth initiatives--such as subsidized work experience, remedial education and training, and direct job creation--was about triple that of the United States. Likewise, the investments of Sweden and West Germany substantially surpassed our own.[23]

A telling aspect of this problem is that America significantly *under*invests in noncollege youth, despite the fact that the majority of today's young people do not pursue post-secondary education in a four-year institution by the time they are age 25, and only one-fifth of those who do graduate. The data in Table 5 are revealing in this regard. The data show the average public investment in education and training for college and noncollege youth in the 16-24 age range. At current rates of expenditure, the overall average is $14,230 per youth. However, the average for college youth is $20,000, more than double the amount for their noncollege counterparts. The disparity is much wider when we exclude high school expenditures and focus on just education and training after high school. In this case, the average public expenditure for noncollege youth ($1,460) is only 14 percent of the average for college youth ($10,440).

Table 5

**Average Public Investment Per Youth
for Education and Training
(Ages 16-24)**

Education Level	Total	Average Expenditure Post High School
College youth	$19,940	$10,440
College graduate	24,700	15,200
Some college	17,100	7,600
Noncollege youth	9,130	1,460
High school graduate	10,840	1,340
High school dropout	5,520	1,720
All youth	14,230	5,770

Source: U.S. General Accounting Office.

None of this is to suggest that the investment in college-bound youth is ill-advised. To the contrary, the acknowledged superiority of our higher education system compared to other countries continues to be a singular national asset. The marked imbalance in investment policy, however, as regards support for college and noncollege youth, is counterproductive. The jobs of the 21st century that will be the backbone of the U.S. economy may not require college educated workers, but they *will* require frontline personnel who possess sound basic skills and aptitudes--in the expanding services sector as well as in manufacturing industries.

The reductions in human resource spending are paralleled by declining investment in the physical infrastructure. Between 1964 and 1988, total infrastructure spending in the United States dropped from 2.3 percent of the GNP to about 1 percent.[24] Federal cutbacks have spearheaded the curtailment. Thus, federal outlays for infrastructure improvements went from 10.9 percent of total nondefense spending in 1962 to 4.5 percent in 1987. In the 1980s alone, federal aid to states and localities for public works projects was reduced by 18 percent--from $24.5 billion to $20.1 billion--in constant dollars.[25]

Although the nation's investment practices differ by category, the overall situation leaves much to be desired. Adjusting for depreciation, America's *net* public investment in core infrastructure (i.e., streets and highways, water and sewer systems, mass transit, airports, and electrical and gas facilities) had all but ceased by 1982. The depreciation adjustment generates a total net investment of less than 0.5 percent of the GNP for that year.[26] For the decade, net federal outlays for physical infrastructure were a steep decline from the levels of funding extant in the 1950s and 1960s.

These retrenchments run counter to the infrastructure investment practices of our major competitors. Japan, Germany, and France, among other industrial nations, have pursued much more progressive development and maintenance initiatives. Particularly impressive are the initiatives by our competitors to develop and apply advanced telecommunications technology within the framework of infrastructure improvement. For example, Japan is constructing a $250 billion fiber-optic communications network designed to transmit video, voice, and data nationwide 1,000 times faster than existing systems. Germany is transforming its autobahn system into superhighways that regulate traffic flow by computer. France already provides a videotext system at no charge to telephone subscribers and recently instituted an electronic library and information bank intended to be accessible to every household.[27] Meanwhile, the United States ranks ninth among industrialized nations in the amount invested annually to upgrade the public telephone system.

Compared to our principal competitors, U.S. policy in recent years suggests little appreciation of the role of infrastructure in the performance of the economy. However, evidence establishing its value grows.[28] Among the more significant findings:

- A 1-percent increase in infrastructure investment raises the GNP by as much as 0.24 percent and brings about a 0.4 percent gain in the rate of productivity growth.
- Eighty percent of America's productivity decline between 1971 and 1985 was due to low spending on infrastructure.
- A $50 billion increase in infrastructure investment would boost the nation's economic output by $62.5 billion in the first year alone.
- For every $1.00 we spend on infrastructure, we realize a $10.00 return on investment.

The essential point of this discussion is that the lack of investment in our human and physical capital--people and facilities--largely accounts for America's deteriorating economic productivity and competitiveness. Rectifying the problem requires a comprehensive, sustained, well-financed investment program in human resource and infrastructure development, targeted to maximize the payoffs.

MARSHALL PLAN FOR AMERICA

The National Urban League's Marshall Plan for America is a multifaceted strategic investment program for economic growth. It is premised on the belief that people are our greatest asset and that good people and good facilities assure the nation's economic success. In its basics, the Marshall Plan for America is characterized by investment initiatives that:

- address both long-term economic productivity goals and short-term improvements in social well-being;
- maximize returns by concentrating on areas of greatest need;
- involve sustained, programmed collaborations on the part of government, the private sector, and nonprofit organizations; and
- operate under rigorous accountability systems for monitoring, assessing, and adjusting results over time.

It bears emphasizing that the Marshall Plan for America is not a "social" program, as popularly conceived, but an economic investment program designed to serve overriding national interests. At the same time, however, the Plan fully acknowledges the disadvantaged conditions of African Americans that militate against economic productivity. How well and how soon these conditions are improved will greatly influence the entire nation's economic well-being.

This section outlines some of the main initiatives encompassed by the National Urban League's Marshall Plan, discusses the all-important question of financing, and describes how the program would be structured to ensure its integrity over time.

Human Resource Initiatives

In human resource development, the Marshall Plan for America combines expansion of existing programs of proven effectiveness with new investment initiatives believed to have high potential for success, with a heavy emphasis on youth. There are three principal proposals that relate to the areas of education and training.

1. That all disadvantaged children be provided quality preschool learning opportunities. Early childhood education is universally recognized as being crucial to a child's success in school. However, all too many of America's children do not benefit from such experiences, and a disproportionate number of them are African Americans. A well-tested, effective mechanism for delivering preprimary services to disadvantaged children is already in place in the form of the Head Start program. However, only about 20 percent of the eligible population currently is being served. The Marshall Plan for America provides for expanding the program to include all eligible children and for making it available on a full-time basis year-round.

It is reassuring to note that having all children start school ready to learn has been established as the number-one goal in the Bush Administration's new education initiative, "America 2000." This action is long overdue. It remains for the Administration and the Congress to commit the resources needed to carry it out.

2. That all disadvantaged elementary and secondary students be provided the supports they need to ensure the acquisition of a sound basic education in the public schools. The problems of underachievement in the public schools, particularly those in poor urban school districts, are widely known. Even the benefits of preschooling are often undermined by the regular school experience and the larger complex of adversities disadvantaged students face. Thus, the Marshall Plan for America emphasizes the provision of supplementary instruction for needy students in reading, math, and science courses.

Again, there is already in place a system for delivering the kinds of educational supports disadvantaged elementary and secondary students need. It consists of the programs administered under Chapter 1 of the 1965 Elementary and Secondary Education Act. However, as is the case with Head Start, only a fraction of eligible students is served. And those who are served do not receive assistance throughout their school years, often losing progress as a result. The Marshall Plan for America would make Chapter 1

24

assistance available to all who need it, expand the scope of supplementary instruction, and maintain the support over time.

The Administration's "America 2000" initiative at least recognizes the special needs of African American and other disadvantaged youth, but the commitment of federal dollars to meet these needs has not occurred. The gap between rhetoric and resources must be closed if "America 2000" is to bring about more than superficial improvements in the academic achievement of American youth in general, and disadvantaged youth in particular.

3. That the nation's employment and training system be expanded and restructured to deliver more relevant and viable job skills to today's youth. The Job Training Partnership Act (JTPA) remains the centerpiece of our job training system. In principle, the training needs of the economically disadvantaged are addressed through Title IIA and Title IIB, the summer youth employment and training components. However, JTPA serves fewer than 6 percent of the eligible disadvantaged population, greatly underserves the most needy among this larger group, and places little emphasis on remedial education and actual preparation for employment. The Marshall Plan for America calls for extending JTPA coverage to at least 50 percent of all eligibles, targeting those with the most severe barriers to employment, and emphasizing basic and occupational skills training over job placement activity.

The Plan also provides for substantial expansion of the Job Corps program, a highly regarded residential program renowned for its intensive, long-term job training, remedial education, counseling, and job placement assistance. The Marshall Plan for America would increase Job Corps enrollments from the present 70,000 youths per year to 400,000.

The types of expansion outlined above are necessary but not sufficient to meet the nation's employment and training needs and to improve significantly the quality of the work force. More fundamental changes in approach are required if we are to upgrade the skills of American workers in the longer-term to match or exceed the standards of our chief international competitors. The present limited provision for training the large population of noncollege youth is a critical factor here.

As discussed earlier, competitor nations such as Japan, Germany, the United Kingdom, and Sweden have instituted much more efficacious strategies to prepare noncollege youth for work. Compared to their practices, the U.S. employment and training system is inefficient and largely unproductive. For one thing, American schools tend to be detached from the labor market and only nominally assist noncollege-bound youth to transition from school to work. Even vocational education programs are widely seen by employers to be ineffective in preparing youth for jobs that do not require a college degree. In addition, vocational education can be criticized for neglecting the development of academic skills, for training youth for low demand occupations, for using obsolete equipment, and for providing limited placement assistance.[29]

Given the deficiencies in the present system and the urgent need for a basic change in approach, the Marshall Plan for America endorses the recommendations of the Commission on the Skills of the American Workforce[30]:

- A new educational performance standard should be set for all students, to be met by age 16. This standard should be established nationally and benchmarked to the highest in the world.

- The states should take responsibility for assuring that virtually all students achieve the Certificate of Initial Mastery. States, with federal assistance, should create and fund alternative learning environments for those who cannot attain the Certificate in regular schools.

- A comprehensive system of technical and professional certificates and associate's degrees should be created for the majority of our students and adult workers who do not pursue a baccalaureate degree.

- All employers should be given incentives and assistance to invest in the further education and training of their workers and to pursue high productivity forms of work organization.

Physical Infrastructure Initiatives

Initiatives to rebuild and upgrade our physical infrastructure promise to bring greater efficiencies to business and industry as well as to promote public safety and our overall quality of life. Each of these outcomes is clearly in the national interest. Their long-term benefits are impossible to calculate. At the same time, there are more immediate payoffs from infrastructure investment that also have important implications for the general welfare in the coming decades.

Infrastructure projects create jobs, providing well-paying employment for workers at all skill levels. They also offer opportunities for apprentice-type skills training in a wide range of areas. Given the geographic distribution of infrastructure needs, which are particularly acute in urban areas, African Americans would be prime beneficiaries of these expanded employment and training opportunities.

The Marshall Plan for America's potential for quickly generating thousands upon thousands of well-paying jobs and worthwhile skills development opportunities where they are most needed is one of its foremost rationales. This opportunity-creation capability distinguishes the Marshall Plan for America as being both an effective approach for achieving long-term productivity gains and a much needed program for improving the current economic well-being of large numbers of disadvantaged families and communities. It has been estimated that each billion dollars of construction contracts generates from 15,000 to 22,000 jobs. This estimate does not even take into account the increased purchasing power of formerly jobless workers and its effect in stimulating employment in other areas. Other estimates indicate that an additional $25 billion per year in federal highway and bridge spending would create 942,926 jobs in the peak year, 87,000 within the first year, and 448,000 within the first two years.[31]

The Marshall Plan for America includes three basic infrastructure proposals, centering on transportation, utilities, and communications needs.

1. That the nation invest in the development of a world-class transportation system. The proposed program includes efforts to repair, refurbish and upgrade existing highways, bridges, mass transit systems and aviation facilities as well as projects to develop new types of transportation technologies, such as the high-speed magnetically levitated ("Maglev") train systems now operating in prototype in Germany. The highway system, in particular, including the 43,000 miles of interstate, is critical to the transportation of goods and services in today's economy and to the movement of people to and from the workplace. It is imperative that we check the deterioration and reduce the high congestion-related costs of this mode of transport.

A key part of the larger highway improvement program is the rehabilitation or renewal of the nation's bridges. Under the Marshall Plan for America, the approximately 240,000 unsound or obsolete bridges around the country would be repaired or replaced, beginning with the 77,000 structures on the federal aid system. Also, the Plan calls for a reassessment of the pattern of federal assistance for mass transit and adjustments where necessary to ensure that systems in older, heavily populated metropolitan areas are able to achieve and/or maintain a viable level of operational efficiency.

It is important to mention that the Surface Transportation Efficiency Act (STEA) contains provisions that go a significant way toward achieving the kinds of transportation improvements that are necessary. While STEA should be regarded as responsible and responsive, two conditions must be met if the initiative is to produce maximum returns on investment. First, there must be safeguards to guarantee that African Americans and other disadvantaged residents of areas subject to highway and transit improvement are equitably represented as workers and contractors on these projects. Second, there must be similar provisions to have the new projects provide meaningful, long-term apprenticeship opportunities for African American and other disadvantaged youth.

Finally, the Marshall Plan for America proposes to accelerate spending on new airports, airport capital improvements, and modernized air traffic control systems so as to reduce air travel delays by 75 percent over the next ten years. Expanding and upgrading the aviation infrastructure is also crucial to reversing the decline in economic productivity.

2. That major investments be made to improve the nation's water supply and treatment facilities as well as to relieve the crisis in solid-waste disposal. If transportation infrastructure has a dominant role in addressing the nation's productivity requirements, water supply and treatment systems and facilities for the disposal of solid-waste products are supremely important to our quality of life. The quality of the water we consume directly impacts physical health and well-being. In addition, efficient removal of wastes from the water used by individuals and industry before it is returned to the natural environment is necessary to control pollution and to keep the environment safe for human exposure.

Initiatives under the Marshall Plan for America would include repairing or replacing decayed sewer lines as well as upgrading existing sewer plants and building new ones. The potential health benefits from such investments need no further emphasis. However, it is necessary to stress the direct economic returns. By one estimate, sewer line construction generates 17,500 jobs, about 42 percent of them in the construction industry itself and the rest in other industries. Similarly, nearly 18,000 jobs result from building sewer plants, with the majority being in nonconstruction fields.

With regard to solid-waste disposal, the Marshall Plan for America calls for upgrading existing landfills and more investment in the development of modern resource recovery facilities. Again, both types of projects would further quality of life interests and expand economic opportunities.

3. That the nation pursue more aggressively the development and application of advanced telecommunications technology. Much of this effort would center on the installation of avant garde voice, video, and information processing systems patterned after the Japanese model. The substitution and diffusion of modern fiber-optics technology as the chief communications medium of the future should be paramount.

The possibilities offered by fiber-optics are virtually unlimited. For example, the technology could be used to support the development of so-called Intelligent Vehicle-Highway Systems (IVHS), which would vastly improve the transportation efficiency. Also, fiber-optics promises impressive efficiency gains for business and commerce by cutting travel costs and expenses for office space. Other benefits include improved worker retention, access to talent and training, more expansive employee interaction across sites, and simply speedier transmitting and receiving of information.

All of the advantages of advanced telecommunications translate into higher economic productivity and international competitiveness. Increased investment in this area, therefore, is key to the Marshall Plan strategy for securing our economic well-being in the next decade and beyond.

The proposals outlined above do not exhaust the human resource and infrastructure initiatives covered by the Marshall Plan for America. Nevertheless, there should be no doubt about the magnitude of the challenge confronting us. The Marshall Plan strategy represents a viable, high payoff approach to serving priority national interests and the urgent needs of the disadvantaged.

FINANCING AND ADMINISTRATION

Obviously, the Marshall Plan for America must be funded adequately if the program is to achieve its objectives. A base allotment of $50 billion per year over a ten-year period is considered a minimal requirement. These funds would be *above* monies presently allocated to human resource and physical infrastructure purposes.

In view of the budget deficit and the current economic downturn, some will argue that the cost is too high. But the cost of not making the investment is sure to be much higher. As indicated, our major competitors are being bold and visionary in preparing themselves for the 21st century. The proposed investment for the Marshall Plan is moderate, indeed, compared to the resource commitments of these other countries.

Cost is not the issue. The real issue is the nation's priorities and our appreciation of what best serves the national interest. We found a way to finance the savings-and-loan bailout, at an estimated total cost of up to $500 billion, because it was in our national interest to do so. The need to enhance America's economic productivity and competitiveness is no less compelling. Diversion of planned cuts in defense spending, transfers from existing programs, taxes, debt financing, or some combination of these and other revenue alternatives are options that should be considered.

Public support for the overall Marshall Plan strategy could be jeopardized by the failure to apply high standards of efficacy and cost effectiveness to given components. The program must be fiscally responsible. Accordingly, program implementations would be regularly monitored and rigorously assessed to determine whether existing resource allocations should be maintained or modified.

As important as adequate financing is maintaining the structural integrity of the program over time. To this end, it is proposed that the president appoint a Cabinet-level Marshall Plan Administrator. Also, it is proposed that an Interagency Council be formed to carry out the Marshall Plan's multifaceted programmatic components. The Council would consist of the secretaries of designated departments within the federal government that have major jurisdictional responsibilities under the Marshall Plan for America design. Coordinating the Council's activities would be one of the principal functions of the Marshall Plan Administrator.

The proposed financial and administrative provisions distinguish the Marshall Plan for America as being a special national investment program, having its own resource base, mandates, accountabilities, and long-term implementation schedule. Although the final mix of specific investment initiatives is subject to debate, the importance of adequately funding and securely organizing the effort is indisputable.

CONCLUSION

America faces some very serious challenges as we move toward the new century. None is more serious than the challenge of economic competitiveness. The stakes are very high, and the longer we wait before launching an initiative that is equal to the challenge, the more at risk we are of being relegated to second-class status in the global marketplace and suffering a major decline in our standard of living. In this regard, the Marshall Plan for America is much more than an idea whose time has come. It is a strategic imperative, and we should waste no time in getting it implemented.

The Demographic Revolution: Diversity in 21st Century America

Bernard C. Watson, Ph.D.

Ominous currents are swirling across the nation's landscape, and they presage profound and disturbing questions about the future of these United States. David Duke's recent emergence as a political force in Louisiana represents only the most visible sign of widespread discontent. Recent polls, focus groups, and annual surveys provide evidence of deteriorating racial and ethnic relations in this country. Demagogues, bigots, and political chameleons of both major political parties fan the flames of divisiveness by using code words like "crime in the streets," "welfare mothers," and "quotas." Much of white America has come to equate affirmative action and civil rights with preferential treatment for African Americans, and has come to believe that "unqualified minorities" are taking jobs, promotions, or seats in college classrooms from "qualified white males."

The current recession and continuing reductions in public expenditures for social services, health, and education have exacerbated the situation by forcing more and more individuals to scramble for a share of a diminishing pie. Meantime, immigration policies, differential fertility rates, and dramatic global economic developments are transforming this country, increasing the number of competitors for apparently limited resources. All minorities are vulnerable during a period such as this, but no group is as vulnerable as African Americans. It behooves all of us to pay attention, to understand, and to prepare for the opportunities--and the dangers--wrought by these changes.

How ironic it would be if minority groups in this country were to become the enemies and oppressors of newly arrived immigrants who seem to obtain the employment, housing, educational, and other opportunities long denied to themselves!

How tragic it would be if African Americans, who have suffered more egregiously than any other minority save Native Americans, were to become adversaries and opponents of people who have come to this country seeking the rights and freedoms so long denied to former slaves!

How sad it would be if this country were to become a battleground of competing, snarling, angry groups, separated along lines of race, ethnicity, religion, or language!

It could happen. It has happened in the past in this country; it is happening right now in countries around the world. But this scenario, which seems so imminent, can also be rewritten. One way to start is to educate ourselves about the demographic revolution that is literally changing the face of this country. Knowing about this revolution and reacting appropriately are important for all Americans. For minorities and the poor in this country, its significance can hardly be overestimated.

INTERNATIONAL DEMOGRAPHIC CHANGE

In the 1990s, Americans are being forced to recognize that no matter *where* something happens, the effects will be felt throughout the world and certainly in the United States. Those pictures of our planet taken from outer space are instructive illustrations of global interdependence, reminding us that events occurring thousands of miles from the United States may have an impact on our own cities, businesses, and even neighborhoods.

The developments in Europe during the past few years--the tearing down of the Berlin Wall and the reunification of Germany; the fragmentation of the Soviet Union; renewed hostilities in such historic tinderbox areas as the Balkans--may be particularly astonishing. But political upheaval and technological revolution are to be found almost everywhere. In some parts of the world, such as the Middle East, Sri Lanka, or Northern Ireland, war between opposing tribes or religions has become a way of life. The predictable result? People fleeing for their lives, people seeking employment that is not available in their homelands, people determining to give their children better opportunities in a new country. It has been estimated that up to 10 percent of the population of the *entire world* will have moved from one country to another in the last one-third of this century. That is approximately 52,000,000 people exchanging the familiar for the unknown, voluntarily or involuntarily, in search of better jobs or driven by political necessity.

Unfortunately, immigrants, particularly in large numbers, are resented and feared more often than welcomed by the people of host countries. The current population shifts are provoking vehement and even violent response from native-born majorities almost everywhere they are occurring. The tensions are exacerbated by the rising militancy and racial pride of ethnic minorities *within* many national boundaries.

- In France, although Algerians now comprise some 8 percent of the population, fascist movements on both the left and right encourage anti-black, anti-Arab, and anti-semitic sentiments and actions.
- Italy has one million foreign residents, perhaps half there illegally. Most of them, Africans and Asians, are street vendors or in low-level service jobs. In early 1991, after thousands of Albanian refugees had crossed the Adriatic, Italy closed its ports.

32

• The first anniversary of German reunification was accompanied by continuing outbreaks of racist insults and violence directed toward "guest workers" from Vietnam and Mozambique. While neo-Nazi skinheads are usually on the front lines of such attacks, they represent many others who are unhappy about the high unemployment in the East or the huge influx of easterners into the West.

• The United Kingdom has been struggling for years to accommodate the stream of immigrants from its far-flung former empire. Many of them are "people of color," such as Pakistanis and West Indians, and the racism from which many Britons thought they were immune has surfaced in graffiti and demagogic speeches. Resented for upsetting "the English way of life," immigrants have been attacked physically by mobs, especially in the depressed industrial North where they are seen as competitors for jobs, housing, and social services.

• Out of the ruins of the once monolithic Soviet empire, the newly independent republics--their names still unfamiliar to many Americans--are struggling to build political and economic stability amid outbreaks of historic hostilities, such as that between Armenians and Azerbaijanis. Hundreds of thousands have become refugees as a result.

• Similar problems beset the former eastern bloc countries, as attempts to shift from state-run to free-market economies lag behind popular demands for a higher standard of living. The resulting dislocation and frustration find a ready outlet in attacks on rival ethnic groups or even in outright warfare, such as that between Serbs and Croats in Yugoslavia.

• Saddam Hussein's invasion of Kuwait created a flood of refugees--and thereby revealed some astonishing demographic facts about that tiny country. In 1910, Kuwait's population was only 35,000; it had grown to somewhere around 1.5 million by the late 1980s--only 40 percent of whom were native Kuwaitis! The other 60 percent comprised people from many countries, drawn by the tremendous labor requirements of the oil fields: 9 percent were from Southeast Asia (India, Pakistan, and Sri Lanka), another 9 percent were from East Asia, but by far the largest of the non-native groups were the Palestinians, numbering as many as 400,000.[1] Post-war Kuwaiti policy, however, called for evicting many of the foreign laborers who had not already fled the war zone.

• Japan, experiencing a severe labor shortage, is a magnet for immigrants from other parts of Southeast Asia.

• The emergence of a Japanese presidential candidate provoked racial tension and demonstrations in Peru in 1990. (Despite the opposition of many members of the Latino majority, Alberto Fujimori won the election.)

• Australia received some 130,000 immigrants in 1989, and as many again in

1990. Originally settled by English-speaking people, Australia is now being forced to cope with many different languages.

- Taiwan illegally imported tens of thousands of unskilled laborers from Malaysia, Thailand, the Philippines, and even mainland China, to work on government projects.

- Thousands of residents of Hong Kong, which will soon revert to China after nearly a century as a British crown colony, have moved elsewhere. Some 80,000 have gone to Canada--usually Toronto or Vancouver--where 50 percent of the school students claim Chinese as their first language.

- Canada, long preoccupied with the claims of French Canadians for cultural recognition if not outright independence, has recently been jolted by reports of anti-black bias and violence in Montreal.

The list could go on . . . but what is its significance to us? Why should we concern ourselves with international demographic changes and the ensuing difficulties? There are at least two possible answers:

1. People leaving war-torn or depressed areas elsewhere may well become our newest immigrants, adding to our already volatile mix of ethnic groups.

2. The kind of ethnic battles taking place in other countries could be replicated here, with equally dire consequences.

By being better informed, we may be better prepared to address continuing demographic changes in positive ways, and to forestall or ameliorate the kind of intergroup tensions that such changes ignite.

DEMOGRAPHIC CHANGE IN THE UNITED STATES

The United States is already involved in the challenge of coping with an influx of new people--housing and employing and educating them, coming to terms with alien languages and customs. The results of the 1990 census have only recently begun to establish the amazing extent of domestic demographic changes.

Table 1
Ethnic Composition of Five Largest Metropolitan Areas, 1980 and 1990

		Total	African American	Hispanic*	Asian & Pacific Islanders
New York	1980	17,539,000	2,825,102	2,050,998	370,731
	1990	18,087,251	3,289,465	2,777,951	873,213
	% change	3.1	16.4	35.4	135.5
Los Angeles	1980	11,498,000	1,059,124	2,755,914	561,876
	1990	14,531,529	1,229,809	4,779,118	1,339,048
	% change	26	16.1	73.4	138.3
Chicago	1980	7,937,000	1,557,287	632,443	144,626
	1990	8,065,633	1,547,725	893,422	256,050
	% change	1.6	-0.6	41.3	77.0
San Francisco	1980	5,368,000	468,477	660,190	454,647
	1990	6,253,311	537,753	970,403	926,961
	% change	16	14.8	47.0	103.9
Philadelphia	1980	5,681,000	1,032,882	147,902	53,291
	1990	5,899,345	1,100,347	225,868	123,458
	% change	3.8	6.5	52.7	131.7

*Note: Persons of Hispanic origin may be of any race.
Sources: U.S. Census Bureau Release 91-229; Statistical Abstract of the U.S., 1990.

The scope and significance of these demographic changes have yet to penetrate very deeply into the American consciousness, although some people have been alerted by articles such as the one that appeared in *Time* magazine in 1990. Entitled "Beyond the Melting Pot," it had the following lead: "In the 21st century--and that's not far off--racial and ethnic groups in the United States will outnumber whites for the first time. The 'browning of America' will alter everything in society, from politics and education to industry, values and culture."[2]   The report gave details: by 2020, the Hispanic or nonwhite population will have more than doubled, while the white population will not be increasing at all. By 2056, the average citizen "will trace his or her descent to Africa, Asia, the Hispanic world, the Pacific Islands, Arabia--almost anywhere but white Europe."

The trends described by *Time* are already being noted around the country. A recent story in *USA Today*[3] reported that the schools in the suburban New Jersey town of Bound Brook have students who speak 20 different languages--Laotian, Greek, Urdu, Hmong, Arabic, Tagalog, Tamac, and Japanese, among others--and have caused the system's bilingual and TESOL (Teaching English to Speakers of Other Languages) programs to expand each year. The newcomers are educationally and economically diverse: some of the children's parents are poor; others are professionals who work at Princeton University, Johnson & Johnson, or AT&T.

Asians--people from China, the Philippines, Japan, India, Korea, and Vietnam, as well as other countries--comprise the fastest growing ethnic group in the United States, expanding at a rate seven times faster than the general population. In 1960, there were well under one million Asians in this country, and 50 percent were on the West Coast. Today, there are over seven million spread across the nation. This dramatic increase resulted largely from changes in immigration law: in 1965, the long-term ban on Asian immigration was lifted, and in 1980, the Refugee Act permitted entry for persons--e.g., from Laos and Cambodia--seeking political asylum.

Even small-town profiles are changing. For instance, in one Philadelphia Main Line suburb, census figures revealed that 700 of the 1,000 new residents are Asians. In the city of Philadelphia, 90 percent of the local businesses in the Olney section are owned by Koreans; the Cambodian New Year is celebrated in a Buddhist temple in South Philadelphia, once referred to as Little Italy; and Asian restaurants are no longer confined to Chinatown --or to Chinese cuisine.

Along the Alabama coast, Vietnamese, Laotians, and Cambodians are taking over the shrimp and crab business abandoned by both whites and blacks who have moved to Mobile. Texas, too, has seen an influx of Asian refugees, whose willingness to work long hours in the fishing industry has earned them not only prosperity but also the resentment (in some cases expressed with guns) of the more easy-going native fishermen. The eastern Los Angeles suburb of Monterey Park is now a Chinese enclave, and at the University of California at Berkeley, Asian student enrollment ranges from 25 to 30 percent.

Asian Americans have become widely known as superachievers or academic whiz kids. Unfortunately, the undeniable academic success of *many* has created expectations that place inordinate pressure on *all* Asian American students: parents and teachers assume that they will succeed and even excel, while classmates resent their presumed superior ability.

In fact, Asian Americans differ enormously from one another in every conceivable way, including country of origin, length of time in the United States, and level of education; and they are increasingly irritated by the label of "model minority." Reports that Asian incomes are higher than those of whites are misleading: their families often include several breadwinners, not just the traditional one or two, and most are in urban areas where salaries are normally higher. Even for the upwardly mobile, there is still a promotion "ceiling," while many others, far from being "rich," are in desperate need of basic human services.

Hispanics, or Latinos, are second only to Asians in the rate of population growth, and many believe they will become America's largest minority group (displacing African Americans) within the next 25 years. The increase is due not only to immigration (legal and illegal) but also to a birth rate higher than that for any other group in the United States. In California, nearly one-third of school students are Hispanic, and when Asians and African Americans are added, the nonwhite school population is well over 50 percent. Forty-nine percent of Dade County (Miami), Florida, is Hispanic (mostly Cuban), while several California metropolitan areas have Hispanic populations well over 30 percent, among them Los Angeles, Fresno, Monterey, and Merced. New Mexico is nearly 40 percent Hispanic. In Corpus Christi, Texas, the Hispanic population now constitutes a majority. In New York City and Jersey City, the figures are 22 percent and 33 percent, respectively.

Like Asians, Hispanics cannot be lumped together as though they were all the same or spoke with a single voice. The majority--over 13 million of the more than 22 million Hispanics in the population--comes from Mexico. The Hispanics' roots are in both pre-Columbian America and in European Spain. The second largest group is comprised of Caribbean Hispanics--Puerto Ricans or Cubans--whose heritage is both European and African. Almost equally as large (nearly three million) is the group from Central and South America. Also like Asians, Hispanics display wide differences on such measures as income level and educational attainment.

Table 2
Major Metropolitan Areas Ranked by Proportion of
Minority Group Population (in millions), 1990

Total	African Americans	Hispanics*	Asians & Pacific Islanders	American Indians/et al.
New York 18.1	New York 3.3	Los Angeles 4.8	Los Angeles 1.3	Los Angeles 0.087
Los Angeles 14.5	Chicago 1.5	New York 2.8	San Francisco 0.9	Tulsa 0.048
Chicago 8.1	Los Angeles 1.2	Miami 1.1	New York 0.87	New York 0.046
San Francisco 6.3	Philadelphia 1.1	San Francisco 0.97	Honolulu 0.53	Oklahoma City 0.046
Philadelphia 5.9	Washington, DC 1.0	Chicago 0.89	Chicago 0.26	San Francisco 0.041

*Note: Persons of Hispanic origin may be of any race.
Source: U.S. Census Bureau Release 91-229.

There are numerous other demographic changes of which we should be aware:

• Islam is this country's fastest growing religion, its ranks swelled by converts in the United States and by immigrants who are already adherents of the faith.

• The "greying" of America (i.e., the increasing number of senior citizens in proportion to other age groups) has been confirmed by the 1990 census and raises serious questions about the adequacy of Social Security and Medicare in the 21st century. According to Social Security Administration projections, by the year 2060, there will be only 1.8 workers for each beneficiary (contrasted with 50 workers in 1945, 5.1 workers in 1960, and 3.3 workers in 1990).

• The population shift from the northeast to the southeast (from Rust Belt to Sun Belt) continues, along with explosive growth in many suburban areas and the virtual abandonment of some small towns.

• The prison population, which is disproportionately black, is increasing. The incarceration rate in the United States is one of the highest in the world: in 1990, it was reported that there were 407 people in U.S. prisons for every 100,000 citizens--compared with estimates of 350-400 per 100,000 people in the Soviet Union.

How well we and other leaders understand the implications of these developments may well determine the health and welfare of American society in the 21st century. Major demographic changes have always been accompanied by clashes of culture and language, by new demands on schools and social services, and particularly by economic conflicts. When an adopted country experiences downturns in its economy, newcomers become convenient scapegoats, competitors for a scarce commodity--work --and urged, verbally and even violently, to "go home."

ETHNIC HOSTILITIES OF THE PAST

As countless orators have reminded us, the United States is a nation of immigrants. But, despite the glowing rhetoric and genuine idealism about welcoming strangers, the story of this country's growth is marred by incidents of ethnic warfare and recurring attempts to restrict immigration.[4]

- In 1705, Massachusetts prohibited intermarriage between blacks and whites, and in 1729, Rhode Island tried to limit immigration to Britons only.
- Anti-Catholicism, prevalent in America from the outset, turned violent in the mid-19th century. Irish immigrant laborers, fleeing by the thousands from the potato famine in Ireland, were seen as dangers both in the job market and at the ballot box. In 1844, for instance, the fledgling Native American party organized street rallies in the Irish district of Philadelphia. Before long, people were killed; a Catholic church and several homes were burned--and the Irish were held responsible for the riots.
- Throughout the pre-Civil War period, "Know Nothings" agitated for the election of only native-born Americans and a 25-year residence qualification for citizenship, while regularly provoking riots to prevent Irish Catholics from voting.
- In 1863, a Conscription Act was passed, allowing men to avoid military service by paying $300 or by obtaining a substitute. This so infuriated the working-class Irish in New York--who could do neither--that they turned on local blacks whom they held responsible for the Civil War. After four days of rioting, hundreds of people had been killed, and millions of dollars in property damage had been done.
- By the 1890s, immigrants from southern and eastern Europe had become the new threat. "The Italians have replaced the Irish as Boston's most unwanted ethnic group," pronounced one newspaper, in one of the more polite summaries of nativist views. Another described the latest immigrants as "scum" and "slime . . . being siphoned upon us from Continental mud tanks."
- On the West Coast, Chinese laborers, who comprised 90 percent of the

construction crews for the Union Pacific Railroad, were initially termed by the governor of California the "most desirable of our adopted citizens." Soon, however, the popular cry was "The Chinese must go," and Chinese immigration was prohibited by law in 1882.

• In 1905, a Japanese and Korean Exclusion League was formed, and warnings about the "Yellow Peril" were common. Hotels put up signs saying "Positively No Filipinos Allowed," and the San Francisco School Board ordered Japanese, Chinese, and Korean children to be segregated in a separate Oriental school. Under the terms of a 1907 "Gentleman's Agreement," Japan was persuaded to limit emigration to the United States.

• From 1924 to 1965, fixed quotas and other restrictions in U.S. immigration law favored immigrants from northern European countries and effectively excluded Asians altogether.

As Ronald Takaki points out in his excellent study of migration across the Pacific Ocean, *Strangers from a Different Shore*,[5] U.S. sentiment was forever changing from welcome (when cheap labor was needed) to abuse (when conditions changed). In hard times, there was always a receptive audience for accusations that there were (or soon would be) too many foreigners, that they were taking jobs away from the native-born, and that they were disrupting the peaceful homogeneity of white America.

CONTEMPORARY INTERGROUP HOSTILITY

Historic patterns of intergroup strife continue, as current immigration trends and other demographic changes alter the American scene. Complicating the problem is the fact that immigrant/minority groups may be heavily concentrated in small areas. As shown in Table 3, the population profile of a given state may be very different from the profile of the state's largest metropolis.

Table 3
Comparisons of Percentages of State and Metropolitan Area Populations, 1990

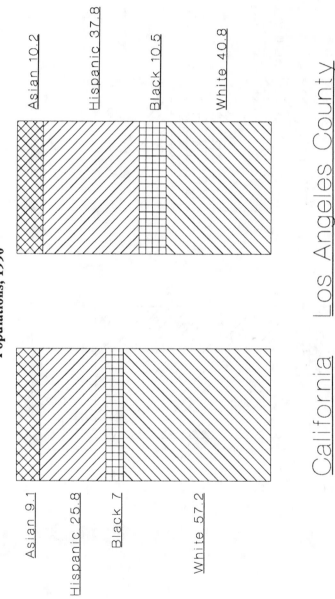

California   Los Angeles County

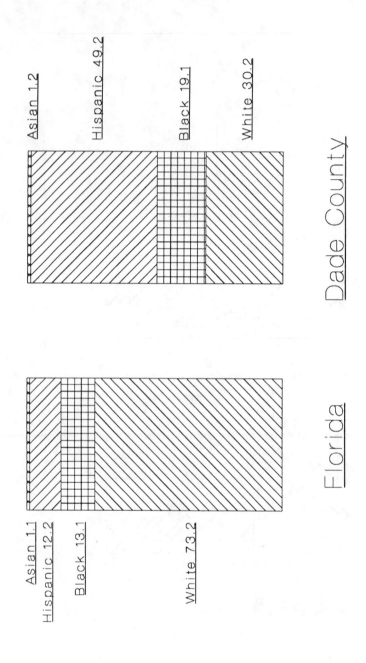

Asian 1.2
Hispanic 49.2
Black 19.1
White 30.2

Dade County

Asian 1.1
Hispanic 12.2
Black 13.1
White 73.2

Florida

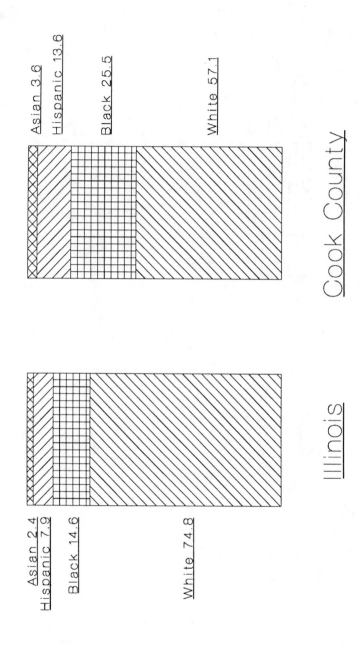

Cook County

Asian 3.6
Hispanic 13.6

Black 25.5

White 57.1

Illinois

Asian 2.4
Hispanic 7.9

Black 14.6

White 74.8

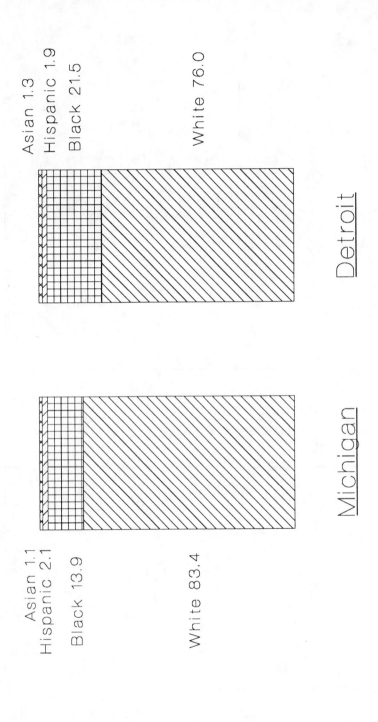

Asian 1.3
Hispanic 1.9
Black 21.5

White 76.0

Detroit

Michigan

Asian 1.1
Hispanic 2.1

Black 13.9

White 83.4

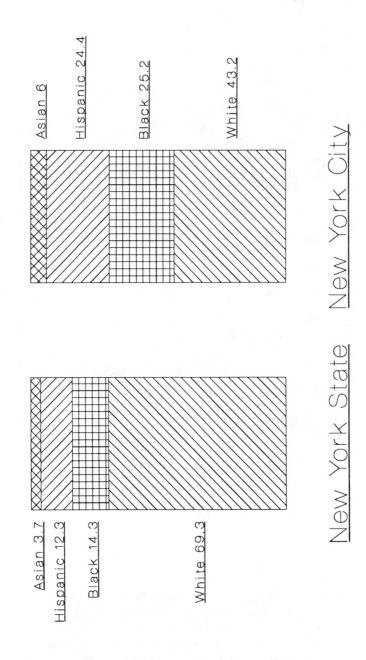

New York State   New York City

Asian 3.7
Hispanic 12.3
Black 14.3
White 69.3

Asian 6
Hispanic 24.4
Black 25.2
White 43.2

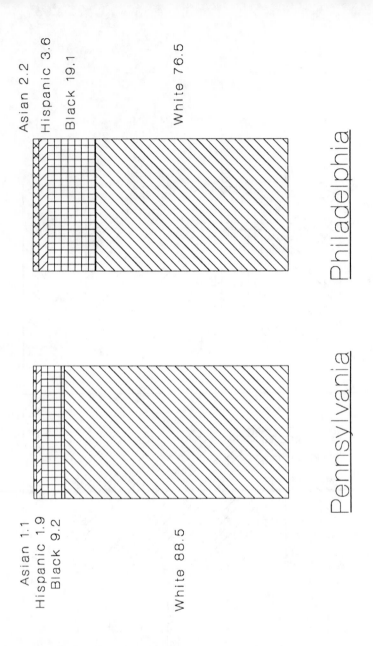

Philadelphia

Asian 2.2
Hispanic 3.6
Black 19.1
White 76.5

Pennsylvania

Asian 1.1
Hispanic 1.9
Black 9.2
White 88.5

Notes: (1) Persons of Hispanic origin may be of any race.
      (2) American Indians and Other Races are not shown, as together
          they comprise less than 1 percent.
Sources: Unpublished charts provided by U.S. Census Bureau, 1991:
             Census Bureau Releases 91-215 and 91-229.

In the light of data such as these, it is no wonder that there are rural/ suburban/urban political and economic tensions, as well as conflicts among individuals who find themselves in areas very different from the ones they had known.

* During a playground brawl between white and Asian youths in southwest Philadelphia, an 18-year-old white youth was killed. At a neighborhood meeting called to ease tensions, whites charged that the police had not responded to earlier calls for protection against "Asian thugs," while Asian youths privately said that racial trouble has been brewing for years, fueled by white anti-Asian insults.

* The increasing numbers of young Asians of undoubted ability and achievement who are applying to institutions of higher education have revived the practice of setting admissions quotas, similar to those imposed some years ago to restrict the number of Jewish students. Harvard was cleared of anti-Asian bias charges, because its relatively higher admission rate for whites was due to its "legally permissible" preferences for children of alumni and for athletes.

* After hours of anti-Asian taunts and slurs, a white man in Raleigh, North Carolina, fatally injured a Chinese American who was playing pool with six Vietnamese friends. The successful federal civil rights prosecution in the summer of 1991 was only the second involving Asian American victims.

* In Waterbury, Connecticut, a Chinese restaurant delivery boy was killed in a planned execution by teenagers, who invited neighborhood kids to watch.

* Hispanics in the southwestern United States are the victims of resurgent nativism that blames them for, among other things, taking away jobs. Many of the jobs "taken" were available only because no one else would consider such backbreaking work as picking lettuce or such appalling living conditions as migrant shacks.

* In an eastern mushroom growing center, crimes are unreported, accusations are falsely made, and criminals go free because Mexican migrant workers cannot speak English and officials cannot speak Spanish. Although Hispanics (first Puerto Ricans, now Mexicans) have worked in this area for some 40 years, "the local McDonald's restaurant does a better job of translating its menu into Spanish than the nearby district justice court does with its official documents."[6] Spanish-speaking court officers have recently been hired, and the state police are now recruiting bilingual candidates throughout the state.

* Arabs have also been subjected to harassment and negative stereotyping. Long before the Persian Gulf crisis began, they were being caricatured as either greedy oil-rich sheiks or crazy terrorists. Said one Arab activist: "Whenever there is a conflict in the Middle East, there is a corresponding backlash against Arab-Americans."

A NEW ROUND OF "LET'S YOU AND HIM FIGHT"

The countless instances, past and present, of majority group antagonism toward immigrants--or anyone who is "different"--are depressing and disturbing. Equally troubling is the reappearance of the "Let's you and him fight" phenomenon. Having made its debut during Reconstruction, when poor whites were pitted against the newly freed slaves in a struggle for economic survival and political power, this scenario is again being played out all over the country.

- It has been evident in the bipartisan machinations connected with the political redistricting mandated by the 1990 census results. A *Wall Street Journal* article described the process at both federal and state levels as not only "fueling bickering between Democrats and Republicans (and) intensifying the strains between incumbents and challengers," but also "breeding new tensions among blacks, Hispanics, Asians, and whites."[7]
- In a near-perfect example of this game, the white owner of a store in a black community took advantage of the anti-Arab sentiments aroused by Desert Storm by placing an enormous sign in his window proclaiming that no Arabs would be involved in the remodeling.
- In lower Manhattan, a Vietnamese gang "Born to Kill" has been encroaching on traditionally Chinese territory; fatal shootings have resulted.
- In Los Angeles, the Martin Luther King, Jr., Hospital has become the site of battles between blacks and Hispanics for a "fair share" of the 3,500 jobs. The hospital was built in response to the 1960s riots in the Watts area of Los Angeles, then nearly 100 percent black. Now, however, the area has become about 50 percent Hispanic--but the hospital staff is only 11 percent Hispanic.
- In Houston, as *Newsweek* describes it, "[a]fter decades of struggle, blacks have finally achieved some measure of political clout, and don't want to give it up. Now Hispanics are demanding their share of political representation." Ben Reyes, the only Hispanic city council member, was quoted as saying: "We can't and won't avoid pitting minority against minority. . . . This is not about being racist toward blacks or blacks being racist toward me. This is about power. It's our turn."[8]
- In Washington, DC, in the spring of 1991, there was a two-day riot, which highlighted tensions between the District's black power structure (mayor and police chief) and its growing Hispanic community. As usual, the conflict was chiefly over jobs--in local government, in construction--but it was complicated by the fact that many of the aggrieved Hispanics were recent immigrants from Central America who do not speak English. One reporter noted, "For those who remember 1968, this week in Washington has brought eerie and disheartening echoes of that year, when white politicians,

merchants, and journalists admitted that they had been totally surprised by the explosions in the black community."[9]

- When a Hasidic Jew struck and killed a black youngster in the Crown Heights section of Brooklyn, it unleashed New York's worst racial violence in more than 20 years. There had been few points of contact for the many recent immigrants from the Caribbean area and members of the close-knit and ultra-traditional Jewish community.
- South Central Los Angeles has been the scene of violence between Koreans and African Americans. In a six-month period in 1991, two Korean shop owners and three black customers have been killed. Similar incidents have been reported in New York and Philadelphia.

Commenting on the growing number of hate-inspired incidents, one expert said: "The rapid increase of a minority population in an area almost invariably leads to conflict."[10] Yet time and time again, when violence breaks out, government officials are as baffled as ordinary citizens. Did no one see the significance of the arrival of numerous new people? Did no one notice that tension was brewing? Why should anyone be "surprised" when people who have been hurling epithets begin throwing rocks as well?

Table 4
Metropolitan Areas with Greatest Increases in Minority Group Populations, 1980-1990

African Americans		Hispanics		Asian & Pacific Islanders	
Sacramento (49)	65.5%	Orlando (31)	271.2%	Merced, CA (46)	423.3%
San Diego (33)	52.5%	DC (16)	136.7%	Modesto, CA (36)	368.2%
Miami (10)	50.1%	Las Vegas (33)	136.3%	Atlanta (19)	332.7%
Orlando (38)	47.1%	Atlanta (42)	135.8%	Austin, TX (37)	303.5%
Seattle (43)	40.1%	W. Palm Beach (38)	133.7%	Dallas, TX (13)	298.4%
Atlanta (7)	40.0%	Providence, RI (50)	114.6%	Fresno, CA (17)	287.4%

Notes: (1) Numbers in parentheses show area rank by 1990 minority population.
(2) Persons of Hispanic origin may be of any race.
Source: U.S. Census Bureau Release 91-229.

Another student of intergroup relations states: "As diversity grows, hate-crime statistics rise, and dealing with tensions caused by competition for jobs and housing, exacerbated by language barriers and cultural misunderstandings, becomes increasingly complicated."[11] Ironically, the warring individuals and groups usually have similar problems: how much better if they could be allies instead of rivals, and make common cause in the struggle for decent housing or employment or education. Instead, the simplest incident of cultural misunderstanding--a Korean or Arab shopkeeper's not making eye contact or engaging in small talk--can be a spark that ignites violence.

The warnings about the nature and dimensions of the changes we are facing have been sounded, but in many quarters, the news seems to have gone largely unheeded. California Tomorrow, an organization that recognizes the already great diversity of that state's population, is one of the few that is attempting to prepare the people and leaders for a peaceful, multicultural future.[12]

THE NEED TO ADDRESS CHANGE: IN BUSINESS

Some business leaders are among those who *are* taking note of demographic change. Government legislation and changing popular attitudes have no doubt contributed to new corporate policies, but so has the recognition that an effective operation is impossible when cultural differences get in the way of customer relations or staff communications.

- Max DePree, chairman and retired CEO of Herman Miller, office furniture manufacturing company: "In our plant in Irvine, California, we have to communicate in English, Spanish, and Vietnamese. . . . We've had a bit of backlash to deal with. . . . We said transfer or leave, diversity is here to stay. It's morally right--and it happens to be pragmatically right."[13]
- James R. Houghton, CEO of Corning: "Companies simply can't prosper in a diverse, multicultural world unless they reflect that diversity to some degree. . . . A company that successfully draws on the talents and abilities of all its employees as individuals will be best positioned for success."[14]
- Richard A. Clarke, chairman of Pacific Gas and Electric Company: "To be an effective business, we've got to have employee groups that are effective in dealing with . . . customers." P.G.& E., which serves an ethnically diverse population of 7.5 million people in Northern California, has placed hundreds of blacks, Hispanics, Asians, and women into jobs once reserved for white males.[15]

In 1987, *Workforce 2000*, the Department of Labor/Hudson Institute study of the forces shaping the American economy, appeared. It was followed in 1988 by *Opportunity 2000*, outlining appropriate strategies.[16] Pointing out that employers are already experiencing a shortage of qualified applicants for job openings, these and similar reports suggest that an increasing proportion of the labor force will be minorities and immigrants, many of whom will be poorly prepared for 21st-century employment. "These changes mean that the ability of companies to effectively compete in the years ahead will be determined in large measure by their success in employing productive workers in a labor market characterized by scarcity, skills deficiencies, and demographic diversity. The most successful companies will be those that meet this challenge creatively and aggressively."[17] Unfortunately, not all employers are as enlightened as those just cited. Three years after the publication of *Workforce 2000*, Towers Perrin surveyed some 645 organizations to see what, if anything, they had done in response to "this challenge." Among the findings:

- 75 percent of the organizations had some level of management concern about the issues; only 42 percent had a minority recruitment program;
- 57 percent claimed that diversity issues affected management decisions; only 29 percent trained managers to value and manage diversity;
- greater numbers of women and minorities were on the payrolls, but there was not a comparable increase in promotions.[18]

THE NEED TO ADDRESS CHANGE: IN THE PROFESSIONS

The social services are far from adequately prepared for diversity. A few years ago, a young white drifter with a history of mental problems shot five children and then himself in a Stockton, California, schoolyard. Most of the children in this school, however, were Cambodian refugees. The mental health and social service systems, eager as they were to ease the traumatic injuries, found that they were all but helpless: the problem was not simply language barriers, but cultural barriers. They had no way of understanding Cambodian family life or religion or sense of privacy, and the Western medical models in which they had been trained were irrelevant and misleading.

What a contrast with another schoolyard tragedy! The mid-air collision that killed U.S. Senator John Heinz and several others took place over an elementary school in a Main Line suburb of Philadelphia. For days afterwards, the local media carried stories about the massive rallying of professionals to assist the children, their families, and their teachers in coming to terms with their sorrow, anger, and fear. Here, however, helpers and helped spoke the same language, shared similar cultural values, and understood one another well.

In courts or offices or hospitals, even the best of intentions can go awry in the face of lack of education about and lack of understanding of minority groups. In one Philadelphia high school, for example, a retired police official, who had had lengthy training and experience in dealing with "difference," was the only person able to resolve continuing student unrest. He discovered that Asian students, many of them recent refugees from war-torn countries, felt threatened simply by being crowded or jostled. Once

51

this cultural difference was understood, school authorities were able to defuse the tensions, and peace has been maintained ever since.

A recent report by the New York State Judicial Commission on Minorities recommended "cross-cultural sensitivity training" as one of the many measures directed at reducing the subtle and overt racism that it found to pervade the state court system. Noting that "while 82 percent of the prison population is nonwhite, 81 percent of court personnel is white," the report stated that "most black litigators . . . say they are frequently confronted by court personnel who assume they are not lawyers."[19]

THE NEED TO ADDRESS CHANGE: IN EDUCATION

Unfortunately, many of today's young people are unacquainted with the history of their own ethnic group and are therefore unaware that their ancestors may well have been on the receiving end of prejudice and hatred. Bob Suzuki, long active in multicultural studies, relates his experience at the University of Massachusetts-Amherst with students from working-class Irish families in South Boston, the center of resistance to the desegregation of the Boston public schools. "Most were ignorant of the Irish experience in the United States and were surprised to learn of the discrimination faced by the early Irish immigrants. . . . When these students learned this history, they could relate more empathetically to the problems of people of color and became more open to understanding their experiences and perspectives."[20]

Bilingual education, usually meaning in Spanish, is frequently recommended as a means of easing acculturation of immigrants and allowing them to preserve their ethnic identity. Although the federal government has funded bilingual programs for some time, there are several reasons why this approach is of questionable value. For one thing, there is little evidence that even several years of instruction in the native language assist students in making a smooth transition to classes in English, increase their subsequent achievement levels, or prevent their dropping out of school.

There are also questions of practicality. School districts already have a difficult time finding bilingual teachers (no doubt a reflection on the sorry state of foreign language training in this country); increased funding would only exacerbate their problem. Consider the consequences, however, if bilingual education were proposed for the fastest growing immigrant group, the Asians. Unlike Hispanics, they do *not* share a common language, and chaos would ensue in any school that tried to offer instruction in the great variety of Asian languages. (The U.S. Census Bureau counts 17 specific Asian groups and eight specific Pacific Islander groups.)

The most important reason for limiting bilingual education, however, is the fact that English is the common language of citizenship, culture, and business in this country. Without English, newcomers are isolated from the mainstream, vulnerable to misunderstanding and being misunderstood. Despite the rhetoric of "English only" groups, the issue is not one of national hegemony but of what is ultimately in the best interests of non-English-speaking immigrants. Moreover, in this era of instantaneous global communication, English has become the world's standard language as well. It has replaced French among diplomats, Latin among theologians, and--in the course of a single generation--German among scientists. Assisting immigrants in becoming proficient in English, quickly and easily, is a key means of enhancing their self-sufficiency and increasing their range of choices.

This is not to say that we have no responsibility to assist non-English speakers, adults as well as children, with interpreters and written translations. Nor is it to suggest that all languages but English should be eradicated: far from it. The ability to communicate with fluency in more than one language has traditionally been the mark of the well-educated person, and students who are bilingual or even trilingual should be honored.

EDUCATIONAL REFORM: THE KEY TO THE FUTURE

Studies of demographic change and its implications for the economy tell us that a very large proportion of new entrants into the labor force of the near future will be immigrants and native-born minority group members; many of these jobseekers will be poorly educated. Simultaneously, economists describe the job market as changing rapidly because of the continuing technological revolution, and demanding "ever-higher levels of education and competency." As has been noted by many, including David Halberstam in his recent book, *The Next Century*, the mismatch is a recipe for disaster. "The line between those who will be winners and those who will be losers seems sharper than ever, and the line is the product of education. . . . Slowly and steadily we are creating a new class system."[21]

One expert after another has reached the same conclusion: the need for dramatic improvements in American education. Of course, educational reform is justifiable on many grounds other than the desire to ensure a qualified work force or to maintain America's position in the world economy. Education is the proven way out of poverty and into a life of dignity and choice, as generations of immigrants and former slaves can testify, but we are very far from providing that opportunity on an equal basis. There is no dearth of evidence that the American educational system is in trouble, particularly in urban areas. Throughout the 1980s, any number of task forces and commissions and blue-ribbon committees studied American schools and colleges, amassed data, and produced recommendations ranging from more homework for students to higher pay for teachers.[22]

Unfortunately, there is little sign that the "Education President" either recognizes one *fundamental* problem--enormous differences in funding levels among public school systems--or is prepared to provide the leadership and determination required if American education is to be reformed. It is naive or cynical to suggest that students be held to "world-class standards" in core subjects without focusing on how students will be able to bring their performance up to those standards. We need to develop, in tandem with the standards, initiatives to help students improve their performance. Without renewed attention to this, efforts to revitalize our educational system run the risk of becoming just another obstacle in the path of underachieving students.

If President Bush expects his education strategy to be taken seriously, he should begin by taking it seriously himself. He should immediately abandon the charade that remarkable public education--with or without choice--can be achieved without additional resources. It may very well be true that funds can be used in more efficient ways and/or reassigned to priority areas. But more money is essential to any effort to create improvement and maintain quality for *all* of this country's children and youth, not just those who already have distinct advantages. The president would never suggest that the Pentagon could develop new weapons without additions to its budget, and he should not imply that schools can or ought to do what is not expected of the Pentagon.

Mr. Bush's call for educational improvement and reform is important, but it displays no sense of urgency, no sense that improved education is crucial to both individuals and the nation. No distinction is made between schools in grave need and those that are relatively well-off, between students who are disadvantaged and those who are not, between those who are fluent in their native language or in two languages and those who have failed to master any language.

President Bush and many governors call for testing, more research, the development of model schools. The irony is that we already know so much about what "works."[23] Examples abound of schools that are succeeding, even in the least promising of circumstances. Recognizing their central and critical role in disintegrating neighborhoods, they have redefined and broadened their mission, their range of services, their staffing, and their hours.

- Teen health and pregnancy clinics, day care centers, and employment assistance can support the academic curriculum.
- Children who come to school hungry can be given breakfast; a laundry can be provided for dirty clothes; a school social worker can visit parents who are unable or unwilling to visit the schools.
- Head Start, one of the most cost-effective programs ever devised, can be made available to *all* the children who are eligible.
- Employers can expand on-the-job training, apprenticeships, and mentor programs, paying attention to the German models that have proven success-

ful in bridging the school-to-work transition for noncollege-bound students. The William T. Grant Foundation's Commission on Work, Family and Citizenship has done outstanding work in this area; particularly relevant is its 1988 report, *The Forgotten Half: Non-College Youth in America.*[24]

Neither the problems nor the urgent calls for solutions are new, of course. *Thirty years ago,* the National Committee on Children and Youth convened a Conference on Unemployed Out-of-School Youth in Urban Areas. Among the persons in attendance were Vice President Lyndon Baines Johnson, U.S. Attorney General Robert Kennedy, Secretary of Labor Arthur Goldberg, and Secretary of Health, Education and Welfare Abraham Ribicoff. James Bryant Conant, President Emeritus of Harvard, who chaired the conference, warned in his keynote address of the dangers posed by great numbers of minority young people who were uneducated, unskilled, and unemployed. Terming the situation "SOCIAL DYNAMITE" (the title given to the Conference proceedings), Conant and the other participants concluded: "This is the Number One domestic problem and can be solved only with multiple resources; there are no easy solutions."

Three decades later, the problems are even more serious--exacerbated by drugs, teen pregnancies, a massive federal budget deficit, and an influx of Asians and Hispanics eager to grab the bottom rung on the economic ladder --but solutions still elude us. Additional rhetoric, research, and reports have been unable to procure the resources necessary for breaking the cycle of poor prenatal care, inadequate education, and poverty. And reason, morality, and common sense have been equally powerless to persuade the American public or its leaders of the wisdom of educational and social reforms.

It is said that for every $1,000 expended on prenatal care, we may be saving up to $100,000 in the cost of treating low birth weight, multi-problem babies. Yet the United States is almost alone among industrialized nations in having no family policy, and there is no sign that we are about to develop one. The cost of a year in an institution--a prison or mental hospital--is greater than a year at an Ivy League college. Yet all over the country, cities and states are unable to fund even basic human services and are cutting back on promising programs, such as the collaboration between the Chelsea, Massachusetts, school system and Boston University.

America needs scientifically trained workers; it needs literate service workers; it needs highly skilled manufacturing workers. But America also needs citizens who understand what America has been, what she is now, and what she is becoming. The education reform movement of the last decade has cast its net out into the global economy, but has given only lip service to the needs of the citizens of the real America. Education for employment is important, but without a revitalized sense of an American civilization, successful reform may prove to be a hollow victory.

A UNIFYING VISION OF AMERICA

For more than two centuries, the United States has attracted and absorbed millions of immigrants, holding out the promise of participation in building a new country, a more just society. Assimilation was expected, not only by those already here but also by the newcomers themselves, and the concept of the melting pot was both accepted and understood. (It helped, of course, that until the mid-20th century, most newcomers had white skin and similar facial features.)

Inexorably, however, the consequences of national and international upheavals, and particularly demographic changes, have contributed to the decline of WASP preeminence and the disintegration of a common culture. Now, the key issue is national survival, not merely as an economic power but as a *nation*. In 1992, how can we maintain our unity while celebrating our diversity? "The national ideal had once been *e pluribus unum*," wrote Arthur Schlesinger in his recent book, *The Disuniting of America*. "Are we now to belittle *unum* and glorify *pluribus*? Will the center hold? Or will the melting pot yield to the Tower of Babel?"[25] Schlesinger's concern--which is not his alone--about *what* will define the new America is important. But *who* will help to define her is at least as important. We need to ensure the participation of people and the inclusion of ideas formerly excluded from the process of definition as we search for a unifying national vision.

Some people are wondering whether there is *anything*--other than the shared experience of televised events, particularly crises--which can tie Americans together in the post-melting pot period of our history. Award-winning American writer Joyce Carol Oates frames the questions well: "Can a secular, consumer-oriented society, rapidly fragmenting into subsocieties of ethnic, cultural, professional, and religious diversity, be united in any but the most abstract political way--guaranteed, and enforced, by law? Or is the very idea of 'community' in America . . . outdated; has it undergone a radical transformation from its origins in a largely agrarian and ethnically homogeneous culture?"[26]

Somewhere between the idea of America as a land of unfettered opportunity and the America that is unrelentingly hostile to her poorest citizens lies the real America. This real America is in desperate need of a new way of apprehending herself: her traditional self-image offers little to help us connect the past to the present, or either to our very different future. The real America has not done much to define her *common* heritage, despite the rising popularity of the trinkets of patriotism. She has done even less to distinguish the part of her common heritage that is worthy of accompanying us into the 21st century, or to separate her from what should remain, as history, in the past.

If America is a beacon, it is because so many of us understand the irony of having to say "we have come, over a way that with tears has been watered." The struggle over multicultural curricula and diversity is heated and angry because our schools, our leadership, and our institutions have not paid enough attention to the defining features of American life: America has been continuously reinvented by streams of people encountering, interpreting, and trying to reconcile their lives with American ideals. The philosophical and political documents that gave this country legal life did not create the nation; that has been done by the people who have struggled to live their lives here. We need to find a new myth or symbol or ritual around which *all* of us can rally, while recognizing that reciting slogans and waving flags can never substitute for new attitudes and actions.

As this nation faces the implications of increased diversity, it is important to understand that the vision of a truly multicultural society is an *ideal*. Even while we work for harmony and justice, we must realize that perfection is not attainable, that not all positive values are compatible, that conflict cannot be wholly eliminated.

WHAT CAN BE DONE?

1. *Distinguish between race and class as the dominant determinant.* Racism is a fact of American life, but not every problem affecting minorities can or should be explained entirely in terms of racism. Poverty is more likely to be the key factor in determining whether people succumb to such diseases as breast cancer or tuberculosis, or whether patients respond well to surgery, or whether children are properly immunized. Similarly, learning difficulties are almost always associated with low family socioeconomic levels. African Americans are disproportionately poor relative to their numbers in the population, but there are in fact more poor whites than blacks.

2. *Devise strategies to fit the times.* Coalitions must be formed around issues, rather than racial groups. Poverty, injustice, poor education, and inadequate health care affect citizens and immigrants, blacks and whites. Successful confrontation and action will be far more likely if strategies of cooperation and inclusion are adopted. It is as unreasonable to expect total agreement as it is to require a perfect solution. Unfortunately, enemies of social progress are always pleased to see groups who ought to be allies fighting each other over turf or status.

3. *Distinguish between policy imperatives and "good works."* As history demonstrates, appeals to morality are seldom effective by themselves. Strategies for change must be aligned with the self-interest of those in power, and ways must be found to overcome the American preference for "instant" solutions.

4. *Refuse to apply "bandaids" when major surgery is required.* Not every strategy, no matter how well-planned, will succeed. And there may

well be emergency situations, when "bandaids"--temporary palliatives--are appropriate. Nevertheless, it is always better to identify and address the underlying causes of a problem, and to devise long-term solutions.

5. *Demonstrate the reality and horror of lives on the edge.* Appeals to alleviate poverty, to provide better health care, or to improve public schools often fall on deaf ears because so many Americans are almost completely insulated from poverty. Ways must be found to make more visible the human face of suffering--as well as the quiet gallantry--in inner city ghettos or forgotten Appalachian towns. One example is Alex Kotlowitz's *There Are No Children Here*[27]; another is Nicholas Lemann's *The Promised Land.*[28] There are many others. A story can illuminate statistics and break down stereotypes more effectively than dozens of well-documented research studies, and we cannot forget that the battle is not simply for people's minds, but for their hearts.

6. *Talk to the people; listen to the people.* The problems confronting African Americans may have diminished somewhat in their severity, but ironically they may very well have increased in magnitude and complexity. It is critical, then, that this recommendation be the guiding principle for all African American leaders, and particularly for the National Urban League.

We cannot assume that everyone understands the complexity of current and persistent issues. We cannot assume that because the policy alternatives are clear to the leadership, they are clear to our constituencies. Someone has said: "New occasions teach new duties, time makes ancient good uncouth. . . ." That truth should guide leaders as they negotiate the dense thicket of competing ideas and confusing information. Leaders must listen, talk, engage in dialogue, analyze, critique--and repeat the process on a continuing basis.

The United States is the only country in history that was founded by immigrants and that said to the entire world:

Give me your tired, your poor,
Your huddled masses yearning to breathe free,
The wretched refuse of your teeming shore.
Send these, the tired, the tempest-tossed, to me:
I lift my lamp beside the golden door.[29]

Despite the failures--there were and are many--to live up to her own generous ideal, America has always been a symbol of hope for millions of people, a place where better jobs could be found, children could be educated, religious and political freedom could be enjoyed. The historic national welcome to newcomers needs to be reaffirmed and extended, but we must also make good on old promises to those of us who have been here for years.

We know from the newspapers, as well as from the history books, that hard times make people desperate, prone to turn on one another and especially on "strangers." African Americans, the largest of the minority groups, are still very much engaged in a centuries-old struggle for equal rights and equal opportunities. Some progress has been made, but much remains to be accomplished--as can be seen from the other essays in this publication. Will the efforts to adapt to increasingly diverse employees and customers work to the advantage or disadvantage of African Americans? Will new fashions in domestic or foreign policy endanger the gains already made and prevent further progress? Suppose that the federal government decides to undertake a massive aid program to assist the former states of the Soviet Union in their attempt to establish economic stability. Will there be any hope of *also* mounting the domestic "Marshall Plan" called for by the National Urban League's John Jacob? What about the current immigration policy, which encourages the admission of thousands of workers already equipped with the special skills needed by business and industry? Will their arrival deflect attention and resources from government- and employer-sponsored efforts to train or retrain native-born American workers?

The changes are inevitable. The choices are ours. For African Americans, the struggle goes on.

The Economic Status of African Americans: Limited Ownership and Persistent Inequality

David H. Swinton, Ph.D.

INTRODUCTION

The annual reports on the economic status of African Americans presented in these pages over the last decade and more have repeatedly shown that African Americans have low and unequal economic status. Moreover, as indicated in the last edition of this report, this pattern has taken on the characteristic of a permanent feature of the American economy. For two decades, there has been no consistent progress in improving the relative position of the African American population as a whole. To be sure, there is a distribution of economic well-being within the African American population. Naturally, some African Americans fare better than others. However, in comparison to Americans of European descent, African Americans experience substantially lower economic status throughout the income distribution. As we have noted on several occasions, relatively well-off blacks are much less well off than well-off whites, and relatively poor blacks are much poorer than poor whites. Moreover, all standard measures of central tendency have consistently revealed the relatively low economic status of the population as a whole.

This year is no exception. Despite a few wrinkles due to the impact of the business cycle, the overall evidence from the latest data shows the persistence of second-class economic status for African Americans. The indicators of absolute and relative current economic status will be reviewed in some detail. These data will once again reveal that blacks continue to have low current incomes, high rates of poverty, low participation in the higher income classes, and low labor-market status.

In the past, we have concluded most of our reviews with the observation that the current economic status of blacks was inextricably tied to the past through the influence of the past on current levels of ownership of human and nonhuman capital. Indeed, we have generally asserted in concluding remarks that the cause of the persisting disparities was the persistence of the large gaps in ownership that African Americans inherited from the past.

Moreover, we have also generally concluded that little progress would be made in closing racial gaps between African Americans and European Americans until there is significant reduction in the ownership gaps. The proposition is very simple. In a market-driven free enterprise economy, **CIVIL RIGHTS IS NOT ENOUGH.** Parity in **OWNERSHIP IS RE-QUIRED** to ensure parity in economic outcomes.

We have also generally concluded that inequality in ownership is not self-correcting. There are no known market forces that will eliminate disparities in ownership once established. Indeed market forces would tend to perpetuate and even exacerbate racial gaps in ownership once they have been established. Thus, some form of extra market intervention would be required to eliminate gaps in ownership and the resulting gaps in economic status.

In this year's paper, we will start our discussion of current economic trends with a discussion of the importance of ownership and a review of the latest available evidence concerning ownership disparities. This reversal of the usual order of presentation is intended to focus more attention on the wealth ownership aspects of African American economic status. After the wealth and ownership disparities are presented, we will again review the latest data and recent trends concerning current economic outcomes. As usual, we will have a few concluding remarks concerning the implications of the analysis for strategy to bring about racial parity in economic life.

AFRICAN AMERICAN OWNERSHIP OF WEALTH, BUSINESS, AND HUMAN CAPITAL

Ownership of human and nonhuman wealth is crucial to the economic well-being of individuals and groups in a capitalistic system. Although this statement is transparently obvious, very little attention is devoted to questions of ownership by those interested in promoting racial equality. Wealth or capital is a stock concept; it refers to all of those things that one inherits from the past that are useful in earning a living.

Ownership of wealth is important to individual or group well-being for two reasons. First, employed capital assets earn current income or provide current consumption benefits. Thus, the group or individual that owns and employs more assets will have higher current earnings or consumption. Second, ownership of wealth is important because wealth holders organize production in a capitalistic system. They determine the employment of human resources. They also determine trading relationships with other economic entities. Thus, an individual or a group that owns sufficient wealth or businesses can better ensure more remunerative employment for the human resources and nonhuman resources that they own or favor. Limited ownership of wealth by African Americans would imply lower direct earnings from wealth ownership and possibly lower earnings from the employment of black human and nonhuman resources. Indeed, as we shall see below, African Americans experience both impacts from their limited ownership.

Current Wealth Ownership

Wealth disparities between blacks and non-Hispanic whites are extremely large. Table 1 displays the latest Census Bureau data on wealth ownership. Census data on wealth ownership have a number of well-known shortcomings. However, these shortcomings probably result in an understatement of the relative ownership disparities. In any case, the disparities are so large that the qualitative conclusions would probably not be significantly impacted by data improvements. Moreover, the census data are the only readily available data on wealth holdings of households.

A number of facts about the black disadvantage in wealth ownership stand out quite clearly from this table. First, blacks who have wealth have much lower average holdings than whites. Thus, the mean black net worth of $26,130 is only 23 percent of the mean white net worth of $111,950. The disparity is even greater if we use median data not shown in Table 1. In 1988, median wealth holdings for blacks was only $4,606, which was less than 10 percent of white median wealth holdings of $47,815. Moreover, as is apparent from the table, mean holdings are lower for each type of wealth. Thus, for example, while blacks who own stocks and mutual funds have average portfolio values of $4,050, whites have average portfolio values of $31,266. The reader can review the other means from the table.

Second, smaller proportions of blacks own each type of asset. Thus, for example, while 76.58 percent of whites own interest-bearing assets at financial institutions, only 44.48 percent of blacks have such holdings. The reader can note the disparity in each of the other types of assets. Moreover, it is also clear that blacks own fewer of the consumer assets as well as fewer of the investment assets. Thus, blacks have lower mean holdings and smaller proportions owning motor vehicles and houses as well.

Third, the combined impact of smaller mean holdings and smaller proportions owning each type of asset results in significantly smaller per capita holdings in the black community. The per capita value of black net wealth holdings of $8,981 is only 21 percent of white per capita holdings of $43,164. Indeed, as is apparent from the B/W column in Table 1, equality is greatest for motor vehicle ownership, and even here the per capita value of black motor vehicles is only 40 percent of the per capita value of white motor vehicles. The per capita value of black stock portfolios is only 3 percent of the per capita value of white stock portfolios. The reader can see from the table that the disparity in black and white wealth holdings of each type of wealth is glaring.

The last three columns translate these notions into aggregate terms. As

Table 1
Wealth Ownership 1988
(in Millions of 1990$)

	Mean		% Wealthholders Owning		Per Capita		Aggregate		B/W	Aggregate Gap
	Black	White	Black	White	Black	White	Black	White		
Total Net Worth	26,130	111,950	100.00	100.00	8,981	43,164	268,568	8,862,993	.21	1,022,208
Interest-Earning at Financial Institutions	4,806	20,870	44.48	76.58	735	6,162	21,979	1,265,262	.12	162,289
Regular Checking	789	1,193	30.11	50.92	82	234	2,452	48,048	.35	45,454
Stock & Mutual Funds	4,050	31,266	6.97	23.92	97	2,884	2,901	592,180	.03	83,342
Equity in Business	27,880	73,511	3.66	13.57	351	3,846	10,496	789,711	.09	104,515
Equity in Motor Vehicle	4,384	7,080	64.67	89.15	974	2,434	29,127	499,781	.40	43,660
Equity in Home	40,624	70,888	43.46	66.72	6,068	18,236	181,458	3,744,453	.33	363,872
Equity in Rental Property	45,031	92,090	4.55	9.61	704	3,412	21,052	700,596	.21	80,980
Other Real Estate	18,132	42,505	4.37	11.35	272	1,860	8,134	381,919	.15	47,488
U.S. Savings Bond	1,118	3,444	11.01	18.47	245	203	1,256	50,307	.17	60,705
IRA or Keoghs	6,136	18,242	6.87	26.43	1,859	1,714	4,336	381,714	.08	51,255

Aggregate gaps = white per capita – black per capita * 1988 black population.
Inequality Index (B/W) = black per capita/white per capita

Source: U.S. Department of Commerce, Bureau of the Census, *Household Wealth and Asset Ownership: 1988*, December 1990.

one would expect, the aggregate wealth holdings of whites dwarf the wealth holdings of blacks. The aggregate value of wealth owned by African Americans in 1988 was about 269 billion dollars compared to $8,863 billion owned by whites. Thus, while the number of white households was about 7.7 times the number of African American households, the wealth ownership of white Americans was over 33 times the wealth ownership of African Americans. Disparities for some individual types of wealth are even more glaring, as can be derived by the reader.

In any case, the aggregate wealth gaps are shown in the final column. Overall, the gap in wealth ownership in the aggregate for African Americans is estimated to be about 1,022 billion dollars. Large aggregate wealth gaps exist for each type of asset. For example, there is an 83 billion dollar disparity in stock ownership, and a 104 billion dollar disparity in the ownership of equity in businesses. Other disparities can be easily read from the table. Given the importance of wealth ownership, these data make it apparent why blacks have made so little progress in attaining economic parity.

Current Ownership of Business

Table 2 provides a different overview of African American ownership. This table displays information about the share of businesses owned by African Americans. Again, there are some difficulties with the data. Starting with the 1987 survey, the Census Bureau excluded regular corporations. This results in somewhat of an understatement of the ownership position of African Americans. However, this understatement is relatively small for African Americans, given the relatively few large corporations owned by this group. The total data cover all firms. However, since they also include black ownership, the inequality indexes somewhat understate the degree of inequality between blacks and whites. However, in view of the very large ownership disparities, this is at best a minor problem.

The data in Table 2 make it abundantly clear that African Americans own a very minuscule share of American businesses. For example, blacks owned 424,000 business firms out of a total of 17.5 million. The B/T column indicates that black per capita ownership was only about 19.8 percent of per capita business ownership for the total population. The last column shows that African Americans own more than 1.7 million fewer businesses than would be required for parity in the number of businesses owned.

A quick perusal of the table will reveal that the number of businesses owned by blacks falls short of parity for each industry classification. For example, blacks have greatest equality in the numbers of construction firms owned. Here, blacks own 37,000 firms, which is a little better than half as many required for parity in numbers of construction firms owned. Blacks are relatively furthest from parity in the ownership of wholesale trade

Table 2
Receipts (in Millions of 1990$) and Number of Firms (1,000's) in 1987 by Industry

	Black Receipts	Total Receipts	B/T**	Receipt Gap	Black Firms	Total Firms	B/T**	Firm Gap
Total	22.8	$11,413	0.016	1,369	424	17,526	0.198	1,713
Construction	2.6	591	0.037	70	37	560	0.539	32
Manufacturing	1.2	3,056	0.003	372	8	642	0.102	70
Trans. and Public Util.	1.8	872	0.017	104	37	735	0.412	53
Wholesale Trade	1.5	1,407	0.009	170	6	641	0.070	73
Retail Trade	6.7	1,729	0.032	204	66	2,658	0.204	258
Finance, Ins. and Real Estate	0.9	1,741	0.004	212	27	1,426	0.155	147
Selected Services	7.1	956	0.060	110	210	7,095	0.242	656
Other Industries*	0.9	1,060	0.007	129	34	3,769	0.075	425

Note: 1987 dollars were converted to 1990 dollars using CPI-U
*Includes Agriculture, Mining, and Industries not elsewhere classified.

**This is black receipts or firms per capita divided by the complement for total per capita.
   Black population in 1987: 29,417,000; total population in 1987: 241,187,000.

Source: U.S. Department of Commerce, Bureau of the Census, *Survey of Minority-Owned Businesses: Black, 1987*, and *The Statistical Abstract of the United States, 1990.* Table 859, p. 521.

businesses. Here, blacks own only 6,000 firms, which is about 7 percent of the number required for parity. The reader can easily review the data for the other industries.

However, the disparity in business ownership is much greater than indicated by the number of businesses owned. Black firms on average tend to be significantly smaller than white-owned businesses. The receipts data in Table 2 provide some indication of the volume of business conducted by African American-owned firms. As can be seen, the total receipts for black-owned businesses in 1987 was only 22.8 billion dollars, compared to 11,413 billion dollars for all American businesses. Black-owned businesses in the aggregate had receipts that were only about 1.6 percent of what would be required for ownership parity. The aggregate receipt gap was about 1.4 trillion dollars.

Table 2 makes it clear that in terms of the share of business volume originating in the black-owned sector, black businesses are minuscule in every industrial sector. While the number of black-owned firms in the construction sector was over 50 percent of the number required for parity, the receipts generated by these firms is less than 4 percent of the amount required for parity. The service sector, which generated only 6 percent of the amount required for parity, is the most equal sector by this measure.

Black ownership of businesses and nonhuman wealth is obviously very limited. The gaps in wealth and business ownership are obviously much larger than the disparities in current labor market outcomes. These large disparities indicate that blacks have little capacity through ownership to ensure equal returns on their resources. Black resource owners are thus very vulnerable to discrimination. Moreover, the low levels of ownership will have a direct impact on reducing black well-being through smaller amounts of earnings from nonhuman assets.

Recent Trends in Wealth and Business Ownership

The evidence concerning trends in black wealth ownership is very sparse. However, available evidence suggests that little if any progress has been made in the past two decades in reducing gaps in the ownership of businesses and nonhuman assets. Although there may be problems with the statistical significance of the measured differences, comparison of the results of the 1984 and the 1988 survey of wealth ownership indicates a small increase in racial inequality at least as measured by the ratio of black-to-white per capita holdings. Overall, while the inequality index for total net worth was about 23 percent in 1984, it had fallen to 21 percent by 1988. While the direction of change in the inequality index varied somewhat by wealth category, the majority of the changes were in the direction of

67

Table 3
Distribution of Persons 25 Years and Older by Years of School Completed

Male

	1990 W	1990 B	1985 W	1985 B	1980 W	1980 B	1970 W	1970 B
0-8 yrs.	10.30	17.01	12.75	20.76	15.67	26.66	25.47	43.98
1-3 yrs. HS	9.86	16.33	10.77	17.73	12.27	20.11	15.40	21.93
4 yrs. HS	36.07	38.33	35.17	34.28	34.10	31.10	31.64	23.25
1-3 yrs. COL	18.42	16.94	17.26	16.02	15.73	13.92	11.76	6.02
4 yrs. COL	13.99	7.66	13.26	7.15	11.94	5.23	15.73	4.81
5+ yrs. COL	11.36	3.75	10.79	4.04	10.30	2.98	15.73	4.81
Med	12.70	12.50	12.80	12.30	12.60	12.10	12.30	9.80

Female

	1990 W	1990 B	1985 W	1985 B	1980 W	1980 B	1970 W	1970 B
0-8 yrs.	9.54	13.83	12.36	18.01	15.58	25.00	23.60	38.71
1-3 yrs. HS	10.49	19.44	11.78	19.02	13.26	22.40	17.12	25.55
4 yrs. HS	41.83	37.22	42.54	36.64	42.39	32.06	39.47	25.16
1-3 yrs. COL	18.78	17.93	16.87	15.61	14.93	12.39	10.85	6.22
4 yrs. COL	12.10	7.61	10.24	6.97	8.87	5.38	8.96	4.36
5+ yrs. COL	7.22	3.96	6.20	3.76	4.96	2.77	8.96	4.36
Med	12.80	12.40	12.60	12.40	12.50	12.10	12.20	10.30

Source: U.S. Department of Commerce, Bureau of the Census, *Money Income of Households, Families, and Persons in the U.S.: 1990*, September 1991, Series P-60, No. 174, Table 29.

increasing inequality. Indeed, the calculated aggregate wealth gap increased from $733 billion to the already noted $1,022 billion.

It is difficult to establish a time trend on the ownership of business because the Census Bureau has changed methodologies with each successive survey since the first one in 1969. There may have been some small improvement in relative business ownership since 1969. However, the gain is at best marginal. Current disparities are so large that it is apparent that there has been no significant reduction in the business ownership disparity in the past two decades.

Recent Trends in Education or Human Wealth Ownership

The discussion so far has briefly reviewed the facts concerning ownership of nonhuman wealth and businesses. Of course, human capital is also an essential ingredient for economic prosperity. The most prominent form of human capital is education. Our brief discussion of human capital shall be restricted to presenting limited information about the educational attainment of African Americans.

Table 3 displays information about recent trends in the educational attainment of the prime working-age population. As can be seen from the data in the 1990 columns, African Americans have lower educational attainment than have whites. This is true for both African American males and females. More African Americans have an elementary school education or less. In 1990, 13.83 percent of African American females and 17.01 percent of African American males had no high school education in comparison to 9.57 and 10.30 percent of white males and females, respectively. Likewise, fewer African Americans had completed at least four years of college. For African American males, the percentage completing college is 11.41 percent versus 25.35 percent for white males; for African American females, the percentage completing four or more years of college is 11.57 versus 19.32 for white females. In 1990, the median educational attainment for black males is estimated at 12.5 years versus 12.7 years for white males, while the median educational attainment for black females is 12.4 years versus 12.8 for white females.

In aggregate terms, these numbers imply a large educational gap. Black males have an excess of 1,002,388 persons who have not completed high school and a shortage of 1,052,388 persons completing at least four years of college. For black females, the excess number of high school dropouts is 1,252,881 persons, and the shortage of college graduates is 753,812 persons. These large educational disparities contribute both directly and indirectly to the continued economic inequality experienced by African Americans.

However, as the historical data make clear, blacks have made substantial educational progress during the past two years. The proportion of males and

69

females that had no high school education has fallen by 75 percent. In 1970, 43.98 percent of black males and 38.71 percent of black females 25 years and older had no high school education. By 1990, these proportions had fallen to 17.01 and 13.83 percent, respectively. The proportion of black high school dropouts had also fallen for both males and females. On the other hand, the proportion of high school completers and those with a college education had increased significantly. Thus, the educational distribution among blacks has improved significantly since 1970.

However, the distribution among whites has also improved over the past two decades. As a result, the relative gaps have declined very little. For example, in 1970, 64.26 percent of black females and 40.72 of white females had less than four years of high school. By 1990, these numbers had fallen to 33.3 percent for black females and 20.06 percent for white females. While the absolute gaps had fallen, the relative disparity had actually increased. In 1990, black females were 66 percent more likely than white females to not have completed high school, but in 1970, black females had been only about 58 percent more likely to not have completed high school than their white counterparts.

Similarly, the gains among white college graduates were also large. While the proportion of black males who graduated from college increased from 4.81 percent to 11.41 percent--an absolute gain of 6.60 percentage points, the proportion of white male college graduates increased from 15.73 percent to 25.35 percent, a gain of 9.62 percent. Thus, the absolute gap between black and white males increased from 10.92 to 13.94 percentage points. However, the relative disparity in college graduates declined, since African American males were only 31 percent as likely as white males to be college graduates in 1970, and 45 percent as likely in 1990.

Calculations reveal similar trends for the change in college graduate proportions among black and white female populations. The absolute disparity between the proportion that were college graduates increased from 4.60 percent to 7.75 percent. However, the relative gap improved, since the ratio of black to white proportions of college graduates improved from 48.7 percent to 59.8 percent between 1970 and 1990.

In order to have a summary measure of the relative educational attainment of African Americans, indexes of occupational similarity were constructed, using the wages of full-time year-round white workers for weights. This index had a value for black males of 87.89 in 1990. This means that if everything else were equal, black males would have an education that was equivalent to 87.89 percent of the education of white male workers in 1990. Another interpretation of this index is that black males would earn 87.89 percent of what white males earn, if all workers worked full-time year-round and the average wage of black workers at each educational level were equal to the average wage of white workers.

This index was also calculated for 1970, still using 1990 wages as weights.

The 1970 value of the index was 83.60 percent. Thus, this measure indicates that educational equality has increased during the past 20 years. In fact, the index increased by 4.29 percent. This is equivalent to a 26 percent decline in the educational disparity since 1970.

Similar calculations for females produced indexes of 92.53 in 1990 and 89.70 in 1970. Thus, by this measure, at least there is less educational inequality between black and white females. The degree of educational similarity also increased between 1970 and 1990 for females. The index increased by 2.83 percent, which is a 27 percent improvement for black females.

Table 4 provides evidence on future prospects for improving the educational distribution. This table displays the educational distributions in 1990 of the population aged 25 to 65 and of the population aged 25 to 34. As can be seen from this table, the younger populations have significantly better educational distributions. This is true for both black and white persons of both sexes. The better educational distributions for younger age groups

Table 4
Years of School Completed in 1990
by Race, Sex, and Age

| | Male | | | |
| | 25 to 65 | | 25 to 34 | |
	B	W	B	W
8 yrs.	10.66	7.19	2.92	4.70
1-3 yrs. HS	16.29	8.80	13.70	9.27
4 yrs. HS	41.96	37.07	50.40	40.66
1-3 yrs. COL	18.70	19.81	21.03	20.80
4 yrs. COL	8.46	15.08	8.89	16.20
5 + yrs. COL	3.93	12.06	3.08	8.38
4 + yrs. COL	12.39	27.14	11.97	24.58

| | Female | | | |
| | 25 to 65 | | 25 to 34 | |
	B	W	B	W
8 yrs.	7.31	5.84	2.65	3.98
1-3 yrs. HS	18.87	8.97	16.75	8.61
4 yrs. HS	40.66	42.53	42.58	40.21
1-3 yrs. COL	20.37	20.63	25.63	21.99
4 yrs. COL	8.47	13.78	9.39	17.97
5 + yrs. COL	4.31	8.26	3.02	7.23
4 + yrs. COL	12.78	22.04	12.41	25.20

Source: U.S. Department of Commerce, Bureau of the Census, *Money Income of Households, Families, and Persons in the U.S.: 1990*, September 1991, Series P-60, No. 174, Table 29.

imply that there will be a continuing absolute improvement in the educational attainment of the population.

Younger blacks have made significant gains at reducing the proportions with no high school. Indeed, both black males and females in the 25-to-34 age group have proportions with less than a high school education that are half what they are for the total black population. In fact, as one can see from the table, the proportion of black males and females with only an elementary school education is actually smaller than the proportion of whites with such limited education among the youngest age group. This implies that the future black population will have a significantly smaller proportion with the lowest levels of education.

However, the progress for blacks has been much lower at the higher end of the educational scale. Younger black males have only marginal larger proportions with college degrees than has the entire black male population. Indeed, the small differences are probably not statistically significant. The ratio of the proportion of black males to white males with college degrees is almost identical to the population over 25, at 45.1 percent, and to the population of males 25 to 65 at 45.7 percent. The ratio is only slightly higher at 48.7 percent for the 25-to-34 age group. Thus, there is no evidence that the proportion of black males with college education will be higher in the future.

The ratio of black to white females is actually lower among the younger age groups. The ratio is 59.6 percent for the entire population, including those over 65; it is 57.9 percent for the 25-to-65-year-old population, and only 49.2 percent for the 25-to-34 age group. The decline in the ratio is due to much faster progress in attaining a college education for white women. In fact, the proportion of white women with college degrees exceeds the proportion of white men with college degrees for the youngest age group. In any case, if recent trends continue, we can expect a slight erosion in the relative proportion of black females with college degrees in comparison to white women.

The index of educational similarity for black males aged 25 to 64 is 86.7, and the index of educational similarity for black males ages 25 to 34 is 91.9. Thus, the educational position of blacks aged 25 to 65 is slightly worse relative to all blacks whose index was 87.9. The educational position of the youngest black males has actually improved relative to the youngest white males. This is caused principally by the educational decline among the youngest white males at the college level and the improvement among young black males at reducing the proportions of their population with the lowest levels of education. If these trends continue, there will be slight improvements in the relative education of the black male population in the future. However, much of this gain may be due to the attrition of the least educated parts of the black male population.

The index of educational similarity for females is 92.6 for women aged 25 to 65 and 92.5 for women aged 25 to 34, while it was 92.5 for all women over 25. Thus, educational inequality by this measure is constant across the three age groups. This constancy for younger groups is the result of the large gains at lower educational levels offsetting the small declines for younger black women at the higher educational levels.

To summarize, the data reveal that blacks continue to have substantially less human capital than whites. Both black males and females have more persons with low amounts of education and fewer persons with high levels of education than do their white counterparts. Blacks have made absolute gains in attaining higher quantities of educational capital since 1970. Based on the index of educational similarity, the educational capital gaps were lowered by as much as 27 percent for females and 26 percent for males between 1970 and 1990. However, recent trends suggest that only marginal additional improvement can be expected in the future.

Using the index of educational similarity as a summary measure, the average black male educational capital in 1990 was about 87 percent of white male educational capital, and the average value of educational capital for black females was about 92 percent of the educational capital for white females.

The shortfall in black earnings due to the educational gap was estimated to be about $40.8 billion. According to McConnell, rates of return from investments in schooling ran 10 to 13 percent for secondary education and 8 to 10 percent for higher education during the 1970s and the early 1980s. Assuming a rate of return of 11 percent for investments in education, the above cited earnings shortfall implies a human capital deficiency of $371 billion. Thus, the aggregate shortfall of human capital for blacks is very large.

RECENT TRENDS IN INCOME, POVERTY, AND LABOR MARKET STATUS

Income, poverty, and labor market status are the result of current economic operations. These concepts measure flows as opposed to the wealth concepts discussed up to this point, which measure stocks. As we have indicated, African Americans are severely disadvantaged with respect to ownership of human and nonhuman capital stocks. The indicated shortfalls of capital ownership measured into the hundreds of billions of dollars. These capital ownership shortfalls would be expected to result in large disadvantages in current economic status. They should produce lower incomes, higher rates of poverty, and lower labor market status. Therefore, we will turn to a review of the current flows to the African American community. These flows may be viewed as a consequence of their current stocks of capital.

73

Recent Income Trends

Income is derived primarily from the earnings of human and nonhuman assets. The data in the next few tables report recent trends in annual flows of income to African Americans. Relatively low incomes are a direct consequence of the relatively low levels of wealth ownership.

Per Capita and Aggregate Income

Table 5 contains data on the flows of per capita and aggregate income since the early 1970s. During 1990, the African American population received an aggregate of 278.6 billion dollars in current income. Aggregate income for African Americans fell slightly in constant dollar terms during that year. Given the continued stagnation of the economy during 1990 we can expect a further real dollar decline in income to be recorded for 1991 when the data are in. The aggregate black income equaled only 7.78 percent of the total aggregate income, even though the African American population was 12.45 percent of the national population.

African American per capita income in 1990 was $9,017, compared to $15,265 for whites. Both African American and white per capita income fell during 1990 by 2.2 and 2.8 percent, respectively. This was the first decline in real per capita income in seven years for both races. White per capita income fell at a slightly faster rate than black per capita income. As a result, inequality fell slightly during 1990. However, if historical patterns follow, inequality will increase again during the early stages of the recovery. In any case, blacks had only 59.1 percent as much income per capita as whites had during 1990. This amounted to an income deficit of $6,248 per black person. In the aggregate, the black community had an income deficit of $193 billion.

These income gaps provide the most comprehensive measure of the impact of the wealth and business ownership gaps on the current economic position of blacks. These low income flows are direct and indirect consequences of the low levels of human and nonhuman wealth and business ownership. As is evident from the data in Table 5, there has been no improvement in the per capita income disparity for the past 20 years. Inequality climbed rapidly during the early 1970s recession and recovered somewhat during the long 1980s recovery. However, as we enter the 1990s, inequality--as measured by the inequality index--is still higher than it was during the mid-1970s. The small gains during the 1970s were due to reduced discrimination and not to increased equality in wealth ownership.

Income of Persons

The limited wealth ownership means that fewer blacks than whites have capital to employ, and those who do own capital have less of it to employ on

	Aggregate Black Income (Billions)	Per Capita Income			Parity Gap	
		Black	White	B/W	Per Capita	Aggregate (Billions)
1990	$278.6	$9,017	$15,265	59.1%	$6,248	$193.0
1989	280.2	9,220	15,701	58.7%	6,481	197.0
1988	273.3	9,138	15,353	59.5%	6,215	185.9
1987	258.8	8,796	15,121	58.2%	6,325	186.1
1986	248.6	8,594	14,730	58.3%	6,136	177.5
1982	197.9	7,260	12,903	56.2%	5,643	153.8
1980	201.6	7,620	13,059	58.4%	5,439	143.9
1978	202.5	8,087	13,625	59.4%	5,538	138.7
1974	181.6	7,636	12,399	61.6%	4,763	113.3
1972	173.2	7,470	12,407	60.2%	4,937	114.7
1970	146.2	6,296	11,298	55.7%	5,002	116.1

Source: U.S. Department of Commerce, Bureau of the Census, *Money Income of Households, Families, and Persons in the U.S.: 1990*, September 1991, Series P-60, No. 174, Table B-8. Calculations of aggregates and gaps done by the author.

average. We have discussed these average disparities previously. The result of these disparities is reflected in the fact that smaller proportions of the black population receive income during any given year, and those who do receive income receive smaller amounts of it. Tables 6 and 7 contain data for the income recipiency of persons, which verify this situation.

Table 6 shows two important pieces of information. The first four columns show the proportions of men and women of each race who receive income. As can be seen during 1990, black men and women were less likely to receive income than white men and women. Only 87.6 percent of black men versus 96.1 percent of white men received income, while 88.1 percent of black women and 92.3 percent of white women received income during 1990. Thus, black men and women were only 92.6 and 95.4 percent, respectively, as likely as white men and women to be income recipients during 1990.

The relative disadvantage for black men has been nearly constant for the past 20 years. However, as can be seen, the situation for black women has generally declined, relative to the position of white women since the early 1970s. In fact, up until 1978, a higher proportion of black women were income recipients. In 1970, black women were about 10.5 percent more likely to be income recipients than white women, while during 1990, they were about 4.6 percent less likely to be income recipients. The last two columns show the ratio of males to females in the black and

Table 6
Percent of Persons With Income and Ratio of Male to Female
1970–1990, by Race and Sex

	Male		Female		Ratio of Males to Females	
	Black	White	Black	White	Black	White
1990	87.6	96.1	88.1	92.3	83.1	93.5
1989	88.5	96.1	88.4	92.2	83.1	93.4
1988	87.8	96.2	88.1	92.2	83.2	93.1
1987	87.8	96.0	87.1	92.1	82.9	93.0
1986	87.5	95.6	85.8	91.1	82.7	93.0
1985	87.3	95.6	85.3	90.6	82.7	93.0
1984	85.9	95.6	85.3	90.7	82.4	92.5
1983	84.4	95.2	83.5	89.8	82.4	92.5
1982	83.2	95.2	83.5	89.5	81.9	92.5
1981	86.6	97.1	81.0	89.9	82.0	91.0
1980	87.4	95.8	83.3	89.6	81.9	92.0
1979	87.9	96.3	81.4	89.7	82.0	92.3
1978	85.6	94.3	80.4	81.3	82.3	92.5
1977	84.1	93.7	78.1	74.6	83.2	92.4
1976	84.0	93.4	75.8	73.1	83.4	92.4
1975	84.0	92.8	75.2	71.2	83.3	92.2
1974	85.4	93.4	74.9	71.0	83.0	92.3
1973	86.2	93.3	73.7	68.8	83.9	92.1
1972	83.9	92.6	72.8	66.7	83.6	91.8
1971	85.6	92.4	73.0	65.4	83.5	91.9
1970	86.0	92.8	72.7	65.8	84.5	91.6

Source: U.S. Department of Commerce, Bureau of the Census, *Money Income of Households, Families, and Persons in the U.S.: 1990*, September 1991, Table B-6.

white working-age populations. As can be seen, the black population has relatively fewer males among its working-age population. In 1990, the ratio of black males to females was only 83.1 percent compared to 93.5 percent for the ratio of white males to females. Since both populations start off with roughly the same proportions of males to females, this number indicates that there is a relatively high rate of attrition for black males. Indeed, the data indicate that, in 1990, there were about 1,111,440 missing working-age black males. This is one of the most basic measures of the impact of the unequal wealth on the black population. These missing black males of working age have a significant impact on the current income deficit.

Table 7 displays the data for the median income of income recipients by race and sex from 1970 through 1990. During 1990, the median incomes for black males and females were lower than the median incomes for corresponding whites. The black male median income was $12,868, which was only 60.8 percent of the white male median income. The black female median income of $8,328 was only 80.7 percent of the white female income. The constant dollar median incomes of both black and white males has declined since the early 1970s. Both black and white male median incomes in 1990 are only about 85 percent of the peak male median income level reached in 1972. On the other hand, female incomes have increased across the decade. Black female median income during 1990 was about 19.8

Table 7
Median Income of Persons With Income by Race and Sex
1970–1990 (in 1990 Dollars)

	Male Black	Male White	B/W	Female Black	Female White	B/W
1990	$12,868	$21,170	60.8%	$8,328	$10,317	80.7%
1989	13,290	21,990	60.4	8,301	10,342	80.3
1988	13,306	·22,051	60.3	8,119	10,057	80.7
1987	12,903	21,751	59.3	7,995	9,788	81.7
1986	12,905	21,537	59.9	7,830	9,254	84.6
1985	13,080	20,784	62.9	7,625	8,936	85.3
1984	11,885	20,715	57.4	7,754	8,741	88.7
1983	11,836	20,240	58.5	7,308	8,552	85.5
1982	11,970	19,975	59.9	7,128	8,082	88.2
1981	12,223	20,555	59.5	7,050	7,935	88.8
1980	12,704	21,140	60.1	7,265	7,847	92.6
Decade Average	12,610	21,074	59.8	7,638	8,953	85.3
1979	13,713	22,152	61.9	7,198	7,909	91.0
1978	13,754	22,959	59.9	7,431	8,253	90.0
1977	13,570	22,868	59.3	7,452	8,629	86.4
1976	13,743	22,825	60.2	7,805	8,283	94.2
1975	13,507	22,593	59.8	7,548	8,308	90.9
1974	14,544	23,473	62.0	7,460	8,264	90.3
1973	15,051	24,883	60.5	7,501	8,310	90.3
1972	14,799	24,433	60.6	7,642	8,180	93.4
1971	13,928	23,355	59.6	6,922	7,900	87.6
1970	14,003	23,617	59.3	6,949	7,633	91.0
Decade Average	14,061	23,316	60.3	7,391	8,167	90.5

Sources: David Swinton, "The Economic Status of Blacks," in Janet Dewart (ed.), *The State of Black America 1990*, New York: National Urban League, 1990, Table 5, page 32; and U.S. Department of Commerce, Bureau of the Census, *Money Income of Households, Families, and Persons in the U.S.: 1990*, Series P-60, No. 174, September 1991, Table B-7.

percent greater than it was during 1970, while white female median income was about 26.3 percent greater than it was during 1970. The ratio of female-to-male income increased from 49.6 to 64.7 for black females, and from 32.3 to 48.7 for white females. Thus, sexual inequality in income recipiency abated significantly during the past 20 years.

However, the B/W columns for males and females in Table 7 make it clear that racial inequality in income did not abate during the past two decades. The relative level of inequality between black and white males remained about constant with the ratio of black-to-white male median income, fluctuating in a fairly narrow band from 57 to 62 percent. If there is any trend, it may be slightly higher inequality for males during the most recent ten years. There has been a clear increase in income inequality between black and white females during the 1980s. Black females earned 92.6 percent as much as white females in 1980, but they earned only 80.7 percent as much in 1990. Thus, overall racial inequality in income recipiency clearly increased during the 1980s. Since our earlier analysis indicated that the human capital

Table 8
Median Family Income and Inequality Indicators
for Selected Years
(1990$)

Year	Median Family Income Black	White	B/W	Median Family Income Difference	Aggregate Gap (in billions)
1990	$21,423	$36,915	58.0%	$15,492	$126.8
1989	21,301	37,919	56.2	16,618	133.8
1988	21,355	37,470	57.0	16,115	122.7
1987	21,177	37,260	56.8	16,083	122.3
1986	20,993	36,740	57.1	15,747	115.4
1985	20,390	35,410	57.6	15,020	109.4
1984	19,411	34,827	55.7	15,416	167.8
1982	18,417	33,322	55.3	14,905	101.3
1980	20,103	34,743	57.9	14,640	91.6
1978	21,808	36,821	59.2	15,013	85.2
1976	21,229	35,689	59.5	14,460	83.3
1974	21,225	35,546	59.7	14,321	79.8
1972	21,462	34,757	61.7	13,295	79.8
1970	21,151	34,481	61.3	13,330	63.2

Note: Aggregate gap is defined as the difference in mean income (not shown) times the number of black families (not shown). Median family income is in 1990 CPI-U adjusted dollars.

Source: U.S. Department of Commerce, Bureau of the Census, *Consumer Income, 1990: Money Income of Households, Families, and Persons in the U.S.: 1990*, Series P-60, No. 174, Tables 13, B4, and B-11. Calculations of aggregates and gaps done by the author.

gaps have closed, this increase in inequality from the early 1970s to now is primarily due to discrimination, which is facilitated by the low levels of business ownership and wealth.

Family Income Trends

The next several tables examine recent trends in income from the perspective of families. Table 8 contains data on median family income and the aggregate family income gap for selected years since 1970. In 1990, African American families had a median income of $21,423. This was a slight increase over the median income for the previous year. However, median black family income in 1990 was below its level in 1972. Black family income has stagnated since the 1970s and was generally lower during the 1980s than it was during the 1970s. The slight increase in black median family income in 1990 contrasted with a decline in median white family income. However, this one-year improvement is slight and may be a statistical fluke. The possibility of this is increased by the fact that most other measures of black income declined during 1990. In any case, the small measured improvement brought about a small decline in relative inequality.

All three inequality indicators improved slightly during 1990 because of the deterioration in white family income. During 1990, African American median family income was 58 percent of the median family income of white Americans. The difference in African American and white American median family income was $15,492. Thus, the typical or median African American family had a considerably lower income. The difference in black and white mean or family income was $16,978 in 1990 (not shown in this table). This produced an aggregate family income deficit of $126.8 billion.

As can be seen from Table 8, family income inequality has increased since 1970. The B/W index has declined significantly since the early 1970s; the median family income difference and the aggregate family income gap especially have all grown significantly since the early 1970s. If African Americans had the same degree of inequality in 1990 that they had in 1972, the median family income would be about 6.3 percent higher, and the aggregate income deficit would be about 6 billion dollars lower.

Table 9 displays data about the distribution of family income among black and white families. These data provide additional evidence of the relative disadvantaged status of African Americans. First, the table provides additional evidence that family income deteriorated for blacks and whites during 1990. The proportion of both groups receiving very low income increased slightly. For blacks, the proportion of families with income under $5,000 per year increased from 10.5 to 11.5 percent, while for whites, the increase was slight--from 2.4 to 2.5 percent. At the same time,

Table 9
Percentage of Families Receiving Income
Selected Ranges and Years by Race
1990, 1989, 1988, 1970

	1990		1989		1988		1970	
	Black	White	Black	White	Black	White	Black	White
Under $5,000	11.5	2.5	10.5	2.4	10.5	2.6	6.8	2.3
$5,000–9,999	14.1	4.7	14.1	4.7	14.7	4.8	14.1	5.1
Less than $10,000	25.6	7.2	24.6	7.1	25.2	7.4	20.9	7.4
$10,000–14,999	11.3	7.0	12.6	7.0	12.8	6.9	13.6	6.9
$10,000–34,999	44.8	39.5	45.8	38.8	45.1	39.1	55.1	44.4
$35,000–100,000 and over	29.5	53.3	29.6	54.0	29.6	53.6	23.8	48.2
$50,000–100,000 and over	14.5	32.5	15.5	33.5	15.7	32.6	9.9	24.1
$100,000 and over	1.3	5.9	1.4	6.1	.5	3.1	.3	2.7

Note: Totals will not equal 100.0 due to overlap of categories. Data is 1990 CPI-U adjusted dollars.

Source: U.S. Department of Commerce, Bureau of the Census, *Money Income and Poverty Status in 1990*, September 1991, Table B-3.

there were small decreases in the proportions receiving over $50,000 per year. For blacks, the drop was from 15.5 to 14.5 percent, and for whites, the drop was from 33.5 to 32.5 percent. Obviously, the proportionate increase by this measure was greater for blacks.

The more important point, however, is that the family income distribution among blacks is considerably worse than it is among whites. The proportion of black families with extremely low income, under $5,000 per year, at 11.5 percent is 4.6 times the proportion of white families receiving such low incomes. At the other end of the distribution, the 1.3 percent of black families receiving $100,000 or more per year was 4.5 times smaller than the proportion of white families with incomes as high. At the extreme, the latest Forbes list of the 400 wealthiest Americans appears to contain only ONE African American--Reginald Lewis, Chairman of TLC Beatrice International Holdings Co. of New York.

The income distributions for both blacks and whites have been becoming more unequal since 1970, and especially since 1980. Indeed, according to Census Bureau data, the Gini ratio--a standard measure of the degree of inequality in a distribution--for all American families rose by 12.2 percent, from .353 in 1970 to .396 in 1990. The proportion of the black population with the very lowest incomes has been increasing at the same time that the proportion of the black population with the very highest incomes has also been increasing. Between 1970 and 1990, the percent of the black population receiving under $5,000 increased by 4.7 percent, from 6.8 to 11.5 percent, while the group receiving more than $50,000 increased by 4.6 percent, 9.9 to 14.5 percent. The lower end of the white income distribution has not deteriorated. However, the proportions receiving low incomes remained nearly stable, while the proportions receiving the highest incomes increased significantly. Thus, while both family income distributions have become more unequal, the black family income distribution has deteriorated relative to the white family income distribution.

In the aggregate, there is an excess of 1.4 million extra black families receiving incomes under $10,000, and an excess of 672 thousand black families with incomes below $5,000. At the other extreme, 1.3 million fewer black families have incomes over $50,000, and 344 thousand fewer families have incomes over $100,000.

African American families throughout the African American income distribution do worse than white American families at all points along the white family income distribution. This statement is confirmed by the data in Table 10. The data in this table represent the upper limits of the first four quintiles and the lower limit of the top 5 percent. The first black/white index is the ratio of these limits, and the second B/W index is the ratio of within quintile mean incomes not shown in the table.

As can be seen at each quintile of the black family income distribution, black families have lower incomes than corresponding white families. For example, in 1990, the upper limit for blacks in the lowest fifth of the income distribution was $8,064 as compared to $18,656 for corresponding whites. Thus, the upper limit for the poorest blacks was only 43.2 percent of the upper limit for the poorest whites. As can be seen, the relative position of blacks is worse for the lowest income blacks. Thus, while the upper index for the lowest fifth is 43.2 percent, the index for the highest fifth is 70.0 percent.

Between 1980 and 1990, the absolute income of black families in the lowest two quintiles declined by this measure. The absolute income of the third quintile rose slightly, while the absolute income of the fourth quintile and the top 5 percent rose more substantially. This confirms the already mentioned absolute decline in the position of the poorest blacks and the absolute improvement in the position of the better-off blacks. However, it is also evident that the position of black families at all points in their distribution deteriorated in comparison to corresponding white families between 1980 and 1990. This is revealed by the decline in the B/W index for all positions of the distribution. The trend in the decline for the lowest two-fifths of the black family income distribution observed between 1970

Table 10
Family Income at Selected Positions of the Income Distribution
1990, 1980, 1970
(in 1990$)

1990	Black	White	Black/White
Lowest Fifth	$ 8,064	$ 18,656	43.2%
Second	16,251	30,660	53.0
Third	27,816	43,986	63.2
Fourth	43,900	63,020	69.7
Top 5%	73,506	105,000	70.0

1980	Black	White	Black/White
Lowest Fifth	$ 9,420	$ 17,971	52.4%
Second	16,843	29,304	57.5
Third	27,694	40,489	68.4
Fourth	42,584	56,249	75.7
Top 5%	68,962	87,711	78.6

1970	Black	White	Black/White
Lowest Fifth	$10,021	$ 18,545	54.0%
Second	16,689	29,425	60.1
Third	26,638	39,421	67.6
Fourth	39,450	53,712	73.4
Top 5%	62,450	84,031	74.3

Source: U.S. Department of Commerce, Bureau of the Census, unpublished data, 1991.

and 1980 continued at an accelerated pace. However, the decline for the upper three positions reverses the improving trend for these groups observed between 1970 and 1980. In fact, as can be seen from Table 10, the relative position of black families in the third quintile, the fourth quintile, and the top 5 percent fell below their 1970 levels between 1980 and 1990. Thus, all of the gains in the relative position of blacks in the top part of the distribution observed in comparing their 1970 and 1980 positions were lost during the 1980s.

Table 11 shows family household income by region of residence. The data for 1990 reveal that blacks fared absolutely best in the West, with a median income of $27,947. They have their absolute lowest income in the Midwest, with a median income of $20,512. The South trails right behind the Midwest with a median family income of only $20,805. The income of black families in the Northeast is second highest at $24,881.

Racial inequality obviously exists in all regions. Outside of the West,

Table 11
Median Family Income by Region
(in 1990$)

	Northeast			Midwest		
	Black	White	B/W	Black	White	B/W
1990	$24,881	$41,092	60.5%	$20,512	$37,370	54.9%
1989	26,763	43,205	61.9	19,290	37,723	51.1
1988	27,108	41,599	65.2	19,333	37,901	51.0
1987	23,833	40,697	58.6	19,311	37,053	52.1
1986	24,938	39,822	62.6	20,732	36,435	56.9
1982	19,801	34,692	57.1	16,628	33,278	50.0
1978	23,181	37,264	62.2	27,195	37,818	71.9
1970	26,213	36,806	71.1	26,024	35,432	73.4

	South			West		
	Black	White	B/W	Black	White	B/W
1990	$20,805	$34,242	60.8%	$27,947	$36,837	75.9%
1989	20,057	34,719	57.8	26,763	38,097	70.2
1988	20,011	35,417	56.5	28,598	37,051	77.2
1987	19,388	34,788	55.7	23,774	37,470	63.4
1986	17,531	31,030	56.5	26,449	37,470	70.6
1982	18,478	32,781	56.4	27,227	35,934	75.8
1978	19,566	34,055	57.5	21,476	37,450	57.3
1970	17,621	31,157	56.6	26,979	35,009	77.1

Sources: David Swinton, "The Economic Status of Blacks," in Janet Dewart (ed.), *The State of Black America 1991*. New York: National Urban League, 1991, Table 5, page 32, and U.S. Department of Commerce, Bureau of the Census, *Money Income of Households, Families, and Persons in the U.S.: 1990*, Series P-60, No. 174, September 1991, Table 13. pp. 52-54.

relative black family income ranges from 54.9 percent of white family income in the Midwest to 60.8 percent in the South. It is interesting to note that by this measure, inequality in the South is below inequality in the Midwest and the Northeast. The relative position of the South has improved slightly in the past two decades due to deterioration in the relative position of blacks in the Northeast and Midwest and a slight improvement in the South.

Blacks have higher measured equality in the West. However, we note that Hispanics constitute about 14 percent of the white population in the West, and since their incomes are almost as low as black incomes, this results in an understatement of the relative gap versus non-Hispanic whites. Moreover, because the black population in the West is so small, the data are less precise. Finally, there has been a suspicious decline in the number of black families reported in the West for the past three years. If this drop in population count represents attrition at the low end, this would overstate the position of blacks in the West.

As is evident from the time series in Table 11, the trend over the past two decades has varied by region. In absolute terms, income has essentially stagnated in every region outside of the Midwest for most of the past two decades. The level of income may have increased in the South and may be slightly up for the past few years in the West and the Northeast as well. However, black family income in the Midwest has definitely declined relative to the levels obtained during the 1970s. Even for the past few years, median family income in the Midwest continues to remain below the levels observed during the 1970s.

In all regions, a high level of racial inequality has persisted. The degree of racial inequality has increased markedly in the Midwest for the two decades taken as a whole. The best generalization for the other regions is that the degree of racial inequality has been relatively constant. Racial inequality may have increased overall in comparison to the 1970s in the Northeast. Moreover, if the big jump in the inequality index in the South observed for 1990 persists, then racial inequality would have improved slightly in this region. The data for the West are too erratic from year to year to judge the underlying trend.

Income of Households by Selected Characteristics

Indeed, the limited black ownership of businesses and wealth generally means that blacks of all characteristics fare worse than whites of all characteristics. Table 12 contains data that illustrate this situation for households in 1990.

Both blacks and whites overwhelmingly have nonfarm places of residence. In 1990, more than 99.8 percent of blacks and 98 percent of whites had nonfarm residences. However, black nonfarm residents had a median

Table 12
Percent of Households and Median Income of Households
by Selected Characteristics and Race

Characteristics	Percent of Households Black	Percent of Households White	Median Income Black	Median Income White	B/W Income
All Households	100.0	100.0	$18,676	$31,231	59.8
Type of Residence					
Nonfarm Residence	99.8	98.0	18,734	31,216	60.0
Inside Metro Areas	84.0	76.4	20,121	33,460	60.1
Inside Metro Areas-Large	58.9	47.6	21,086	35,837	58.8
Inside Central Cities	40.8	16.2	18,156	29,630	61.3
Outside Central Cities	18.0	31.4	28,444	39,670	71.7
Inside Metro Areas-Small	25.2	28.7	17,562	30,043	58.5
Inside Central Cities	17.5	11.5	16,402	26,845	61.1
Outside Central Cities	7.7	17.3	21,517	31,881	67.5
Outside Metro Areas	16.0	23.6	13,119	24,887	52.7
Type of Household					
Family Households	70.0	70.2	21,899	37,219	58.8
Married-Couple Family	33.4	58.1	33,893	40,433	83.8
Single-Male Headed	4.4	2.8	24,048	32,869	73.2
Single-Female Headed	32.1	9.3	12,537	20,867	60.1
Nonfamily Households	30.0	29.8	11,789	18,449	63.9
Male-Householder Nonfam.	14.3	12.7	15,451	23,778	65.0
Female-Householder Nonfam.	15.6	17.1	8,661	14,629	59.2
Age of Householder					
Under 65	83.2	77.2	21,011	35,646	58.9
15-24	6.4	5.0	9,816	19,662	49.9
25-34	24.3	21.1	18,339	31,859	57.6
35-44	24.2	22.2	26,011	40,423	64.3
45-54	15.9	15.5	26,910	44,098	61.0
55-64	12.5	13.4	19,226	34,249	56.1
65 and over	16.8	22.8	9,902	17,539	56.5
65-74	10.5	13.2	11,974	21,089	56.8
75 +	6.3	9.6	7,831	13,714	57.1
Number of Persons in Household					
One	26.0	25.1	10,156	15,981	63.6
Two	25.2	33.2	20,122	32,561	61.8
Three	18.9	16.8	21,474	38,930	55.2
Four	15.7	15.2	25,683	43,363	59.2
Five	7.5	6.4	24,342	40,715	59.8
Six	3.5	2.1	26,742	40,420	66.2
Seven or More	3.2	1.2	22,361	40,822	54.8
Number of Earners					
No Earners	24.4	20.8	5,870	12,395	47.4
One Earner	39.1	32.5	17,040	25,801	66.0
Two Earners or More	36.5	46.6	36,404	45,705	79.6
Two Earners	20.4	35.9	33,657	42,498	79.2
Three Earners	5.9	7.9	42,897	54,264	79.1
Four Earners or More	2.2	2.9	60,323	66,876	90.2
Work Experience of Householder[1]					
Total	100.0	100.0	18,471	31,212	59.1
Worked	67.1	73.1	25,683	37,441	68.6
Worked Year-round, Full-Time	44.7	53.5	31,042	42,010	73.9
Did Not Work	32.9	26.9	7,249	15,144	47.9

[1]Restricted to civilian householders.

Source: U.S. Department of Commerce, Bureau of the Census, *Money Income of Households, Families, and Persons in the United States: 1990*, September 1991, Table 1.

income of $18,734, which is only 60 percent of median household income for white nonfarm residents.

Blacks are more likely than whites to live in metropolitan areas; within metropolitan areas, they are more likely to live in the larger cities. However, within metropolitan areas of all sizes, blacks are more likely to reside in central cities while whites are more likely to reside in the suburbs. The choice of size of area appears to be an economic choice. Incomes are higher for both races in large metropolitan areas than in small areas and higher in small metropolitan areas than in nonmetropolitan areas. Blacks in large metropolitan areas have incomes that are 20 percent higher than those of blacks in small metropolitan areas and 61 percent higher than the incomes of blacks in nonmetropolitan areas; whites in large metropolitan areas have corresponding advantages of 19 and 43 percent, respectively. As a consequence, blacks are relatively more likely to live in larger places.

On the other hand, the choice of suburban residence appears to be more a consequence of economic success than a cause. Thus, although blacks who live in the suburbs have higher incomes, relatively fewer blacks live in the suburbs than in central cities.

In any case, blacks have lower incomes than have whites, regardless of their place of residence. Inequality as measured by the B/W index is least in the suburbs where the better-off blacks choose to live. The inequality index is 71.7 percent in the suburbs of large metropolitan areas versus 61.3 percent in the central cities, while the corresponding figures for small metropolitan areas are 67.5 and 61.1 percent, respectively, for suburbs and central cities. Inequality is about the same in small and large metropolitan areas where the inequality index is 58.8 percent in large areas and 58.5 percent in small areas. Inequality is greatest in the nonmetropolitan areas, where blacks have only 52.7 percent of the white median household income.

The next panel displays the median income of blacks by household type. Here, blacks have much higher proportions of female-headed family households and lower proportions of married-couple households. Moreover, as is evident from the table, married-couple households of both races have higher incomes than other household types. Blacks and whites have roughly the same proportions of family and nonfamily households and, as might be expected, family households have higher median incomes than nonfamily households.

It is also evident from the data that blacks have lower incomes than whites in every type of household. Inequality is least for married-couple households where the relative median income is 83.8 percent of the white median income. Racial inequality is considerably higher for all other household types. Single female-headed black family households have incomes that are only 60 percent of the incomes of single female-headed white families. Black nonfamily households have median incomes only 63.9 percent of

86

white nonfamily households.

Moreover, it seems likely that the distribution of black households by type is more a consequence of their relative disadvantage than a cause. For one thing, a close reading of the data will show that black male householders are only slightly more likely to be in family types other than married couple than white male householders. Indeed, only 3.2 percent more black male householders have nonmarried couple status than have white males. (This percentage difference is calculated by adding the difference between black and white single-male headed households--1.6 percent--to the difference between black and white male-householder nonfamily--also 1.6 percent.) More black than white male adults probably live as secondary members of other households. But this difference adds fewer than another 5 to 7 percentage points. In any case, if black males had the same proportions living in other than married-couple status as white males, this would not eliminate half of the gap in the proportion living in married-couple households. The missing black males prevent blacks from attaining equal married-couple proportions. Moreover, the economic status of black males restricts their ability to form and maintain stable married-couple families.

The next panel shows that income increases with age up to age 55 for black and white households. Black householders of all ages have lower incomes than white householders of corresponding ages. The youngest black householders, age 15 to 24, experience the most disadvantages. Their median income of $9,816 is only 49.9 percent of corresponding white income. The greatest equality is for the 35-to-44 and 45-to-54 age groups whose median incomes are 64.3 and 61.0 percent of the corresponding white incomes, respectively. Black household median income for all other age groups is between 56 and 58 percent of the corresponding income for whites.

The next panel shows median income by size of household. Income generally increases with household size, primarily because larger household sizes generally have older heads and more earners. As can be seen, as usual, blacks are disadvantaged at each household size. The range of variation in inequality across this characteristic is relatively small. Black households of every size category have incomes ranging from 54.8 to 66.2 percent of corresponding white incomes.

The next panel shows income by the number of earners. As already indicated, the income of households generally increases as the number of earners increase, for obvious reasons. Black households have fewer earners on average. Thus, 24.4 percent of black households versus 20.8 percent of white households have no earners. Thirty-nine percent of black households have only one earner, compared to only 32.5 percent of white households, and 46.6 percent of white households compared to 36.5 percent of black households have two or more earners. In general, there is greater equality in median income for multiple-earner families. Nonetheless, black households have lower median earnings for every number of earners category. Finally, the last panel in Table 12 shows median household income by work experience. As can be seen, blacks once more are disadvantaged. First, fewer blacks work than whites--67.1 percent versus 73.1 percent. Second, fewer blacks than whites work year-round full-time--44.7 percent versus 53.5 percent. Third, more blacks than whites do not work at all--32.9 percent versus 26.9 percent. Furthermore, blacks in all work experience categories have lower median incomes than corresponding whites. The range of the B/W index is from 47.9 percent for those not working at all to 73.9 percent for those working year-round full-time.

Trends in Poverty Rates

The income disadvantages for blacks lead directly to higher rates of poverty. The information in Tables 13 and 14 will be used to discuss poverty trends. Table 13 provides data on three national poverty rates. The first panel provides the poverty rate for all persons. As can be seen during 1990, 31.9 percent of blacks and 10.7 percent of whites were in poverty. For both races, this was a slight increase over the previous year. For blacks, 9.8 million persons were in poverty in 1990, up by 500 thousand over 1989. For whites, 22.3 million were in poverty, up 1.6 million from the previous year.

The all-persons poverty rate for blacks has fluctuated between 30 and 36 percent since 1970. The all-persons poverty rate for whites has fluctuated between 8.7 and 12 percent. The poverty rate for whites is clearly much lower than it is for blacks. However, white poverty has drifted slightly up since the late 1970s at a somewhat higher rate than for black poverty. The changes in the poverty rates have been small in percentage terms. However, in 1990, over 2.2 million more blacks and about 6.1 million more whites were in poverty than in 1978. The faster rate of growth of white poverty has lowered the B/W index from the 3.5 to 1 range to the 3 to 1 range. Blacks typically have three times the poverty rate of whites.

The net impact of this is that there is a huge poverty gap. In 1990, there were 6.5 million more blacks in poverty than would have been if blacks and whites had equal poverty rates. This gap has grown in absolute terms since the 1970s. As can be seen, the gap in 1990 is one million persons larger than it was in 1978.

The second panel presents similar data for poverty among children. As the table shows, the rate of poverty among black and white children was 44.8 percent and 15.9 percent, respectively, during 1990. Thus, over 44 out of every 100 black children and about 16 of every 100 white children lived in poverty during 1990. Both rates represent increases over the previous year. There were 4,550,000 black children and 8,232,000 white children in

Table 13
Selected Poverty Rates by Race for Selected Years

Persons In Poverty

| | Percent of Number[1] | | Percent | | | |
	Black	White	Black	White	B/W	Poverty Gap
1990	9,837	22,326	31.9	10.7	2.98	6.5 Million
1989	9,302	20,785	30.7	10.0	3.07	6.3 Million
1988	9,356	20,715	31.3	10.1	3.10	6.3 Million
1987	9,520	21,195	32.4	10.4	3.12	6.5 Million
1986	8,983	22,183	31.1	11.0	2.83	5.8 Million
1982	9,697	23,517	35.6	12.0	2.97	6.4 Million
1978	7,625	16,259	30.6	8.7	3.52	5.5 Million
1970	7,548	17,484	33.5	9.9	3.38	5.5 Million

Children in Poverty

| | Percent of Number[1] | | Percent | | | |
	Black	White	Black	White	B/W	Poverty Gap
1990	4,550	8,232	44.8	15.9	2.82	2.9 Million
1989	4,375	7,599	43.7	14.8	2.95	2.9 Million
1988	4,296	7,435	43.5	14.5	3.00	2.9 Million
1987	4,385	7,788	45.1	15.3	2.85	2.9 Million
1986	4,148	8,209	43.1	16.1	2.68	2.6 Million
1982	4,472	8,678	47.6	17.0	2.80	2.9 Million
1978	3,830	5,831	41.5	11.3	3.67	2.8 Million
1970	3,922	6,138	41.5	10.5	3.95	2.9 Million

Persons in Female-Headed Families

| | Percent of Number[1] | | Percent | | | |
	Black	White	Black	White	B/W	Poverty Gap
1990	6,005	6,210	50.6	29.8	1.70	2.5 Million
1989	5,530	5,723	49.4	28.1	1.76	2.4 Million
1988	5,601	5,950	51.9	29.2	1.78	2.6 Million
1987	5,789	5,989	54.1	29.6	1.83	2.6 Million
1986	5,473	6,171	53.8	30.6	1.76	2.4 Million
1982	5,698	5,686	58.8	30.9	1.90	2.7 Million
1978	4,712	4,371	54.2	25.9	2.09	2.5 Million
1970	3,656	3,761	58.7	28.4	2.07	1.9 Million

[1]In thousands.

Source: U.S. Department of Commerce, Bureau of the Census, *Poverty in the United States: 1990*, September 1991, Tables 2 and 3.

poverty during 1990.

The rate of poverty among both black and white children has increased since the 1970s. Once again, the relative increase has been higher among whites. The ratio of black-to-white children in poverty has fallen from over 3.5 to 1 in the 1970s to under 3 to 1 during the 1980s. However, as noted, this is due entirely to a deterioration in the situation of white children, since the already high poverty rates among black children also have gone up significantly during the 1980s. The children poverty gap is significant. In 1990, there was an excess of 2.9 million more black children in poverty. This gap has persisted at around the same level for the past 20 years.

The final panel of Table 13 shows data for the poverty rate of persons living in female-headed families. As can be seen during 1990, more than half of all persons who live in female-headed black families and almost 30 percent of all persons living in female-headed white families live in poverty. For blacks, this amounted to 6,005,000 persons, and for whites, this amounted to 6,210,000 persons. The number of persons living in poverty among female-headed families increased by about 2.35 million for blacks and 2.45 million for whites since 1970.

Racial inequality is marked here as well. However, the poverty rate for female-headed white families has drifted slightly upward, while the rate for female-headed black families has drifted downwards. As a result, the B/W

Table 14
Poverty Rates by Regions:
Selected Years, 1970–1990

| | Northeast | | | Midwest | | |
	Black	White	B/W	Black	White	B/W
1990	28.9	9.2	3.1	36.0	9.5	3.8
1989	24.7	8.0	3.1	36.4	9.0	4.0
1988	22.9	8.4	2.7	34.8	8.7	4.0
1987	28.8	8.9	3.2	36.6	9.9	3.7
1986	24.0	8.9	2.7	34.5	10.6	3.3
1982	32.2	10.7	3.0	37.9	11.5	3.3
1978	29.1	8.2	3.5	24.8	7.4	3.4
1970	20.0	7.7	2.6	25.7	8.9	2.9

| | South | | | West | | |
	Black	White	B/W	Black	White	B/W
1990	32.6	11.6	2.8	23.7	12.2	1.9
1989	31.6	11.4	2.8	23.5	11.3	2.1
1988	34.3	11.6	3.0	23.6	11.3	2.1
1987	34.5	11.5	3.0	24.3	11.5	2.1
1986	33.6	11.8	2.8	21.7	12.3	1.8
1982	33.6	12.0	2.8	26.6	11.8	2.3
1978	34.1	10.2	3.3	26.1	8.9	2.9
1970	42.6	12.4	3.4	20.4	10.6	1.9

Sources: David Swinton, "The Economic Status of Blacks," in Janet Dewart (ed.), *The State of Black America 1990*. New York: National Urban League, 1990, Table 5, page 32, and U.S. Department of Commerce, Bureau of the Census, *Poverty in the United States: 1990*, September 1991, Table 9.

index has declined from around 2 to 1 to 1.7 to 1. Nonetheless, the excess number of black persons living in female-headed families in poverty is still quite large. In 1990, the excess poverty gap for black female-headed families was 2.5 million persons. This gap has fluctuated around this level since the late 1970s.

We should also note that the proportion of black and white families headed by females has been increasing. The increase has been very sharp for blacks. The proportion is up from 30 to 45 percent of all persons living in families since 1970. For whites, the proportion has increased from 8 to 12 percent over the same period. Thus, the problem of female-headed poverty is of a much larger magnitude for blacks. Indeed, if the excess proportion of female-headed black families were taken into account in calculating the gap, this would increase the poverty gap for female-headed families to 5,080 persons for 1990.

Table 14 displays data for poverty rates by regions. Poverty rates for blacks during 1990 were highest in the Midwest at 36 percent, followed by the South at 32.6 percent. Poverty was lowest in the West at 23.7 percent, followed by the Northeast at 28.9 percent. In general, poverty was up in all regions outside of the South in comparison to 1970. Poverty has generally been higher for blacks in each region during the 1980s compared to the 1970s. The poverty rate for blacks in the South was lower than it was at the beginning of the 1970s. However, even here, poverty has been relatively stagnant since the late 1970s.

White poverty rates were lowest in the Northeast and the Midwest. Thus, inequality as measured by the B/W index was highest in these two regions. In the Midwest, the ratio of black-to-white poverty had gone up to nearly 4 to 1. In the Northeast, the ratio has been around 3 to 1, and in the South, the ratio has fluctuated from 2.8 to 3.0. In the West, the ratio of black-to-white poverty has generally been around 2 to 1.

SOURCES OF INCOME INEQUALITY

The extensive income inequality presented above originates in the differences in ownership of wealth and human capital previously discussed. Some insight into the roles of these factors can be obtained by examining income by sources. Limited ownership of businesses and financial assets directly reduces income from property and self-employment. Limited ownership of human capital directly reduces earnings from labor. Moreover, limited ownership also indirectly reduces earnings by limiting opportunity to employ whatever assets are owned in their best use.

Tables 15 and 16 will enable us to gain some insight into the direct role that property ownership plays in generating inequality. Table 15 shows income in 1990 by source of income. Several facts are clear from this table. First, blacks have smaller proportions of their population who receive every

Table 15

Percentage of Persons With Income and Aggregate Per Capita Income By Race, 1990

	Black				White				B/W Mean Income	B/W% With Income
	Percent with Income	Mean Income	Aggregate Income (Billions)	Percent of Income	Percent With Income	Mean Income	Aggregate Income (Billions)	Percent of Income		
Wage & Salary	61.42	$16,266	$221.8	79.61	64.91	$21,559	$2,303.1	72.28	$875.45	94.62
Nonfarm Self-Employed	2.83	11,267	7.1	2.54	7.07	16,748	194.8	6.11	67.27	40.03
Farm Self-Employed	.10	—	—	—	1.09	9,415	17.0	0.53	—	9.17
Property Income	27.34	924	5.6	2.01	61.88	2,475	252.0	7.91	37.33	44.18
Govt. Transfer Payments	33.10	4,832	35.5	12.70	28.88	6,505	309.1	9.70	74.28	114.61
Pensions	3.86	7,583	6.5	2.33	8.16	8,836	118.7	3.73	85.82	47.30
Soc. Security or RR Ret.	15.43	4,878	16.7	6.00	19.29	6,121	194.3	6.10	79.69	79.99
Public Assistance or SSI	13.00	3,186	9.2	3.30	3.33	3,192	17.5	0.55	99.81	390.39
All Income Sources	87.87	14,281	278.6	100.00	94.21	20,552	3,186.5	100.00	69.49	93.27

Aggregate Gap = per capita gap * 1990 population (30,895,000).

Source: Calculated by author from data in U.S. Department of Commerce, Bureau of the Census, *Money Income of Households, Families, and Persons: 1990*, September 1991, Table 34.

type of income except welfare income. Second, black income recipients receive smaller mean incomes from every source--including welfare.

Most black income--79.61 percent--comes from wage and salary employment. More black individuals, 61.42 percent, receive this type of income than any other type. The average amount received from this source, $16,266, is also the highest. Wage and salary income is also the most important income source for whites. However, slightly larger percentages of whites receive wage and salary income (64.91 percent), and they receive significantly larger mean incomes ($21,559) from this source. As indicated by the B/W indexes in the last two columns, blacks are 94.62 percent as likely as whites to have wage and salary income, and their mean incomes are only 72.28 percent of white mean incomes. Nonetheless, whites receive a smaller share, 72.28 percent, of their income from this source. This inequality is due to smaller amounts of human capital and limited opportunities to employ human capital because of the limited ownership of businesses.

Looking at the rest of the table, one can see the direct impact of the limited ownership of business and nonhuman wealth. The inequality in the property, self-employment, and retirement income sources was much higher than the inequality in the wage and salary source. Only 2.83 percent of blacks compared to 7.07 percent of whites received income from nonfarm self-employment. The mean income received from this source was only $11,267 for blacks compared to $16,748 for whites. Thus, the inequality index for the percentage with nonfarm self-employment income was 40.03 percent, and the inequality index for the mean income was 67.27. Only 27.34 percent of blacks versus 61.88 percent of whites had income from property. The mean amount received by black property owners was only $924 versus $2,475 for white property owners. Inequality indexes for percentages with income and the mean income were 44.18 percent and 37.33 percent, respectively. The reader can also observe the situation for pensions and retirement income from the table. Property income is clearly racially more unequal than wage and salary income.

A greater proportion of blacks received government transfer income than did whites--33.10 percent versus 28.88 percent. However, the mean amount of government transfer income received by blacks, $4,832, is only 74.28 percent of the mean amount received by whites ($6,505). Of course, one reason for this is that many government transfer programs are means tested. Nonetheless, the primary reason why blacks have a higher proportion receiving government transfers is the greater proportions of blacks who receive public assistance income. Whites are either equally as likely or more likely to receive the other transfers as blacks. Thus, in 1990, whites were more likely to receive Social Security, veterans' benefits, and survivors benefits, and about equally as likely to receive unemployment compen-

Table 16
Per Capita Income and Per Capita Income Gaps by Source of Income
1990

	Black Per Capita	White Per Capita	B/W	Per Capita Gap	Aggregate Gap (Billions)	% of Gap
Wage & Salary	$7,178.21	$11,032.52	65.06	$3,854.32	$119.1	61.7
Self-Employment	232.26	1,014.53	22.89	785.50	24.2	12.6
Property Income	181.48	1,207.34	15.03	1,025.86	31.7	16.4
Govt. Transfer Payments	1,149.08	1,480.77	77.60	331.70	10.2	5.3
Other Income	277.28	529.30	52.39	252.02	7.8	4.0
Total	9,016.51	15,264.40	59.07	6,247.89	193.0	100.0

Aggregate Gap = per capita gap * 1990 population (30,895,000).

Source: Calculated by author from data in U.S. Department of Commerce, Bureau of the Census, *Money Income of Households, Families, and Persons: 1990*, September 1991, Table 34.

sation, workers' compensation, disability benefits, and educational assistance.

A considerably higher proportion of blacks received welfare income. In 1990, 13 percent of the black population and 3.33 percent of the white population received public assistance or supplemental security income. Only about 6.5 percent of blacks received AFDC payments, and 5.3 percent of them received supplemental security income (SSI). In any case, blacks are 3.9 times as likely to receive welfare income of some type than are whites. Blacks and whites who receive welfare income receive almost equal mean amounts--$3,192 for whites and $3,186 for blacks. Given the above discussion about the much higher proportions of blacks with extremely low incomes and the much higher proportions in poverty, these differences make sense. However, it should be pointed out that only a minority of all persons in poverty received welfare income.

Table 16 summarizes the impact of inequality in the main sources of income on per capita and aggregate income inequality. As can be seen, blacks and whites received the greatest amount of per capita income from wage and salary employment. However, the inequality in this source is high. Blacks received only 65.06 percent as much per capita from wage and salary employment as did whites. The per capita gap in wage and salary income was $3,854.32, and the aggregate gap was $119.10 billion. Inequality in the amount of per capita income derived from wage and salary employment accounted for 61.7 percent of overall income inequality.

Self-employment income was a much smaller source for both blacks and whites. However, inequality in self-employment income, which is a direct consequence of differences in business ownership, was much more pronounced. Blacks received $232.26 per capita from self-employment, which is only 22.89 percent of the $1,014.53 received by whites from this source. The per capita gap in this source was $785.50, and the aggregate gap was $24.2 billion. Inequality in self-employment income accounted for 12.6 percent of the overall inequality gap.

Property income, which is primarily returns to nonhuman assets, was even more unequal than self-employment income. Blacks received $181.48 per capita from this source, 15.03 percent of the $1,207.34 received by whites. The per capita and aggregate gaps were $1,025.86 and $31.7 billion, respectively. Inequality in property income accounted for 16.4 percent of the overall income gap. Given the low rate of ownership of productive assets discussed earlier, all of this gap can be attributed to the direct impact of differences in property ownership.

The transfer source was the second most important source of income for both races and was also the most equal of the four principal sources of income. Nonetheless, blacks were still disadvantaged with respect to receipt of government transfers as well. Blacks received $1,149.08 per capita from this source in 1990, compared to $1,480.77 per capita received by whites in government transfers. Thus, blacks received only about 78 cents from government transfers per capita for every dollar whites received per capita. The per capita gap in transfer payments was $331.70, and the aggregate gap was $10.2 billion. Inequality in government transfer payments accounted for 5.3 percent of the overall income gap.

As we noted above, blacks received more of one type of transfer--welfare--than did whites. The per capita gap for welfare income is in blacks' favor by $213.82, and in the aggregate, the favorable gap is $6.6 billion. Welfare income, thus, reduces income inequality by 3.4 percent. However, whites received $545.52 per capita more than blacks from other government transfer programs. This created an aggregate gap of $16.8 billion. Thus, transfers other than welfare accounted for 8.7 percent of the inequality gap. The net impact of government transfers was to increase racial inequality. (The figures cited in this paragraph are not isolated in Table 16; they are included, however, in the total "Govt. Transfer Payments" category in the table.)

Finally, to be complete, we have included a row for the residual income sources. Other income included alimony, child support, private pensions, and income not accounted for in the major sources. There was significant inequality from these residual sources as well. Blacks received only 52.39 percent as much per capita from the other sources as did whites ($277.28 versus $529.30). These sources produced a per capita gap of $252.02 and an aggregate gap of $7.8 billion. Other income contributed 4.0 percent to the inequality gap.

It is apparent from the above discussion that limited ownership accounted for a sizable proportion of racial inequality in income. About 38.3 percent of income inequality originated in sources other than wage and salary employment. This inequality was primarily a direct result of lower levels of ownership of businesses and other nonhuman property. If we attributed 90 percent of the gap from the property and other sources to differences in ownership, about 35 percent of overall inequality could be attributed to the direct impact of lower levels of ownership of nonhuman capital.

Moreover, as we have seen, a sizable proportion of the gap in wage and salary income was a direct result of lower amounts of human capital. We estimate that the aggregate earnings gap in 1990 due to differences in mean earnings of male and female workers was $87.9 billion. Thus, 73.8 percent of the per capita aggregate wage and salary gap was due to differences in the mean earnings of black and white workers. The remainder was due to demographic factors. We estimate that 33.9 percent of the male earnings difference was due to lower levels of human capital and all of the female differences and more were due to lower amounts of education. Overall, about 46.4 percent of the difference in mean earnings could be attributed to the direct impact of lower amounts of human capital. Thus, about 21.3 percent of the overall income gap (46.4 percent times 73.8 percent times

61.7 percent) was due to the direct impact of smaller amounts of human capital.

Combining these two estimates yielded a total of about 56 percent of overall income inequality due to the direct impact of differences in ownership of businesses and human and nonhuman wealth. Given that the total income gap was about $193 billion, this means that about $108 billion of the 1990 income deficit was due to the direct impact of limited ownership and wealth.

Of the remaining inequality, some portion--maybe up to 20 percent--was due to the cumulative demographic impacts of the legacy of inequality. The rest can be considered an indirect impact of the limited ownership of businesses, wealth, and human capital. This part of the gap--about 35 percent or $68 billion--could be attributed to the unequal treatment of black resource owners. This gap is the indirect consequence of limited ownership. This portion of inequality could in principle be eliminated without eliminating the wealth gaps through antidiscrimination and equal opportunity policies. However, eliminating the wealth gap would also eliminate this portion of inequality as well as the portion directly attributed to unequal ownership.

CURRENT AND RECENT LABOR MARKET TRENDS

National Employment and Unemployment Rates

Much of the inequality, as we have seen, originated in the labor market. For that reason, we turn now to a review of the current and recent labor market trends. The data for this review are contained in the next several tables.

Tables 17 through 20 contain the latest data on employment rates (employment to population ratios) and unemployment rates. As can be seen, the most recent data in Tables 17 and 18 reflect the continued stagnation in the national economy. Black employment rates for the total population in the latest six months have fluctuated between 54.1 and 55.7 percent; this range is about 1 to 2 percent below the averages observed during the past three years. The overall employment rate for the first three quarters of 1991 averaged 55.1 percent. The dip in employment has been experienced by men, women, and teenagers. However, the decline relative to 1990 has been greatest among teenagers.

Black employment rates fell sharply during the early 1980s, but they have fluctuated between 55 and 57 percent since that time. While this is a low employment rate, it is higher than the historical average. This is primarily due to the increasing participation and employment of black women. Employment rates for black women have risen from the mid-40 percent range to 54 percent of the population over the past two decades.

Table 17
Civilian Employment—Population Ratio
by Race, Sex, and Age
1991

1991	Total Population		
	Black	White	B/W
November	54.1	62.4	86.7
October	54.5	62.5	87.2
September	55.7	62.5	89.1
August	54.5	62.2	87.6
July	55.1	62.4	88.3
June	54.8	62.6	87.5
1991	Men (20 and over)		
November	65.0	73.1	88.9
October	65.1	73.2	88.9
September	65.6	73.3	89.5
August	64.1	73.1	87.7
July	64.9	73.2	88.7
June	64.5	73.3	88.0
1991	Women (20 and over)		
November	51.6	54.6	94.5
October	52.3	54.8	95.4
September	54.2	54.7	99.1
August	53.5	54.7	97.8
July	53.6	54.9	97.6
June	53.2	55.0	96.7
1991	Both Sexes (16 to 19 years old)		
November	22.0	46.9	46.9
October	21.1	47.1	44.8
September	22.4	47.1	47.6
August	19.3	43.9	44.0
July	22.4	43.7	51.3
June	23.0	45.6	50.4

Note: Data are seasonally adjusted.

Source: U.S. Labor Department, Bureau of Labor Statistics, *Employment Situation*,
November 1991.

Employment rates for black men declined sharply during the early 1980s,
but they have begun to recover somewhat since the mid-1980s. However,
the employment rate of black men continued to decline for the two decades
taken as a whole. The black male employment rate was 73 percent in 1972;
it began to rally back and forth in the 1980s, reaching a maximum of 67

Table 18
Civilian Employment—Population Ratio
By Race, Sex, and Age
Selected Years

Total Population

	Black	White	B/W
1991*	55.1	62.6	0.880
1990	56.2	63.6	0.884
1989	56.8	63.8	0.890
1988	56.3	63.1	0.892
1982	49.4	58.8	0.840
1978	53.6	60.0	0.893
1970	53.7	57.4	0.936

Men (20 and over)

	Black	White	B/W
1991*	64.9	73.4	0.884
1990	66.1	75.0	0.881
1989	66.9	75.4	0.887
1988	67.0	75.1	0.892
1982	61.4	73.0	0.841
1978	69.1	77.2	0.895
1972	73.0	79.0	0.924

Women (20 and over)

	Black	White	B/W
1991*	53.5	54.8	0.976
1990	54.2	55.3	0.980
1989	54.6	54.9	0.995
1988	53.9	54.0	0.998
1982	47.5	48.4	0.981
1978	49.3	46.1	1.069
1972	46.5	40.6	1.145

Both Sexes (16 to 19 years old)

	Black	White	B/W
1991*	22.9	46.6	0.491
1990	26.6	49.8	0.534
1989	28.8	51.5	0.559
1988	27.5	51.0	0.539
1982	19.0	45.8	0.415
1978	25.2	52.4	0.481
1972	25.2	46.4	0.543

*Averages of the first three quarters of 1991.

Sources: Bureau of Labor Statistics, *Handbook of Labor Statistics,* June 1985, pp. 46 and 47; *Employment and Earnings,* January 1991 and October 1991, Table A-44.

percent in 1988. The employment rate of black men has been slowly declining since then.

Black teenagers continue to have severe employment difficulties. Their employment rate has not exceeded 30 percent for the past two decades; it fluctuated around the 25 percent level most of the time. There has been no trend to speak of.

Unemployment rates have also been high for the past six months for all black demographic groups.

Table 19
Unemployment Rates by Sex, Race, and Age
Selected Months
1991

1991	Total Population Black	White	B/W
November	12.1	6.1	1.98
October	12.7	6.0	2.12
September	12.1	6.0	2.02
August	12.3	6.1	2.02
July	11.8	6.2	1.90
June	13.1	6.2	2.11
1991	Men (20 and over)		
November	10.4	5.8	1.79
October	10.8	5.9	1.83
September	10.8	6.1	1.77
August	11.5	5.9	1.95
July	11.6	6.0	1.93
June	12.7	5.9	2.15
1991	Women (20 and over)		
November	11.4	5.1	2.24
October	11.6	4.9	2.37
September	10.3	4.7	2.19
August	10.3	5.0	2.06
July	9.4	4.8	1.96
June	11.0	5.2	2.12
1991	Both Sexes (16 to 19 years old)		
November	34.3	16.5	2.08
October	39.3	16.1	2.44
September	37.8	15.3	2.47
August	39.7	16.2	2.45
July	34.6	18.5	1.87
June	33.7	17.5	1.93

Note: Data is seasonally adjusted.

Source: U.S. Labor Department, Bureau of Labor Statistics, *Employment Situation*, November 1991, News Release, Table A-2, December 1991.

Table 20
Unemployment Rate by Sex, Race, and Age
Selected Years

Total Population

	Black	White	B/W
1991	12.4	6.0	2.074
1990	11.3	4.7	2.404
1989	11.4	4.5	2.533
1988	11.7	4.7	2.489
1987	13.0	5.3	2.453
1982	18.9	8.6	2.198
1978	12.8	5.2	2.462
1972	10.4	5.1	2.039

Men (20 and over)

1991	11.7	5.8	2.031
1990	10.4	4.3	2.419
1989	10.0	3.9	2.564
1988	10.1	4.1	2.463
1987	11.1	4.8	2.313
1982	17.8	7.8	2.282
1978	9.3	3.7	2.514
1972	7.0	3.6	1.944

Women (20 and over)

1991	10.2	4.9	2.099
1990	9.8	4.1	2.390
1989	9.8	4.0	2.450
1988	10.4	4.1	2.537
1987	11.6	4.6	2.522
1982	15.4	7.3	2.110
1978	11.2	5.2	2.154
1972	9.0	4.9	1.837

Both Sexes (16 to 19 years old)

1991	36.2	14.9	2.425
1990	31.1	13.4	2.321
1989	32.4	12.7	2.551
1988	32.5	13.1	2.481
1987	33.4	13.3	2.511
1982	34.7	14.4	2.410
1978	48.0	20.4	2.353
1972	35.4	14.2	2.493

Note: 1991 data represent average of first three quarters.

Sources: Bureau of Labor Statistics, *Handbook of Labor Statistics,* June 1985, pp. 69, 71-73. *Employment and Earnings,* January 1991, Table 5: October 1991, Table A-44.

Overall, unemployment has fluctuated between 11.8 and 13.1 percent for the past six months. Unemployment for blacks averaged 11.3 and 11.4 percent in 1990 and 1989, respectively. Thus, overall unemployment has been up by 1 or 2 percent, or 10 to 20 percent over the past six months. The overall unemployment rate for the first three quarters of 1991 averaged 12.4 percent.

A review of the time series data will show that black unemployment has been high throughout the past two decades. The overall rate has been above 11 percent for every year since 1978. Adult black men have had unemployment rates above 10 percent for every year since 1980, and adult black women had unemployment rates above 10 percent in every year except 1989 and 1990, when their unemployment rate was 9.8 percent. The lowest unemployment rate experienced by black teenagers since 1980 was 31.1 percent in 1990.

It is also apparent from the data in Table 16, as well as those in Tables 17 through 20, that there has been persistent racial inequality in employment and unemployment. In the latter six months, the overall black employment rate was only about 87 percent of the white rate. The disparity was greatest for black men and teenagers. Black men's employment rates have ranged from 87.7 to 89.5 to 89 percent of white men's employment rates and 44 to 51 percent of the employment rates of white men. Black teenagers have had from 44 to 51.3 percent of the employment rates of white teenagers. Black women's employment rates have generally been between 94 and 99 percent of the employment rates of white women.

The data in Table 16 make it clear that the inequality in employment rates is a permanent feature of the American economy. Indeed, during the past two decades, this inequality probably increased. The increases have been greatest for black women. During the early 1970s, black women had considerably higher employment rates than did white women. However, during the 1980s, white women overtook black women for the first time since such statistics have been kept. Moreover, there has been a slow erosion in the position of black women over the two decades. Inequality in relative employment rates for black men has crept up very slightly, as the employment rates of white men has also declined for the past two decades. The relative rate of employment for black teenagers fluctuates with the cycle around 50 percent of the employment rate of white teenagers (Tables 18-19). However, there is no noticeable trend. The net result overall has been a slight increase in inequality, as the B/W index shows. This index had a value of .936 in 1970 and stood at .880 in the latest year.

As Table 20 shows, unequal unemployment rates have also been a permanent feature of the American economy. Inequality for all of the demographic groups has generally crept upwards for the past two decades. For the 1980s, each of the black demographic groups and the population as a whole generally had about 2.5 times the unemployment rate of corresponding white demographic groups. The relative rise has been sharpest for black females who, up until the 1980s, generally had unemployment rates that were slightly less than two times the white female unemployment rate. Black teenage unemployment rates have typically been over 20 percentage points higher than those for white teenage unemployment.

We should note in passing that the degree of racial inequality in unemployment rates has fallen rather sharply as measured by the B/W indicator in 1991 for black men and women. An examination of the data in Tables 19 and 20 will reveal that the B/W index for the first three quarters was 2.031 for black men and 2.099 for black women. Table 20 also shows a slight decline in the B/W index for 1990 for men, women, and teenagers, although teenagers lost some of their gain in 1991. This situation was brought about by the fact that the unemployment rate for blacks has risen at a relatively slower pace than the unemployment rate for white men during the current slowdown. Moreover, data for the past five months suggest that the unemployment rate for black men has been recovering since July, while the unemployment rate for white men has been at best stagnating. This is a very anomalous situation and bears watching. This phenomenon could result from the fact that the industry and occupational mix affected by the current recession has reached higher into the middle class. However, if past recessions provide any guide, this situation will lead to a sharp rise in black unemployment in the months ahead if the slowdown continues.

In any case, the continuing inequality has large aggregate impacts. The 1990 employment rate differential implied that blacks had a shortfall of 1.6 million jobs. The 1990 unemployment differential implies an excess of about 900 thousand unemployed persons.

Employment and Unemployment in Regions and Places

The next two tables provide information on unemployment and employment rates by regions. In 1990, blacks continued to have their worst labor market experiences in the Midwest. Blacks in that region had the lowest employment rates at 51.1 percent and the highest unemployment rates at 15.1 percent. The 15.1 percent unemployment rate in the Midwest represents the best year for blacks in that region for over a decade. Black employment rates were highest in the South and West at 57.8 and 57.7 percent, respectively. The employment rate for blacks in the Northeast was 56.2 percent. The South had the second highest unemployment rate in 1990 at 10.8 percent, the Northeast and the West had unemployment rates of 9.8 and 9.6 percent, respectively.

All of the demographic groups also experienced their worst unemployment and employment rates in the Midwest, except that the employment rates for black teenagers were about the same in the Northeast and the

Table 21
Employment Population Ratio by Sex and Race, by Region (1990)

	Total Black	Total White	B/W	Black Male	White Male	B/W	Black Female	White Female	B/W	Black 16-19	White 16-19	B/W
Northeast	56.2	62.3	90.2	60.6	72.1	84.0	52.7	53.4	98.7	24.4	47.1	51.8
Midwest	51.1	65.4	78.1	55.9	74.5	75.0	47.2	56.9	83.0	24.5	56.5	43.4
South	57.8	62.6	92.3	63.9	72.5	88.1	52.8	53.6	98.5	27.7	46.5	59.6
West	57.7	64.6	89.3	65.1	74.0	88.0	51.5	55.6	92.6	30.1	48.8	61.7

Source: U.S. Department of Labor, Bureau of Labor Statistics, *Geographic Profile of Employment and Unemployment: 1990*, July 1991, Table 1.

Table 22
Unemployment Rates by Region, 1990

	Total Black	Total White	B/W	Black Male	White Male	B/W	Black Female	White Female	B/W	Black 16-19	White 16-19	B/W
Northeast	9.8	4.9	2.000	11.9	5.2	2.288	7.7	4.5	1.711	28.5	12.6	2.262
Midwest	15.1	4.6	3.283	16.5	4.9	3.367	13.6	4.4	3.091	37.6	11.9	3.160
South	10.8	4.5	2.400	10.5	4.3	2.442	11.1	4.7	2.362	30.2	15.0	2.013
West	9.6	5.1	1.882	10.2	5.2	1.962	8.9	5.1	1.745	24.6	14.2	1.732

Source: U.S. Department of Labor, Bureau of Labor Statistics, *Geographic Profile of Employment and Unemployment: 1990*, July 1991, Table 1.

Midwest. Black males had their best experiences in the West, with an unemployment rate of 10.2 percent and an employment rate of 65.1 percent. The South followed with an unemployment rate of 10.5 percent and an employment rate of 63.9 percent. Black males in the Northeast had an 11.9 percent unemployment rate, and their employment rate was only 60.6 percent. Black females had their lowest unemployment rate in the Northeast with 7.7 percent, followed by the West at 8.9 percent and the South at 11.1 percent. The employment rates were close in all three regions, as can be seen from Table 21. Black teenagers fared best in the West for both employment and unemployment rates. The Northeast followed the West with respect to unemployment rates, while the South was second best with respect to employment rates.

As can be seen from the B/W indexes in Tables 21 and 22, inequality is large in all regions. However, once again, inequality was worst in the Midwest. Here, the B/W index was over 3 for all demographic groups for unemployment. Thus, all black demographic groups were more than three times as likely as corresponding white groups to be unemployed in the Midwest. Overall, blacks were only 78.1 percent as likely to be employed as whites in the Midwest. The data clearly reveal that each of the groups fared much worse with respect to the employment rate in the Midwest than in the other three regions.

Racial inequality in employment rates was least in the South and the West for men and teenagers and least in the Northeast and the South for females. All black demographic groups, except females in the Northeast, were over two times as likely to be unemployed as whites in the Northeast and the South. Black females in the Northeast were only about 1.711 times as likely to be unemployed. In the West, black teenagers and females were around 1.75 times as likely to be unemployed, while black males were just under 2 times as likely to be unemployed.

Tables 23 and 24 provide data on the labor market experiences of blacks in those standard metropolitan statistical areas (SMSAs) that had large enough black populations to be reported. The most noticeable fact about these data is the wide range of unemployment and employment rates for blacks. In general, blacks appear to fare best where whites have low unemployment rates and high employment rates. There are even several SMSAs where the relative black employment rate is higher than the relative white employment rate. In most cases, these are places where blacks have very high participation rates relative to whites. As can be seen from the data in Table 24, there is only one place where blacks have a lower unemployment rate than have whites. This is in San Antonio, Texas, where there is a large Hispanic population with a high unemployment rate, and the city has a relatively small black population. We note that the black unemployment rate in San Antonio has a high standard of error and that the difference in the black and white unemployment rates is not statistically significant. The places with the worst labor market experience for blacks continue to be predominantly in middle America. This situation has persisted throughout the past decade. We note that the labor market situation for blacks in San Francisco has continued to deteriorate. This labor now ranks as the third or fourth worst location for black workers with respect to unemployment and employment rates. San Francisco is also one of the most unequal markets. Buffalo-Niagara Falls, New York, brings up the rear as the worst labor market for blacks.

Occupational Distribution, 1990

Table 25 contains the latest data on the occupational distribution of black and white males and females. This table tells the same story that we have told in these pages for the past 15 years. Blacks are clearly disadvantaged occupationally. As can be seen, blacks are less likely to be employed in the best jobs and more likely to be employed in the worst jobs. This is particularly true for men but is noticeable for women as well.

In 1990, black males were less than half as likely to be in executives, administrators, managers, or sales occupations. They were just over half as likely to be in the professional specialty occupations. They were around 75 percent as likely to be employed in technician or craft, precision production, or repair occupations. These five occupational groups offer the best jobs for men. In total, these five groups employed 36.9 percent of black males and 61.8 percent of white males. This leaves a good job gap for black males of about 1,472,835 good jobs. On the other hand, black men were significantly more likely to be employed in administrative support, laborers, other service workers, and transportation and material movers occupations. These less desirable occupations employed 45.2 percent of black males and only 23.9 percent of white males. This implies a surplus of 1,259,895 persons employed in the less desirable occupations.

Similarly, black women were less likely to be employed in professional, managerial, or sales occupations. In 1990, 40.8 percent of white women and only 28.1 percent of black women were employed in these good jobs. Thus, there was a good job gap for black females of 768,477 jobs. On the other hand, black women were more likely to be employed in household service, other service, laborer, and operative occupations. In 1990, 37.3 percent of black women and only 22.9 percent of white women were employed in such occupations. Thus, there was an excess of 871,344 persons employed in the less desirable jobs.

The final table provides information on recent wage trends. Table 26 displays the median weekly earnings of full-time wage and salary workers. As can be seen, there was a small decline in real wages in 1990 for all demographic groups except white females. Overall, the median wage for

106

Table 23
Employment to Population Ratios for Selected SMSA's by Race, 1990

Metro Area	Black Emp/Pop Ratio	White Emp/Pop Ratio	B/W
Phoenix, AZ	77.4	66.3	1.167
Hartford, CT	72.6	67.3	1.079
Washington, DC	69.4	72.6	0.956
Dallas-Ft. Worth, TX	69.1	72.5	0.953
Charlotte, NC	67.5	69.8	0.967
Bergen-Passaic, NJ	68.8	63.5	1.083
Kansas City, KS	68.6	69.9	0.981
Indianapolis, IN	68.2	69.8	0.977
Atlanta, GA	67.7	71.6	0.946
Fort Lauderdale, FL	67.5	69.8	0.967
Seattle, WA	66.1	70.4	0.939
San Antonio, TX	64.9	55.6	1.167
Nassau-Suffolk, NY	64.3	64.2	1.002
Norfolk, VA	60.9	66.7	0.913
Newark, NJ	60.6	63.3	0.957
Houston, TX	60.6	68.0	0.891
Riverside, CA	59.7	61.6	0.969
Columbus, OH	59.7	67.1	0.890
Denver-Boulder, CO	57.3	71.7	0.799
Baltimore, MD	57.0	66.5	0.857
Miami, FL	56.8	61.3	0.927
Los Angeles, CA	56.5	63.7	0.887
Louisville, KY	56.2	68.4	0.822
Tampa-St. Petersburg, FL	56.1	59.7	0.940
Sacramento, CA	55.7	64.4	0.865
Philadelphia, PA	55.1	63.1	0.873
Providence, RI	54.2	63.4	0.855
Cincinnati, OH	54.0	68.4	0.789
Boston, MA	54.0	67.1	0.805
New York, NY	52.1	55.2	0.944
Milwaukee, WI	51.6	69.3	0.745
Oakland, CA	51.0	64.4	0.792
Memphis, TN	49.5	63.3	0.782
New Orleans, LA	48.6	61.7	0.788
St. Louis, MO	47.6	63.5	0.750
Chicago, IL	47.4	68.3	0.694
Pittsburgh, PA	47.4	56.0	0.846
Cleveland, OH	47.0	63.1	0.745
Dayton, OH	46.8	62.2	0.752
San Francisco, CA	45.9	66.4	0.691
Detroit, MI	44.0	63.6	0.692
Oklahoma City, OK	43.5	68.3	0.637
Buffalo-Niagara Falls, NY	36.8	60.2	0.611

Source: Bureau of Labor Statistics, *Geographic Profile of Employment & Unemployment: 1990*, Table 23.

Table 24
Unemployment Rates for Selected SMSA's
by Race, 1990

Metro Area	Black Unemployment Rate	White Unemployment Rate	B/W
Bergen-Passaic, NJ	5.2	4.2	1.238
Nassau-Suffolk, NY	5.5	3.2	1.719
Seattle, WA	5.6	3.6	1.556
Phoenix, AZ	6.1	4.8	1.271
Charlotte, NC	6.2	2.8	2.214
Washington, DC	6.3	2.6	2.423
Louisville, KY	6.5	3.6	1.806
Sacramento, CA	6.7	3.8	1.763
Riverside, CA	6.7	6.2	1.081
Indianapolis, IN	7.3	2.6	2.808
Philadelphia, PA	8.7	3.7	2.351
Los Angeles, CA	8.8	5.7	1.544
Fort Lauderdale, FL	8.8	4.2	2.095
Hartford, CT	8.9	4.5	1.978
Atlanta, GA	9.0	3.4	2.647
San Antonio, TX	9.2	9.5	0.968
New York, NY	9.6	5.4	1.778
Dallas-Ft. Worth, TX	10.3	3.8	2.711
Norfolk, VA	10.9	3.6	3.028
Tampa-St. Petersburg, FL	11.0	4.6	2.391
Denver-Boulder, CO	11.0	3.8	2.895
Boston, MA	11.2	5.5	2.036
Memphis, TN	11.3	4.1	2.756
Miami, FL	11.6	6.5	1.785
Kansas City, KS	11.6	5.1	2.275
Columbus, OH	11.7	3.5	3.343
New Orleans, LA	12.1	3.6	3.361
Newark, NJ	12.2	4.8	2.542
Baltimore, MD	12.4	3.8	3.263
Houston, TX	13.3	4.8	2.771
Oakland, CA	13.5	5.2	2.596
Cincinnati, OH	13.7	3.7	3.703
Dayton, OH	15.1	4.9	3.082
Cleveland, OH	15.1	3.4	4.441
Providence, RI	15.5	6.2	2.500
Oklahoma City, OK	15.7	4.1	3.829
Pittsburgh, PA	16.2	5.5	2.945
Detroit, MI	16.4	6.3	2.603
Milwaukee, WI	16.6	3.0	5.533
Chicago, IL	16.8	4.2	4.000
San Francisco, CA	16.9	4.7	3.596
St. Louis, MO	17.1	4.0	4.275
Buffalo-Niagara Falls, NY	17.8	4.9	3.633

Source: Bureau of Labor Statistics, *Geographic Profile of Employment & Unemployment: 1990*, July 1991, Table 23.

black workers was $329 per week versus $427 per week for white workers. Thus, blacks earned on average 77 percent as much as whites. Black male weekly earnings of $360 was 72 percent of white male earnings of $497. Black females earned $308 per week in 1990, which was 87 percent of the median weekly earnings of white females.   Overall, the earnings of males have increased a bit during the past three years, although the median weekly earnings for black males is still below the 1979 level. Earnings for white males is above the 1979 level. In general, black male inequality has increased since the late 1970s. There has, in fact, been a decline in the B/W index for black males throughout the 1980s. Thus, wage inequality is not only a permanent feature for black males but also it has been rising.

The wages of both black and white females trended upwards throughout the 1980s, as can be seen from the table. However, racial inequality in earnings has been slowly drifting upwards and was generally higher in the 1980s than it was during the 1970s. Currently, black female earnings are only 87 percent of white female earnings. This is the lowest ratio since 1979.

Table 25
Occupational Percent Distribution of Employed Workers, 1990

	Male			Female		
	Black	White	B/W	Black	White	B/W
Exec., Admin., & Managerial	6.8	14.6	0.47	7.5	11.6	0.65
Professional Specialty	6.5	12.3	0.53	11.2	15.6	0.72
Technicians & Related Support	2.2	3.1	0.71	3.6	3.5	1.03
Sales Occupations	5.8	11.8	0.49	9.4	13.6	0.69
Administrative Support	9.1	5.5	1.65	26.1	28.2	0.93
Private Household	0.1	—	NA	3.1	1.2	2.58
Protective Service	4.4	2.5	1.76	1.2	0.5	2.40
Other Service	13.7	6.2	2.21	23.0	14.7	1.56
Precision Pro., Craft & Repair	15.6	20.0	0.78	2.3	2.1	1.10
Mach. Operators, Assem., & Insp.	10.3	7.2	1.43	9.1	5.5	1.65
Trans. and Material Movers	11.6	6.4	1.81	1.0	0.8	1.25
Handlers, Cleaners, Helpers, Labor	10.8	5.8	1.86	2.1	1.5	1.40
Farming, Forestry, and Fishing	3.2	4.6	0.70	0.3	1.1	0.27

Note: Data are not shown where base is less than 35,000. NA means not applicable.

Source: U.S Department of Labor, Bureau of Labor Statistics, *Employment and Earnings*, January 1991, Table 21.

The next two tables provide information about the impact of education on the labor market experiences of blacks. Table 27 shows the impact of education on work experience. The first panel shows the impact of education on the probability of working at all during the year for persons aged 25 to 64 years. First, it is apparent that education significantly increases the probability of working for both race and sex groups. Black females with an elementary school education had only a 39.69 percent probability of working or having earnings at all during 1990. This increased to almost a 90 percent probability for those with college degrees. The probability for white females went from 43.51 to 88.47 percent as education increased from the elementary school level to the graduate school level.

Education had a similar though less pronounced impact on employment probabilities for males. Black male elementary school workers had a 55.76 probability of working, while white elementary school dropouts had a 73.64 percent probability of working. These probabilities increased to 94.12 and 95.95 percent for black and white male college graduates, respectively.

It is also apparent from the table that human capital increased the probability of working full-time all year as well. In the lower panel, one can see that impact. The probability of working full-time year-round increased with education for all groups. For example, only 17.01 percent of black females who had attended only elementary school worked year-round full-time, while 67.26 percent of black female college graduates did. Only 62.59 percent of the black male high school graduates compared to 80.69 percent of those with a graduate school education worked year-round full-time. Thus, education clearly has a major impact on work experience.

Education also has a significant impact on racial inequality in work experience. As can be seen, black females who had not attended college were less likely than corresponding white women to have had work experiences, whereas black women with some college were more likely to have had work experience. Table 27 also shows that black women with high school diplomas or better were significantly more likely to work full-time year-round than white women, while black women below the high school graduate level were less likely to work year-round full-time. Black women college graduates were 27 percent more likely to work year-round full-time in 1990. Considering just those with four-year degrees, black women were 36 percent more likely to work year-round full-time. Thus, although black women have lost their overall employment advantage, they still have an employment advantage at higher educational levels. This probably reflects white women's choices.

Racial inequality in employment was more marked among males. However, education also decreased racial inequality for black men. While black

Table 26
Median Weekly Earnings of Full-Time Wage and Salary Workers
By Race and Sex, 1979-1990

	Black	White	B/W
1990	$329	$427	0.77
1989	336	431	0.78
1988	331	415	0.80
1987	317	404	0.79
1986	318	404	0.79
1985	308	394	0.78
1984	306	391	0.78
1983	307	383	0.80
1982	304	377	0.80
1981	307	381	0.81
1980	298	381	0.78
1979	328	406	0.81

Males

	Black	White	B/W
1990	$360	$497	0.72
1989	367	508	0.72
1988	366	490	0.75
1987	344	474	0.72
1986	347	473	0.73
1985	339	465	0.73
1984	351	465	0.76
1983	356	472	0.75
1982	343	459	0.75
1981	344	459	0.75
1980	535	460	0.77
1979	370	492	0.75

Females

	Black	White	B/W
1990	$308	$355	0.87
1989	317	352	0.90
1988	304	335	0.91
1987	290	324	0.90
1986	287	321	0.89
1985	281	314	0.90
1984	279	305	0.92
1983	275	303	0.91
1982	262	298	0.88
1981	266	286	0.93
1980	264	292	0.90
1979	272	296	0.92

Source: Bureau of Labor Statistics, *Handbook of Labor Statistics*, June 1985, p. 94; *Employment and Earnings*, January 1986-1991.

elementary school workers were only 75.72 percent as likely to work as were their white counterparts, black college graduates were 98.10 percent as likely to work as were white college graduates. Racial inequality declined as education increased through the college graduate level. Racial inequality in the probability of working year-round full-time also decreased with education except for the anomaly at the one to three years of college level. While black high school dropouts were less than 80 percent as likely as white high school dropouts to work full-time all year round, black males with four or more years of college were about 96 percent as likely as corresponding whites to work full-time all-year. Indeed, black males with five or more years of college had a 2.1 percent higher probability than corresponding white males to work full-time all year. Thus, human capital also reduces racial inequality in employment rates.

Table 28 provides data concerning the impact of education on the earnings of workers in 1990. The top panel shows the overall impact on education and earnings of all workers. It is the result of the impact of education on work experience and wage rates. As can be seen, education clearly increased the earnings of workers from each demographic group. Earnings for all groups increased steadily with more education. Black males who had attended only elementary school earned $11,026, while median earnings for those with four years of college was $28,827. Thus, black males with four years of college earned 2.6 times the salaries of those with only an elementary school education. Similar gaps existed for all groups. Indeed, the differential was even more dramatic for females. Black female college graduates earned four times as much as black female high school dropouts.

More education also attenuates racial inequality in earnings. The effect was most dramatic for females, where the earnings gap was relatively low in any case. The median earnings of black females increased relative to the median earnings of white females up to the five or more years of college category. Indeed, black females who were high school graduates or better had higher median earnings than did corresponding white females. The median earnings of white females were higher only for the high school dropout levels. As we will see below, the earnings advantage for black females and the attenuation of inequality with education were primarily the result of the impact of education on employment.

Racial inequality in earnings was much greater for black males. Overall, black male earnings were only 69.4 percent of white male earnings, while the overall black female median was 94.21 percent of the white female median. The most equal earnings for black males was for the elementary school group. However, this group was small, and the statistics are probably subject to error. Racial inequality was about the same level for the two high school groups. Racial inequality in earnings of all workers declined as

Table 27
Percent of Persons 25 to 65 Years Old With Earnings
by Work Experience, Race, Sex, and Years of School Completed
1990

All Workers

	Females			Males		
	B	W	B/W	B	W	B/W
0-8 yrs.	39.69	43.51	91.23	55.76	73.64	75.72
1-3 yrs. HS	51.23	55.45	92.39	74.67	85.38	87.46
4 yrs. HS	72.20	72.91	99.01	86.01	91.81	93.69
1-3 yrs. COL	81.17	79.58	102.00	90.11	94.18	95.67
4 yrs. COL	89.91	83.42	107.70	94.44	96.07	98.31
5 + yrs. COL	89.80	88.47	101.50	93.44	95.80	97.53
4 + yrs. COL	89.87	85.30	105.30	94.12	95.95	98.10
All Levels	69.96	73.73	94.89	82.70	91.53	90.35

Year-Round Full-Time Workers

	Females			Males		
	B	W	B/W	B	W	B/W
0-8 yrs.	17.01	18.84	90.28	35.70	45.71	78.11
1-3 yrs. HS	24.25	27.88	86.99	43.38	56.14	77.46
4 yrs. HS	45.39	41.69	108.80	62.59	70.96	88.21
1-3 yrs. COL	55.56	46.76	118.80	64.48	75.98	84.84
4 yrs. COL	69.73	51.10	136.40	75.81	82.01	92.44
5 + yrs. COL	62.10	55.97	110.90	80.69	78.99	102.10
4 + yrs. COL	67.26	52.92	127.00	77.36	80.67	95.89
All Levels	44.19	42.63	103.60	58.77	71.47	82.24

Source: U.S. Department of Commerce, Bureau of the Census, *Money Income of Households, Families, and Persons in the U.S.: 1990,* September 1991, Series P-60, No. 174, Table 29.

education increased beyond the high school graduate level. Blacks with five or more years of college earned 84.16 as much as did corresponding whites.

The second panel in Table 28 provides data on the earnings of workers who worked full-time throughout the year. These data, therefore, remove the impact of employment differences. These data can be taken as annual wage rates. As can be seen, by comparing the data in the bottom panel to the data in the top panel, education is still positively related to annual wage rates. For all demographic groups, the wage rate increased with the level of education. For example, black males with four or more years of college had annual median wages of $32,145, while black male high school graduates had wages of only $20,271. However, the impact of education on annual earnings was smaller once the employment effect was removed. For example, black males with four years of college earned about 2.6 times as much as those with only an elementary school education, when all workers were included. However, when annual wage rates were used, the advantage dropped to 1.8 times. A similar decline was seen for black females, where the advantage of those with college degrees over those with elementary school educations dropped from 4.1 to 1 down to 2.4 to 1. Thus, a great deal of the earnings advantage of more educated workers is due to their more favorable employment experience.

The second panel also makes it clear that education in general does not reduce wage inequality, as measured by the B/W index. In general, wage inequality was lower than overall earnings inequality for males with less than a college degree and females with less than a high school degree. Racial inequality in wages was generally greater than racial inequality in earnings for all male workers with college degrees and females with high school degrees or better. All of the advantages of black females in earnings of all workers vanished when the earnings of full-time year-round workers only were considered. Indeed, except for those with four years of college, all black female educational groups had lower annual wages than had their white counterparts.

It is apparent from the table that racial inequality does not decline with education. For both males and females, racial inequality in wages are about the same across educational levels. For females, racial inequality increases slightly with education up to the college degree. Females with four years of college have equal wages. Males who have no high school have equal wage rates and those with one to three years of college have a B/W index of 82.53. All other groups have B/W indexes that range from 76.42 to 79.80. Wage inequality is higher for those with five or more years of education than for those four years of education for males and females. In any case, it is apparent that much of the inequality reducing impact of education comes through its impact on employment rates.

Table 28
Median of Persons 25 Years and Older
by Years of School Completed, 1990

All Earners

	Males			Females		
	W	B	B/W	W	B	B/W
0-8 yrs.	$12,300	$11,026	89.64	$7,107	$6,118	86.08
1-3 yrs. HS	16,926	12,396	73.24	9,015	8,685	96.34
4 yrs. HS	23,557	17,181	72.93	12,368	12,675	102.48
1-3 yrs. COL	28,392	22,095	77.82	16,270	16,496	101.39
4 yrs. COL	35,596	28,827	80.98	21,429	24,784	115.66
5+ yrs. COL	42,071	35,405	84.16	27,268	28,224	103.51
4+ yrs. COL	37,996	30,282	79.70	23,598	25,874	109.64
Med	26,365	18,299	69.41	19,972	14,105	94.21

Working Year-Round Full-Time

	Males			Females		
	W	B	B/W	W	B	B/W
0-8 yrs.	$16,906	$16,961	100.33	$11,826	$11,364	96.09
1-3 yrs. HS	21,048	16,778	79.71	14,010	13,643	97.38
4 yrs. HS	26,526	20,271	76.42	17,552	16,531	94.18
1-3 yrs. COL	31,336	25,863	82.53	21,547	19,922	92.46
4 yrs. COL	38,263	20,532	79.80	26,822	26,881	100.22
5+ yrs. COL	47,787	36,851	78.19	31,119	31,991	97.27
4+ yrs. COL	41,661	32,145	77.16	29,109	28,094	96.51
Med	30,598	22,176	72.48	20,759	18,838	90.75

Source: U.S. Department of Commerce, Bureau of the Census, *Money Income of Households, Families, and Persons in the U.S.: 1990*, September 1991, Series P-60, No. 174, Table 29.

115

CONCLUSIONS

In this paper, we have explored the low and unequal economic status of African Americans that has been a permanent feature of American economic life. As in previous years, we have again found pervasive and unrelenting poverty and inequality. The gaps in income, poverty rates, and labor market status have not generally abated in the latest data. However, we did note a fluctuation in relative unemployment rates during the past year. It seems, however, that this is probably not indicative of any secular change in the situation of blacks.

We have formulated our presentation in the context of the large differences in ownership of businesses and human and nonhuman wealth. Our analysis suggests that much of the persisting disparities in economic status can be traced to the direct or indirect impact of the large ownership gaps. Indeed, we suggested that at least 35 percent of the gap in aggregate income can be attributed to the direct impact of lower ownership of nonhuman wealth and businesses. Another 21 percent of the gap was attributed to the direct impact of lower levels of human capital ownership on wage and salary earnings. Thus, 56 percent of the aggregate income gap, $108 billion, is caused by the direct impact of limited ownership. An additional $68 billion was attributed to the indirect impact of limited ownership.

The net upshot of the argument is that a significant share of racial inequality in economic life can be eliminated if ownership differences are eliminated. Perhaps, more importantly, the majority of racial inequality cannot be eliminated without eliminating racial differences in ownership. Moreover, even though in principle the portion of inequality attributed to the indirect impact of limited ownership can be eliminated by diligent use of equal opportunity policies, the practical ability to implement such policies in face of the large-scale ownership disparities is limited.

Disparities in ownership are the legacy that the history of inequality in economic life has left to current living generations. Moreover, this disparity is perpetuated by the normal operations of the economic system. Indeed, it is the fact that the normal operations of the market perpetuate ownership disparities from generation to generation that cause racial inequality to be a permanent feature of the American economic system. Equality cannot be obtained without breaking the cycle of self-perpetuating wealth inequality.

It is for the above reason that we end this paper as we have ended this analysis for the last several reports--with the observation that large-scale capital infusions are required to end the poor and unequal status of blacks. These capital infusions may be called reparations in the sense that their function is to repair the disadvantaged ownership position that the living African American generation has inherited as a consequence of the legacy of slavery, Jim Crowism, segregation, and discrimination in economic life. The alternative to reparations is to develop and implement much stronger affirmative action and equal opportunity regulations to regulate the behavior of those who currently have disproportionate ownership. Even if successful, however, this strategy could not eliminate the majority of inequality. Moreover, the past two decades have indicated the difficulty of successful regulation of discriminatory behavior. A policy of reparations would eventually reduce if not eliminate the need for such efforts and, therefore, eventually eliminate one source of rising racial antagonism.

A do-nothing policy would perpetuate and perhaps result in increasing racial inequality and a consequent rise in racial tensions and antagonisms. Such a policy would also prevent America from achieving its full potential as a nation. Moreover, a do-nothing policy or a continuation of the same strategies currently in place will perpetuate the continued tenuousness of African Americans and maintain their second-class status in perpetuity.

Racial Earnings Inequality into the 21st Century

William A. Darity, Jr., Ph.D.
and
Samuel L. Myers, Jr., Ph.D.

INTRODUCTION

Racial earnings gaps among family heads have widened in recent years. The ratio of black-to-white average wage and salary earnings dropped from .63 in 1976 to .59 in 1985. The ratio of black-to-white family incomes, which include the wage and salary earnings and other income of all family members, also declined. The ratio was almost .65 in 1970; it was about .64 in 1976 and about .62 in 1985.

As Figure 1 graphically demonstrates, the ratio--ranging between .61 and .62 in 1989 and 1990--was below what it was for *every single year from 1967 through 1980*. (Throughout this chapter as well as in the various figures, we have based our calculations on data extrapolated from the *Current Population Survey*, published regularly by the U.S. Census Bureau.)

Ratio of Black-to-White Family Income
1967-1990

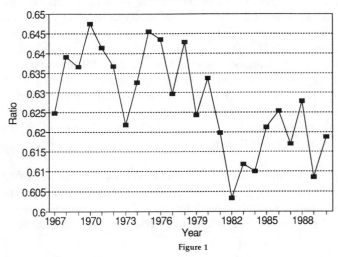

Figure 1

119

In relative terms, black families are losing economic ground. If this decline in the relative economic status of black families is projected into the next decade, the result will be a persistence of racial income inequality that turns the clock back to the income position black families experienced 30 years ago. Moreover, because of changes in family structure, the black family is more vulnerable today than it was at the start of the 1960s. Until recently, policy analysts gave little recognition to widening racial inequality among families in America. The victories of the Civil Rights Movement seemed to translate into considerable gains for black men and women in the labor force. One of the dominant themes in explanations of narrowing earnings inequality after the 1960s was the role of improved education. Either because of desegregation in southern school systems or because of direct increases in educational completion arising from antidiscrimination legislation, increased education among blacks helped to reduce racial earnings disparities. Indeed, nearly every analysis of racial earnings gaps using post-1960s data shows a positive impact of black educational progress on black economic progress.

And yet, today, nearly everyone agrees that inner-city schools are a mess; that drop-out rates are at an all-time high; and that drugs and violent crimes are turning many of our schools in the poorest minority neighborhoods into war zones. If education is improving the relative economic position of blacks, is it doing so by way of class bifurcation within the black community? Is the observed impact of education on reduced inequality an artifact of the widening of the gap in educational opportunities between the black middle class and the black poor?

In fact, among family heads, economic advancement has been uneven over much of the post-Civil Rights era. In recent years, moreover, racial disparity has widened in earnings of family heads and in family incomes. And, when one accounts for the differential labor force participation and unemployment experiences of blacks and whites, especially among young males, the evidence of "improvement" disappears. How can this be, in light of convincing evidence that the racial gap in the educational attainment has all but disappeared? And what does it portend for the future?

This chapter examines the effects of educational achievement on changing earnings inequality among family heads and nonfamily householders. The aim is to establish how it is possible that returns to education are increasing and the average black educational performance is improving while the relative earnings position of blacks is deteriorating. The central conclusions are the following:

(a) The explanations for the alleged convergence of racial earnings during the 1960s and 1970s are of limited use in explaining the recent divergence in earnings. Educational improvements persisted in the 1980s even as the relative position of black families continued to deteriorate.

(b) At least part of the explanation for the decline in the economic status of black families in recent years is related to the increasingly marginalized status of black males, as evidenced by increases in incarceration and violent deaths. This marginalization translates into fewer marriageable mates and thus fewer opportunities for the formation of two-parent families.

(c) Improvements in education, evident for those with earnings and black male heads of families as well as black single females, were accompanied by increased returns to education to blacks with earnings. The reason earnings inequality did not diminish as a result is that there were increases in the number of blacks without earnings at all.

(d) The earnings gaps increased for young black males with less than a high school education. The ratio of black-to-white earnings for this cohort dropped from 1.11 in 1970 to .35 in 1988. This astonishing decline--more pronounced than the drop from .86 to .59 in the ratio of black-to-white earnings among all males under 25 years of age--meant that, by the late 1980s, young black males without high school degrees became one of the most disadvantaged groups in society relative to the same age-education peer group among whites. While some other age and education cohorts showed improvements, the outcomes were not dramatic enough to reverse the overall deterioration in black economic well-being.

(e) If the present patterns persist, wherein there is continued marginalization of young black males and continued growth of younger families headed by females whose educations are curtailed, then economic disparities will persist into the next century, even as black middle-class families experience continued improvements.

BLACK-WHITE EARNINGS CONVERGENCE?

Concerns about how and why racial earnings inequality is narrowing while family life is deteriorating have been addressed by sociologists examining class bifurcation. Wilson and Aponte (1985) and Wilson (1987) see these conflicting indicators of economic progress as evidence of a widening intraracial inequality.

This perspective, however, has been challenged by Farley (1985). Among sociologists, Farley (1985, 1984) recognized the mixed message cast up by data about the economic progress of blacks during the post-Civil Rights era. As we will show below, there is a marked discrepancy between the implications of available data on earnings differences between black and white *individuals* and income differences between black and white *families*. The two types of data lead to quite different implications about trends in the relative economic status of blacks in the United States.

Farley (1985) also found that a third gap continues to persist virtually without change since passage of the Civil Rights legislation in the early

1960s: the racial gap in unemployment rates. Wilson (1987) contended that black male joblessness lies at the heart of familial deterioration among blacks. Joblessness leads to fewer marriages and fewer opportunities to reap the economic benefits of stable families. The result is increased polarization within the black community between middle-class families and poor families. The former are overwhelmingly husband-wife families; the latter are predominantly single-parent, female-headed families.

However, Farley (1985, 24) questioned "the view that the black community is increasingly polarized into a black elite and a black underclass . . . ." He argued, instead, that there long have been class differences among blacks and that today's situation is not unique. Wilson and Aponte (1985) and Wilson (1987) argued, in contrast, that in the post-Civil Rights period, desegregation facilitated the movement of the black middle class out of inner-city ghettos. Thus, a spatial separation between the black middle class and the black underclass evolved that had not existed before.

A parallel debate among economists over the nature and condition of the black underclass has not come to grips with the issue of class bifurcation among blacks. Indirectly, however, the "illusion of progress" hypothesis, in suggesting the heterogeneity of black labor, reaches similar Wilsonian conclusions. The most well-known version of the argument that an illusion of racial economic progress has been created by voluntary labor force withdrawal is that of Richard Butler and James Heckman. They argued that generally there has been no change in the gap in the average productivity between blacks and whites. They suggest that the apparent improvement in the economic status of blacks has resulted from those blacks at the lowest levels of human capital removing themselves from the labor market while the most productive blacks have remained. They propose that the particular mechanism that propels low-earning blacks to leave the labor market is the work disincentives associated with public assistance incomes. This process results in a rise in the ratios of black-to-white earnings, and thus leads to the illusion of black economic progress.

Various attempts to test this sample selection process have challenged the hypothesis. Only mixed support emerges for this argument.[1]

Regardless, the question before us now is no longer why have earnings ratios improved, but--at least among family heads--why have earnings ratios deteriorated in recent years? Labor force participation rates have declined among black family heads, but if the *lowest* earners withdrew, then black earnings ratios should not have declined in a Heckman world. We argue that the marginalization of black males has caused the rise in female-headed families and contributed to the fall in labor force participation of otherwise higher-earning family heads. This, in turn, has resulted in a widening of racial earnings differentials.

EVIDENCE

Figure 2 reveals the conventional story that prompted a decade of debate about the sources of black-white earnings convergence. The ratio of black-to-white male earnings rose from a low of about 50 percent at the end of the 1940s to more than 75 percent during the 1980s among full-time, year-round workers. The ratio is lower when part-time workers are included, but the positive trend still is evident. A similar finding emerges with respect to women, as revealed in Figure 3, and although the relative improvement for women peaked during the late 1970s, black and white women nearly reached parity in earnings by 1980.

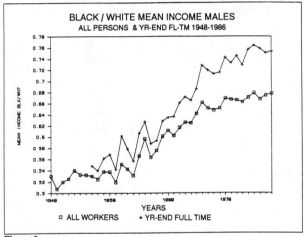

Figure 2

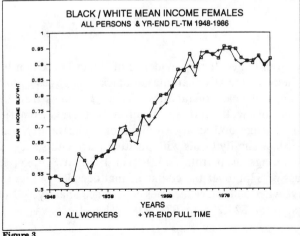

Figure 3

The decade since the mid-to-late 1970s, however, has also seen the growth of poverty and inequality. For example, Table 1 shows that a growing proportion of black and white families, particularly female-headed families, sank into poverty between 1976 and 1985. In part, the rising poverty rate is due to increases in the percentage of all families headed by females--families that begin with higher than average poverty rates. Another part is due to an increase over time in the poverty rates among female-headed families. Thus, any discussion of trends in racial earnings inequality must address changes in both black and white family structures.

Table 1
Poverty Rates Among Primary Families,
1976-1985

White	1976	1985
Male Headed	5.60%	6.00%
Female Headed	26.60%	27.70%
Total	7.80%	9.60%
Black		
Male Headed	13.90%	13.90%
Female Headed	50.80%	52.40%
Total	27.20%	31.90%

Source: Authors' computations from *Current Population Survey* (CPS) tapes.

The apparently conflicting evidence of rising black family poverty in the face of increased relative earnings of blacks can be resolved by focusing on the earnings of heads of families. Table 2 shows that the wage and salary incomes of black family heads fell in real terms from 1976 to 1985, while the real wage and salary earnings of white family heads actually increased. Black family heads with positive wage and salary incomes saw their real earnings drop from $15,012 in 1976 to $14,654 in 1985, an absolute loss of $356 over the course of that decade. White family heads with positive wage and salary incomes experienced nearly a $1,000 increase in earnings, from $23,704 to $24,660. The effect was to leave black families relatively worse off, as the ratio of black-to-white family earnings fell from .63 to .59. Thus, despite the evidence that racial earnings gaps among individual workers seemed to continue to narrow in the past decade, the gap widened among family heads. This conclusion helps to explain why the ratio of black-to-white family incomes exhibits an essentially flat overall trend from the mid-1970s through the 1980s.

Table 2
Wage and Salary Incomes
Family Heads, 1976-1985

	1976	1985
Whites	$23,704	$24,660
Blacks	$15,012	$14,654
B/W	.633314	.594241

Source: Authors computations from CPS tapes. Data for family heads with positive earnings, expressed in 1984 earnings.

In 1976, 36 percent of black families were headed by females. In 1985, almost 45 percent of black families were female-headed. Tables 3 and 4 provide a regional breakdown of family structures among blacks. All regions experienced sharp increases in female-headed families among blacks. In the West, the fraction of black families headed by females jumped from 25 percent in 1976 to 44.6 percent in 1985. In the North Central states, the percentage of black families headed by females increased from 38.6 percent to 51.8 percent.

The absolute *and* relative decline in black family heads' incomes also has been accompanied by a decline in labor force participation rates. While 70.5 percent of black family heads of household worked or were looking for work in 1976, only 65 percent were in the labor force in 1985. The highest

125

Table 3
Family Structure, Sex-Ratios and Earnings, Blacks 1985

Estimated* Sex-Ratios	U.S.	West	North Central	North East	South
Males/Female	0.7999	0.8699	0.8676	0.7629	0.7756
Unmarried Males/ Unmarried Females	0.6064	0.6770	0.7054	0.5626	0.5720
Wilson-Neckerman MMPI	0.4756	0.5443	0.4212	0.4250	0.5063
Darity-Myers Marriageable Males	0.4091	0.4859	0.4222	0.3767	0.4041
Female-headed Families	0.4483	0.4463	0.5180	0.4816	0.4096
Expected Welfare	$567	$717	$956	$939	$243
Wage & Salary Income	$9,493	$10,352	$8,982	$9,996	$9,372
Wage & Salary Income Positive Earners	$14,654	$15,602	$15,701	$16,737	$13,519
Labor Force Participation Rate	0.6495	0.6218	0.5752	0.6152	0.6951

*Refers to individuals. All other computations refer to family heads.
Incomes expressed in 1984 dollars.
Source: Authors' computations from *Current Population Survey, March Supplement* tapes.

Table 4
Family Structure, Sex-Ratios and Earnings, Blacks 1985

Estimated* Sex-Ratios	U.S.	West	North Central	North East	South
Males/Female	0.8689	0.9724	0.7718	0.8020	0.9179
Unmarried Males/ Unmarried Females	0.6728	0.7495	0.5787	0.6772	0.6978
Wilson-Neckerman MMPI	0.4935	0.5297	0.4410	0.3921	0.5489
Darity-Myers Marriageable Males	0.4594	0.5513	0.3763	0.4692	0.4747
Female-headed Families	0.3605	0.2538	0.3856	0.3730	0.3640
Expected Welfare	$760	$605	$1,137	$1,188	$459
Wage & Salary Income	$10,359	$12,311	$12,359	$11,630	$8,675
Wage & Salary Income Positive Earners	$15,012	$17,150	$18,260	$17,594	$12,362
Labor Force Participation Rate	0.7051	0.6995	0.6897	0.6824	0.7213

*Refers to individuals. All other computations refer to family heads.
Incomes expressed in 1984 dollars.
Source: Authors' computations from *Current Population Survey, March Supplement* tapes.

labor force participation rates were registered for black family heads in the South during both years; the lowest were found in the Northeast and North Central states. In summary, despite the appearance of convergence of earnings among individuals, black-white earnings differentials among family heads are widening. This is occurring as black family heads' labor force participation rates are declining and as female-headship among black families is on the rise. To understand how this process works, it is necessary to place the problem of changing family structure within the broader context of changes in the economy from industrial manufacturing to a new managerial age.

A MODEL OF RACIAL EARNINGS INEQUALITY

We have specified and estimated a comprehensive model linking earnings, labor force participation, and family structure equations. Figure 4 describes the process. Our model is premised on the view that the managerial elite, which evolved and expanded under the transformation from the earlier capitalistic state, has a vested interest in the newly emergent institutions designed to control, contain, or eradicate the underclass. The black managers who run the welfare bureaus and the local governments have at best ambivalent attitudes toward the poor. In our model, increased marginality feeds back upon the behaviors that contribute to or at least justify the expansion of institutionalization.

Figure 4

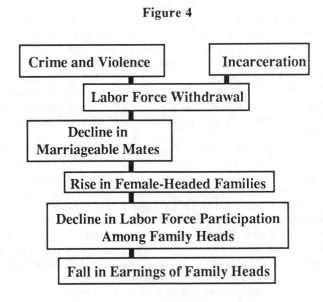

We have detailed the role of the managerial elite in contributing to the marginality of the black poor. We noted:

> Black Americans overwhelmingly are part of the working class, but they also are disproportionately part of the *inactive portion* of the working class. For among their numbers are a large percentage of persons rarely employed, deeply entrenched in poverty, most likely to be imprisoned, most likely to be the military's foot soldiers, and least likely to have a sense of optimism about the opportunities offered to them by American society . . .
>
> The managerial class . . . will find less and less reason to retain such an excess population at all. For its rational view of production--unvarnished by anything but pure efficiency considerations--leads it to see no major reason to maintain a reserve of the unemployed. Over the shorter term, the social work bureaucrats will uphold maintenance of the welfare apparatus and resist reforms that eliminate their administrative and supervisory positions. But in the longer term, the managerial class will restructure itself, reducing class dependence on positions within the welfare bureaucracy and increasing class reliance on more purely technocratic positions. The sheer "planning" impulse will overwhelm the "helping" impulse. The current assault on the welfare system by capital could prove fortuitous for the technocratic core of the managerial elite, insofar as it creates a pretext to pare away relatively weaker and less indispensable fractions of its class. In the meantime, however, the fraction of the managerial class that is ensconced within the welfare bureaucracy will fight to maintain the welfare system regardless of whether or not the system uplifts the poor. Moreover, the "helping" element of the managerial class provides the help of the paternalist.
>
> Over the long term, the managerial class is likely to move to eradicate "useless" layers of the working class. Since those layers most likely to be deemed superfluous are disproportionately black, then the fates have grim times in store for the black underclass. The managerial class in its more humanitarian guise will advocate programs to change members of the black underclass into people more like members of the managerial class (manpower training, educational programs, etc.). As frustration accelerates with such a project, the managers will push for racially targeted population control measures.
>
> The superfluity of the black underclass--from the perspectives of both elites--is reinforced not only by technological developments that reduce the social necessity of all labor, inclusive of black labor, but also it is aggravated further by the new immigrants. The latter stand as replacements. They are less jaded, more enthusiastic, less rebellious, and cheaper workers, unaccustomed to the "cushion" provided by the American social transfer scheme.
>
> In the short term, the managerial class may promise and even deliver a renewed expansion of social programs to garner black political support--in part because of the interests of the social welfare bureaucracy. But the longer-term tendency is for the broader managerial class to prune away superfluous elements of other classes as well as its own. Once power is consolidated, the voting power of blacks no longer will be required and the non-accommodative

black poor may be viewed as simply *too* expensive. Steps will be taken to prune away the black underclass and, subsequently, an equally superfluous, weaker fraction of its own class, the black social managers.[2]

Marginality also contributes to self-destruction--partly explaining the rise in homicides--which we have found in our empirical work directly contributes to the decline in marriageable mates. The decline in two-parent families, then, is a result of declines in the availability of marriageable mates that ultimately flows from structural transformation in the labor markets. The labor market transformation in question is the technical and managerial changes that result from and contribute to the rise of managerial society. Surplus labor--unemployed, underemployed, or never employed-- is now socially unwanted; institutional mechanisms arise to contain, control, and ultimately eliminate the superfluous labor.

Two mechanisms illustrated in the figure are institutionalization and crime. These two feed upon one another and contribute to labor force withdrawal, siphoning off the least productive and undesirable elements of the surplus pool. At the same time, even potentially productive members of the community are drawn off in this process as crime, drugs, violence, and, for some, imprisonment or death further erode the capability to reproduce stable family forms in black communities.

EDUCATIONAL GAINS OR LOSSES?

We have assembled data and have specified an estimated empirical counterpart of this model. From the model, it is possible to derive the returns to education and to estimate the impacts of increased education on earnings inequality. Table 5 presents a range of estimates of the returns to education.[3]

Table 5
Returns to Education, Family Heads

	Blacks 1976	Whites 1976	Blacks 1985	Whites 1985	Change in Inequality
Estimates	.027085	.043778	.06816	.065603	-0.01925
Average Years Completed	10.056	11.901	11.095	12.414	

Source: Authors' computations from *Current Population Survey, March Supplement* tapes

Educational completion rose for black and white family heads from 1976 to 1985, but the increase was sharper for blacks than for whites. Also evident is the fact that the returns to education rose considerably for blacks from 1976 to 1985. By returns to education, we mean the percent change in earnings as a result of a one-year increase in education. Our estimates of the returns to education for whites were 4.3 percent and 6.5 percent in 1976 and 1985, respectively. The estimates for blacks were 2.7 and 6.8 percent. In other words, the returns to education rose dramatically for blacks to the point where they approximated those for whites in 1985. Black returns to education improved in the decade of the 1980s.

There is no reason to believe that the near equalization of education between individual blacks and whites nor that the convergence in their returns to education means the elimination of discrimination that has pervaded labor markets for decades. At least among family heads, the racial gap in educational completion persists. As Table 5 shows, the average white family head in 1985 had 12.414 years of education, while the average black family head had only 11.095 years of education. This divergence is due in part to the wide differences in family structure between blacks and whites. But other factors contribute to the disparity as well. Blacks are far less likely than whites to have access to wealth; they are more likely to be discriminated against in credit markets; they are less likely to be self-employed and to be business owners.[4] These factors result in a cumulative disadvantage whereby the low income and wealth in present generations spill over to handicap future generations.

One can compute the impact of these increasing educational returns on earnings inequality. The ratio of black-to-white earnings in year t to black-to-white earnings in year $t+1$ is one measure of inequality. As this ratio rises, inequality increases, or the racial earnings gap widens.[5] We find that earnings gaps widened by 5 percent from 1976 to 1985. Table 5 shows that a uniform increase in one year of education ought to reduce inequality. However, ignoring the selective withdrawal of marginalized young black men--as well as the subsequent impact this will have on the rise in female-headed families and labor force participation of family heads--leads to a significant overstatement of the degree of reduction in racial earnings gaps attributable to education. This suggests that there exists a nontrivial class of persons who may not be beneficiaries of improved education and the earnings improvements that follow. These persons are the nonearners who necessarily are not included in published statistics on earnings.

Table 6 provides additional insights about the distribution of educational advances among blacks and whites. The table details two important breakdowns. One is positive earners versus nonearners. This dichotomy reflects those with and without positive wage and salary incomes. A second breakdown is family heads versus nonfamily heads. The former consists of heads of families; the latter consists of heads of nonfamilies and largely represents single heads of households.

Table 6
Educational Attainment of Earners and Nonearners, 1976-1985

	1976		1985		Percent Change 1976-1985	
	Black	White	Black	White	Black	White
Positive Earners						
Family Heads						
Male	10.48	12.37	12.02	12.94	14.69%	4.61%
Female	11.08	11.93	11.95	12.58	7.85%	5.45%
Nonfamily Heads						
Male	10.47	13.29	11.83	13.58	12.99%	2.18%
Female	10.91	12.82	12.77	13.58	17.05%	5.93%
Nonearners						
Family Heads						
Male	7.93	10.84	9.09	11.41	14.63%	5.26%
Female	9.28	9.85	9.74	10.64	4.96%	8.02%
Nonfamily Heads						
Male	9.12	10.35	9.09	11.72	-0.33%	13.24%
Female	7.53	10.19	8.92	10.67	18.46%	4.71%

Source: Author's computations from the *Current Population Survey,*
March Supplement tapes

Among those with positive incomes, the educational attainment of family heads as well as nonfamily heads increased, whether male or female. The percentage increase was larger for blacks than for whites and was largest for black female nonfamily heads. This group, which experienced an increase in educational attainment of 17 percent, completed 10.91 years of schooling in 1976 but 12.77 years by 1985, surpassing the educational attainment of black and white female family heads and black male family and nonfamily heads and nearly equaling the educational attainment of white male family heads. This group of mostly single black women, slightly older than their white counterparts and older than female family heads in 1985, was a younger group in 1985 than it was in 1976. The average age of black female nonfamily heads with positive earnings in 1976 was 45; in

131

1985 it was 40. This suggests impressive educational gains among younger black women *without family responsibilities*. This group certainly outdistanced all other groups of black women and was the only group of blacks, save for male family heads, that had an average level of education exceeding high school.

In sharp contrast with the educational gains of single black women is the deterioration of the educational prospects for black male nonfamily heads without earnings. These men, who had completed 9.12 years of schooling in 1976, completed an average of only 9.09 years of schooling by 1985. This educational completion was lower than that for whites in any category and even for black female family heads. Yet, these men were not young like the single females with positive earnings. Their average age was 54 in 1985 and 56 in 1976. The youngest men had some earnings but were not family heads. The average age of black male nonfamily heads with earnings was 39 in 1976 and 37 in 1985. Still, neither the black male nonearners nor the black male earners had managed to attain an average level of educational attainment equivalent to high school graduation.

The implication is that, outside of families, education completion diverged between black males and females--black males being burdened with educational levels below high school degrees and black females blessed with sharp increases in educational attainment, obtaining high school degrees and some college education. And, within families, black males saw educational growth substantially exceed that of black females or white family heads. This is the backdrop against which we must examine the impacts of educational attainment on earnings inequality. It is a perverse impact due to the intraracial distribution of educational attainment.

EARNINGS RATIOS BY AGE, EDUCATION, AND OCCUPATION

To underscore the fact that not all blacks have benefited from educational improvements over the past quarter century, we computed earnings ratios for selected years by age and education. Table 7 displays these computations.

Table 7
Ratio of Black-to-White Earnings, By Age and Education, 1970-1988

	1970		1973		1976		1979		1982		1985		1988	
	Males	Females	Males	Females	Males	Females	Males	Females	Males	Females	Males	Females	Males	Females
Less than 25 years	0.86	0.69	0.70	0.73	0.64	0.63	0.64	0.63	0.57	0.57	0.51	0.57	0.59	0.59
Elementary through High School	1.11	0.90	0.74	0.94	0.87	0.91	0.87	0.91	0.51	0.66	0.36	0.46	0.35	0.72
High School Graduate	0.88	0.86	0.80	0.91	0.72	0.67	0.72	0.67	0.61	0.58	0.60	0.62	0.70	0.56
Some College	0.95	0.84	0.90	0.77	0.75	0.68	0.75	0.68	0.87	0.75	0.70	0.72	0.74	0.79
College Graduate and More	1.07	1.03	1.57	0.85	0.76	0.83	0.76	0.83	0.69	0.61	1.11	0.71	1.31	1.03
25 to 40 years	0.64	1.30	0.66	1.23	0.71	1.17	0.71	1.17	0.68	1.00	0.63	0.98	0.67	0.90
Elementary through High School	0.73	1.23	0.67	1.17	0.79	1.00	0.79	1.00	0.74	1.16	0.62	0.83	0.78	0.76
High School Graduate	0.69	1.43	0.72	1.46	0.77	1.39	0.77	1.39	0.72	1.11	0.66	1.06	0.69	1.04
Some College	0.73	2.00	0.80	1.44	0.80	1.51	0.80	1.51	0.77	1.10	0.73	1.13	0.82	1.02
College Graduate and More	0.77	1.82	0.88	1.69	0.80	1.33	0.80	1.33	0.73	1.19	0.80	1.18	0.73	1.08
Over 40 years	0.62	0.87	0.62	1.00	0.61	1.01	0.61	1.01	0.60	1.04	0.61	1.18	0.66	1.11
Elementary through High School	0.78	1.02	0.83	1.14	0.85	1.07	0.85	1.07	0.83	1.19	0.88	1.43	0.80	1.18
High School Graduate	0.74	1.16	0.76	1.28	0.76	1.33	0.76	1.33	0.81	1.34	0.78	1.39	0.80	1.49
Some College	0.82	1.39	0.58	1.62	0.90	1.63	0.90	1.63	0.83	1.70	0.89	1.52	0.97	1.40
College Graduate and More	0.70	1.65	0.78	1.53	0.82	1.70	0.82	1.70	0.68	1.49	0.77	1.62	1.00	1.40
TOTAL	0.62	0.95	0.61	1.01	0.62	0.98	0.62	0.98	0.60	0.94	0.58	0.99	0.63	0.93

Source: Authors' computations using the *Current Population Survey, March Supplement* tapes. Ratios obtained for individuals over 16 years.

133

These findings emerge:

(a) There were drastic declines in the relative earnings of young black males with education attainment of elementary through high school. These males, under 25 years of age who were not high school graduates, had earnings that were 1.11 times that of similarly situated white males in 1970. In 1979, they had earnings that were 87 percent of white males' earnings. By 1982, they had earnings that were about 50 percent of the earnings received by lesser educated young black males. And, by 1988, they earned only 36 percent of what comparably situated whites earned.

(b) There was some improvement in relative earnings among older, better educated black males. For male college graduates over 40 years of age, the ratio of black-to-white earnings rose from .70 in 1970 to 1.00 in 1988. These educated black men moved from earning less than three-quarters of what similarly situated white men earned to a point where there was earnings parity.

(c) Older black women, especially high school graduates, closed substantially the earnings gap, and by the 1980s, enjoyed an earnings advantage over whites.

(d) Black women in the age group 25 to 40 years saw their earnings advantage erode. While the ratio of black-to-white earnings dropped from 1.30 to .90 in 1970 and 1988 respectively, among all women in this age group, the drop was most acute among less-educated women. For them, the ratio dropped from 1.23 in 1970 to .76 in 1988.

The upshot of these findings is that just as older educated black men and women seem to be improving their lot comparatively, younger black males, and even to a lesser extent black females under 40 with little education, are slipping badly. This suggests not only the development of a generational wedge but also a wedge based on education.

Figure 5 shows another dimension of the wedge being driven between the haves and have-nots among blacks. We display ratios of black-to-white earnings of all family heads and of those with professional and managerial jobs. The numbers above each bar represent the black-white earnings ratio among professionals/managers as compared to the earnings ratio for all occupations. Among male family heads, professionals and managers did not face racial earnings ratios greater than the average in 1970. The ratio for them was .65; for all male family heads it was .68. Thus, the index of .96 (calculated by dividing the professional/manager's earnings ratio by that for all male family heads) indicates no real relative earnings advantage among professional and managerial male heads of family in 1970. This changed in the late 1970s, and by 1988, the ratio rose to .88 for those with professional and managerial jobs and to only .74 for the average male family head. Thus, a significant relative earnings advantage of being a black male head of family with a professional or managerial job in the late 1980s emerged. In 1985 and 1988, the "relative advantage" index for these family heads rose to 1.17 and 1.19. With the exception of the dip in the relative earnings during the 1982 recession, black male heads of families with professional and managerial jobs narrowed the gap between their white counterparts and widened their advantage over other black males.

Figure 5

Ratio of Black-to-White Earnings
Professional/Managerial Family Heads

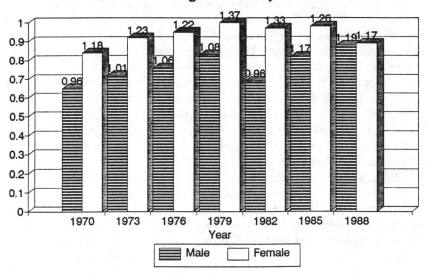

The ratio of black-to-white earnings was greater for professional or managerial female heads of families. Parity of the earnings of comparably situated blacks and whites was attained by the end of the 1970s. However, the advantage that black professional or managerial female heads of families held over all other black female heads of families diminished throughout the 1980s, with the index of relative advantage falling from 1.37 in 1979 to 1.17 in 1988. Thus, while professional black women who were heads of families enjoyed greater earnings equality with professional white female

135

heads of families than did the average black female-headed family, this advantage--less than the advantage held by black male-headed families in 1988--was by far less substantial at the end of the 1980s. The relative advantage of black female-heads of families who held professional and managerial jobs disintegrated during the past decade.

PROSPECTS FOR THE FUTURE?

Earnings inequality, particularly among family heads, is not likely to diminish in the years ahead. There are several factors at work. First is the fact that, as the fraction of black families headed by females continues to grow, the share of lower-earning family heads among blacks increases. Even if the next generation of female heads were disproportionately drawn from the professional and managerial ranks--unlikely as that may seem--the effect would not necessarily be to reduce racial inequality. If present trends continue, whereby even professional black women who head families are losing ground relative to professional white women and are losing their relative advantage over other black female-headed families, racial inequality among family heads will continue to worsen.

A second factor at work is the continued decline in the relative earnings and the educational prospects of young black males. These individuals--should they become family heads--are not likely to be positioned to experience significant earnings growth over the years. More likely, they will either be nonearners or nonfamily heads, further contributing to the growth of female-headed families.

Perhaps more intriguing is the factor of education. The educational gains of the past decades were unevenly shared among family heads and earners and nonearners. Among black males, educational gains were limited to those with jobs and those who headed families. Some of these employed family heads held good-paying managerial and professional positions. Yet, those nonfamily heads without jobs--including the increasing number of black males incarcerated or deeply scarred by arrest records and criminal involvement--saw no educational gains. And black female-heads of families--whether they received wage and salary income or not--only realized modest educational gains. It was black females who did not head families, who often had good jobs in professional and managerial occupations, whose education rose substantially. Yet, since these women's education lagged slightly behind that of comparably situated whites, there was little additional advantage conveyed to them. Thus, although uniform increases in educational completion ought to reduce racial inequality, the unevenness of educational gains within the black community results in muted progress.

Blacks suffer a major disadvantage with respect to advanced education masked by mean years of schooling convergence. Among persons 25 years and older in 1990, 46 percent of whites had some college education compared to only 37 percent of blacks.[6] Blacks will lack access to professional-managerial positions in the future as a result of this continuing gap in advanced education. For example, there remains a major racial gap in the receipt of scientific degrees.[7] Whereas whites comprised 75 percent of the population in 1990, they received 88 percent of science and engineering doctorates in 1987. Blacks comprised 12 percent of the population in 1990 but received only 1.5 percent of science and engineering doctorates in 1987. Blacks will be excluded from the managerial age--an age of science and technology--with this significant underrepresentation in advanced degrees.

The net effect of continuing inequality in more advanced education--even in the face of apparent convergence in average education completion--is to leave the black community underdeveloped. Darity (1991) has computed a separate Human Development Index score for African Americans. The living standard for the average black in the United States is found to compare to that of persons living in Portugal, Singapore, and Korea. It is below that of Argentina, Poland, Hungary, Costa Rica, and Hong Kong.[8]

Recall Figure 1, which describes the trends of family incomes over the past decades. Part of the long-term decline in the ratio of black-to-white family incomes is due to the reduction in the relative wage and salary earnings of black family heads. But since there are mixed effects involved in the determination of black family heads' earnings--some positive and some negative--then it is useful to extrapolate to the year 2000, using the entire family incomes and using information on past and current trends. Estimating a straight line from 1967 through the year 2000 shows a predicted drop in the ratio of black-to-white family income to .60. That is, black families in the year 2000 can expect to earn 60 cents for every dollar that white families earn if the quarter-century trend continues. Figure 6, with the results plotted as Forecast 1, reveals this outcome.

Ratio of Black-to-White Family Income
1967-1990 and Forecasts to Year 2000

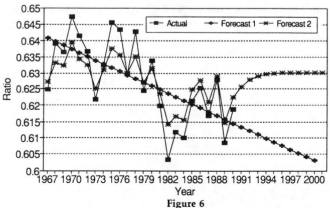

Figure 6

137

The past trend, however, shows several periods of slight improvement in the ratio of black-to-white family income. For example, family income rose from .625 in 1967 to almost .65 in 1970. After dropping to nearly .62 in the early 1970s, it rose again above .64 by the mid-1970s. There was a prolonged skid during the late 1970s until the recession of 1982, when the ratio fell to just above .60. The overall assessment, then, of the period between the end of the Great Society and the beginning of the Reagan Revolution was a deterioration of relative black family incomes. However, the 1980s recovery from the recession and the rebound of the ratio of black-to-white family incomes, albeit only up to the level of the late 1960s, suggest that there may be a separate positive trend. This upward swing, led in part by the gains of male-headed families in managerial and professional occupations, may be short-lived if the recessionary years of the early 1990s pull down the relative earnings of these male managers and professionals along with those of females.

Nevertheless, it is possible to obtain estimates and forecasts based on a more sophisticated rendering of the ups and downs of relative incomes.[9] The results are displayed in Figure 6 as Forecast 2. The recent trend dominates the forecast, suggesting an upward growth in the ratio of black to white family income, but a growth which tapers off by the end of the century. The upshot is that even in this more optimistic scenario--no recessionary effects, no offsetting effects via the growth of female-headed families and the deteriorating plight of young black males--the ratio of black-to-white family earnings will still be only .63: Black families will earn at best 63 cents for every dollar white families earn by the year 2000.

This sad conclusion can be averted if the growth of poor, female-headed families is curbed. As long as young men continue to be marginalized, however, the prospects for increasing the share of black families with male heads seems remote. Strengthening female-headed families, while obviously beneficial in the short-run, offers little hope for reducing the earnings gap further. Since the culprit in this link remains the deteriorating position of young black males with little training or education beyond high school, the solution must lie in salvaging what otherwise could be a lost generation of men. Failure to reverse the neglect of these disadvantaged members of our communities will only mean that future inequality will be more difficult to eradicate.

* * * * *

Support from the W.E. Upjohn Institute for the data analysis reported in this article is gratefully acknowledged, although the findings do not necessarily reflect the views of the Upjohn Institute. Able research assistance was provided by Helen Banks, Lisa Cook, Kevin Hart, and Ruby Taylor-Lewis. Programming and computer analysis was expertly provided by Dr. Tsze Chan. Technical details of the analysis discussed in this chapter are available in "Black-White Earnings Gaps Have Widened: The Problem of Family Structure, Earnings Inequality, and the Marginalization of Black Men," *AASP Working Paper Series: Policy Research, Analysis and Minority Communities*, Vol. 1, No. 5, August 1991, University of Maryland at College Park.

The Condition of African American Education: Changes and Challenges

Shirley M. McBay, Ph.D.

INTRODUCTION

Education is the historic gateway to a better life for all Americans, especially for African Americans. However, as we begin 1992--some 37 years after *Brown* v. *The Board of Education of Topeka*--most African American children remain in schools that are separate and decidedly unequal. Nineteen hundred and ninety-two marks the second anniversary of another decision with potential to alter radically the education of African Americans: the decision by President Bush and the governors to establish national education goals to be achieved by the year 2000 for every child, every adult, and every school in America. What will be the outcome for African Americans under this decision? Is there reason to believe it will be any different than that under *Brown*?

In April 1991, President Bush announced "America 2000," a four-part strategy, as the Administration's plan for achieving the national educational goals. What is in America 2000 for African Americans? For example, will America 2000 enable every African American child to start school ready to learn as called for in the national educational goals? Will African American students, under America 2000, achieve the national goal of having U.S. students be the first in the world in mathematics and science achievement? Does the president's strategy address the national educational goal that every school, including those attended by African American students, will be free of drugs and violence by the year 2000?

A context is needed in which to address these questions. Let us consider where African Americans were and are in education (1980-1991), where we want to be ("A Vision for 2001"), why we are not there ("Challenges to be Met"), and how we get there ("Strategies to Achieve Vision 2001"). The implications of America 2000 for African Americans can then be realistically examined.

WHERE WE WERE AND ARE IN EDUCATION

Educational achievement among African Americans continues to lag behind that of all other racial and ethnic groups, despite numerous examples of individual accomplishments under segregated circumstances. Inadequate preparation in unequal schools and continued racial prejudice have trapped more than a third of African Americans in a cycle of poverty and a quality of life comparable to that of many Third World countries.

Historically, low educational achievement among African Americans has resulted not only from poverty and prejudice, but also from the structured expectation in our schools that African American children will fail. As a consequence of this self-fulfilling prophecy, millions of African American youth are left behind and are unprepared for the future. The injustice is painfully clear. Poverty rates for African Americans are the highest of any group in America: 31.6 percent (9.43 million people) in 1988, nearly two-and-a-half times the national average and more than three-and-a-half times that of white Americans (a ratio that has not changed since 1969).

Among African American children under 18 in 1988, the situation was far worse: 42.2 percent (4.2 million) living in poverty, more than twice the poverty rate for all American children. Forty-eight percent (1.6 million) of African American children under the age of six, nearly one in two, were living in poverty in 1987. This percentage is higher than that for any other racial or ethnic group. When these African American children enter school, they will be unprepared for success. They will attend segregated schools with significantly smaller per-pupil expenditures and fewer educational resources than those attended by their white and their more affluent African American peers.

Once in school, "ability" testing, sometimes as early as pre-kindergarten, will disproportionately place African American children into low-ability or special education classes from which it will be almost impossible to escape. Such assignments essentially seal the fate of many of these children for a lifetime. As early as the third grade, a divergence in achievement appears, relative to their white peers, in reading, writing, mathematics, and science. The gap widens to as much as four years by the junior year in high school. Clearly, our current system produces a large proportion of African American students who are, at best, only marginally prepared for success in college or the work force. It leads, instead, to an educated elite that does not include significant numbers of African American students. This factory model educational system also produces a group of dropouts that is disproportionately low-income and minority (African American, American Indian, Mexican American, and Puerto Rican).

Drop-out rates among African American students have declined somewhat over the last decade. However, about 15 percent of African Americans aged 16-24 in 1988 had not graduated and were out of school.[1] Most high school dropouts are essentially unemployable in a workplace that requires increasingly higher skills.

African American youth who drop out are worse off because they are

142

more likely to have only minimal academic skills. Their ability to find work is significantly affected by the increasing proportion of work exported by U.S. companies to other countries where large numbers of workers are available and eager to perform low-skill jobs, previously performed by Americans, at considerably lower wages. These alternative sources of cheap labor minimize the need to invest in the education of poor children, as enlightened self-interest might have led to in the past.

Several factors combine to create a powerful urgency for major systemic changes in the approach to educating low-income children and youth, especially those who are African American: America's factory model approach to education with its structured expectation that African American children cannot and will not achieve; the major shift in demographics occurring in this country; the increasing need for higher levels of skills in the workplace; and America's challenge to compete internationally.

The urgency is brought further into focus by the unabated violence in America's inner cities, the disproportionately high number of African American males in prison, the increasing percentage of African American children living in poverty, and the alarming spread of hopelessness and despair in African American communities. Quality education and marketable skills are key to solving these problems.

Clearly, ignorance and bigotry outside of our community fuel overt acts of racism that deny African American students equal access to education (witness the significant rise in racist behavior in schools and on predominantly white college campuses around the country; attacks on affirmative action in admissions and on race-specific scholarships; the raising of college admissions standards, including at many public institutions; and an increasing call for merit-based, rather than need-based, financial aid). While we should continue seeking remedies for such acts, we cannot wait for others to do what is morally right. Time is not on our side.

Population and Selected Social and Economic Measures

According to the 1990 census, the African American population increased more than 13 percent since 1980, reaching close to 30 million persons. Thirty-three percent (10 million) were under 18 years of age, while the median age was 27.9 years. Among African American children under 18, the proportion living only with their mothers increased significantly, from 43.9 percent in 1980 to 51.2 percent in 1990. Almost 54 percent of this group of children were living in poverty.

More encouraging is the fact that the number of African Americans graduating from high school and college increased sharply during the 1980s. A new Census Bureau study reports that the percentage of African American men in the 35- to 44-year-old age group completing four years of high school or more increased to 78.9 percent in 1990, up from 62.2 percent in

1980 (a 26.8 percent increase). African American women showed similar gains, with an increase of 28.5 percent in high school completion rate (to 80.7 percent, up from 62.8 percent).[2]

The proportion of African American males 35 to 44 years old who had completed four or more years of college more than doubled, from 7.3 percent in 1980 to 16.7 percent in 1990. Among African American women, the increase was 68.6 percent (from 8.6 percent in 1980 to 14.5 percent in 1990).[3]

Although there have been gains in education, the gap in income between African Americans and white Americans remains significant. For example, the 1989 median family income for African Americans was only $20,210, while for white Americans it was $35,980. African American men continued to earn about 75 percent of what white men earned, regardless of whether they had a high school or a college education. On the other hand, the earnings gap between African American women and white women almost closed, with African American women earning 98 percent of the median earnings of white women.[4] In the latter case, it should be kept in mind that white women earn only 61 percent of what white men earn; and more years in the work force coupled with longer working hours may help to explain the comparable average salaries of African American women and white women.

Preschool Opportunities

The low socioeconomic status of a third of African Americans, with its attendant myriad problems, has continued to erode the well-being of preschool-aged African American children, as evidenced by the increasing percentage of these children who live in poverty (48 percent in 1987, up from 41 percent in 1975).[5] As a consequence, one out of every two African American children may not be prepared to learn when they enter school. In 1987, at least 800,000 African American children were in need of post-natal and preschool intervention to ensure that they entered school healthy, emotionally secure, and sufficiently developed socially in order to succeed in school. However, only 171,000 African American children between the ages of three and five were served by Head Start, a federal program that began in 1965 to provide comprehensive services including health, education, and social services to preschool children of low-income families.

Elementary and Secondary School

In 1984-85, African Americans represented slightly more than 16 percent of the 39 million students enrolled in the nation's public elementary and secondary schools. This percentage is projected to increase 13 percent between 1985-86 and 1994-95.[6] The majority of these children will likely attend schools that are predominantly minority. There are no signs of increased school desegregation since 1980, when 64 percent of African American students attended schools that were more than 50 percent minority and 33 percent were enrolled in intensely segregated schools with fewer than 10 percent white students.[7]

Without intervention, these students will disproportionately attend schools that lack academic rigor; experienced, well-prepared, and caring teachers; meaningful parental involvement; and a supportive environment characterized by high expectations.

They will be tracked into low-level reading, English, mathematics, and science courses without, for example, the opportunity or preparation to complete the "gatekeeper" courses of algebra and geometry by the ninth grade and to enroll subsequently in more advanced courses in mathematics while in high school.

Preparation and Plans for College

African American youth continued to make gains on the Scholastic Aptitude Test (SAT), the widely used college entrance examination, as reflected in Table 1 below.

Table 1
Average SAT Scores for African Americans, 1982, 1991

	1982	1991	Change
SAT-Verbal	341	351	+10
SAT-Math	366	385	+19
Total	707	736	+29

Sources: Admissions Testing Program of The College Entrance Examination Board and *The Chronicle of Higher Education Almanac,* August 28, 1991.

The average composite score of African American students on the American College Test (ACT) has also continued to improve. In 1991, for example, the average composite ACT score for African Americans was 17.0, up from 16.5 in 1987. Student performance on both tests continues to correlate strongly with family income. However, an analysis of the academic preparation of students who took the ACT in 1991 revealed that "low-income students who took a more rigorous high school curriculum also posted better results. The average score for students with an annual family income of less than $18,000 who took college preparatory classes was 20.1, compared with 17.6 for students with the same family income who took a less difficult curriculum."[8]

The preparation of African American students in mathematics and science bears special examination, given forecasts of national needs and the historic under-preparedness and underrepresentation of African Americans in the sciences and engineering. Success in college in these fields requires strong academic preparation at the precollege level in mathematics and science.

An examination of the scores of college-bound African American seniors who took advanced placement tests in 1988 in nine science and mathematics subject areas reveals scores below 2 in four of the areas and between 2 and 3 (2.16 to 2.98) in the remaining five. A score of 3 qualifies for college credit, while a score of 2 indicates possible qualification. In comparison, the average scores for all college-bound seniors taking these tests were between 2 and 3 (2.56 to 2.94) in four subject areas, and above 3 in the five remaining areas.[9]

Interestingly, almost 34 percent of the African American college-bound seniors who took the SAT that year indicated science and engineering as their intended major in college (in comparison with 32 percent of students overall). The average SAT-mathematics score among this group of African American students was 416, some 100 points less than that of all college-bound seniors in 1988 with similar interests.

Only 12 percent of the African American college-bound seniors that year had enrolled in science honors courses in high school (compared to 20 percent of all college-bound seniors) and 13 percent in honors courses in mathematics (compared to 22 percent for all college-bound seniors). Although the interest in mathematics, science, and engineering majors existed among one-third of the 1988 college-bound African American seniors, their low enrollment in honors science and mathematics courses in high school and their performance on achievement tests raise concerns about their ability to persist in these fields in college, and, if they do persist, about their ability to graduate in four years.

Participation in Post-Secondary Education

The representation of African Americans in higher education continues to be below their representation in the college-age population. African Americans were approximately 15 percent of the 18- to 24-year-old population in 1990, while comprising 13 percent of high school graduates and 10 percent of first-time college freshmen in 1988.[10]

The table below provides information on the enrollment of African American students in college in selected years.

146

Table 2
College Enrollment of African American Students, Selected Years

	1980	1982	1984	1986	1988
All	1,107,000	1,101,000	1,076,000	1,082,000	1,130,000
Men	464,000	458,000	437,000	436,000	443,000
Women	643,000	644,000	639,000	646,000	687,000
Public	876,000	873,000	844,000	854,000	881,000
Private	231,000	228,000	232,000	228,000	248,000
4-Year	634,000	612,000	617,000	615,000	656,000
2-Year	472,000	489,000	459,000	467,000	473,000
College	1,028,000	1,028,000	995,000	996,000	1,039,000
Grad.	66,000	61,000	67,000	72,000	76,000
Prof.	13,000	13,000	13,000	14,000	14,000

Source: *The Chronicle of Higher Education Almanac*, August 28, 1991.
Note: Because of rounding, details may not add.

The large percentage of African American students in two-year colleges merits special notice. Although many factors explain this high enrollment (e.g., costs, convenience of location, open enrollment, and availability of remedial courses), there is cause for concern. For example, of all students enrolled in two-year colleges in 1980, only 28.7 percent had transferred to four-year colleges by October 1983. For African Americans, the transfer rate was 18.35 percent, the lowest of all student groups.

The participation of African American students enrolling in college continues to lag behind that of all high school graduates. For example, of the 337,000 African American high school graduates in 1989, only 178,000 (52.8 percent) were enrolled in college in October 1989. This compares with a 59.6 percent enrollment in college for all 1989 high school graduates.[11]

While more than 50 percent of African American high school graduates enroll in college, college enrollment does not always lead to graduation. Attrition remains a major problem for African American students. For example, during the 1986-87 academic year, African Americans represented 9.2 percent of the undergraduate enrollment, but received only 5.7 percent of the bachelor's degrees awarded that year. At the graduate level, they represented 5.0 percent of the total enrollment but earned only 3.1 percent of the doctorate degrees awarded that year.

The situation is especially acute in mathematics, science, and engineering fields, where African Americans are severely underrepresented. African

Americans received only 5 percent of the baccalaureate degrees awarded in these fields and 1 percent of the doctorates.

A major determinant of college enrollment and graduation of African Americans is the availability of financial aid. Given the median family income of African Americans ($20,210 in 1989), it is not surprising that these families require substantial financial assistance to enable their children to attend college. The following table provides some insight.

Table 3
Financial Aid to Undergraduates, Fall 1986

Proportion of students receiving Financial Assistance, by Source			Type of Assistance		
Total	Federal	Other	Grants	Loans	Work-study
African Americans					
63.8%	55.7%	33.2%	56.6%	35.0%	9.8%
White Americans, non-Hispanic					
43.3%	32.0%	28.4%	35.1%	23.6%	5.6%
All Undergraduates					
45.5%	34.9%	28.8%	37.6%	24.4%	6.1%

Source: *The Chronicle of Higher Education Almanac*, August 28, 1991.

Although gains were made in the number of African Americans who graduated from college during the 1980s, the participation of African Americans in college dropped more than 3 percent between 1980 and 1984. Many attribute this drop to uncertainty about the availability of federal financial aid as well as to an actual decrease in federal funds available.

The relatively low persistence-to-degree rates by African Americans enrolled at all levels of higher education are of serious concern, given the (1) increasing demand for workers with technical skills, (2) increasing representation of African Americans and other minorities in the U.S. population generally and in the 18- to 24-year-old group in particular, (3) percent of jobs projected by the year 2000 to require some college (50 percent), (4) percent expected to require a bachelor's degree (30 percent), and (5) dearth of African American mathematics, science, and engineering faculty.

Overall Degree Attainment

Table 4 provides a snapshot of the educational attainment, six years later, of students who were seniors in high school in 1980. It demonstrates clearly that the higher one goes up the educational ladder, the fewer African Americans one finds.

Table 4
Educational Attainment* of 1980 High School Seniors by 1986

No high school diploma	High school diploma	License	Assoc. degree	Bachelor's degree	Professional/ Graduate degree
African Americans					
1.2%	69.4%	13.9%	5.3%	9.9%	0.2%
Whites, non-Hispanic					
0.8%	60.0%	11.5%	6.6%	20.2%	0.9%
All Undergraduates					
0.9%	61.8%	11.9%	6.5%	18.2%	0.7%

* - Highest level of education achieved by spring 1986.
Source: *The Chronicle of Higher Education Almanac,* August 28, 1991.

The following table provides data on the actual numbers of African Americans receiving various post-secondary degrees.

Table 5
Degrees Earned by African Americans, 1988-89

Associate	Bachelor's	Master's	Doctorate	Professional
Men	Men	Men	Men	Men
12,826	22,365	5,200	497	1,608
Women	Women	Women	Women	Women
21,585	35,651	8,876	574	1,493
Total	Total	Total	Total	Total
34,411	58,016	14,076	1,071	3,101

Source: *The Chronicle of Higher Education Almanac*, August 28, 1991.

A VISION FOR 2001

Despite claims by supporters of such schemes as educational choice and publicly funded vouchers being used to support parental choice of schools for their children, the overwhelming majority of children from low-income families, including low-income African American families, will continue to attend second-rate public schools. As in the past, these families will have to look to the public schools to equip their children and youth with the knowledge and skills required for future success and security as workers, as citizens, and as leaders in their communities.

The intellectual and leadership capabilities of these children will develop fully only if:

1. there is early intervention to ensure adequate nutrition and health care, parental education, day care, and preschool education; and

2. our public education system is restructured so that the academic achievement of those students most under-served by the present system becomes the primary measure of accountability.

The public schools envisioned for 2001 in the Quality Education for Minorities Project Report, *Education That Works: An Action Plan for the Education of Minorities,* will instill in African American and all other children such lifelong values as:

- the intrinsic joy of learning
- the pleasure of using one's mind to solve problems and come up with ideas
- an appreciation and respect for one's own accomplishments as well as those of others
- the self-confidence to make decisions based on one's own ideas and experiences
- a willingness to work with others toward a common objective
- respecting points of view that may be different from one's own
- taking responsibility for doing things that need to be done and doing them well, from beginning to end
- understanding that helping others is a responsibility and is its own reward
- understanding that learning is a lifelong process and the best way to have the most control over one's life

When these students graduate from high school, they will be well-grounded in biology, chemistry, physics, mathematics, history, geography, social studies, and the arts. They will be fluent in English and in at least one other language. They will have strong communications, analytical, and problem-solving skills. Their educational achievements will be due, in no small part, to the increased value placed by their parents on learning and achievement, evidenced in part by their parents own involvement in educational and training programs. They will have been taught by well-trained and enthusiastic African American and non-African American teachers who expect all of their students to achieve at the highest level.

Such students will have restored America's faith in public education, for they will enter college and the work force fully prepared to be successful. Support for early intervention programs, the restructured school system, and incentives that attracted more talented individuals to the teaching profession (including significantly more African American men and women) will have proved to be essential investments in America's future. A renewed faith will exist in African American communities regarding the power of education to advance their children as families witness the increased self-confidence and pride in academic achievement their children now reflect.

Community institutions and organizations will once again serve as safety nets for all of the community's children. Young people will have greater exposure to role models who have persisted in school, who have launched successful and fulfilling careers, and who have seen their incomes rise steadily. Students will see, through these individuals, that education can reap rewards commensurate with effort and performance.[12]

CHALLENGES TO BE MET

The crises in the African American community will not end until there is massive and focused intervention and strong leadership from within the African American community. The future of the African American community will be only as strong as the opportunities that exist for African American children to receive quality health care, to grow up in a caring and safe environment, to obtain a quality preschool education, and to attend schools that promote rather than discourage their education.

As the social and economic indicators clearly demonstrate, such opportunities are essentially out of reach for one out of every two African American children. Lack of access to quality education, to health services, and to caring adults threatens the ability of children living in poverty to contribute to their own future well-being or to that of the larger African American community. Factors such as the lack of full funding for effective programs, including the Women, Infants, and Children (WIC) Supplemental Food Act and Head Start; the historic disparity in per-pupil expenditure between low-income communities and more affluent ones; and the failure of efforts to implement the national educational goals to focus on ensuring quality education for those children most in need suggest that the futures of almost half of African American children have been written off, as if their futures were unconnected to that of the rest of the nation's.

Concerns about how well the public school system is serving African American children are not limited to children from low-income families. A recent *Washington Post* article[13] reports on the fears some African American middle-class families have regarding their children's education: their children will not receive an academic program as demanding as the ones they received in racially integrated schools; local tests are used to "sort and dump" African American boys "like so many defective spare parts"; and schools expect less of their children and do not provide African American role models.

The results of an analysis of 219 major metropolitan areas that were reported in *USA Today*[14] cause further concern. The study found that African Americans are highly segregated in 31 of the 47 areas where they comprise at least 20 percent of the residents. Middle-class and affluent African Americans, according to the study, are only slightly more likely to live next door to whites than to poor African Americans. Unlike many other racial and ethnic groups, succeeding generations of African Americans have not prospered as their children moved out of the neighborhood for higher paying jobs and better schools. Instead, their children must attend predominantly minority or intensely segregated schools where resources are extremely limited and teachers are the least experienced and the least prepared to meet their needs.

African Americans, nevertheless, view education, and a college degree in particular, as more important than ever.[15] Although African American students are more likely to experience feelings of isolation and marginality on predominantly white college campuses,[16] more than 80 percent of those enrolled in college are attending predominantly white institutions. African American students from low socioeconomic backgrounds tend to be less well-prepared academically because the public schools they attended are of poorer quality than public schools in more affluent neighborhoods. Lack of academic preparedness, feelings of alienation, faculty with little time for undergraduates, and the lack of adequate financial aid all help to explain the large drop-out rate among African American college students (63.3 percent within six years of college entry).

There is hope, however. There are educational programs in place all over America that are effectively educating African American students. They provide signposts and direction for the fundamental restructuring that must occur in schools serving African American children--restructuring that uses the academic achievement of those students most underserved by our current system as the primary measure of a school's effectiveness; restructuring that leads to an educational system that values and holds high expectations of African American youth.

Despite the problems that exist along the educational continuum for African American children and youth, we do know what kinds of services, programs, and resources result in successful, highly motivated students; we do know that early success in mathematics and science is critical to the later pursuit of majors in these fields; and we do know that African American children achieve when they are given the same recipe for success that others receive.

152

America 2000[17]: Implications for African Americans

It is important to distinguish between the national educational goals and America 2000. The national educational goals for the year 2000 were established by the president and the governors following an educational summit in September 1989. The six goals (commonly referred to as school readiness; school completion; student achievement and citizenship; mathematics and science; adult literacy and lifelong learning; and safe, disciplined, and drug-free schools) were announced in February 1990. America 2000 is a broad strategy for achieving the national educational goals that were developed by the Administration and announced in April 1991 by President Bush. Although the national educational goals, announced in February 1990, were influenced by the goals contained in the report of the MIT-based Quality Education for Minorities Project, *Education That Works: An Action Plan for the Education of Minorities*, America 2000 clearly was not.

America 2000's four-part strategy (better and more accountable schools, a new generation of American schools, a nation of students, and America 2000 communities) and the very limited implementation role envisioned for the federal government ("setting standards, highlighting examples, contributing some funds, providing flexibility in exchange for accountability and pushing and prodding--then pushing and prodding some more"), hold little hope for addressing the barriers to quality education for low-income African American children. The strategy does not, for example, provide for the $4.5 billion needed annually to ensure full funding of Head Start or the $1.6 billion required annually to fund fully the WIC program. How then does America 2000 propose to ensure that all children, including all low-income African American children, will start school ready to learn by the year 2000 as called for in the first national educational goal?

The strategy calls for the development of a new set of "voluntary" tests (American Achievement Tests) to be administered at the fourth, eighth, and twelfth grade levels to measure achievement in core subjects; yet, it does not address the problems that make it almost impossible for African American children to perform well on such tests: (1) low per-pupil expenditures in schools that are attended predominantly by African American and other students from families living below the poverty line; (2) the tracking of African American students disproportionately into low-level classes in reading, mathematics, and science beginning in elementary school; and (3) the poor quality of instruction, the weak curriculum, and the inadequate resources available in the schools these children attend.

Instead of addressing these issues and identifying ways to ensure that these children have a safe, drug-free environment in which to learn (the sixth national educational goal), America 2000 promotes educational choice for parents and students, a strategy that will not benefit significant numbers of children from low-income families and will only further segregate our schools. America 2000 is silent on multicultural education: it fails to call for an education that enables all students to recognize and value the contributions to America's greatness made by all racial and ethnic groups that make up this country; it ignores the need for an education that binds rather than divides.

America 2000 calls for the creation of 535+ schools (at least one per congressional district) referred to as "New American Schools" whose design, development, and funding are all under the control of the private sector. It is reasonable to ask how likely are these 535+ schools to reach the children most underserved by our current system, when there are almost 1,000 schools in the predominantly minority (39 percent African American) New York City school district alone and more than 5,000 schools in the 22 largest predominantly minority school districts in the country (16 of these districts have student enrollments that are more than 30 percent African American).

STRATEGIES TO ACHIEVE VISION 2001

Our goal must be to bring about change at the scale necessary to break the cycle of poverty in which a third of African Americans are trapped. We must ensure that African American children start school prepared to learn and that, once in school, they receive a quality education in an environment of high expectations. We must ensure that they leave school with the skills necessary to pursue successfully post-secondary education in fields of interest to them or to enter the work force fully prepared to be successful.

Accomplishing such an ambitious goal requires that we adopt broad new strategic principles as well as replicate and scale up specific existing programs that have proved effective in meeting the educational, health, and emotional needs of children and youth at various levels along the educational continuum. Any such strategy must be holistic, viewing each part of the educational experience (pre-/post-natal, early childhood/preschool, elementary/middle school, high school/undergraduate, and graduate/professional) as linked to the next.

Success depends upon many factors:

1. Early intervention to ensure a healthy start for African American children and to enable parents to be effective in their roles as first teachers of their children. This means pressing for full funding of such successful programs as the Special Supplemental Food Program for Women, Infants, and Children (WIC) and Head Start, and for training and licensing of day care and other early childhood workers.

2. Restructuring our public schools to shift major responsibility for education to local schools, whose success will be measured on the basis of student achievement. Nothing is more important to the education of African

Americans than the restructuring of schools.

3. The elimination of tracking as a pedagogical strategy and replacing it with more effective approaches such as cooperative learning and group study.

4. The establishment of core competencies at the elementary school level that African American and all other children will be expected to achieve.

5. The existence of a rigorous high school curriculum with the opportunity for all students to take advanced course work.

6. A curriculum that reflects, respects, and values the cultures of all children.

7. The creation of incentives to attract to the teaching profession a larger number of talented African Americans and others concerned about equity and equality of educational opportunities.

There are other actions that we must take as well. We must ensure that:

- provisions for quality education for African Americans are explicitly included in plans to restructure schools, upgrade teaching standards, and reform undergraduate education. This means that African Americans must assume leadership roles in educational reform efforts to ensure that the educational needs and interests of African American and other children and youth who have historically been underserved by our current system are at the forefront. Only if we are present and participating can we insist that adequate resources be allocated, that the curriculum be rigorous and pluralistic, and that the best teachers be made available to those who need them the most;
- educational strategies proven effective with African American youth are broadly publicized and replicated for the benefit not only of African American children but also of all children;
- the public understands and appreciates the fact that quality education for African Americans is essential to improve education for *all* students;
- an educational system is in place that values and holds high expectations of African American youth and that inspires African American families and communities to take greater responsibility for the education of their children; for raising expectations; and for promoting the values of discipline and hard work required to succeed in school, in the workplace, and as citizens.

Polls suggest that the American public is ready to act. Based on its extensive polling in 1989, the Gallup organization concluded that the public is ready for "tradition shattering" changes in policies that govern public education. More than 80 percent expressed the belief that we must step up our efforts to improve the quality of education in poorer communities. By a two-to-one margin, they said they were willing to pay higher taxes to finance such improvements.

While it is clear that new money will be required to establish a quality educational system for everyone, all the necessary funds would not have to be through new appropriations. A restructured system would use existing resources more efficiently. Even a fraction of the proposed cuts in the defense budget would go far to finance the educational improvements America so critically needs. So too would a major shift to public education of the billions of dollars now spent annually by the private sector to retrain entry level workers and of the millions of dollars spent by colleges and universities to fund remedial programs for underprepared students. *We must understand that expenditures on human resources are high yield investments, not just budget costs.*

In our efforts to ensure quality education for African American children and youth, we must form partnerships on several levels: across the educational pipeline that have students and faculty at historically black colleges and universities joining with other community organizations to help provide support to parents, teachers, and students in local schools (with a special focus on housing developments and low-income communities); across racial and ethnic groups to ensure that the needs of all children are known and met; and across local, state, and regional boundaries to have school districts, minority and nonminority colleges and universities, national laboratories, and business and industry join together to develop and implement a national agenda for ensuring quality mathematics, science, and engineering education for African American and other groups seriously underrepresented in these fields.

President Bush and the nation's governors ended their education summit in September 1989 with a call to action. They said, "The time for rhetoric is past; the time for performance is now." African Americans could not agree more. We know that "the door to the future for every child is first and foremost the door to the schoolhouse."[18]

Science, Technology, and Human Resources: Preparing for the 21st Century

Walter E. Massey, Ph.D.

The advent of the 21st century brings with it a diverse and interrelated set of challenges and opportunities. The issues at hand run to the core of our nation's ability to provide a high quality of life and adequate living standard to all of its residents. Meeting the challenges in vital areas such as economic competitiveness, health care, environmental conservation, and energy efficiency will require advances in science and technology and a strengthening of the nation's human resource base. Furthermore, our ability to meet these challenges will determine the value and viability of future opportunities--and the stakes are greatest for African Americans.

One way to imagine this connection between the challenges and opportunities is to think of them as forming the two sides of an equation—where the opportunities are a function of the challenges. The crucial parameters that will determine the overall magnitude of the equation are related to the strength of the nation's knowledge base--the research enterprise, the human resource base, and the work-force skills, as well as the necessary infrastructure to connect people and ideas.

In other words, the future opportunities that await us depend on the investment and emphasis we devote to building the knowledge base. If our response, on the one hand, is insufficient, future opportunities will be mediocre: the available jobs will pay low wages and provide little security; adequate health care will be out of reach of most citizens; and our land, water, and air will be under siege from pollution. On the other hand, we can ensure a secure future by strengthening our national stock of knowledge and, in particular, that aspect of knowledge derived from science and technology.

For example, one of the challenges in the environmental area stems from the use of pesticides and fertilizers on crops; these substances, though beneficial, can threaten groundwater supplies and ecosystems. Research on crops that naturally resist pests and disease could provide an inexpensive solution to this problem. The end result would be a safer drinking water, a cleaner environment, and more affordable food supply. There is a similar story in the energy area, where new materials such as photovoltaic cells and superconductors could lead to a cheaper, nonpolluting, and more efficient generation of electricity, which thereby would reduce our dependence on fossil fuels.

Nowhere is the connection between challenges and opportunities more obvious--or more relevant to African Americans--than in the area of economic competitiveness. To state the matter quite simply, whether or not good jobs with good wages are plentiful in coming decades depends entirely on whether the work force is educated and can adapt to new production processes.

Economic Transformation

We are in the midst of an economic transformation--many people refer to it as the knowledge revolution or the third industrial revolution--and its leading characteristic is that the resources most critical to progress are no longer mined from the earth but instead are created in the human mind. Knowledge and human talent are now the hallmark of a modern, competitive, and healthy society. The inputs that determine productivity now depend on human resources and not on the capacities of machines.

Robert Reich, in his book *The Real Economy*, presents a number of points that illustrate this transformation:

- The trade balance is an outdated measure of a nation's ability to compete and produce because "the value a nation's work force adds to the global economy is no longer measurable in terms of products shipped across borders."[1] The value actually lies in the strength of the human resources found within the country's borders.
- The idea of "goods" as distinct from "services" is also becoming obsolete, because much of the value-added in any product is derived from services. For example, only 10 to 15 percent of the purchase price of an IBM personal computer reflects the actual cost of manufacture. The rest of the value comes from activities such as design, programming, and support that are traditionally considered services.[2]
- At the bottom line, Reich's analysis emphasizes that America's ability to produce and compete in the 21st century will depend on her human resources, or as he puts it: "educated brainpower--along with the roads, airports, computers, and fiber-optic cables linking them up--determines a nation's standard of living."[3]

The companies, particularly manufacturers, that survive and thrive in the coming decades will be those that adopt what are often called "best practices"--an interdependent set of principles and policies that yield productivity gains, greater efficiency, higher wages, and job security. The common elements of these organizations are flat structures; a focus on cost, quality, and responsiveness; and the use of team concepts that require employee involvement and empowerment. Unfortunately, businesses could be hamstrung and unable to adopt these best practices if the work force is not equipped with a solid foundation of scientific and technical knowledge.

The National Center on Education and the Economy, in its report, *America's Choice: high skills or low wages!*, constructed a story of two factories to illustrate the two directions that the nation's economy can take.[4]

Both factories operated on assembly line principles. As automation and high technology were introduced, the operators faced a dilemma. Productivity could increase, but the characteristics of the work force would have to change. The operators could maintain the assembly line type of operation and shift to lower skilled/lower wage workers, the kind that could be found easily overseas or in Latin America. Or the companies could adopt a best practices approach to production, one that relies on team concepts and gives more autonomy to production workers. In this model, workers participate in design processes, coordinate orders with suppliers, and help devise marketing strategies. Both of these approaches will improve productivity, but the latter is much stronger in the long run because it preserves well paying jobs in the United States and yields a more flexible organization.

For the best practices model to succeed, workers must be well-grounded in science, mathematics, and problem-solving techniques. The high in-house training costs would probably deter companies from taking this approach. In effect, businesses will shape their production processes to match the pool of available workers:

- If our educational system produces a poorly trained work force, companies will be forced to adopt production processes based on low skills.
- If the available workers are well educated, however, the up-front costs of adopting the best practices approach will be reduced.

A good example is that when General Motors constructed a factory, the Saturn facility, around the best practices model, it made the strength of local schools and the level of work-force skills one of the highest priorities in the site selection process.

Both sides of the challenge/opportunity equation are greater for the groups of our society that have traditionally been underrepresented in scientific and technical activities: women, African Americans, Hispanics, Native Americans, Alaska and Pacific Island natives, and the disabled. Beyond a requirement for secure and satisfying employment, equipping our citizens with an understanding of science and technology is fast becoming a necessity for the functioning of our democracy. As complicated public policy issues, such as global change, come to the forefront, all citizens need to understand and evaluate the issues. The implications of the decisions made by our representatives could easily bypass the interests of the underrepresented groups if they are not fully informed and involved at each stage of the decision-making process.

African Americans, who historically have been bypassed by social, economic, and political institutions, know the full extent of this challenge. Beginning in elementary school, the achievement of African Americans in scientific and technical areas trails that of the majority population. Without improvement, the differentials will remain, which in turn will widen the social and economic disparities. Furthermore, because of their increasing share of the population, the achievement of African Americans will play a large role in determining if the nation is able to thrive in the new economic climate.

SNAPSHOT OF AFRICAN AMERICAN EDUCATIONAL PERFORMANCE

A glance at a variety of indicators suggests that the performance of African Americans in scientific and technical areas is not sufficient to help the nation meet the challenges of the 21st century, nor will it enable African Americans to realize future opportunities. From precollege achievement through career placement, African Americans continue to trail the white majority on test scores, and their representation in scientific and technical fields is well below their share of the population.

Many studies have documented the interest in science and engineering of African American students, although their preparation in these areas is often less than that of other students. It is encouraging that the performance of black students on several tests has improved over recent decades and has begun to close the gap with white students, but the differential between these groups remains unacceptably large.

- On mathematics achievement tests taken by 9-, 13-, and 17-year-old students, the average scores of black students have improved by 7 percent to 10 percent since 1973. The scores of white students have not changed greatly over this period.[5]
- The scores of African American college-bound high school seniors on the Scholastic Achievement Test (SAT) have increased considerably in the 1980s: the average combined (verbal and math) score increased by 42 points between 1981 and 1991 for African Americans, compared to a five point increase for white Americans.[6] It is also encouraging that the number of African Americans taking the SAT has increased and that the interest of these college-bound students in majoring in a quantitative field in college remains higher than that of their white counterparts.[7]

160

• Still, the gap between these groups remains large. For combined SAT scores, the difference in 1991 was nearly 200 points, or 21 percent. On precollege mathematics achievement tests, the 9-, 13-, and 17-year-old black students have average scores that are 7 percent to 11 percent below white students.[8]

What happens to African American students who go to college and are interested in majoring in a science/engineering field? *Figure 1* provides an overview of representation at different points in the undergraduate science/engineering process. At each step of the "pipeline," the percentage of African Americans drops further and further below their proportion of the total population. There are large losses between the freshman year and college graduation for African Americans. While the share of African Americans graduating from high school, 12 percent, is now close to the share of the total population share, 14 percent, representation falls to roughly 5 percent of science and engineering bachelor's degrees, and to just over 2 percent of the Ph.D. degrees in these fields. The result for which we should strive is to make the height of each bar shown in Figure 1 equal to the population share.

An important point not shown on the graph is that the bachelor's degree completion rate (within 4.5 years after high school) of students intending to major in a science/engineering field was 16 percent for blacks, compared with 34 percent for whites. It is also worth noting that African Americans earn their undergraduate degrees at different types of institutions than do whites. Blacks were much less likely than white Americans to earn a science or an engineering degree at the 70 major research universities.[9] The historically black colleges and universities (HBCUs) play a major role in producing black science and engineering bachelor's degree recipients; in 1989, the 81 four-year HBCUs accounted for three out of ten black science and engineering baccalaureates.[10]

Problems in College Retention

The above data on retention show the major "leaks" from the pipeline. The fact that our society has made the college degree a passport to career opportunities makes it important that we understand the causes of this trend.

Some suggest that the drive, desire, and ambition to succeed are not as strong as they should be among black youth. This is clearly not a complete explanation, for many ambitious and motivated black youth are seeking routes other than college for advancement; a significant number, for example, are enrolling in proprietary schools or joining the armed forces. African Americans also join the work force at a faster rate than do their white counterparts.

Financial concerns loom large. For many minority students, the

Figure 1: Retention Problems

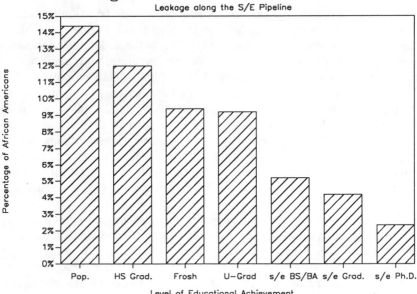

Leakage along the S/E Pipeline

LEGEND:

Pop.	=	18 to 19 year old population (1983)
HS Grad.	=	High School graduates (1983)
Frosh	=	Full-time freshman in 4-year colleges intending to major in science/engineering (1983)
U-Grad	=	Undergraduate enrollment (1984)
s/e BS/BA	=	Bachelors degree recipients in s/e (1989)
s/e Grad.	=	First time s/e graduate enrollment (1989)
s/e Ph.D.	=	Ph.D.s (U.S. citizens) received in s/e (1990)

Source: National Science Foundation, Division of Science Resources Studies, "Blacks in Undergraduate Science and Engineering Education" (Washington, DC: NSF, forthcoming), Table 1.

prospects of a heavy loan burden make it a rational decision to seek other alternatives. Recent evidence shows that nearly half (48 percent) of all African American freshmen had to take out loans in order to complete their freshman year, and that one fifth had major concerns about how they would pay for their college education.[11]

There are also intangible and "less rational" reasons for this trend. Many minority youths lack the confidence and vision to commit themselves to what they view as a difficult undertaking--being accepted, matriculating, and succeeding at a college or university. A minority student is more likely to drop out of college if a chosen major in a scientific or technical field does not prove possible. Lack of preparation at elementary and secondary school levels and feelings of inadequacy, disaffection, and disillusionment lead many minority students to believe they will not succeed in college, which deters them from taking the risk. They feel it is best to take a more secure route to employment, such as vocational school or the armed forces. Poor education, as well as less than adequate counseling and teaching, is surely a contributory factor--if not the major one--in developing this tendency.

The severe attrition of African Americans during undergraduate education is also caused by the lack of black faculty in natural science and engineering fields; blacks currently hold fewer than 1 percent of these faculty positions. Many studies have noted the importance of mentors and role models in attracting and retaining students. Dr. Eugene Cota-Robles at the University of California at Santa Cruz found that the success of certain graduate departments with minority students is strongly correlated with the presence of minority faculty.[12]

One disquieting note related to this particular issue is that the number of black American citizens receiving the doctoral degree is 26 percent less than it was in 1977.[13] This raises further questions about whether there will be an adequate number of minority professors at American universities to attract and train future generations of students.

All of these data show that there is a need for action and intervention strategies at all levels of the educational and career development process. There is a need to adopt new approaches to education--those that seek to cultivate the interests of all students and to improve the participation of women, African Americans, and other minorities in science and engineering activities.

IMPROVING EDUCATIONAL OPPORTUNITIES FOR AFRICAN AMERICANS

Whereas interest in the plight of minority students was once motivated largely by notions of benevolence and equity, it is now accepted as a matter of national need. During the 1980s, business groups dropped their reflexive opposition to tax increases when it came to education; corporate executives exerted leadership in education policy; and outreach and "adopt-a-school" programs became commonplace. These changes were part of a recognition that schools are not producing a work force that can meet future requirements.

As a nation, we are in the process of restructuring our approach to education in general, and to mathematics, science, and engineering education in particular. Programs are being revamped so that they will no longer serve as a filter to weed out all but the best prepared students, but instead will kindle and cultivate the interest of all students. Common elements in these programs are that they will make science more accessible, more enjoyable, and more relevant to students' interests and needs.

The dual problems of education quality and quantity are most acute for those groups that traditionally have been underrepresented in these areas. The manifold needs in this particular challenge revolve around the inadequate training of science and math teachers in predominately minority schools, a lack of resources and facilities, and the undeniable shortage of mentors and role models for minority youths interested in these disciplines.

THE ROLE OF THE NATIONAL SCIENCE FOUNDATION

To address these issues, the National Science Foundation (NSF) has implemented an innovative set of programs in the education and human resources area: The National Science Foundation has adopted innovative programs that are aligned with our national needs and this program of reform. The NSF role is that of a catalyst--fostering connections among institutions, disseminating knowledge, and bringing together talented people. At all levels of education--precollege, undergraduate, graduate, and postgraduate/career development--NSF has specific programs to increase the participation and performance of African Americans and others from underrepresented groups in future science and engineering efforts.

These programs aim to provide all American youths with the needed level of proficiency in mathematics, science, and technology. The NSF has put in place a framework of programs and a strategy based on the understanding that education is a series of interdependent and interconnected stages, with links from preschool to grade 12, to undergraduate and graduate study and beyond. These programs build upon an idea of "sweeping and drastic change: in the breadth of student participation, in our methods and quality of teaching, in the preparation and motivation of our children, in the content of our courses, and in our standards of achievement."[14]

Elementary and Secondary Education Programs

Precollege science and mathematics courses must meet the future needs of all students: those who will perform technical jobs crucial to the nation's economy, those who will become scientists and engineers, and all of us who as citizens must make decisions on the science- and technology-based issues facing society. NSF employs a range of strategies to address these diverse needs. Programs funded by the Foundation emphasize hands-on activities that connect coursework to real-life activities and experiences, and strive to create an enjoyable, accessible, and nurturing educational environment. Technology and informal methods are often used to reach students who, in standard teaching environments, might not realize their interest in science.

Through the **Statewide Systemic Initiative** (SSI), NSF is forging partnerships among the higher education community, state and local governments, industry, teachers unions', and parent organizations in the comprehensive restructuring of primary and secondary education. Ten states recently were selected for and have initiated this program: Connecticut, Delaware, Florida, Louisiana, Montana, Nebraska, North Carolina, Ohio, Rhode Island, and South Dakota. The SSI program will focus on the special needs of underrepresented groups by requiring states to:

- include female and minority students in all aspects of the project,
- make special efforts to include historically minority institutions of higher education and organizations serving underrepresented groups outside of formal educational structures, and
- make efforts to locate projects in predominately minority areas.

For example, of the first ten states with SSI awards, Connecticut has made urban districts a priority under its initiative, and Louisiana's SSI will have a significant impact on its school system's 40 percent minority population through the collaborations between universities and the school districts.

The Foundation's **Career Access Opportunities** program is designed to give minority students an overview of science and technology careers. This program supports **Comprehensive Regional Centers for Minorities**, which help colleges and universities take steps to improve precollege education in regions with a high minority population; and **Science Summer Camps**, which use nontraditional settings to increase students' interest in science and technology.

NSF is also relying on new technologies and informal programs to lessen inequalities that may exist within and across school districts. In the **Application of Advanced Technology Program**, NSF supports research, development, and demonstration in the use of state-of-the-art computer and telecommunications technologies. NSF's **Informal Science Education** programs provide an enjoyable and accessible learning experience by working with science museums and other community-based organizations.

In the area of teacher preparation and enhancement, NSF sponsors several programs, including **Teacher Preparation Centers**, which focus on the math and science content of undergraduate education curricula.

Undergraduate Programs

As was shown in Figure 1, the "last straw" for many minority students in science and mathematics achievement occurs during their undergraduate years. Freshman year at many colleges and universities has served as a filter preventing all but the most dedicated from pursuing studies in mathematics, the sciences, and engineering. While this approach may have served the nation in an earlier era of increasing enrollments, it is no longer productive or appropriate. In particular, it cuts us off from the very groups we need to attract—women, African Americans, and other minorities—who often enter college less interested or less prepared to pursue studies in technical fields.

At a conference sponsored by the Foundation, Denice Denton, an assistant professor of electrical and computer engineering at the University of Wisconsin-Madison and recipient of the prestigious Presidential Young Investigator award, described her undergraduate experiences:

> My mother was a single parent trying to raise three children. I didn't eat mathematics for breakfast. I ate pop tarts while watching Gilligan's Island. I'm a prototype for the people you are teaching.
>
> In my sophomore year, I took a signals and systems course at MIT. I found it sort of interesting, but I kept wondering what I was doing in it. I failed to see the utility. That's because I had no knowledge base. I managed to go 17 years without knowing the numbers on a radio dial were frequencies; no one ever mentioned that to me.[15]

Colleges and universities have a responsibility to reach out to all undergraduates, including the unprepared and uninterested. In general, this means that universities will need to pay greater attention to undergraduate curriculum and instruction. Sheila Tobias identified the challenge in her path-breaking study of learning in introductory chemistry and physics classes, "No college student should be permitted to say 'no' to science without a struggle."[16]

To help reform introductory courses, the Foundation supports four specific programs—one focused on calculus instruction, another aimed at a major revision of engineering curriculum, a faculty enhancement program, and a new **Undergraduate Course and Curriculum Development** program encompassing all fields of science, mathematics, and engineering. The latter encourages institutions to rethink professional and preprofessional curricula and courses for nonscientists, to strengthen the transition from high school to college mathematics and science, to integrate new knowledge and technologies, and to involve more research-oriented faculty in undergraduate instruction.

Alliances for Minority Participation (AMP) is another new NSF program designed to create partnerships--that is, public and private sector alliances addressing the special issues involved in attracting and retaining minority students in science and engineering fields. Only about a third of the minority freshmen interested in science and engineering fields are still enrolled in these studies by their junior year. The AMP program promotes retention of minority students throughout the undergraduate years as well as during the transitions from high school to college and graduate studies. AMP programs may employ a variety of specific activities, including apprenticeships with industry, academic and career awareness programs, as well as graduate level teaching and research assistantships.

Through NSF's **Research Careers for Minority Scholars** program, Jackson State University (Mississippi) is preparing high ability minority undergraduates to pursue advance degrees and professional careers in environmental and marine sciences. This project provides financial support, research experience, career counseling, and opportunities for off-campus research during the summer.

Partnerships are a key aspect of the Foundation's approach to educational improvement. In a series of colloquia to discuss "what works," NSF is bringing together faculty, administrators, federal officials, industry representatives, and others with experience and interest in improving undergraduate education in mathematics, the sciences, and engineering. They are able to share their approaches with interested colleagues. For example, the University of Houston-Downtown offers math majors an opportunity to participate in a "senior practicum" in local research laboratories. At the Texas Medical Center, students have analyzed blood chemistry and height-weight data in order to establish the equations needed to determine the level of drug delivery for cancer patients undergoing chemotherapy.[17] And through high speed computer and communication networks, such as NSFNET and the proposed National Research and Education Network, academicians actively engaged in improving undergraduate education can disseminate their knowledge and experiences to a broader audience via high speed computer networks.

The Foundation's programs also attempt to strengthen the partnership between research and teaching. Research demonstrably enriches mathematics, science, and engineering education at all levels. The **Research Experiences for Undergraduates** program supports the creation and operation of undergraduate research sites in established industrial and academic laboratories. The program also provides a mechanism by which NSF principal investigators can receive additional support to include undergraduates in their research team.

Graduate Level and Career Development Programs

African American students who successfully complete their undergraduate education often face difficulties continuing down the science and engineering career path. Through programs that focus on graduate education and career development, the Foundation assists minority students at crucial stages of their career development. These programs are intended to deliver multiple benefits because these scholars will serve as mentors and role models to future generations of scientists and engineers. Highlights of current NSF activities in this area include:

- Plans by NSF to provide roughly over 300 **Minority Graduate Fellowships** in 1992. A new program component, two-year **Career Development Fellowships**, will be aimed at seniors in predominately minority colleges and universities.
- The **Minority Research Initiation** program, which helps talented minority faculty members start their research careers by providing one-time grants for investigators who have not previously received federal research support.
- The **Research Improvement in Minority Institutions** program, which provides opportunities for institutions with substantial minority enrollments to improve their research infrastructure.
- The continuing **Minority Research Centers of Excellence** that have been supported by the Foundation for over a decade in an effort to strengthen the nation's minority colleges and universities.

Because the number of African American Ph.D.'s is so small, and has been meager for so long, any improvement would have dramatic long-term effects. In any given year, the number of African Americans receiving the Ph.D. degree in important fields such as mathematics, physics, or computer science can be counted on one hand, and rarely is above the low teens. A modest goal that could make a huge difference would be for every graduate department in the country to double plus one the number of African Americans it had graduated over the previous decade. A simple doubling of the previous number would be insufficient because in the great majority of cases, the base would be zero.

This testifies to the serious need for measures to attract and retain students in the sciences. The programs described here do not have a long history and have yet to make their full impact; over time, through a thorough process of assessment and evaluation, we will find out what works and what does not. A strong reason for optimism rests in the simple fact that these programs will reach tens of thousands of students and teachers at the undergraduate and graduate levels, and countless others at the precollege level each year.

CONCLUSION

Societal change can widen or narrow existing disparities, especially when it pertains to African Americans. The current transformations now underway--the restructuring of the economy, the increasing importance of science and technology in many social and political endeavors--are no different. Will these changes yield increased opportunity for African Americans? Or will they do little to neutralize the gaps that exist between African Americans and the majority populations?

The nation as a whole and African Americans, both as individuals and as a community, will determine the answers to these questions. As a nation, we must continue to make investments that pay dividends in human knowledge and ideas. These investments, when strategically focused on the needs of minorities, will make long strides toward remedying past inequities.

Improving the educational achievement of minorities is an accepted national goal. While no one can guarantee that the future will bring a plentiful supply of opportunities, it is clear that the future will not bring any at all if we--as a nation and as African Americans--do not accomplish this goal.

Clear and Present Danger: The Decay of America's Physical Infrastructure

Sylvester Murray

INTRODUCTION

History has shown that governmental policies and programs make a significant difference in the economic well-being of the country as a whole and in the opportunities and conditions of African Americans in particular. Perhaps the greatest example during this century is the Works Progress Administration (WPA) of the New Deal. The WPA was a social and an economic program of the federal government from 1935 to 1941. In those six years, more than eight million unemployed persons built thousands of schools, libraries, water lines, sewer lines, roads, and bridges. The country and African Americans benefited.

A more recent example is the decades of the 1950s and 1960s, when the country witnessed significant national economic growth. During that era, a plethora of government programs and policies enabled many African Americans to achieve middle-class status through employment and educational programs and government enforcement of nondiscrimination laws.

On the other hand, slow overall growth of the economy during the 1970s and 1980s and a retrenchment in government policies and programs are impediments to African American conditions today. If policies and programs that promoted economic well-being have been essential for the past progress of our nation, then further progress is unlikely without them. The lack of government actions has significantly affected social and economic opportunities for all Americans. A case in point is the government's lack of funding for the maintenance and upgrading of the nation's infrastructure.

For at least the past two decades, America has neglected to maintain and improve her physical infrastructure. Taken as a whole, the condition of the infrastructure is an indication of the health and economic well-being of our society. Our society's well-being is at risk because the infrastructure of our cities, states, and nation is in decay. Consider the following:

- The Office of Technology Assessment of the U.S. Congress placed the value of the capital stock represented in the nation's infrastructure at about $1.4 trillion. The Joint Economic Committee of the U.S. Congress placed the amount of money needed to rehabilitate the existent infrastructure and to provide for needed new facilities by the year 2000 at $1.2 trillion.

- The Secretary of Transportation reported to Congress in 1989 that the cost of rehabilitating the nation's highways and bridges, in real terms, is estimated to be $40 billion per year from 1989 to 2000. In 1987, real spending on rehabilitation was about $16 billion less than the estimated annual requirement.

- A 1991 infrastructure survey by the American Public Works Association in Michigan found only 50 percent of the roads and 48 percent of the sidewalks rated at adequacy levels. Storm water systems in the state were rated at a 49 percent level. With only 22 percent of the infrastructure population surveyed, the study found that $16 billion is required to make improvements that will make Michigan's infrastructure adequate.

- The Ohio Environmental Protection Agency related that, in 1983, 39 counties in Ohio had an insufficient landfill capacity. In 1988, 70 percent of Ohio's counties had insufficient capacity. The Ohio EPA defines "insufficient capacity," in terms of the expected life of a solid-waste disposal landfill, to be five years or less.

- The Commission on Budget and Financial Priorities of the District of Columbia reported in November 1990, that the District has not kept pace with its infrastructure maintenance needs for several years, and that it has a backlog of projects totaling $1.6 billion. As an example, the District resurfaces 25 miles of streets per year, but at least 40 miles per year are required.

- The Cleveland, Ohio, *Plain Dealer* (July 12, 1989) reported that the city of Cleveland's water system has four plants that produce an average of 320 million gallons of water per day (MMGD). However, because of a 30 percent shrinkage due to leaks and other factors, about 100 MMGD never reach customers' meters.

- A December 1987 report of the city of Cincinnati, Ohio, Infrastructure Commission recommended that $109.4 million should be invested as a one-time catch-up investment, and $42 million annually, to restore to good condition those infrastructure assets that have deteriorated from deferral of maintenance. The city invested $2.9 million in 1987.

The above examples represent a dismal picture of the decline in the quantity and quality of public infrastructure at the national, state, and local levels. Public infrastructure is the foundation for our way of life because it is the permanent physical installations and facilities supporting socioeconomic activities in a community, region, or nation. Infrastructure systems are identified as those physical structures that support growth and development--roads, streets, bridges, water and wastewater facilities, solid-waste disposal, public buildings, and structured open spaces.

Why should America be concerned about infrastructure decay? Because public capital investments are important aspects of economic development, there should be a national interest in ensuring that urban public facilities are in place to support economic growth and that they are maintained in good working order. There should be a national interest in ensuring that the infrastructure is provided, that it adds up to a *national* system, and that it is kept in good operating condition.

In fact, many economists have shown that America's decline in productivity growth is partially due to delayed investment in her public infrastructure.

Much of the research linking infrastructure investment with economic growth has been generated by economists at the Federal Reserve Banks (FRBs) in Cleveland and Chicago. According to Randall Eberts (Cleveland FRB), two characteristics distinguish infrastructure investments from other types of investment. First, public infrastructure provides the basic foundation for economic activity; and second, it generates positive spillovers. David Aschauer (Chicago FRB) argues that productivity decreases are linked to the secession of infrastructure investment; he then asserts that every $1.00 in infrastructure invested nationally results in a $4.00 increase in the nation's gross national product.[1]

To what extent has the decline of investment in public infrastructure affected the performance of the U.S. economy as a whole? Economist Aschauer states that if the United States had continued to invest in public capital after 1970 at the rate maintained for the previous two decades, we could have benefited in the following ways:[2]

- Our rate of productivity growth could have been up to 50 percent higher--2.1 percent per year, rather than the actual rate of 1.4 percent.
- Our rate of profit on nonfinancial corporate capital could have averaged 9.6 percent instead of 7.9 percent.
- Private investment in plants and equipment could have increased from 3.1 percent to 3.7 percent.

Why should African Americans be concerned about infrastructure decay? The answer is simple: because severe infrastructure problems are being encountered in cities, particularly in central cities. At the same time that our cities' infrastructures are decaying, the African American population of central cities is increasing. And, not surprisingly, unemployment figures show a disturbing correlation between central cities with high unemployment and those that have the most need for infrastructure improvements. Examples: The Cincinnati African American population is 34 percent, with a 13.7 percent unemployment rate; the Cleveland African American population is 49 percent, with a 15.1 percent unemployment rate.

African Americans, especially those in central cities, could enjoy a better quality of life if they were the recipients of jobs produced by a greater investment in infrastructure.

The clear and present danger of a decaying infrastructure is evident:

(a) because the neglect in infrastructure investment has been so severe, the investment needed for improvement will increase at an exponential rate; what could cost x dollars today, could cost twice as much in a few years, and several times as much in ten years;

(b) America's declining productivity will become more and more difficult to turn around; and

(c) the large African American population in central cities will become disproportionately disenfranchised from a decent quality of life.

EXTENT OF THE PROBLEM

The infrastructure renewal movement probably had its origins in New York City's effort to get federal aid for infrastructure rehabilitation after its fiscal crisis in 1975. However, most of the in-depth studies took place during the 1980s, beginning with Pat Choate and Susan Walter's *America in Ruins: The Decaying Infrastructure* in 1983. Other researchers included Professor Ralph Gakenheimer of M.I.T., Professor Marshall Kaplan of the University of Colorado-Denver, and Federal Reserve Bank economists Randall Eberts and David Aschauer. In addition, the National Council on Public Works Improvement, the American Public Works Association, the Joint Economic Committee, and the Office of Technology Assessment of the U.S. Congress performed extensive infrastructure studies. They all basically agreed that our nation's infrastructure is in decay and that the decay is due to significant shortfalls in public infrastructure investment. This shortfall began in the 1970s.

Choate and Walter reported that the nation's public works investments, measured in constant dollars, fell from $38.6 billion in 1965 to less than $31 billion in 1977--a 21 percent decline. On a per capita basis, public works investments in constant dollars dropped from $198 per person in 1965 to $140 in 1977--a 29 percent decline. When measured against the value of the nation's gross national product, public works investments declined from 4.1 percent in 1965 to 2.3 percent in 1977--a 44 percent decline.[3] Each of these measures reflects that, although government expenditures significantly increased during that 12-year period, federal investments in public infrastructure declined significantly, both relatively and absolutely.

In a 1984 study by *American City & County* magazine, 78 percent of the local government officials surveyed listed at least one infrastructure area as one of the top three issues facing local governments.[4]

The National League of Cities surveyed the nation's small cities and towns in 1987; it found that the top problems facing these localities were maintenance of streets, roads, and sidewalks, and overall economic conditions.[5]

America's infrastructure includes all of her physical foundations. The value of the capital stock represented in the nation's roads, bridges, mass transportation, airports, ports, water and sewer, and solid-waste facilities is estimated to be about $1.4 trillion. And although federal, state, and local governments currently spend about $140 billion annually on building, operating, and maintaining these facilities, it is generally acknowledged that infrastructure systems across the United States are outdated, inadequate, and poorly maintained.[6]

The federal government has historically played a large role in financing infrastructure improvement through direct construction and grants (see Table 1).

Table 1
Federal Infrastructure Expenditures
1980 and 1989
(in millions of 1982 adjusted dollars)

	1980	1989
Total	$29,863	$23,609
Transportation Infrastructure:		
Highways	10,584	11,392
Mass transit	3,732	2,838[a]
Rail	3,531	483
Aviation	4,334	5,378
Ports, harbors, waterways	1,365	1,137
Environmental Infrastructure:		
Water supply	1,017	284[b]
Wastewater	5,300	2,097

[a]Drop in expenditure reflects the sale of Conrail.
[b]Low spending figure for water supply in 1989 reflects repayments of Farmer's Home Administration water supply loans.

Source: Office of Technology Assessment, 1991. Based on preliminary Congressional Budget Office estimates, Office of Management and Budget historical data, and U.S. Army Corps of Engineers' estimates.

The United States has failed to invest sufficient funds in its infrastructure. However, in 1989, federal contributions totaled about $24 billion, a considerable reduction from the nearly $30 billion spent in 1980. Investment generally has not kept pace with the growth of the gross national product (GNP). For example, total public spending on infrastructure dropped from 3.6 percent of the GNP in 1960 to 2.6 percent in 1985. While spending on operations and maintenance has remained a constant share of the GNP, capital spending has dropped from 2.3 percent of the GNP in 1960 to 1.1 percent in 1988. The relative share of public works spending decreased from nearly 20 percent of total expenditures in 1950 to less than 7 percent in 1984.[7]

The Joint Economic Committee of the U.S. Congress released a report in 1985 that estimated that $1.157 trillion will be needed by the year 2000 to rehabilitate the nation's existent infrastructure and to provide for new facilities necessitated by growth. However, financial resources are expected to fall $443 billion short of projected needs (see Table 2).

Table 2
Projected U.S. Infrastructure Needs, Resources, and Shortfalls
1983-2000
(in billions of 1982 dollars)

	Needs	Resources	Shortfalls
Highways and Bridges	$720	$455	$265
Other Transportation	178	90	88
Water Supply and Distribution	96	55	41
Wastewater Collection and Treatment	163	114	49
Totals	$1,157	$714	$443

Source: From the Report to the Joint Economic Committee of Congress, *Hard Choices: A Report on the Increasing Gap between America's Infrastructure Needs and Our Ability to Pay for Them,* Washington, DC: Government Printing Office, 1984).

Included in the Joint Economic Committee study were costs associated with the rehabilitation and construction of streets, highways, bridges, water supply systems, wastewater collection and treatment facilities, and mass transit. Significantly, not included were costs for solid-waste collection and disposal, airports, energy production and distribution systems, parks and recreation needs, traffic engineering networks, public buildings, and schools.

A good illustration of the extent of the infrastructure problem in just the areas of highways and bridges comes from the government itself. In a 1989 report to Congress, the Secretary of Transportation stated that full constrained needs through 2005 on the existing highway and bridge systems ranged from $34.7 to $39.4 billion annually in 1987 dollars. Even at these investment levels, the Secretary indicated that full constrained needs do not imply system perfection, and although overall conditions may improve, congestion may worsen in some of the larger urbanized areas. The extent of our infrastructure investment needs range from $52.6 billion, estimated by the Congressional Budget Office, to $118.2 billion, estimated by the Association of General Contractors (see Table 3).[8]

Table 3
Annual Infrastructure Investment Needs
(in billions of 1982 dollars)

Infrastructure Category	AGC	JEC	CBO
Highways and bridges	62.8[a]	40.9	27.2
Other transportation (mass transit, railroads, airports, ports, locks, waterways)[b]	17.5	9.9	11.1
Drinking water	6.9	5.3	7.7
Wastewater treatment	25.4	9.1	6.6
Drainage	5.6	—[c]	n.a.
Total	118.2	64.3	52.6

Sources: The National Council on Public Works Improvement, *Fragile Foundations: A Report on America's Public Works;* from the Association of General Contractors, *America's Infrastructure*; Joint Economic Committee, *Hard Choices* (February 1984); and Congressional Budget Office, *Public Works Infrastructure* (May 1983).

Notes: n.a. = not available.
AGC = Association of General Contractors; JEC = Joint Economic Committee; and CBO = Congressional Budget Office.

[a]Highways only. Bridges were estimated separately at an additional, one-time repair cost of $51.7 billion.

[b]The JEC study excluded needs for locks and waterways; the CBO study excluded needs for railroads.

[c]Included under wastewater treatment.

THE ANCILLARY ISSUE OF AFRICAN AMERICANS IN CENTRAL CITIES

To this irresponsible trend of infrastructure neglect must be added the human side of urbanism. A recent NBC-*Newsweek* poll (September 9, 1991) showed that 88 percent of the nation see America's cities in negative terms. According to *Newsweek*, there is a sense of gloom and even helplessness at the dimensions of the urban dilemma; that dilemma is race and poverty.[9]

One of America's most perplexing but important urban problems concerns the future of large U.S. cities containing sizable minority populations--especially African Americans. The 1990 census indicated that African Americans now make up at least 30 percent of the population in eight of the ten most populated cities (Los Angeles excepted; see Table 4).

Table 4

1990 Racial Composition
8 of Top 10 Most Populated Cities

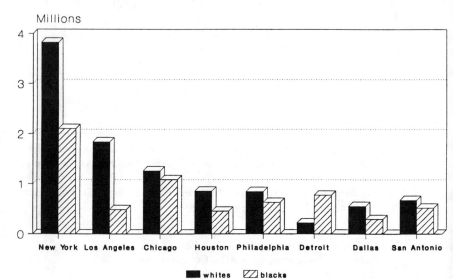

Source: U.S. Bureau of the Census.

In each of these cities, including Los Angeles, the African American unemployment rate far exceeds that of whites (see Table 5). For all of the country, unemployment rose to 5.5 percent in 1990 from 5.3 percent in 1989. The unemployment rate stood at 6.8 percent in the fall of 1991. The National Urban League reported in its September 1991 *Quarterly Economic Report* that between the first and second quarters of 1991, unemployment rose substantially for African Americans, to 12.8 percent--the highest level since the second quarter of 1987.

Table 5

1990 Unemployment Rates
7 of Top 10 Most Populated Cities

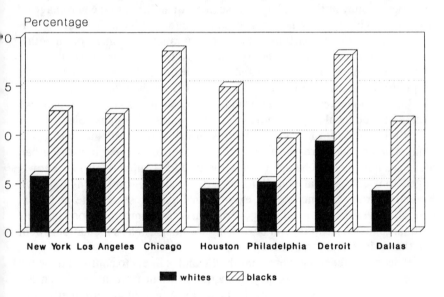

Source: U.S. Dept. of Labor.

Unemployment translates into poverty. In 1990, the poverty rate in the United States rose to 13.5 percent from 12.8 percent a year earlier. The 1990 poverty rate of 13.5 percent is higher than at any time in the 1970s. For whites, the poverty rate rose to 10.7 percent in 1991 from 10.0 percent in 1990; for Hispanics, from 28.1 percent to 26.2 percent. For African Americans, the rate stands at 31.9 percent.[10]

A decaying infrastructure in central cities, high unemployment, and real poverty are affecting the quality of life for African Americans to a degree that should be unacceptable to all.

A SUGGESTED SOLUTION

There is no easy way to resolve the infrastructure crisis. Although the decay of infrastructures is felt more directly at the subnational level, state and local officials are probably powerless to address the problem sufficiently. At the same time that studies indicate massive increases in public spending are necessary to arrest the rate of deterioration and to develop new facilities, money at the local level is scarce. In addition to the shrinkage of tax revenues by the current recession, many states and localities face legislative or constitutional limits on debt issues, on raising revenues, or on both.

There is a huge gap between state and local fiscal resources and the level of expenditures needed. Choate and Walter estimated that annual spending on public infrastructure must be quadrupled from the $70 billion level of 1983. With no increase in federal aid that would entail a 40 percent increase in all state and local taxes--a prospect that is politically impossible.[11]

While the bulk of new investments in urban infrastructure will come from state and local treasuries, acceptable levels of service in many urban areas are not likely to be achieved without federal support. It is acknowledged that one critical contribution of the federal government to urban infrastructure is the income tax exemption for interest on state and local bonds. However, state and local governments must compete in bond markets with large increases in federal borrowing for items such as the national debt and the savings-and-loan bailout.

Indeed, the federal government should and is likely to continue to be the major source of funding for key elements of urban infrastructure that are directly related to economic development. The federal government recognized this obligation with its enactment of the Surface Transportation Reauthorization Act of 1991. However, this bill--which calls for spending $151 billion over six years--does not go far enough.

Improving the quality of urban labor forces through effective education and job training can best be achieved through a national strategy with substantial federal government involvement. The serious problem of unemployment among economically disadvantaged African Americans should be a part of that national strategy.

The education and job training of African Americans become more acute with the conclusions drawn in the U.S. Department of Labor's *Workforce 2000* report: by the year 2000, the white labor force will grow by 15 percent, but the growth of African American workers in the labor force is estimated to be about twice that of whites.[12]

Our suggested solution is to place the nation's infrastructure on a continuous schedule of repair with federal and local funding, and to accomplish this repair in large part with the human resources that are currently unemployed or underemployed in our metropolitan areas.

In some urban areas, expanding public employment within the framework of infrastructure improvement may be both a necessary and a desirable way to approach local economic development and labor market problems. Such jobs can help the urban poor and dislocated workers who do not find work with private employers. Even more importantly, public infrastructure employment programs should be carefully designed primarily to strengthen basic urban services and facilities. This concentration on adequate quality services and facilities can increase the attractiveness of an area to private business.

One proper function of public employment infrastructure improvement is to train workers so that they can compete for nongovernment jobs as well as for better public jobs. Such public employment can also be used to avoid the most serious consequences for dislocated workers who otherwise are likely to face extended unemployment, and for those who have no other realistic way of entering the work force.[13]

The public jobs approach was recommended by Harvard professor Robert D. Reich in a *Cleveland Plain Dealer* newspaper article on November 6, 1991, titled "What Bush Should Do." Reich proposed:

> Announce an emergency multibillion dollar program to rebuild and repair the Nation's infrastructure. The immediate advantage is that construction jobs would quickly sop up workers who don't need much training and give them fairly good wages and benefits. No need to worry about the impact on the budget. It's perfectly justifiable to add to the public debt to improve the Nation's capacity for future growth.

It was also recommended by Sar Levitan and Frank Gallo of the Center for Social Policy Studies of George Washington University, who argued that a public jobs program is the best way to alleviate joblessness, hardship, and poverty; to promote the work ethic and self-reliance; to provide neglected goods and services; and to help the economy emerge from the recession.[14]

The 1991 Marshall Plan for America proposal of the National Urban League gives the best presentation of a national strategy for investing in our decaying physical infrastructure and our unemployed human resources. It is estimated that each billion dollars of construction contracts generates from 15,000 to 22,000 jobs. The essential point of the Plan is that:

> Lack of investment in our human and physical capital largely accounts for America's deteriorating economic productivity. The Nation's future economic well-being and the quality of life of its citizens require a comprehensive, sustained, well-financed investment program in human resources and infrastructure development targeted to maximize the payoffs.

In summation, the physical infrastructure of our nation, necessary to develop and sustain economic growth and a good quality of life, is in disrepair and decay. Bold strategies with substantial federal funding are necessary to arrest this decay.

Urban Infrastructure:
Social, Environmental, and Health Risks
to African Americans

Robert D. Bullard, Ph.D.

The nation's urban infrastructure is crumbling at the seams. Nowhere is this more apparent than in America's large urban centers where the majority of African Americans are concentrated. More than 57 percent of African Americans live in central cities, the highest concentration of any racial and ethnic group. Even affluent African American families—those with household incomes of $50,000 or more—are more likely to live in central cities than their white counterparts. For example, 56 percent of affluent African Americans live in central cities, and 40 percent live in the suburbs. The patterns for affluent whites reveal that 25 percent live in central cities and 61 percent live in the suburbs.

In general, the physical infrastructure of central cities is old and in need of some repair. The physical infrastructure includes roads and bridges, housing stock, schools, job centers, public buildings, parks and recreational facilities, public transit, water supply, wastewater treatment, and waste disposal systems. Taken as a whole, this infrastructure condition determines the well-being of our society. At present, too many of our cities and their inhabitants are at risk from infrastructure decay, environmental degradation, health threats, and economic impoverishment.

This chapter examines the factors that contribute to the nation's decaying urban infrastructure and the accompanying social, environmental, and health risks to African Americans.

IMPACT OF INSTITUTIONAL DISINVESTMENT

Urban America continues to be segregated along racial lines. The legacy of institutional racism lowered the nation's gross national product by almost 2 percent a year, or roughly $104 billion in 1989.[1] A large share of this loss is a result of housing discrimination. The "roots of discrimination are deep" and have been difficult to eliminate.[2] Housing discrimination contributes to the physical decay of inner-city neighborhoods and denies a substantial segment of the African American community a basic form of wealth accumulation and investment through homeownership. The number of African American homeowners would probably be higher in the absence of discrimination by lending institutions.[3] Approximately 59 percent of middle-class African Americans own their homes, compared with 74 percent of whites.

Studies over the past 25 years have clearly documented the relationship among redlining and disinvestment decisions and neighborhood decline.[4] From Boston to San Diego to the urban centers all across the nation, the pattern is clear: African Americans still do not have full access to lending by banks and saving institutions as do their white counterparts.

A 1991 report by the Federal Financial Institutions Examination Council (FFIEC) found that African Americans were rejected for home loans more than twice as often as Anglos.[5] After studying lending practices at 9,300 U.S. financial institutions and more than 6.4 million loan applications, the federal study uncovered the rejection rates for conventional home mortgages were 33.9 percent for African Americans, 21.4 percent for Latinos, 22.4 percent for American Indians, 14.4 percent for Anglos, and 12.9 percent for Asians.

Loan denial rates for African Americans varied widely among large urban centers (see Table 1). For example, one in three African American loan applicants was rejected in the Boston, Houston, St. Louis, Pittsburgh, and Phoenix metropolitan areas. The lowest loan rejection rate for African Americans occurred in the District of Columbia, Baltimore, Oakland, and San Diego metropolitan areas.

Table 1
Mortgage Rejection Rates in 19 Large Metropolitan Areas

Metro Area	Asian	Black	Latino	Anglo
Atlanta	11.1	26.5	13.6	10.5
Baltimore	7.3	15.6	10.1	7.5
Boston	15.4	34.9	21.2	11.0
Chicago	10.4	23.6	12.1	7.3
Dallas	9.3	25.6	19.8	10.7
Detroit	9.1	23.7	14.2	9.7
Houston	13.3	33.0	25.7	12.6
Los Angeles	13.2	19.8	16.3	12.8
Miami	16.9	22.9	17.8	16.0
Minneapolis	6.4	19.9	8.0	6.1
New York	17.3	29.4	25.3	15.0
Oakland	11.6	16.5	13.3	9.6
Philadelphia	12.1	25.0	21.0	8.3

Phoenix	12.8	30.0	25.2	14.4
Pittsburgh	12.2	31.0	13.9	12.0
St. Louis	9.0	31.8	13.5	12.1
San Diego	11.2	17.8	15.1	9.8
Seattle	11.6	18.3	16.8	10.7
Washington, DC	8.7	14.4	8.9	6.3

Source: Federal Reserve Bank Board, 1991.

Federal regulators continue to ignore discrimination in lending. These alarming loan rejection statistics still leave some government and industry officials in doubt as to whether the culprit is a function of discrimination. Discriminatory lending practices subsidize the physical destruction of African American communities. Today, these same communities must share in the paying the hundreds of billions of dollars to bail out the failed savings and loan institutions, many of whom engaged in redlining African American communities.[6]

THE ROOT OF INFRASTRUCTURE DECLINE

Racism and residential segregation are facts of life in urban America. Eight out of every ten African Americans live in neighborhoods where they are in the majority. Residential segregation decreases for most racial and ethnic groups (not for African Americans) with additional education, income, and occupational status.[7] An African American with an earned income of $50,000 is as segregated as a Latino American who earns $5,000.

African Americans, no matter what their educational or occupational achievement or income level, are exposed to higher crime rates, less effective educational systems, high mortality risks, more dilapidated surroundings, and greater environmental threats because of their race.[8] Institutional barriers make it difficult for many African Americans to buy their way out of health-threatening physical environments. For example, in the heavily populated South Coast air basin of Los Angeles, it is estimated that over 71 percent of African Americans and 50 percent of Latinos reside in areas with the most polluted air, while only 34 percent of whites live in highly polluted areas.[9]

The development of spatially differentiated metropolitan areas where African Americans are segregated from other Americans has resulted from governmental policies and marketing practices of the housing industry and lending institutions. Millions of African Americans are geographically isolated in economically depressed and polluted urban neighborhoods away from the expanding suburban job centers.[10]

The infrastructure conditions result from a host of factors, including the distribution of wealth, patterns of racial and economic discrimination, redlining, housing and real estate practices, location decisions of industry, and differential enforcement of land use and environmental regulations. All communities are not created equal. Apartheid-type housing and development policies limit mobility, reduce neighborhood options, diminish job opportunities for African Americans, and decrease environmental choices.[11]

It is difficult for millions of African Americans in segregated neighborhoods to say "not in my backyard" (NIMBY) if they do not have a backyard.[12] Nationally, only about 44 percent of African Americans own their homes compared to over two-thirds of the nation as a whole. Homeowners are the strongest advocates of the NIMBY positions taken against locally unwanted land uses, or LULUs, such as the construction of garbage dumps, landfills, incinerators, sewer treatment plants, recycling centers, prisons, drug treatment units, and public housing projects. Generally, white communities have greater access to and influence over land use and environmental decision making than their African American counterparts.

The ability of an individual to escape a health-threatening physical environment is usually related to affluence. However, racial barriers complicate this process for millions of African Americans.[13] The imbalance between residential amenities and land uses assigned to central cities and suburbs cannot be explained by class factors alone. Blacks and whites do not have the same opportunities to "vote with their feet" and escape undesirable physical environments.[14] Those who are less fortunate must suffer the double jeopardy of poverty and pollution.

Institutional racism continues to influence housing and mobility options available to African Americans of all income levels—and is a major factor that influences the quality of neighborhoods they have available to them. The "web of discrimination" in the housing market is a result of action and inaction of local and federal government officials, financial institutions, insurance companies, real estate marketing firms, and zoning boards. More stringent enforcement mechanisms and penalties are needed to combat all forms of discrimination.

UNEVEN DEVELOPMENT AND UNEQUAL OPPORTUNITIES

Uneven development between central cities and suburbs combined with the systematic avoidance of inner-city areas by many businesses has heightened social and economic inequalities. For the past two decades, manufacturing plants have been fleeing central cities and taking their jobs with them. Many have moved offshore to Third World countries, where labor is cheap and environmental regulations are lax or nonexistent.

Industry flight from central cities has left behind a deteriorating urban infrastructure, poverty, and pollution. What kind of replacement industry can economically depressed African American communities attract? Some planners have suggested enterprise zones as a development strategy. Many of these communities do not have a lot of choices available to them. Some community leaders and workers have become so desperate that they see even low-paying hazardous industries as better than no industry at all.

These communities and their workers are forced to choose between unemployment and a job that may result in risks to their health, their family's health, and the health of their community. This practice amounts to "economic blackmail."[15] Economic conditions in many African American communities make them especially vulnerable to this practice.

Some polluting industries have been eager to exploit this vulnerability. Some have even used the assistance of elected officials in obtaining special tax breaks and government operating permits. For example, public officials in Robbins, Illinois—a small black village located six miles south of Chicago—are using their enterprise zone to attract industry. Robbins has been selected as the site for an incinerator that will burn garbage from 600,000 south suburban residents.[16] The Illinois Environmental Protection Agency has given its preliminary approval of the $200 million project.

Reading Energy Company of Philadelphia is scheduled to begin burning garbage in 1993 at the Robbins site. The incinerator is being designed to burn 1,600 tons of garbage a day—enough to fill 160 garbage trucks. The incinerator will create 500 construction jobs and 80 permanent jobs. Because of the low skill level of workers in Robbins, it is unclear how many of the construction and permanent jobs will go to local residents. The incinerator, however, will pay the community at least $750,000 a year in taxes, rentals, and fees.[17] Local citizens who oppose having other people's garbage barged into Robbins and burned feel they are having to give up too much in terms of health risks for a new job-producing industry.[18]

Clearly, economic development and environmental policies flow from forces of production and are often dominated and subsidized by state actors. Numerous examples abound where state actors have targeted cities and regions for infrastructure improvements and amenities, such as water irrigation systems, sewer treatment plants, ship channels, road and bridge projects, and mass transit systems. On the other hand, state actors have done a miserable job in protecting central city residents from the ravages of industrial pollution and nonresidential activities valued as having a negative impact on the quality of life.[19]

REGULATING URBAN LAND USE

Racial and ethnic inequality is perpetuated and reinforced by local governments in conjunction with urban-based corporations. In general, "at a certain point in community development . . . trajectories of economic growth and quality of life converge."[20] Race continues to be a potent variable in explaining urban land use, streets and highway configuration, commercial and industrial development, and industrial facility siting. Moreover, the question of "who gets what, where, and why" often pits one community against another.

Competition intensifies for the residential amenities and infrastructure improvements that are not always distributed equitably along racial and class lines. Some residential areas and their inhabitants are at a greater risk than is the larger society from unregulated growth, ineffective regulation of industrial toxins, and public policy decisions authorizing industrial facilities that favor those with political and economic clout.

Zoning is probably the most widely applied mechanism to regulate urban land use in the United States.[21] Zoning laws broadly define land for residential, commercial, or industrial uses, and may impose narrower land-use restrictions (e.g., minimum and maximum lot size, number of dwellings per acre, and square feet and height of buildings).

Zoning ordinances, deed restrictions, and other land-use mechanisms have been widely used as a NIMBY (not in my backyard) tool, operating through exclusionary practices. Thus, exclusionary zoning has been used to "simply zone against something rather than for something."[22] Exclusionary zoning is "one of the most subtle forms of using government authority and power to foster and perpetuate discriminatory practices."[23] With or without zoning, deed restrictions, or other devices, various groups are "unequally able to protect their environmental interests."[24] More often than not, African American communities get shortchanged in the neighborhood protection game.

DUMPING GROUNDS IN A BOOMTOWN

One of the best examples of environmental discrimination against an African American community has been documented in Houston, where well-established waste facility practices allowed black neighborhoods to become the dumping ground for the city's garbage.[25] Houston, the nation's fourth-largest city with a population of 1.6 million inhabitants, had the distinction of being the only major American city without zoning.

From the mid-1920s to the late-1970s, all city-owned landfills were located in African American neighborhoods; six of the eight city-owned garbage incinerators were located in African American neighborhoods during this same period. The city closed its waste disposal facilities in the early 1970s and contracted out this service with private firms. During Houston's booming years, from the early to the late 1970s, four privately owned sanitary landfills were used to dispose of Houston's solid waste. Three of these facilities were located in mostly African American neighborhoods, although African Americans made up just one-fourth of the city's population. The private waste disposal industry followed the discriminatory facility siting pattern that had been established by the Houston city government.

Concentrating landfills, incinerators, and garbage dumps in Houston's African American neighborhoods during the boom era of the 1970s lowered residents' property values, accelerated physical deterioration, and increased disinvestment practices. Moreover, the discriminatory siting of landfills and incinerators stigmatized the neighborhoods as "dumping grounds" for a host of other unwanted facilities, including salvage yards, recycling operations, cement plants, paint shops, and used automobile storage facilities.[26]

PAYING THE PRICE FOR RISKY TECHNOLOGIES

The problems identified in Houston are not unique. Risky technologies such as lead smelters, hazardous waste landfills, and incinerators pose health and environmental threats to African American communities from West Dallas to South Central Los Angeles.

The case of hazardous incinerators is one that has drawn much attention in recent years. For example, communities with hazardous waste incinerators generally have large minority populations, low incomes, and low property values. A 1990 Greenpeace report found that (1) the minority portion of the population in communities with existing incinerators is 89 percent higher than the national average; (2) communities where incinerators are proposed have a minority population 60 percent higher than the national average; (3) average income in communities with existing incinerators is 15 percent less than the national average; (4) property values in communities with incinerators are 38 percent lower than the national average; and (5) average property values are 35 percent lower in communities where incinerators are proposed.[27]

African American residents have begun to treat their struggle for a clean environment as an extension of their struggle for basic human rights. Just as social justice activists fought for equal access to education, employment, and housing, they are now defining the opportunity to live in an unpolluted physical environment as a basic right.

Moreover, many community leaders are now convinced that targeting their communities with risky technologies, such as waste disposal facilities, contributes to urban infrastructure decline comparable to housing discrimination, redlining practices, and disinvestment decisions of lending institutions. Environmental discrimination mirrors other forms of discrimination.

Industries employing risky technologies often make location decisions in African American communities with little or no input from local community leaders. When questions are raised by concerned citizens, the argument of jobs for local residents is used to quell dissent. Promises of jobs and a broadened tax base in economically depressed communities are presented as acceptable trade-offs to potential health and environmental risks. This "dangling carrot" scenario has proven to be the rule for African American people in this country and peoples in the Third World.

Many industrial firms, especially waste disposal companies and industries that have a long history of pollution violations, have come to view the African American community as a pushover, lacking community organization and environmental consciousness. The strong (and sometimes blind) pro-jobs stance—a kind of "don't bite the hand that feeds you" sentiment—has aided in institutionalizing "unacceptable risks" and environmental inequities.[28]

TOXIC TIME BOMBS

The hazardous waste problem continues to be one of the most "serious problems facing the industrial world."[29] The nation's Love Canals persist. Millions of tons of hazardous waste still end up at municipal landfills designed for household garbage; are released from tank trucks onto back roads; or are dumped directly into sewer systems. Sewer treatment plants are not designed for industrial chemicals. Toxic pollutants from these plants are discharged into the environment via wastewater discharge, air emissions, and sludge.

Over one-fourth of the Super Fund sites on the National Priority List had been used as municipal landfills. These toxic time bombs are not randomly scattered across the urban landscape. Nor is it a great mystery as to who is most likely to live next to a municipal landfill, incinerator, or a toxic waste dump. These facilities are often located in communities that have high percentages of poor, elderly, young, and minority residents.[30]

Do waste facilities just happen to end up in poor and minority communities? The nonrandom pattern of waste facility siting is not due to chance or the luck of the draw. Location decisions often involve cooperation between government and industry officials. In the case of siting waste-to-energy facilities (incinerators), Cerrell Associates, a Los Angeles-based consulting firm, advised the California Waste Management Board to push incinerators off on "neighborhoods least likely to express opposition—older and lower socioeconomic neighborhoods."[31] Recommendations of this type offer a green light to government and industry to target African American and other communities of color for incinerators.

The Commission for Racial Justice's landmark *Toxic Wastes and Race* study found race to be the single most important factor (i.e., more important than income, homeownership rate, and property values) in the location of abandoned toxic waste sites.[32] The study also found that (1) three out of five African Americans live in communities with abandoned toxic waste sites; (2) 15 million African Americans (60 percent) live in communities with one or more abandoned toxic waste sites; (3) three of the five largest commercial hazardous waste landfills are located in predominately African American or Latino communities and account for 40 percent of the nation's total estimated landfill capacity; and (4) African Americans are heavily overrepresented in the populations of cities with the largest number of abandoned toxic waste sites, which include Memphis, St. Louis, Houston, Cleveland, Chicago, and Atlanta.[33]

There are hundreds of examples of urban environmental problems confronting African Americans in cities. However, only a few examples will be highlighted in this paper.

Atlanta

Often referred to as the "capital of the New South," Atlanta has a total of 94 abandoned toxic waste sites. Nearly 83 percent of the city's African American population live in zip codes where these sites are found, while 60 percent of white Atlantans live in waste site areas. Atlanta is also one of the most segregated cities in the South. More than 86 percent of the city's African American population live in mostly black areas. Atlanta's residential patterns and waste site location are closely related.

Chicago

Chicago is the nation's third-largest city, with a population of more than 3 million inhabitants. The city's 1.1 million African Americans make up 39 percent of its total population. Chicago has the reputation of being the most racially segregated big city in America. Some 92 percent of the city's African Americans lived in segregated neighborhoods in 1980 (i.e., a figure down from 93 percent in 1970).[34]

Institutionalized discrimination by the housing industry and lending institutions has trapped many of the city's African American residents in deteriorating older neighborhoods. For example, the city's southside neighborhoods are threatened not only by economic stagnation and infrastructure decline, but also must contend with heavy use by polluting industries. Industrial encroachment into residential areas has turned Chicago's southside area into an urban "sacrifice zone."

The Altgeld Gardens housing project, located on Chicago's southeast side, lies within this sacrifice zone. Residents have described the project as a "toxic donut" because it is encircled by municipal and hazardous waste landfills, incinerators, grain elevators, sewer treatment facilities, and a host of other polluting industries.[35] The southeast side Chicago neighborhood is home to 150,000 residents (of whom 70 percent are African American and 11 percent are Latino), 50 active or closed commercial hazardous waste landfills, 100 factories (including seven chemical plants and five steel mills), and 103 abandoned toxic waste dumps.[36] The southeast side area is also scheduled to host the 1,600-ton-per-day Robbins municipal incinerator that will be allowed to release two tons of mercury and a half-ton of lead into the air each year.

191

Los Angeles

Los Angeles is the nation's second-largest city, with a population of 3.5 million persons. It is one of the most culturally and racially diverse big cities in the country. Persons of color (Latinos, Asian and Pacific Islanders, African Americans, and Native Americans) now constitute a majority (63 percent) of the city's population.

Residential segregation continues to be the dominant housing pattern in Los Angeles. For example, eight of every ten African Americans live in segregated areas. The South Central Los Angeles area is one these segregated neighborhoods that are over 52 percent African American and 44 percent Latino. The neighborhood suffers from years of systematic neglect, infrastructure decay, high unemployment, poverty, and heavy industrial use.

A recent article in the *San Francisco Examiner* described the zip code in which South Central Los Angeles lies as the "dirtiest" in the state.[37] The population in the zip code is 59 percent African American and 38 percent Latino. The one-square-mile area is saturated with abandoned toxic waste sites, freeways, smokestacks, and wastewater pipes from polluting industries. South Central Los Angeles is a haven for locally unwanted land uses. Some 18 industrial firms in 1989 discharged more than 33 million pounds of waste chemicals in the environment.

Los Angeles' growing population has meant a mounting municipal solid-waste and hazardous waste problem. In an effort to deal with its bulging garbage problem, the city (under a grant from the federal EPA) developed a plan in 1979 to build three waste-to-energy incinerators.[38] A number of advisory councils and committees were appointed by the Mayor and City Council between 1981 and 1984 to coordinate the Los Angeles City Energy Recovery (LANCER) project. Ogden-Martin was selected to build the incinerators that would handle a capacity of 1,600 tons of waste per day. The first of the three incinerators, or LANCER 1, was to be built in South Central Los Angeles.

Although the LANCER project had been in the works for more than six years, neighborhood residents were informed about the city-sponsored project in August 1985. Local residents organized themselves into a group called Concerned Citizens of South Central Los Angeles and were successful in defeating the controversial proposal. Leaders of Concerned Citizens, along with their allies, clearly demonstrated that it is possible for grassroots groups to defeat discriminatory facility siting proposals.

Richmond (California)

Located in Contra Costa County along the eastern shore of the San Francisco Bay, Richmond has a population of about 80,000 residents. More than half are African American and about 11 percent are Latino. The median income of Richmond residents is one-third of that of all Contra Costa County residents. One in four Richmond residents lives below the poverty line, a figure that is three times the county average.

Richmond is a highly industrialized area with over 350 industrial facilities that handle hazardous materials. These industrial firms generate over 800,000 pounds of toxic air contaminants, nearly 18,000 pounds of toxic pollutants in wastewater, and about 179,000 tons of hazardous waste each year.[39] Most of Richmond's African American population live adjacent to the city's petrochemical corridor. For example, African Americans comprise "72 percent to 94 percent of the local population in 14 Richmond neighborhoods" that are closest to the city's heavy industrial zone.[40] Local residents for years have suspected that pollution from the petrochemical plants is responsible for all kinds of community health problems—from skin rashes to cancer.

In 1987, Richmond residents organized themselves into a group called the West County Toxics Coalition. The group was initiated with support from the Boston-based National Toxics Campaign. Today, the West County Toxics Coalition is the leading environmental and social justice advocate in Richmond.

Dallas

Dallas is the seventh-largest city in the nation, with a population just under one million. The city's African American population grew from 265,594 in 1980 to 296,262 (an 11.5 percent increase) in 1990. African Americans make up about 30 percent of the city's population.

Over the years, Dallas's African American neighborhoods have had to cope with the problem of lead smelters operating in their midst. All of the lead smelters in the city were located in mostly African American and Latino neighborhoods. For example, the 63-acre Murph Metals secondary lead smelter (later known as RSR Corporation) operated in the West Dallas neighborhood, beginning in the mid-1930s.

West Dallas has a population of 13,161 residents, of which more than 85 percent are black. The lead smelter is located next door to an elementary school and across the street from the West Dallas Boys Club and a 3,500-unit public housing project. The housing project is located just 50 feet from the sprawling lead smelter's property line and is in a direct path of the prevailing southerly winds.

During the peak period of operation in the mid-sixties, the plant employed more than 400 persons (few of whom lived in the neighborhood). The smelter pumped more than 269 tons of lead particles each year into the West Dallas air. Lead particles were blown by prevailing winds through the doors and windows of nearby residents and onto the West Dallas streets, ball parks, and children's playgrounds.

Dallas officials were informed as early as 1972 that lead was finding its way into the bloodstreams of children who lived in two mostly African American and Latino neighborhoods: West Dallas (RSR lead smelter) and East Oak Cliff (Dixie Metals smelter). The city health department found that living near the smelters was associated with a 36 percent increase in blood lead level. The city was urged to restrict the emissions of lead to the atmosphere and to undertake a large screening program to determine the extent of the public health problem. The city failed to take immediate action.

The community organized itself into the West Dallas Neighborhood Committee on Lead Contamination in 1981. The city took action only after a series of lead-related articles made the headlines in the local newspapers, triggering widespread concern, public outrage, several class-action lawsuits, and legal action by the Texas attorney general against the smelter. West Dallas plaintiffs won an out-of-court settlement worth over $45 million. The lawsuit was settled in June 1983, with the firm agreeing to a soil cleanup in West Dallas, a blood-testing program for children and pregnant women, and the installation of new anti-pollution equipment.

The pollution equipment was never installed. In May 1984, the Dallas Board of Adjustments—a city agency responsible for monitoring land-use violations—requested the city attorney to order the smelter permanently closed for violating the zoning code. The West Dallas smelter was shut down (but not cleaned up) in 1984 under a zoning ordinance: the smelter operator had never obtained the necessary use permits to operate in the neighborhood.

The Dixie Metals smelter, on the other hand, was allowed to continue operating in the East Oak Cliff neighborhood under a phase-down agreement. The plant was shut in 1990.

CONCLUSIONS

African American communities are beginning to mobilize around quality of life issues. These issues range from fair housing to anti-redlining to environmental equity strategies. Institutional barriers and discriminatory public policies contribute to urban infrastructure decline, reduce wealth accumulation, and add risks to African Americans.

A national urban policy is needed to begin addressing the nation's decaying urban infrastructure. A new form of activism has emerged that is not limited to attacks on well-publicized toxic contamination issues; these activists have begun to seek remedial action on neighborhood disinvestment, housing discrimination and residential segregation, urban mass transportation, pollution, and other urban problems that threaten public safety.

It is in the national interest that we have healthy cities. An economic, environmental, and infrastructure crisis exists in urban America. This crisis has been created in part by the systematic withholding of investments and infrastructure improvements, while allowing some urban neighborhoods to become municipal and hazardous waste dumping grounds. Many African American communities are subsidizing—with their health—the siting of risky industries other communities refuse to accept.

The current emphasis on waste management and pollution control regulations encourages dependence on disposal technologies that are themselves sources of toxic pollution. Pushing incinerators off on people is not economic development. It is, however, a cruel hoax that exploits the economic vulnerability of desperate communities.

Pollution regulations have done little to rid African American communities of toxic pollutants. African American communities have received few tangible benefits from current waste management strategies. Pollution prevention holds the greatest promise for protecting human health and the environment of all communities.

African Americans in urban areas are tired of their communities becoming toxic wastelands for polluting industries that promise jobs and an expanded tax base. Too often, the communities that host landfills and incinerators remain impoverished. All communities must deal with their waste. For example, federal-, state-, and local-mandated garbage prevention programs need to be funded that set goals for recycling, composting, using recycled materials, and eliminating throw-away products. Small and minority businesses should be encouraged to explore the pollution prevention field as a possible expansion market.

Because of the inherent inequities associated with waste facility siting, a national moratorium is needed on the construction of (1) new commercial hazardous waste treatment, storage, and disposal facilities; and (2) new municipal solid-waste incinerators and landfills in communities already saturated with environmental problems.

Clearly, institutional arrangements influence land-use policies and perpetuate the separate and unequal quality of residential areas for whites and African Americans. Racial discrimination reduces the options available to African Americans in terms of where they live, work, and play. The problems associated with a nearby lead smelter and lead in drinking water must be addressed as quality of life issues.

The nation must redefine "environment" to include infrastructure problems that threaten the fabric of our cities and their inhabitants. An inadequate sewer treatment plant is an environmental and a health threat. The repairing or replacing of decayed sewer lines and upgrading existing and building new sewer plants are investments in America.

The rebuilding of urban America must involve people who live in cities. Public officials must take leadership roles in calling for new investments in housing, mass transit, and pollution prevention programs.

Social justice and equity must be incorporated into all infrastructure improvement and pollution prevention plans. No segment of society should have to bear a disproportionate burden of the nation's pollution problem.

In addition to the standard "technical" requirements, equity proposals will need to require implementation of a "fair share" plan that takes into account sociodemographic, economic, and cultural factors of impacted communities.

Finally, the problems associated with environmental racism need to be elevated to the national agenda. The time is long past when institutional racism can be dismissed as a figment of someone's imagination. A number of action steps are recommended to address the problem of environmental injustice and disproportionate impact:

(1) hold congressional hearings;

(2) establish a blue-ribbon commission or think tank;

(3) select the National Academy of Sciences to conduct a comprehensive study; and

(4) create a permanent division within the federal EPA that examines environmental equity, disproportionate impact, and pollution prevention strategies.

Urban Redevelopment: Developing Effective Targeting Strategies

Robert B. Hill, Ph.D.

A major objective of the National Urban League's Marshall Plan for America is to enhance America's competitiveness in the global market by making significant investments in its urban centers. Since African Americans are disproportionately concentrated in these cities and are one of the fastest growing groups, it is clear that the United States will be unable to regain its economic leadership in the 21st century unless it targets the underutilized human and physical capacities of African American communities.

Yet, many policies and programs originally designed to revitalize economically depressed central cities not only have failed to benefit the low-income groups and minorities living there, but also have disproportionately benefited middle-income and upper-income individuals and communities. For example, when Congress created the Resolution Trust Corporation in 1989 to rescue struggling savings and loan institutions, it set aside thousands of foreclosed homes and apartments as affordable housing targeted for low-income people. However, thus far, only a tiny fraction of the foreclosed homes have gone to the working poor. Instead, most of the buyers have been middle-income and upper-income individuals and groups.

What political, economic, and social factors are responsible for subverting many well-intentioned social policies to have such unintended, negative consequences for blacks and low-income groups? Unless special efforts are made to learn from past experiences, any new initiatives to revitalize inner-city areas may continue to bypass those most in need.

Consequently, this paper will address the following four questions:

1. What have been the effects of past targeted programs, such as Public Housing, Urban Renewal, Model Cities, Community Development Block Grants (CDBG), and Comprehensive Employment and Training Act (CETA) programs, on economically and racially disadvantaged groups and communities?

2. What social, economic, and political factors, such as institutional racism, exclusionary zoning, land-use policies, redlining, insensitive government policies, and census undercount, subvert many social policies from reaching their intended beneficiaries?

3. How promising are current targeted initiatives, such as enterprise zones, the Home Mortgage Disclosure Act (HMDA), the Community Reinvestment Act (CRA), linkage programs, public housing resident management, tax credits, and church-based community development corporations for markedly enhancing the social and economic well-being of African American individuals and communities?

4. What recommendations are needed to insure that the domestic Marshall Plan and associated human and physical development programs will have major beneficial consequences for African American communities?

EFFECTIVENESS OF PAST TARGETED EFFORTS

Public Housing

The Low-Rent Public Housing (LRPH) program was established by the Housing Act of 1937 to provide affordable housing for low-income families in central cities. During the initial decade (1937-48) of public housing, blacks were only a small fraction of its residents, since it was designed for "temporarily poor" white immigrants. Blacks made their major inroads into public housing during its second decade (1949-59), mainly as a result of urban renewal. Thus, the proportion of blacks in public housing rose from 38 percent to 46 percent between 1952 and 1961. Although blacks accounted for 52 percent of all public housing residents by 1977, they comprised two-thirds (66 percent) of nonelderly families in public housing.[1] Moreover, while working poor couples were given highest priority for eligibility in public housing during its first decade, the proportion of nonworking poor rose sharply--also as a result of their displacement by urban renewal activities. Thus, between 1952 and 1974, the proportion of public housing residents who worked fell from 71 percent to 27 percent.

Urban Renewal

The "urban renewal" of deteriorating residential areas was established by Title I of the Housing Act of 1949 in which the federal government agreed to provide two-thirds of the funds to cities for such efforts. It should be clearly understood that urban renewal was not a housing program--it was mainly a slum clearance initiative. Very little residential housing replaced the low-income dwellings that were demolished. That is why poor families displaced by urban renewal and related government activity were given the highest priority for relocating to public housing, and the criteria for eligibility for public housing were lowered markedly. As a result, the proportion of low-income single families in public housing rose sharply.[2]

Since blacks comprised about 63 percent of the families relocated from

Title I areas by 1964, it is not surprising that urban renewal has been characterized as "black removal." Yet, it should be realized that since public housing comprises only a tiny fraction (about 2 percent) of all housing units, most of the families displaced did not move into public housing. Although half of the displaced families were eligible for public housing, only one-fifth of them actually moved into the projects.[3]

Subsidized Rent

Since public housing could not accommodate the majority of low-income families, the Housing and Community Development Act of 1974 created Section 8 to increase the accessibility of poor families to affordable housing in the private sector. Section 8 is a type of housing allowance program that provides certificates to very low-income families, i.e., households with incomes no higher than 50 percent of the median income for their local area. Participants in this program are not suppose to pay more than 30 percent of their income for rent, and the government pays the landlord the difference between that amount and the market rent for their units. By 1979, blacks comprised only 39 percent of the total 2.5 million poor households receiving public housing or subsidized rent assistance. Or, only one-third of poor blacks received such housing aid.[4]

In order to offset the rising costs of the Section 8 subsidies, the Housing and Urban-Rural Recovery Act of 1983 created an experimental housing voucher program that provided the poor with a fixed subsidy based on their income and local area fair market rent--regardless of the actual rent for the unit. Low-income families were free to shop for rental housing--but they had to pay any extra money needed if the unit's rent exceeded the fair market value. Or, they could keep the difference, if the unit's rent fell below the fair market level--a much rarer occurrence. Moreover, unlike the 15-year commitment of the Section 8 program, the housing vouchers lasted for only five years. Although President Reagan sought to convert the entire Section 8 existing housing program into vouchers, Congress rebuffed him by restricting the voucher program to a limited demonstration.[5]

Model Cities

One of the earliest initiatives to redevelop slum areas of central cities was the Model Cities program, which was launched in 1966 and expanded in 1968 by the Johnson Administration as part of its "War on Poverty" program. It was designed as a comprehensive interagency effort targeted to a limited number of central cities with high proportions of low-income minority residents. While only 63 cities were initially selected from about 200 applicants, the total number of participating cities was restricted to 150. Since the early years of the Model Cities program were devoted to planning, its funding rose from $86 million to $500 million between 1970 and 1972. However, its major funding, which was to begin flowing in FY 1974, never materialized as a result of being phased out by President Nixon's Community Development Block Grant (CDBG) program.[6]

Community Development Block Grant (CDBG) Program

The Community Development Block Grant (CDBG) was one of several new block grants created by the Nixon Administration as part of its "New Federalism" program to devolve responsibility for major social programs from the federal government to states and cities. Unlike the Model Cities categorical strategy of targeting inner-cities areas with large numbers of the poor and jobless, the block grant approach was based on a "revenue-sharing" concept of providing funds to as many central cities and suburban areas as possible--regardless of their social or economic need. In addition to the Model Cities program, the CDBG also merged other housing-related programs, such as urban renewal, open space, historic preservation, public facilities, rehabilitation, neighborhood facilities, water and sewer, and neighborhood development.

The 1974 legislation creating the CDBG stipulated that 100 percent of its funds were to be used for activities involving the elimination of urban blight that would mainly benefit "low and moderate income" persons. Yet, early audits of CDBGs revealed that many localities were using sizable amounts of their funds to construct hotels, tennis courts, or swimming pools to benefit middle- and upper-income persons. Thus, during the Carter Administration in 1978, HUD Secretary Patricia Harris attempted to retarget the CDBG program to low-income residents by issuing regulations that required localities to use at least 75 percent of the funds for activities that would benefit low- and moderate-income people.

However, Congress strongly fought Secretary Harris' efforts and enacted a 1978 amendment that prohibited HUD from using any percentage threshold as a basis for rejecting CDBG plans. Thus, many localities felt free to continue to use their CDBG funds for the disproportionate benefit of middle- and upper-income persons. Although a 1983 amendment stipulated that localities must use at least 51 percent of their CDBG funds for activities that benefited economically disadvantaged persons, no plans were rejected that failed to meet this threshold.

Comprehensive Employment and Training Act (CETA) Program

The Comprehensive Employment and Training Act (CETA) program was created in 1973 by the Nixon Administration to provide funds for states and localities to use as part of a "revenue-sharing" block grant program in the area of employment. Although the original target group of CETA was the long-term jobless and "hard-core" unemployed, the actual beneficiaries were mainly the short-term unemployed, especially former city government employees who were laid off as a result of the 1974-75 recession. Moreover, an in-depth evaluation conducted by the National Academy of Sciences revealed that the CETA block grant program reached a smaller proportion of low-income persons and minorities than the earlier categorical employment programs under the Johnson Administration. The Carter Administration's attempts to retarget the CETA block grant program to the long-term unemployed were only moderately successful.[7]

INSTITUTIONAL CONSTRAINTS

What social, economic, and political factors have been responsible for subverting many well-intentioned redevelopment programs from reaching the poor and jobless in inner cities? Without a doubt, the major force has been the continuing significance of racism, especially institutional racism.

Institutional Racism

About 25 years ago, Carmichael and Hamilton used the term "institutional racism" to refer to regulations, laws, formal policies, and information practices of organizations or institutions that result in differential adverse treatment or subordination of racial and ethnic minorities.[8] Such racism may be overt or covert. Overt institutional discrimination involves deliberate mistreatment of minorities by organizations or institutions that are based on *explicit* racial or ethnic criteria. Examples of overt racism include: slavery, the Black Codes after emancipation, *de jure* segregation laws, racial housing covenants, and racial steering.

Covert, or subtle, institutional discrimination, however, refers to the intentional mistreatment of minorities by organizations or institutions that are based on *nonracial* criteria that are strongly correlated with race. Covert discrimination is also known as "patterned evasion," the deliberate use of proxies for race in order to deny equal opportunities to racial minorities. Numerous court cases have identified covert intentional institutional discrimination as resulting from: (a) urban renewal practices of public or private agencies that disproportionately displace low-income minorities from their homes; (2) redlining, i.e., the differential refusal of home mortgage loans, commercial credit, and auto and homeowners insurance to minorities living in "redlined" neighborhoods; and (c) exclusionary zoning, i.e., zoning ordinances that prohibit low-income and multifamily dwellings in predominantly white communities.[9]

Fair housing audits have continued to uncover disparate intentional housing discrimination against prospective black renters and homeowners--even when one controls for income, sex, family size, and credit history. The first comprehensive audit was conducted in 40 metropolitan areas in 1977 by the National Committee Against Discrimination in Housing under a HUD contract. The NCDH study revealed that whites received "favorable" treatment in 48 percent of the rental audits, compared to only 21 percent of the rental audits when blacks received "favorable" treatment. Moreover, whites received "favorable" treatment in 39 percent of the sales audits, compared to only 24 percent of that for blacks. Similar patterns of pervasive housing discrimination were revealed by rental and sales audits conducted by the Urban Institute in 25 metropolitan areas in 1989. Such studies underscore the fact that the residential hypersegregation of blacks results much more from intentional housing discrimination than from self-separation.[10]

Structural Discrimination

Yet, Carmichael and Hamilton also underscored the fact that institutional racism may be unintentional. Over 40 years ago, sociologist Robert K. Merton identified "unprejudiced discrimination" as a form of racism that has been neglected by scholars, since they accept the false premise that discrimination can *only* result from malevolent intent or prejudiced attitudes.[11] Baron specifies the covert operation of unintentional institutional discrimination as follows:

> Maintenance of the basic social controls is now less dependent upon specific discriminatory decisions (or intentions). Such behavior has become so well-institutionalized that the individual generally does not have to exercise a choice to operate in a racist manner. The rules and procedures of the large organizations have already prestructured the choice. The individual only has to conform to the operating norms of the organization and the institution will do the discriminating for him.[12] (Author's parentheses.)

Calmore describes how unintentional institutional racism is manifested in housing discrimination:

> . . . discrimination will reflect a "color-blind" decision or practice that has a disproportionate adverse impact on the members of a minority group . . . discrimination comes into housing decisions in ways that are more subtle than a clear desire to harm the victims. Three of the ways emphasized in legal scholarship are "racially selective sympathy and indifference," generalizations and stereotypes, and perpetuation of past discrimination. In each case, victims are subjected to differential treatment because of their race, or other impermissible factors, without any necessary intent on the part of the perpetrator to discriminate.[13]

Accordingly, we operationally define structural or "unintentional" discrimination as racially disparate adverse effects on minorities of social forces or policies that may not have been explicitly designed to have such discriminatory consequences.[14] We contend that structural discrimination plays a major role in subverting the formal goals of redevelopment policies and programs from reaching low-income minorities in inner cities. Baron has identified primary and secondary subsectors of institutions as key mechanisms for perpetuating racial inequality. While white and middle-income persons are overrepresented in the primary subsectors, blacks and low-income persons are overrepresented in the secondary subsectors. We will now illustrate how structural discrimination undermines many urban development policies targeted for the disadvantaged.

Structural Unemployment

High levels of structural unemployment among inner-city minorities are a manifestation of structural discrimination. Inner-city areas disproportionately experience structural unemployment because they are adversely affected by structural transformations in the economy, such as the exodus of industries, the shift from higher-paying manufacturing to lower-paying service jobs, the shift from union to nonunion jobs, and the decline in unskilled and semiskilled jobs due to technological automation.

Yet, because of the dual labor market phenomenon, structural unemployment is more highly concentrated among workers in the secondary labor market than among workers in the primary labor market. Since whites are overrepresented in the higher-paying, high-skilled, stable jobs in the primary sector, and blacks are overrepresented in the lower-paying, low-skilled, unstable jobs in the secondary sector, blacks are more acutely affected by structural unemployment than whites.

Cyclical Unemployment

Workers in the secondary labor market are not only disproportionately affected by structural joblessness, but also they are acutely affected by cyclical unemployment. Between 1970 and 1982, this nation experienced four recessions--1970-71, 1974-75, 1980, 1981-1982--or one every three years. And, black workers are much more likely than white workers to lose their jobs during recessions due to: (a) the seniority principle of "last hired, first fired" and (b) their disparate concentration in secondary sector unskilled and semiskilled jobs. Thus, government policies targeted to the underemployed and jobless may bypass such groups because of structural discrimination resulting from both cyclical and structural unemployment. For example, the 1974-75 recession was a major factor responsible for the ineffectiveness of the CETA program in reaching the long-term unemployed.[15]

Exclusionary Zoning

Exclusionary zoning has been a land-use policy that has undermined the effectiveness of redevelopment programs targeted to low-income residents. Nevertheless, zoning in favor of detached single-family homes has many socially useful goals. It protects open space, preserves historic districts, limits congestion, and reduces sources of pollution. Yet, many white communities in central cities and suburban areas have used zoning policies to exclude "undesirables," especially blacks, low-income people, and the homeless by prohibiting the construction of multifamily dwellings, public housing developments, and other low-income housing.[16]

The Mount Laurel ruling by the New Jersey Supreme Court is a landmark decision in the field of exclusionary zoning policies. The court ruled that Mount Laurel's use of exclusionary zoning to prohibit the construction of low-income housing was racially discriminatory. Similarly, the New Hampshire Supreme Court ruled in July 1991 that the town of Chester had "blatantly exclusionary" zoning policies that restricted the construction of apartments to less than 2 percent of its developable land. The Chester decision may have important national implications, since many suburban jurisdictions, such as Fairfax, Prince George's, and Montgomery counties in the suburban Washington, DC, area restrict apartment construction to about 2 percent or less of their developable land. Such zoning policies severely restrict the ability of localities to revitalize their areas by building affordable housing for low-income residents.

Insensitive Federal Policies

A major political constraint responsible for the inability of many urban redevelopment policies to benefit low-income groups and inner-city minorities has been the hostility of the White House to initiatives by Congress in behalf of the poor. Early examples of this "War Against the Poor" were the moratorium imposed on all subsidized housing programs and the conversion of highly targeted categorical programs to less targeted block grants by the Nixon Administration. The Reagan Administration continued to reduce markedly federal expenditures for low-income housing. Thus, funding for public housing has been reduced by one-third since 1980, while funds to increase the supply of affordable housing have been reduced by 80 percent. For example, between FY 1980 and FY 1988, federal funds for assisted housing plummeted from $27 billion to only $7 billion.[17]

Consequently, the number of low-income housing units is expected to drop from 14 million to 9 million between 1974 and 2003, while the number of households needing low-income housing is expected to soar from 9 million to 17 million. Thus, approximately 8 million households (or 19 million persons) may be homeless or forced to live doubled-up by the year

2003, if the supply of affordable housing is not increased markedly.[18] Clearly, the sharp increase in homeless individuals and families, especially in inner-city areas, must be traced to the insensitive government housing policies of the '70s and '80s.

Census Undercount

Another factor that consistently undermines the effectiveness of government programs targeted to inner-city areas is the disproportionate undercount of minorities in decennial censuses. Between 1790 and 1860, a 40 percent undercount of blacks was legally mandated--five black slaves were counted for every three whites for purposes of political apportionment. The Census Bureau estimated that 5 percent of blacks (4.8 percent) and Hispanics (5.2 percent) were left out of the 1990 census, compared to only 1 percent of whites.

Since census figures are used to allocate about $50 billion from nearly 100 federal programs (many of them targeted to low-income groups) to states and localities, this disparate undercount has major implications for communities with large concentrations of racial minorities. For example, Hill estimated that: (a) the 229,000 persons missed in the 1990 census in New York City will cost the city $325 million per year; (b) the 32,000 persons missed in Washington, DC, will cost the city $91 million per year; and (c) the 36,000 persons missed in Baltimore will cost the city $39 million per year.[19] Thus, the census undercount structurally discriminates against inner-city areas by denying them their equitable share of government aid for vitally needed programs.

PROMISING INITIATIVES

Following are brief descriptions of some promising initiatives designed to revitalize inner cities and to benefit their low-income residents. Each deserves serious consideration.

Home Mortgage Disclosure Act

In order to reduce the redlining of inner-city neighborhoods by lending institutions, Congress passed the Home Mortgage Disclosure Act (HMDA) in 1975:

> . . . to provide the citizens and public officials of the United States with sufficient information to enable them to determine whether depository institutions are fulfilling their obligations to serve the housing needs of the communities and neighborhoods in which they are located.[20]

The HMDA requires financial institutions to produce annual reports documenting the number and dollar volume of residential loans made in each census tract in the communities they serve. Reports must be filed by all federally regulated depository institutions that have $10 million or more in assets and at least one branch in a metropolitan statistical area. A 1980 amendment requires HUD to report information on the volume and location of loans insured by the Federal Housing Administration (FHA). Another 1980 amendment requires the Federal Reserve Board to computerize all the reports and to designate a central depository for each metropolitan area. Each computer tape costs $250 and contains the annual reports for all the metropolitan areas.

Community Reinvestment Act

In order to make lending institutions more accountable to the residents of the communities in which they are located, the Community Reinvestment Act (CRA) was enacted in 1977:

> . . . to encourage regulated financial institutions to fulfill their continuing and affirmative obligation to help meet the credit needs of their communities, including low- and moderate-income neighborhoods, consistent with safe and sound operation of such institutions.[21]

The CRA requires financial institutions to prepare reports that delineate the communities they serve, to list the types of credit they intend to extend within the areas, to indicate the efforts made to meet community credit needs, and to assess their performance in meeting those needs. Citizens have the right to add written comments to the CRA files and to examine comments submitted by other citizens. Federal regulatory agencies rate lending institutions on the basis of their performance in meeting community credit needs.

Most institutions receive very favorable CRA ratings. More than 97 percent of the institutions rated before March 1989 received a rating of 1 or 2, based on a scale in which 5 is the least favorable rating. Citizens who are dissatisfied with institutions' CRA records can file formal protests with the regulatory agencies and can request public hearings as part of the review of the institutions' applications.

Community-based groups have found the HMDA and CRA to be important tools for encouraging lending institutions to invest a significant amount of funds for the revitalization of inner-city neighborhoods. An in-depth analysis of lending patterns in the Baltimore metropolitan area between 1981-84 based on HMDA data was conducted by the Institute for Policy Studies of Johns Hopkins University for the Maryland Alliance for Responsible Investment.[22] This study revealed that the single-family lending market was comprised of three tiers: a high volume market for gentrified neighborhoods; a moderate volume market for white, nongentrified neighborhoods; and a low volume market for black, nongentrified neighborhoods. Interestingly, this study found similar low-volume lending markets for nongentrified black neighborhoods in the suburbs and central cities.

Robinson provided an in-depth description of how the Atlanta Community Reinvestment Alliance (ACRA) used HMDA and CRA data to mount a successful challenge to the redlining activities of lending institutions in the Atlanta metropolitan area.[23] Although the Federal Reserve Board refused to hear ACRA's challenge to the merger proposed by Trust Company, ACRA provided copies of its report to the *Atlanta Journal/Constitution*. A staff writer, Bill Dedman, conducted his own analysis of mortgage lending patterns in black and white neighborhoods in the Atlanta area.

A four-part series entitled "The Color of Money" ran in the *Atlanta Journal/Constitution* from May 1-4, 1988. It revealed that savings and loan institutions made four times as many loans per 1,000 single-family structures in white neighborhoods than they did in black neighborhoods of similar economic status. Moreover, while financial institutions made 31 percent of the home loans in low-income white neighborhoods, they made only 17 percent of the home loans in upper-income black neighborhoods. The widespread publicity from these articles compelled the lending institutions to establish special funding programs to make significant amounts of loans available for homeownership, for housing improvements, and for underwriting the construction of homes for low- and moderate-income families.

Enterprise Zones

Enterprise zones offer another promising approach designed to target special tax incentives and other investments to revitalize inner-city communities. Since the early 1980s, legislation for enterprise zones has been introduced on a regular basis. It has been sponsored on a bipartisan basis-- former Rep. Jack Kemp (R-NY) and Rep. Charles Rangel (D-NY) were among the early cosponsors. Although no bill has been enacted as a federal initiative, the zones have been implemented by 37 states and the District of Columbia. Overall, the zones have saved or created about 180,000 jobs and stimulated about $9 billion in private investment in low-income areas.[24]

However, evaluations of individual states' zones have revealed mixed results. Some of the more successful zones, such as in New Jersey, Connecticut, and Illinois, have used tax incentives of such magnitude to attract private investment. On the other hand, the less successful zones, such as in Maryland, have employed relatively small incentives.

Enterprise zones have not been as effective in stimulating the involvement of minority businesses. Such participation of minority businesses would be enhanced markedly if the tax credits were made refundable in order to help those small businesses during their early stages when they are less likely to make a profit. Furthermore, the enterprise zones should be targeted to encourage the involvement of economic development activities by the residents of inner-city areas to enhance the social and economic development of black and Hispanic communities.

Tax Credits

Several tax credits have proven effective in targeting low-income areas and individuals. The **Low Income Housing Tax Credit** is designed to attract private funding to enhance the production and rehabilitation of low-income rental housing. It already subsidizes about 25 percent of low-income rental housing under construction and is effectively targeted to very low-income families. For example, the 61,200 units financed with 1990 tax credits equaled one-fourth of the 240,000 low-income multifamily rental unit construction starts that year. Unfortunately, since this tax subsidy is renewed on an annual basis, it is expected to expire by the end of 1991--if Congress takes no action. Not only should this important tax credit be renewed, but also it should be made permanent in order to encourage stronger partnerships between nonprofit and private institutions and to stabilize the growth of low-income housing.

The **Earned Income Tax Credit** (EITC) has proven to be very effective in targeting tax relief to working poor families with children--in which black families are overrepresented. Congress enacted the EITC in 1975 as a result of studies that revealed that the poor were paying higher effective tax rates than wealthy individuals. The major feature of this tax credit is its refundability--that is, poor families receive a rebate even if they owe no taxes. The Tax Reform Act of 1986 raised the maximum credit to $800 (or 14 percent of the first $5,714 of earned income). The Omnibus Budget Reconciliation Act of 1990 not only raised the maximum EITC amount but also it created two supplemental tax credits--a young child credit and a health insurance credit.

The **Targeted Jobs Tax Credit** (TJTC), which was enacted in 1978, has also been effective in increasing the employment of disadvantaged groups in the private sector. The targeted groups for the TJTC are economically disadvantaged individuals (youth, veterans, ex-convicts, and summer youth employees), SSI recipients, AFDC recipients, General Assistance (GA) recipients, and the disabled. Of the 452,453 individuals who were certified for private employment in FY 1989, half of them were low-income youth between the ages of 18 to 24, and one-fifth of them were welfare recipients. The credit is equal to 40 percent of the first $6,000 of first-year wages paid to a member of the targeted group, for a maximum credit of $2,400 per individual. However, for summer youth employees, the credit is 40 percent of wages up to $3,000, for a maximum credit of $1,200.

Linkage Programs

Linkage programs are a relatively new approach to increasing the supply of low-income housing that more and more localities have found to be effective. Housing linkage requires that developers of commercial space (usually in downtown areas) also agree to construct or provide financial assistance for the production of low-income housing in other parts of the city. Linkage programs may be optional or mandatory. They may provide funds in a housing trust fund (as in Boston) or may be allowed to build the housing themselves (as in San Francisco). National surveys have found that between 10-18 percent of the cities use some form of linkage.[25]

Another version of linkage is the one-for-one replacement program, which was prompted by Massachusetts Congressman Barney Frank's amendment to the 1987 Housing and Community Development Act. This amendment requires one-for-one replacement of low-income housing units demolished using CDBG or Urban Development Action Grant (UDAG) funds. About 10 percent of the cities have replacement programs. However, there are several legal challenges by private developers to replacement obligation programs. Thus, some localities place a mandatory replacement obligation on the public sector, but an optional obligation on private developers who raze low-income housing. Clearly, linkage programs deserve greater consideration as a mechanism for revitalizing inner-city areas.

Resident Management

The resident management of public housing has also proven to be a very effective mechanism for revitalizing inner-city areas by the residents themselves. With the assistance of the National Center for Neighborhood Enterprise, the number of public housing developments managed by the residents has increased markedly over the past decade. For example, after three years of resident management in Kenilworth-Parkside in Washington, DC, there were sharp declines in vandalism, welfare dependency, school dropouts, teenage pregnancy, and unemployment. In addition to hiring former welfare recipients to manage and repair their developments, the resident management corporations have also created a wide range of small businesses in such areas as maintenance, day care, laundry, tailoring, barbering, beauty salons, catering, thrift shops, and reverse commuting vans. Clearly, greater resources should be given to such community-based groups to participate in the revitalization of their communities.

Church CDCs

Another community-based group that has proven to be effective in stabilizing and enhancing inner-city areas has been the community development corporation (CDC) developed by churches. One of the earliest efforts in this area was launched by a group of ministers in Philadelphia under the leadership of Reverend Leon Sullivan, pastor of Zion Baptist Church. To develop a pool of funds for economic development activities, Reverend Sullivan instituted the "10/36" plan, whereby members of his church would pay $10 a month for 36 months. These efforts resulted in the creation of the Zion Investment Corporation (ZIC)--and subsequently, the Opportunities Industrialization Centers (OIC). Through OIC, Reverend Sullivan developed an international network of employment and training programs targeted to disadvantaged youths and adults. And through ZIC, the consortium of black churches was able to purchase shopping centers, to create numerous small businesses, and to build many units of low-income housing.

Fortunately, there are numerous other examples of black churches playing major roles in the social and economic development of their communities. The United House of Prayer for All People has vested $20 million of its own money in constructing affordable housing and stimulating minority business development in such cities as Washington, DC, Charlotte, NC, and New Haven, CT. Similar successful neighborhood revitalization efforts by church consortiums include Leaders Energizing Neighborhood Development (LEND), Baltimore United in Leadership Development (BUILD), and the Congress of National Black Churches (CNBC). Clearly, one of the most effective mechanisms for targeting inner-city areas is through the churches that are located in them.[26]

Disparate Impact Lawsuits

Our analysis has emphasized the subtle role of structural or "unintentional" discrimination in thwarting the well-intentioned efforts of many government programs to target inner-city individuals and areas for social and economic development. Yet, many persons are unaware of the fact that successful lawsuits can be launched to combat structural discrimination. The basic precedent for such lawsuits is the *Griggs v. Duke Power Company* decision of 1971 in which the U.S. Supreme Court declared that the company's employment tests, which had an unintended adverse impact on hiring and promoting minority workers, violated the Constitution.[27]

In fact, subsequent court cases declared numerous mechanisms that had disparate adverse impact on minorities "racially discriminatory"--even if these consequences were not intended. However, in the *Wards Cove v. Atonio* decree of 1989[28], the conservative majority of the U.S. Supreme

Court attempted to overturn the 28-year-old *Griggs* decision. Outraged by the *Wards Cove* decree, Congress attempted to restore the *Griggs* standing by enacting a civil rights bill in 1990. It failed to override President Bush's veto by only one vote. Yet, Congress successfully restored *Griggs* in the Civil Rights Act of 1991, which the President reluctantly signed--since he knew that Congress had sufficient votes to override his veto. The *Griggs* decree in employment has been used increasingly as a precedent for combating unintentional discrimination in the field of housing as well.

CONCLUSIONS

In summary, we contend that many well-intentioned policies--including the National Urban League's Domestic Marshall Plan, designed to help inner-city individuals and areas--may bypass them because of a number of social, economic, and political constraints. The major constraints are institutional racism, intentional discrimination, structural discrimination, exclusionary zoning, redlining, insensitive government policies, and the census undercount.

In order to revitalize inner-city areas more effectively, we recommend that the following targeting mechanisms be utilized more fully:

- Home Mortgage Disclosure Act;
- Community Reinvestment Act;
- Tax credits;
- Linkage programs;
- Public housing resident management;
- Church-based community development corporations; and
- Lawsuits to combat both intentional and unintentional discrimination.

Public Investment for Public Good: Needs, Benefits, and Financing Options

Lenneal J. Henderson, Ph.D.

INTRODUCTION

African Americans have a disproportionate stake in the nature, process, and results of federal, state, and local public policies. Historically dependent on public sector decisions for household and business income, health, education, and a variety of social services, the African American community grapples with a disintegrating economy, intractable socioeconomic dilemmas, and urban conditions whose larger context is a struggling American economy and a financially beleaguered public treasury.[1] Moreover, African Americans, now nearly 32 million of America's 248 million citizens, compete with emerging Asian, Hispanic, and Native American populations for their share of publicly sponsored programs for addressing the effects of racism and discrimination and with increasingly diverse immigrant populations who are often able to establish themselves economically and commercially much faster than African Americans.[2] The essential dilemma for America and for Black America is how to advance the economic, social, and political aspirations of African Americans in a context of declining federal, state, and local financial resources and in the worst economic conditions America has experienced since the Great Depression.[3]

This article argues that only a vigorous, coordinated, and continuous program of careful and sustained public investment, particularly in cities, can address both America's aggravated economic and fiscal condition and the complex and extensive socioeconomic challenges facing African American communities. It is further argued that not only is public investment essential for the simultaneous reclamation of America's and Black America's aspirations and potential, but also that the ultimate outcome of such investment is a more vibrant and internationally competitive economy. The complex interdependency of economic and public sector vitality requires a conception of public investment that orchestrates public and private, domestic and international, federal and local resources to produce economic gain. Economic gain results in net benefits to both the gross national product (GNP) and, consequently, to reductions in federal, state, and local government deficits.[4]

The first objective of this analysis is to generate definitions of both public investment and public goods. These definitions are considered the ultimate context in which the National Urban League's proposed Marshall Plan should be considered and advocated.[5]

The second objective is to link definitions of public investment and public goods to a national benefit framework inclusive of social, economic, and political returns to the nation. The essential empirical foundation of such analysis is that an investment in any substantial African American context, particularly increasingly large African American urban institutions, is an immediate and ultimate investment in America. Historically, the converse has not necessarily been true.

The third objective of this paper is to relate both the public investment/-public goods framework and the national benefit framework to a series of proposed financing options. These options are proposed as an answer to the questions: How should America initiate investment in Black America and who ultimately pays for such investment?

THE CONTEXT OF PUBLIC INVESTMENT IN PUBLIC GOODS

Public goods are defined multidimensionally. First, public agencies produce public goods. According to Reed and Swain, public goods display the characteristics of indivisibility, nonsubtractability, or both. Indivisibility generally means that a good cannot practically be divided up into pieces and, therefore, is generally available to all citizens nationally or within a defined geographic area. For example, national defense is presumably a public good from which all members of a nation benefit or suffer.[6]

Moreover, nonsubtractability means that one person benefiting from a public good does not subtract from or deny other citizens benefit of that same good. Public highways, bridges, tunnels, and other physical infrastructures sponsored and managed by the public sector are examples of nonsubtractability. Although the persistent legacy of racial segregation and current severe differences in the life chances of inner-city African American communities and their more affluent suburban counterparts suggest a tendency towards divisibility of public goods by race and income and some subtractability of public goods resulting from greater utilization of public goods by more affluent communities and individuals, "public" goods are theoretically available to all citizens.[7]

Another conception of public goods is offered by Nancy Smith Barrett and Paul Samuelson. Barrett characterizes public goods as "the more extreme example of an externality."[8] Given that externalities are the spillover effects of private decisions that are usually addressed by public agencies, such as air pollution, traffic congestion, and inequities in income distribution, public goods not only address externalities but also enhance decisions. Roads induce commerce. Air pollution abatement protects productive employees and arrests costly environmental degradation. National defense provides a security envelope for all productive activities.

Samuelson defines a pure public good as one for which total social consumption is the same as each citizen's consumption: another mode of arguing that a mass transit's value to any citizen represents its value to all citizens. If Y is total consumption of a public good, then:

$$Y = Y_1 = Y_2 = ... = Y_n$$

where Y_1 is consumption of the good by the *ith* individual.[9] National defense and programs to eliminate water pollution are examples of public goods and services that are available to everyone in equal amounts.[10]

The key issue is what governs public decisions about investment in public goods. Rarely are public investment criteria purely, or even primarily, articulated on the grounds of economic efficiency. Any public decision, whether about operating or capital budgets, financing programs or tax policy, is influenced by the politics of competing interest groups. The political status and efficacy of the African American community is therefore as essential as the use of economic criteria influencing public investment in those public goods that not only advance the interests of African Americans but also represent continuous net benefits to the American citizenry at large.[11]

THE FORMULATION OF A NATIONAL BENEFIT FRAMEWORK

To sustain our thesis that investment in the human and infrastructural conditions of Black America is an ultimate and immediate investment in America, it is essential to review key socioeconomic and demographic characteristics of the national African American community. Five key conditions relate to the need for inclusion of African Americans in a national Marshall Plan:

(1) The changing demography of African Americans in a national and an international context;

(2) The deepening crisis in the human resource profile of African Americans, both as a result of structural and cyclical conditions in the national economy;

(3) The increasing proportion of African Americans experiencing poverty, or near-poverty, conditions;

(4) The declining household, corporate, and public infrastructure, particularly in cities with substantial African American populations; and

(5) Overall work-force characteristics of the national African American community.

The Changing Demography of African Americans

The context for a strategy of accelerated and targeted public investment in public goods, particularly in cities, is clearly reflected in the changing demography of African Americans.

The 1990 census indicates that the African American population increased by 3.5 million between 1980 and 1990 to nearly 30 million, or 12.1 percent of the U.S. population. The Population Reference Bureau and a number of cities with substantial African American populations argue that about 5.7 percent of the African American population, or 1.5 million individuals, were undercounted in the 1990 census.[12]

Since World War II, most African Americans have moved to and reside in central cities (Table 1). Consequently, more than 20 American cities have at least 150,000 African Americans or more. In the past 20 years, many of these cities, beset with a combination of declining economies, eroding tax bases, accelerating crime, aggravated environmental problems, and an increasingly large number of female-headed, dependent populations have significantly lost white, affluent populations to the suburban areas, while an increasingly larger proportion of African Americans remain in central cities (Table 2). Although evidence indicates some suburbanization of the African American population, these populations moved to less affluent suburbs or were sparsely represented among more affluent suburbs.[13]

The movement of African Americans to the suburbs was counterbalanced by a growing concentration of blacks in high-poverty areas over the past decade. Between 1980 and 1990, the number of blacks living in high-poverty areas (defined as census tracts with at least 20 percent of the residents in poverty) increased by 19 percent, while the black population as a whole increased by 13 percent.[14] See Table 3.

The Reality of Racial Poverty

The exacerbation of African American poverty is attributable not only to structural economic conditions in the African American community but also to the economic decline in the nation as a whole. Within a ten-year period, from 1980 to 1990, America became a debtor nation with a negative balance of payments and balance of trade, a federal deficit approaching $300 billion, and a national debt approaching $4 trillion. In real dollar terms, the gross national product declined.

The Challenge of Inner-City Employment

Consequently, employment prospects for African Americans, particularly in traditionally menial and semiskilled and emerging technician and professional occupational categories, appear to have worsened within the decade.

216

Table 1
U.S. Cities with Black Populations
of 150,000 or Greater, 1990

Black Rank	Overall Rank	City, State	Total Population	Black Population	Percent Black
			(in thousands)		
1	1	New York, NY	7,322.6	2,102.5	29
2	3	Chicago, IL	2,783.7	1,087.7	39
3	7	Detroit, MI	1,028.0	777.9	76
4	5	Philadelphia, PA	1,585.6	631.9	40
5	2	Los Angeles, CA	3,485.4	487.7	14
6	4	Houston, TX	1,630.6	458.0	28
7	13	Baltimore, MD	736.0	435.8	59
8	19	Washington, DC	606.9	399.6	66
9	18	Memphis, TN	610.3	334.7	55
10	25	New Orleans, LA	496.9	307.7	62
11	8	Dallas, TX	1,006.9	297.0	30
12	36	Atlanta, GA	394.0	264.3	67
13	24	Cleveland, OH	505.6	235.4	47
14	17	Milwaukee, WI	628.1	191.3	31
15	34	St. Louis, MO	396.7	188.4	48
16	60	Birmingham, AL	266.0	168.3	63
17	12	Indianapolis, IN	742.0	165.6	22
18	15	Jacksonville, FL	673.0	163.9	24
19	39	Oakland, CA	372.2	163.3	44
20	56	Newark, NJ	275.2	160.9	59

Source: Bureau of the Census, 1991. Unpublished data from 1990 census.

Sociologist William Julius Wilson attributes the decline to the reduction in stable, higher-paying blue-collar employment in industrial cities.[15] Others focus on the movement of employment opportunities and the changing structure of employment opportunities in suburban areas of the metropolis providing fewer and more transitory job opportunities for central city African American populations.[16] Clearly, as Table 4 indicates, African American men are still substantially represented in the semiskilled labor categories while African American women are making more substantial progress in penetrating some higher paying managerial, technical, and professional occupations.

The Opportunities for Public Investment

Given these critical demographic shifts in the African American national

Table 2
Total U.S., Black, and White Populations by Metropolitan Residence, 1970–1990

	1970 Total	1970 Blacks	1970 Whites	1980 Total	1980 Blacks	1980 Whites	1990* Total	1990* Blacks	1990* Whites
Total number (in thousands)	203,212	22,581	177,749	226,546	26,495	188,372	245,992	30,332	206,853
Percent	100.0	100.0	100.0	100.0	100.0	100.0	100.0	100.0	100.0
Metropolitan areas	68.6	74.3	67.8	74.8	81.1	73.3	77.7	83.7	76.4
Central cities	31.4	58.2	27.8	29.9	57.7	24.9	30.5	56.7	26.2
Suburbs	37.2	16.1	40.0	44.8	23.3	48.4	47.2	27.0	50.2
Nonmetropolitan areas	31.4	25.7	32.2	25.2	18.9	26.7	22.3	16.3	23.6

Note: Metropolitan-nonmetropolitan area classification are as of date in question.
*Civilian, noninstitutional population as of March 1990.

Sources: 1970 Bureau of the Census, Census of Population 1970 PC (1) B1. United States Summary (Washington, DC: Government Printing Office, 1972), Table 48; 1980 Bureau of the Census, Current Population Reports, P-60, no. 168 (Washington, DC; Government Printing Office, 1990), Table 22.

community and the declining physical and household infrastructure[17] of many central cities with large African American populations, three critical public policy issues are evident. First, which public policy strategy, or combination of public policy strategies, is most appropriate to arrest this erosion of urban human and physical infrastructure?

Second, how can such a strategy address fundamental needs and priorities of the nation or be defined as beneficial to the national interest?

Table 3
Poverty Rates for Blacks, 1978–1987

	1978	1986	1987
Nationwide Poverty Rate	11.4	13.6	13.5
Blacks	30.6	31.3	33.1
Whites	8.7	11.0	10.5
Black Children			
Under Age 18	41.2	43.0	45.6
Under Age 6	42.5	45.6	49.0
Black Families			
Married Couples	11.3	10.8	12.3
Female-Headed	50.6	50.1	51.8
Young Black Families			
Head 15-24	49.0	48.6	56.7
Head 25-34	30.4	34.4	39.4
Blacks by Education			
College Education	12.6	10.9	11.2
High School Graduate	18.7	26.7	27.8
Dropout	34.2	35.4	39.4

Note: The poverty rate is defined as the percentage of individuals whose income is less than $11,611 for a family of four.

Sources: Census Bureau; Center on Budget and Policy Priorities.

Third, how will investments in urban human and physical capital be paid for, or pay for themselves, particularly given aggravated socioeconomic and criminal justice conditions in central cities?

Clearly, not only has corporate investment in central cities correlated with demographic shifts in urban African American communities, but also public, particularly federal, investment has precipitously declined. Between 1981 and 1988, for example, critical urban grant-in-aid programs suffered cumulative spending reductions totaling almost $60 billion. By contrast, during the same period, the annual increases in military spending reached a cumulative total of $328 billion.[18]

However, given the dramatic changes in the political landscapes of Eastern Europe and the Soviet Union and the oft-cited prospect of a "peace dividend" to the domestic economy resulting from reductions in military outlays, an opportunity exists to convert military spending to human and physical public investment. It is essential to emphasize that any significant reductions in domestic military installations or human resources with a concomitant conversion to domestic public investment only exacerbate conditions in urban areas.

Conversely, a recent report of the U.S. Conference of Mayors indicates that nationally, a five-year shift of $150 billion from the military budget to urban programs yields a positive net economic effect. The gross national product (GNP) would rise by an annual average of $3.5 billion. Personal disposable income would increase to $2.2 billion annually. Fixed private investment in residential and commercial construction, plants, and equipment would increase to $550 million on average each year. And, most importantly, as a result of the rise in personal income, federal, state, and local tax revenues would increase by $50 million annually. The report suggests an annual average net increase of 197,500 jobs is generated by urban, rather than military, programs and that there is a net gain of 6,600 jobs, on average, for every $1 billion shifted from military spending to urban investment.[19]

The strategy of shifting military to urban expenditures addresses fundamental needs and priorities not only of central cities but also of metropolitan areas. Given the intrinsic interdependencies of central city and metropolitan economies; given that 78 of the 160 largest central cities now have deficits; and given that many suburban communities are experiencing unprecedented deficits and consequent service and employee reductions, it is clear that a federal program of public investment in urban public goods is in the national interest and will benefit many beyond the African American community.

FINANCING OPTIONS FOR THE NATIONAL MARSHALL PLAN

A variety of immediate and longer-term options are available for financing large-scale investment in public goods, particularly in urban areas. First, it should be established that the role of the federal government in promoting investment in urban areas goes well beyond direct or supportive funding mechanisms. The federal government "frequently sets the standards which define 'needs' and which guide the type and method of construction" of infrastructure and other large-scale public investments.[20] To the extent that cities have invested in secondary wastewater treatment facilities, for example, it is clear that federal laws have mandated certain levels of water quality as well as federal assistance to help pay for these facilities. Similarly, federal standards for road construction, bridges, and other infrastructures are important in dictating state and local investment, management, construction, and maintenance practices.[21]

However, the nature and scope of financing options, particularly those of major relevance to the objective socioeconomic conditions of African Americans, depend directly on the objectives, scope, and complexity of the specific public goods communities aspire to provide. Indeed, for each financing option discussed, at least five interrelated criteria for African

American inclusion in the investment must be articulated and incorporated in the public investment mandate and strategy:

1. The incorporation[22] of the African American political community in the policy agenda-setting community into the policy agenda-setting process for public investment in public goods[23];

2. The political support of the African American community for the policy of investment and the financing strategy for its implementation;

3. The inclusion of African American enterprise in the design, development, construction, management, and maintenance of the public goods resulting from public investment strategies;

4. Targeting of public investment in public goods to the struggling central cities of the nation with a focus on the essential interrelationships between investments in physical infrastructure and parallel investment in the human infrastructure actualizing and utilizing the public goods resulting from such investments; and

5. Inclusion of African American human resources at every level of investment from the most menial to the most technical, from the most transitory employment to the most long-term engagement, and from the smallest enterprise and institution to the largest and most complex public and private organizations.

However, specific financing options for public goods investment include a variegated network of carefully orchestrated strategies inclusive of existing revenue sources, the development of large-scale capital plans and budgets, a transition to more enterprise-oriented public-private partnerships, and specific financing strategies tied to specific types of public investment. Although financing approaches may be multidimensional, their coordination is essential to articulate African American human resource capabilities and needs and to revitalize and make productive urban communities that can contribute substantially to the reduction of national economic and social deficits.

Financing Option 1: Use of Existing Fiscal Resources

Elaine S. Sharp has effectively captured the dynamic elements of urban economic and fiscal distress which, in order to be reversed, must utilize existing fiscal resources in a more effective manner. Figure 1 depicts the Sharp Schematic Model of Urban Fiscal Dilemma. Existing state and local revenue sources, such as real and personal property taxes, income taxes, excise taxes, estate and inheritance taxes, and user fees, are either saturated or near saturation.[24] Many cities cannot effectively use municipal obligation bonds, industrial revenue bonds, and other instruments of long-term capital financing because of their aggravated economic and fiscal conditions and low credit ratings. However, most cities can reform and restructure existing financing resources to handle smaller-scale investments in

Table 4: Blacks & Whites by Occupation

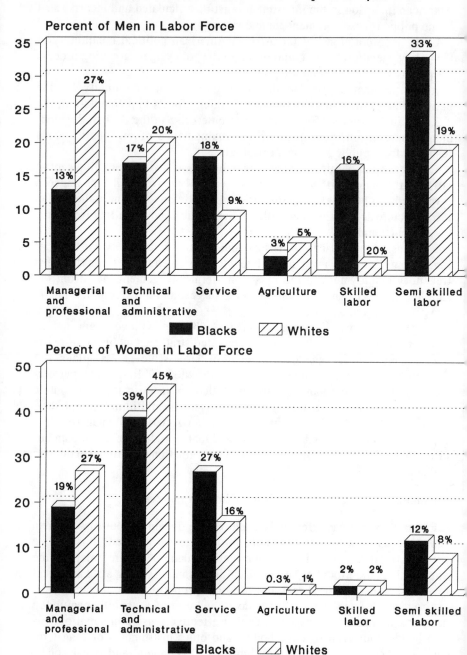

Percent of Men in Labor Force

Percent of Women in Labor Force

Source: Bureau of Labor Statistics, Employment and Earnings 38, no. 1 (1991), table 22.

Figure 1

Economic and Social Environment

Locus: Regional, National, and International Trends

Examples: Job Shifts from Frostbelt to Sunbelt

Private Sector Disinvestment in Center Cities

Change from Industrial to Post-Industrial
U.S. Economy

LEVEL 1 LONG-TERM ECONOMIC DECLINE
Locus: City's Economy and Social Character

Examples: Extent of Dependent Population (elderly, poor)
Population Loss
Job Loss

LEVEL 2 FISCAL DISTRESS
Locus: City Government Actions

Examples: Economic Development Initiatives
Spending Policies
Borrowing

LEVEL 3 FISCAL CRISIS
Locus: Immediate State of Budget

Examples: Capacity to Pay Operating Expenses
Ability to Issue Bonds

ource: Elaine S. Sharp, Urban Politics and Administration

public goods and to match better the investments of federal, state, corporate, foreign, and other sources. Clark, Ferguson, and Sharp use per capita taxes and the volume of short-term debt as a percentage of total revenues as barometers of urban fiscal health.[25] But they also suggest that the continuing groundswell of tax and expenditure reform provides an opportunity to move to the kind of fiscal restructuring that will make better use of scarce fiscal resources. Thus, better and more strategic use of existing shorter- and longer-term fiscal resources is among the financing options that can promote greater public goods investments.

Financing Option 2: Development of Large-Scale Capital Investments

Despite fiscal woes, many cities are involved individually or in collaboration with state, federal, corporate, or foreign investors in the development or improvement of airports, mass transit systems, convention centers, stadia, bridge and tunnel development, wastewater treatment systems, municipal solid-waste disposal and utilization systems, and other large-scale capital development projects. These are financed not only through municipal capital budgets but also through a variety of revenue-generating strategies, such as leasing to private and public agencies, purchase agreements, imposition of admission or user fees, and efforts to attract substantial private investment through the location and relocation of companies in the city.[26] Table 5 describes how companies rank local fiscal and other incentives when relocating their firms. Tax abatements--the deferral of property and other taxes in exchange for the location or relocation of the business to a locality--rank first. The provision of land, often through a municipal redevelopment agency at lower-than-market cost, ranks second. But clearly, a comprehensive review of the city's capital development program and strategy is essential for African Americans seeking greater opportunities to participate in the ordering and development of city infrastructure. Too often deals are concluded, frequently with outside business concerns, long before they attract the attention of the leadership of the African American community. *Thus, a review and restructuring of the capital development program of a city and state represent a second financing opportunity for channeling more investment in public goods in cities with substantial African American populations.*

Table 5

How companies rank local incentives in relocation decisions

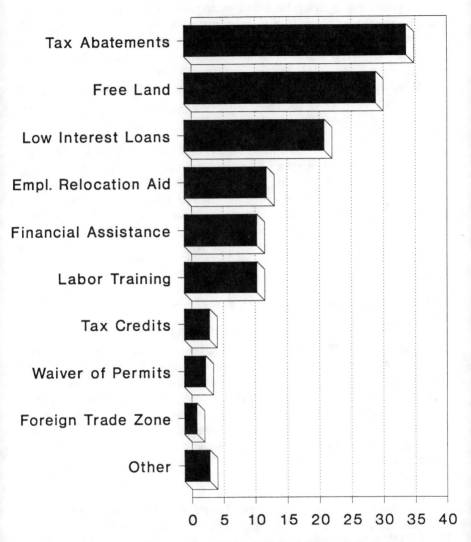

Percentage of respondents

Note: Total exceeds 100 percent due to multiple responses.
Source: *Governing*, Volume 4, Number 11, August 1991.

Financing Option 3: Dedicated "Peace Dividend" Funding

As suggested earlier, most foreign policy/international relations scenarios suggest a sharply declining need for sustaining a Cold War military infrastructure. President Bush has received the recommendations from one commission for military base and weapons-reduction priorities, and recently concluded nuclear arms accords with the Soviet Union. The downsizing of the North Atlantic Treaty Organization suggests the prospect of more than $100 billion in reduced military spending over the next five fiscal years.

A $50-60 billion dedicated Marshall Plan fund resulting from the transfer of military savings can substantially seed a renewed and vital linkage between urban human and physical public investment. Clearly, net losses to local economies resulting from the reduction or elimination of military installations or defense contracts in the United States will need to be offset by such a dedicated Marshall Plan fund not only to advance new investments in public goods but also to replace economic vitality attributable to the presence of military installations. It is important to emphasize that many of the recommended reductions in military installations and defense contracts are located in cities with substantial African American communities, such as Fort Ord, California (the neighboring city of Seaside is all African American), Philadelphia, Pennsylvania, the Washington, DC Naval Yard, and Charleston, South Carolina.[27]

Financing Option 4: Enterprise-Oriented Government

As urban communities with substantial African American populations grapple with serious energy and environmental problems, such as air and water pollution, saturated landfills, accelerating urban waste, toxic and hazardous waste, traffic congestion, radon, lead and other toxic household chemicals and materials, and rapidly rising natural gas and electric utility costs, many are considering cost-saving strategies resulting from both demand-side management and alternative production strategies. The following are examples of many of the government-sponsored enterprises urban governments have initiated with support from such organizations as Public Technology, Inc., the Joint Center for Political and Economic Studies, and Earth Island Institute in California:

(1) Municipal solid-waste disposal plants that incinerate increasing tons of waste and generate compost for direct use or sale by the city;

(2) Wastewater treatment plants focused on the development and distribution of potable water. Adjacent communities have often joined together to build and operate these facilities more cost effectively. Alternatively, special districts often manage and finance such facilities;

(3) Recycling enterprises designed to retrieve, separate, and recycle the

tons of paper, glass, metal, and other reusable materials that often litter urban communities and streets. Often, city-sponsored curbside recycling provides opportunities for small and micro-business enterprises in cities that can generate employment and business experience for thousands of African Americans;

(4) Cogeneration and district heating plants operated or jointly operated by municipalities or counties and private industry use substantial waste heat and steam as a primary, environmentally safe, energy source; and

(5) Special and paratransit systems designed to supplement transportation for the elderly, the disabled, youth, remote populations, or others in the urban community not able to access primary mass transit.

The primary financial characteristics of these enterprises include:

(1) Government sponsorship and/or direct management;

(2) Provision of initial financing from a variety of public, private, and user sources, such as sales tax increases or user fees;

(3) Use of municipal tax-exempt or deferred bonds to acquire rights-of-way, to initiate construction, and to build infrastructure for these enterprises; and

(4) Use of corporate, community development, and nonprofit vendors or contractors to provide or operate the services associated with these systems.

However, it is important to concede that many of these enterprises operate in deficits for many years before becoming profitable. But, what is essential is that they generate productive employment for thousands of urban dwellers who purchase goods and services from the metropolitan economy and they generate cost-effective alternatives to entrenched inner-city problems that provide a collective financial and human payback that can far offset both initial investments and current operating costs.

Financing Option 5: Sales of Government Assets and Use of Proceeds

The federal government generates billions of dollars annually from the sales, auctions, and leasing of real and personal property confiscated by such law enforcement agencies as the Drug Enforcement Administration; from financial recovery mechanisms such as government loan repayments and Resolution Trust Fund proceeds; and from revenues and royalties generated from severance taxes, leases, and other uses of federal property.

A relatively small percentage of these proceeds dedicated to investments in urban public goods could substantially initiate the national Marshall Plan. What more appropriate retribution for the confiscation of real and personal property acquired from drug distribution, particularly in inner cities ravaged by African American drug use, guns proliferation, and accelerating homicides than to reinvest such monies in the restoration of the human and physical capital of these communities!

Given increasingly severe federal, state, and local budgets, large-scale public investments in public goods generation may be limited. A viable alternative is a renewed effort to channel corporate and foreign investment in central cities through clear, tangible, and immediate tax relief. Clearly, current tax laws tend to work against such investments. From a cost-benefit perspective, net short-term loss of revenue from such abatement is very likely to be offset by the longer-term generation of employment and economic and infrastructural vitality.

SUMMARY, CONCLUSIONS, AND RECOMMENDATIONS

This paper argues that vigorous investment in the development and expansion of public goods, particularly in urban communities with substantial African American populations, is a direct, immediate, and significant investment in America's own economic and political revival. Continuous net benefits accrue to the millions of businesses from which an increased African American disposable income, business presence, and economic vitality will inexorably purchase goods and services.

The vital linkage among the public policy strategies for advancing public investment in urban public goods; strategies for addressing chronic and extensive socioeconomic, criminal, and other problems in African American urban communities; and options for financing such strategies requires the bold commitment and articulation reflected in the National Urban League's proposed Marshall Plan.

Despite the expanding economic recession/depression and spiraling federal, state, and local fiscal woes, viable financing options are available that provide resources for higher public investment in urban public goods, which gradually decrease the financial dependency of urban populations on government.

Consequently, specific recommendations include:

(1) The adoption of a national Marshall Plan by the Congress and President Bush, which dedicates the nation to higher levels and more types of public investment in public goods as the engine of American economic revival;

(2) Renewed efforts by state and local governments to not only restructure to make more productive existing fiscal resources but also to focus such resources on the reduction of dependent urban populations through the employment generated by investment in public goods;

(3) Modification of current and projected large-scale capital plans and programs to incorporate more directly and substantially African American human, business, educational, and professional resources;

(4) Direct conversion of savings from military expenditures to public

investment in urban public goods. An essential corollary is the need to actually reduce military costs given changing global conditions and changing U.S. roles in those conditions;

(5) Extended use of local government enterprises to stimulate and make more cost effective the need to address environmental, energy, and transportation problems clearly at the heart of many urban ills; and

(6) Modification of the Tax Reform Act of 1986 and related statutes to provide a national direct tax incentive to stimulate concentrated corporate investment in the urban human and physical infrastructure.

Public-Private Partnerships: Prospects for America . . . Promise for African Americans

In Wood County, West Virginia, students in five separate high schools are taught third-year German from one highly qualified teacher through a fiber-optic network that allows total interaction among students in all five schools. In Dallas, Texas, 425 construction and 800 hotel jobs are created, precipitating a 2,700 percent increase in the tax base. In San Jose, California, 4,800 trained individuals are placed in jobs, saving an estimated $6 million in unemployment benefits and welfare. In Scottsdale, Arizona, a private company has provided fire suppression services for the city and surrounding communities at half the national per capita cost of governmental fire departments.

These success stories are the results of public-private partnerships in those communities and represent the basis for the contention that, while not a panacea for the nation's ills, partnerships are a step in the right direction for America.

For the African American community, public-private partnerships offer a promising means of empowerment--in the areas of housing, education, jobs/job-training and social services. For African Americans, they hold real promise for the future--a promise of an intrinsic, valuable role in the shaping of our local community and economic status.

Public-private partnerships, at their best, have larger societal goals that are trying to be achieved even while the partnership addresses a specific problem. Further, public-private partnerships are stewards of the democratic process, for they challenge communities, states, and the nation to fulfill the mandate of providing equal participation and equal partnership in all aspects of democratic living. The more African Americans are able to participate in public-private partnerships, the more we are a part of that democratic process.

The greatest benefit of the partnership relationship for African Americans comes from the very fact that, in this activity, we have an equal role in building communities.

We still live in a very racist society. Frequently, African Americans are excluded from the real economic and political decision making. For most African Americans and African American communities, the question is-- how do we get to the table?

231

The future success of this country depends on the effective engagement and appreciation of its diversity. Partnerships with economic agendas are needed to stem the tide of the racial hate being fed by the projected demographics of the year 2000 (when 43 percent of the work force will be comprised of minorities) to the people who wish to stay in power and not share it. Partnerships are also vehicles for building trust. Those who participate as equals in them view race problems differently because they have been helped to see issues from another base of understanding brought about through partnership dynamics.

For example, in an urban city, the police computer identified policemen wanting to get together and go out that night and kill "niggers." Except for a small reprimand, the police chief and others in authority chose to do little about the incident. Once the community learned of this, there was outrage expressed by those involved in the partnership involving all three sectors. The group gave the following response: "Up with this we will not put." Because of the level of understanding and trust that had been built among members of the partnership, they were able to respond on behalf of the community, resulting in the policemen's dismissal. This situation provides evidence that public-private partnerships can and do make a difference.

Solutions to problems must be made in cooperation with the people most affected by those problems. The problems of African Americans--problems ranging from affordable housing to job training and creation to quality social services and education--have all proven themselves solvable by the application of the partnership principle. Working together--in cooperative partnership--is an effective community tool with which to confront these problem areas.

Economic empowerment is a key aim. For a partnership to fulfill its defined goal--to "contribute to the benefit of the broader community," it is imperative that efforts to battle a specific problem emphasize the strengths and abilities of the local community. Public-private partnerships must seek to strengthen the African American community's investment through leadership roles, economic empowerment, and consequently, a self-sustaining future.

PARTNERSHIPS AT A GLANCE

Another success story involves Columbia Commons Apartments in Columbia, Maryland, a 200-unit mixed-use project developed jointly by the Enterprise Foundation, Shelter Development Corporation, and the Federal National Mortgage Association (Fannie Mae). Each one-, two-, or three-bedroom apartment in the $14.83 million project is outfitted with a washer and dryer, fully applianced kitchen, and window treatments. Residents have access to the clubhouse with exercise room as well as to an outdoor swimming pool. Market rental rates for 150 of these apartments, located as they are in affluent Howard County, will range from $590 to $890 per month.

The remaining 50 units, however, will rent between $322 to $433 per month, according to Shelter Properties director of marketing Patrick Duffy. "The apartments are priced at rents so that people who work at modest paying professions in Howard County can afford to live near where they work," he explained.

Funding for the apartment complex came from tax-exempt bonds issued by the Howard County Government and the Maryland Community Development Administration as well as from a $1.28 million investment by Fannie Mae. The project is jointly managed by the Enterprise Social Investment Corporation (a subsidiary of the Enterprise Foundation) and Shelter Development.[1]

At the dedication ceremony for this venture, James W. Rouse, chairman of the Enterprise Foundation, said, "The Columbia Commons development is a perfect example of how the public and private sectors of a community can join efforts and resources to provide superior housing for all its residents." This cooperation among public agencies, private foundations, and businesses to provide reasonably priced housing is a classic example of public-private partnership. Such partnerships have a recorded history of success in tackling--and solving--critical socioeconomic issues. They have matured from a period where they were limited almost exclusively to implementing federal programs to their current status, in which community organizations, businesses, and government entities cooperatively utilize partnerships to work for the common good as defined by membership-driven agendas.

Partnerships are viable mechanisms for change in economic development, neighborhoods, and social services. Partnerships, particularly in urban settings (which obviously affect African Americans), have revitalized communities, provided countless new jobs, and created vital, working centers in areas that were once condemned as unsafe and unlivable.

Within the partnership relationship, grassroots organizations and self-help initiatives have gained new prominence and respect. Public-private partnerships intensify the strengths of its member groups, build relationships and a civic infrastructure that can carry over to other community challenges and/or ventures, and open avenues of communications and trust among divergent sectors of the populace. An obstacle to this communication and trust is the fact that, although African Americans are not monolithic, other Americans frequently bring to the partnership table a historical perspective that stereotypes African Americans. It is this perspective that must be erased if a partnership is to develop as a viable entity.

For African American citizens, as well as the entire populace, public-private partnerships are an effective means of initiating positive action to address challenging socioeconomic problems. Because we live in a society where issues are more complicated and resources are scarce, the partnership concept allows organizations to direct available resources more purpose-fully, while at the same time, take advantage of the expertise of each individual member. Partnerships do, in effect, draw on and magnify the strengths of all sectors to address a single problem.

DEFINING PUBLIC-PRIVATE PARTNERSHIPS

The term "public-private partnership" first surfaced in the late 1970s during the Carter Administration to describe ventures between federal programs and private organizations. In those early days, the public sector of such partnerships was, almost exclusively, the federal government, and the joint efforts were looked upon primarily as a ready means to supplement or implement federal programs, usually within urban neighborhoods.[2]

Contemporary partnerships, in contrast, are more apt to involve a state or local government, and are, in fact, sometimes entered into due to the dearth of federal money. The partnership concept itself has matured over time to a point where current partnerships often employ mechanisms like loans, leases, or information sharing--notions that were unheard of 20 years ago.[3]

The partnership relationship has also gained complexity--and a greater scope--with the advent of intermediaries. Launched in the early 1980s, intermediary groups, either local or national, coalesce the partnership prin-ciple by providing new funding streams, technical assistance, and new means of coordinating private efforts with public potential.[4]

In the past 15 years or so, partnerships have become more structured. There are new mechanisms—financial intermediaries like the Local Initia-tives Support Corporation (LISC) and the Enterprise Foundation--that, in fact, are able to attract private money and re-grant or loan it to nonprofit organizations (mostly CDCs--community development corporations) to do projects primarily involving housing.

But if the nomenclature and the mechanics are new, the concept of a cooperative effort between government and private citizens is an old one. There has been a major public-private sector relationship in the delivery of social services before and since the New Deal. In these partnerships, the public sector uses its funds to contract with nonprofit social service organi-zations to deliver services that can better be delivered by private rather than public institutions.

In its 1982 landmark study, the Committee for Economic Development (CED) defined modern day "public-private partnership" as "cooperation among individuals and organizations in the public and private sectors for mutual benefit."[5]

A public-private partnership, the CED study further explains, consists of two primary dimensions: the **policy dimension**, which articulates the goals of the community, and the **operational dimension**, in which these goals are pursued. The purpose of a partnership is "to link these dimensions in such a way that the participants contribute to the benefit of the broader community while promoting their own individual or organizational interests."[6]

A public-private partnership is usually a cooperative venture between private or nonprofit entities and government institutions or programs, most commonly in the areas of housing and economic development.

If the partnerships of the latter twentieth century differ from their predecessors in maturation, they also differ in structure, particularly within the housing area. Massive amounts of nonprofit development geared to closing the side gap of affordable low- and moderate-income housing have attracted the investments of for-profit corporations. These public, private, and corporation or for-profit roles could be the components for many of the future public-private partnerships.

Virtually all the literature concurs on one salient point in their definitions of public-private partnerships: *cooperation.* By cooperating, by contributing to the benefit of the broader community, public-private partnerships offer the distressed urban neighborhood, the homeless, the hard-to-employ, and, most importantly, every citizen a constructive method of marshalling a variety of important resources to work toward a goal--one that will improve the quality of individual lives.

THE ROLE OF VOLUNTEERISM IN PUBLIC-PRIVATE PARTNERSHIPS

Although the concept of public-private partnerships might have originated in the bureaucratic halls of the federal government, it is with individual citizens that the concept becomes reality.

Americans give--whether it is for the local PTA or for a national cause --both monetarily and of themselves. In fact, individuals represent approximately 90 percent of all charitable giving. Fully three-fourths of American families contribute to charities and causes, giving an average of $790 a year. And approximately one-half of all adult Americans average 4.7 hours per week as active volunteers, while 23 million Americans volunteer five or more hours per week.[7] Personal giving and volunteering are growing assets, serving schools, churches, and, in particular, public-private partnerships.

Self-help is at the root of public-private partnerships, since it is these same grassroots organizations that convince, coax, and cajole public organizations to invest in projects for the public good. In fact, it is this spirit of self-determination that has provided much of the major impetus behind the public-private partnerships of the last few years.

Self-help, too, is one of America's oldest and proudest traditions, wrote

Talton Ray in his introduction to *Enterprising Communities* by Neal R. Peirce and Carol F. Steinbach.[8] It is a tradition that is manifested today in the revival of grassroots organizations designed by citizens to renew and improve their local communities, be it through housing renovation, social service projects, and/or involvement with the public school system.

Self-help organizations are often the catalysts that bring together public and private organizations to work for a common goal. They are the cohesive segment of the partnership that provides an effective mechanism for tapping the knowledge and motivation of local residents. Once the need or the project is determined, self-help groups turn to foundations and businesses to provide important sources of money, expertise, and organizational skills, and to government to provide financial incentives, i.e., grants, loans, and/or tax credits or exemptions.[9]

These organizations, community based, exist in all 50 states. Their effectiveness can be measured; a survey of only 834 groups (fewer than one-half the number in existence today) showed that they had:

- produced nearly 125,000 units of housing and repaired an additional 275,000 units;
- developed 16.4 million square feet of retail office space, offices, and industrial parks in economically distressed communities;
- made loans to more than 2,000 enterprises; and
- created or retained close to 90,000 jobs in the last five years.[10]

It is obvious, therefore, that the volunteer sector can make government more responsive and efficient, and that it can catalyze partnership efforts between the public and private sectors. But it is over-simplification to exaggerate exactly what this sector can, and should, be expected to do. Brian O'Connell, founding president of INDEPENDENT SECTOR, said: "Voluntary organizations are approximately 10 percent the economic size of all governments in the United States, but if their money and other assets are efficiently utilized, these organizations have impacts far beyond their proportionate size. On the other hand, if these groups are called upon to do what governments no longer feel they can do or to supplement what governments do, their 10 percent will gradually become just a shadow of governmental functions."[11]

A public-private partnership is established to create a more competent vehicle for change within a given situation. It is not created to shift the burden of responsibility from one agency to another. If the volunteer spirit is to be utilized to its fullest potential, volunteer groups must not be overburdened with responsibility that, ultimately, belongs to government.[12]

THE CORPORATE ROLE IN PUBLIC-PRIVATE PARTNERSHIPS

As mentioned earlier, today's partnerships often merge three, rather than two, diverse sectors. Along with the traditional public and nonprofit partners, many cooperative efforts include the influence and capital of the private, for-profit sector as well. Especially in the cities, where public and private organizations are attempting to infuse new life into decaying neighborhoods and fragile economic systems, the input of the corporate community, with its wealth of funds and expertise, is a welcomed addition. According to a survey by the New School for Social Research in New York, the private business sector provides 15 percent of the funding for local development groups, making it the third largest investor in community development.[13]

For corporations, the partnership relationship marries good business with good citizenship. Motivated by profit, the corporate sector also seeks to acquire long-term assets, to energize the local market, and to give something back to the community by allying itself with the public and nonprofit sectors.[14]

For some corporations, support for community-based initiatives has traditionally taken the form of charitable contributions. In the last ten years or so, corporations have demonstrated an interest in supplementing their charity with investments in programs (often through intermediaries like LISC, the Local Initiatives Support Corporation) that are designed to achieve social objectives. And a few have made the ultimate business commitment --locating their facilities in business parks managed by community groups.[15]

Observers, however, have noted a disturbing trend. Plummeting profits, new CEOs, and a wave of leveraged buyouts and mergers lead some to fear that corporate entities may reduce their support. More than 300 executives told pollster Daniel Yankelovich in the fall of 1988 that uncertainties about the future threaten their corporate giving.[16]

APPLICATIONS OF PUBLIC-PRIVATE PARTNERSHIPS

Public-private partnerships have the most direct impact on three primary areas of urban life (a life in which African Americans comprise a large number): the local economy, neighborhoods, and social services.[17] According to the Center for Employment Training (CET), future job training efforts must concentrate on those groups most in need--primarily minorities and women. By the year 2000, the CET estimates that African Americans and Hispanics together will account for 43 percent of the work force.[18]

Each area benefits from and, indeed, often requires public input, and each is an area where a combination of public and private support serves to enhance the final productivity.

"Economic development today requires conscious effort by local government and private sector organizations to retain existing businesses, to facilitate the openings of new businesses, to attract outside investment, to create jobs for local residents (with special attention to training and placement of the hard-to-employ), and to foster a climate supportive of business expansion that is compatible with other community goals," emphasizes CED's report on public-private partnerships.[19]

One example of a partnership effort designed to foster positive economic growth is the Dallas, Texas' Reunion project, a 50-acre downtown development--including a hotel, municipal sports arena, parks, pedestrian walkways, roads, and public parking--jointly entered into by the city of Dallas and the Woodbine Development Corporation in 1973. Phase I public costs, provided by revenue bonds and sports arena options, came to approximately $35.5 million, while private costs, furnished by Equitable Life and First National Bank of Dallas, totaled $75 million.

As a result of this partnership, 425 construction jobs and 800 hotel jobs were created; the tax base increased 2,700 percent; and a hotel occupancy tax netted $200,000 annually. Along with these primary benefits, downtown Dallas saw increased utilization of nearby public facilities, collateral development, and increased convention business.[20]

It is not enough, however, to stimulate economic development without addressing the issues of job training and job creation. Job training should closely coordinate with other economic development initiatives.[21] One must also accept the challenge of matching training with available jobs. The CED, addressing that point, recommends offering businesses incentives to give first consideration to local residents when hiring.[22]

It is crucial that job training programs address these issues if they are to succeed. Since its inception in 1967, the Center for Employment Training (CET) in San Jose, California, has provided a job training program that has successfully placed 4,800 alumni at corporations such as Hewlett-Packard, Xerox, and Amdahl. Graduates from 1989 alone earned $32 million in 1990--and saved the government more than $6 million in welfare and unemployment payments.[23] CET's program, with an average cost per student of $5,500, is paid for largely by government grants and corporate donations.[24]

Although its typical student has not completed the eighth grade, CET's comprehensive training program "graduates" 85 percent of its students, and of those, 90 percent find employment in jobs for which they were trained.[25]

CET contends that this nation will be able to meet its future labor needs only if it commits itself to developing fully its human resources. "Like it or not," the Center says, "employers, governments, and training agents are forced to serve a highly needy population. Training programs must drop stringent prerequisites and instead develop effective methods for teaching not only vocational skills, but also basic skills, language skills, and job readiness skills. CET's experience indicates that even complex vocational skills can be taught to functionally illiterate persons if sufficient resources are made available."[26]

Neighborhoods

It is within neighborhoods, particularly in the area of urban housing, that public-private partnerships have blossomed as an effective mechanism for collaboration among neighborhood groups, businesses, nonprofit organizations, and government. Community self-help organizations, often in the form of community-based development corporations, offer these partnerships firsthand knowledge of the needs and motivations of local citizens. Social institutions, foundations, and businesses bring funding, expertise, and organizational skills to the partnership relationship, while government provides financial incentives in the form of grants, loans, and tax credits or exemptions.[27]

Neighborhood revitalization in Baltimore, Maryland, is due, in part, to the efforts of the Baltimore Corporation for Housing Partnerships (BCHP)--the corporate entity of the Baltimore Housing Partnership. BCHP is a nonprofit organization established in 1984 in an effort to produce affordable homes, primarily through rehabilitation of existing inner-city properties, for low- and moderate-income families. With a board of directors comprised of business leaders, BCHP works with city agencies and community groups to strengthen neighborhoods and replenish housing throughout Baltimore.[28]

According to its 1991 annual report, BCHP has produced 361 homes for low- and middle-income families at an estimated value of over $17 million. Along with this, the Baltimore organization has worked to perfect its ability to tap public sources of creative financing for every phase of real estate development, including mortgaging. This past year, it has also put real effort into learning how to work successfully with state and city agencies.[29]

Among its 1991 accomplishments, BCHP is currently participating in a state-funded pilot lease-purchase program, which is designed for people who need extra help to buy and keep their own homes. Working with Adopt-a-House, Inc., as well as with the state, this program will cover 40 houses when it is fully operational, and could be expanded if the pilot proves successful.

In brief, the lease-purchase program works as follows: BCHP acquires and renovates a house, then rents it to a qualified individual who agrees to purchase it at the end of a two-year lease. These homebuyers, individuals whose credit records would ordinarily bar them from homeownership, agree in turn to receive financial counseling, to improve their credit worthiness, and to attend BCHP workshops.[30]

Social Services

Many urban communities have trouble providing adequate public coverage of such basic utilities as transportation, education, waste management, and public safety. At the same time, many private entities, both nonprofit and for-profit, cite inadequate mass transit, understaffed schools, unsanitary conditions, and excessive crime as deterrents to locating and/or doing business in the cities.[31] It would seem that the social services could only benefit from a cooperative effort.

While governments have the responsibility to protect public health, safety, and welfare, contends the CED, it does not necessarily have to provide the appropriate service itself. Rather, governments should consider alternatives to conventional public service agencies in carrying out their mandated policies.[32]

The CED emphasizes that "local governments should distinguish between the role of policymaker and that of service provider and should consider more actively alternatives to conventional public-service agencies in carrying out their policies."[33]

In Scottsdale, Arizona, for example, a widely publicized private company provides fire-suppression services by contract to the city and surrounding communities at a cost that is about one-half the national per capita cost of government fire departments. Through sparing use of well-trained personnel--including part-time fire fighters, effective use of technology, and other cost-cutting measures, this private company offers citizens a high-quality service for less than a comparable local public sector implementation.[34]

In the field of education, public school systems have discovered that a partnership with the private sector can extend their limited resources and offer students educational opportunities beyond that of the conventional classroom. In Maryland and Virginia, the District of Columbia, and the city of Baltimore, for instance, junior and senior high school students join educators from the Chesapeake Bay Foundation (CBF) for one-day field trips along the Bay and its tributaries as part of the schools' science and environmental education curricula.

During the 1990-91 school year, the public schools' contract with the foundation accounted for approximately 36 percent of the education program costs. Through grants from foundations, corporations, and private donors, CBF defrayed the remainder of the fees. For the school systems, this program offers students a hands-on, on-the-water experience with qualified instructors that would otherwise be unavailable. For CBF, the program provides an opportunity to educate future generations to protect and save the Chesapeake Bay.

In Wood County, West Virginia, the school system has a partnership with businesses and the community. The school system did not have the money to provide advanced placement and study of foreign languages, math, and sciences in all five high schools in the county. For example, there was not enough money to hire a teacher for a third-year German class for each high school. Transportation alone was time and cost prohibitive. In cooperation with the Chamber of Commerce and a technology company, an interactive fiber-optic network was created and paid for by a community fund drive. Through the use of monitors, this network permitted students in any high school to see and hear the teacher as well as hear the student responding or asking a question. An electronic graphics board broadcast this information to the other participating classrooms. This enabled school systems personnel to offer advanced placement math, science, and language courses to students throughout the county.

In another county, a junior high school principal, teachers, and counselors identified 17 "at risk" students who, without intervention, would drop out of school at 16 years of age. The team determined that these students needed adult friends to care about them and participate in activities with them. They sought the help of the local power company. The executives were reluctant to present the offer to their employees because the personal commitment and responsibility were too great. However, they took the challenge to the company's employees. Seventeen adults were recruited and trained by the school. The employees began by helping the students with homework and celebrating birthdays. In time, they were taking the students to events. All 17 students graduated from high school and some went on to college. While the official commitment was made for the junior high years only, the adults maintained the relationships on their own through high school and college. At the same time, they worked with other students coming into junior high school. The drop-out rate continued to decrease, illustrating the power of personal involvement.

In other school systems across the country, partnerships are providing mentors/tutors for students, staff development for teachers, and administrative support for the schools. The partnerships with schools are only considered partnerships when people from all sectors are involved, power is shared, and financial/material resources are brought to the partnerships after people are engaged and are employed.

THE BENEFITS OF PUBLIC-PRIVATE PARTNERSHIPS

As the preceding examples demonstrate, public-private partnerships hold great potential for positive outcomes. Yet, even beyond the successful resolutions of a specific program or project, a partnership offers many benefits to its members and to the wider community.

Public-private partnerships force government, businesses/corporations, and community leaders/organizations to see their work in a larger context-- that of building communities. When working at their optimum, public- private partnerships bring about an equality of voice, provide leverage for change, and generate the power to move communities forward.

Within successful partnerships, bonds are forged between members and organizations that can far outlast one particular collaboration. A true partnership builds relationships that can be carried over to meet other challenges. By establishing an atmosphere of mutual trust and cooperation in one situation, the potential is there to extend this civic infrastructure to work for other issues too.

The very mechanics of the partnership relationship--determining common goals, working through conflict, formulating workplans, and establishing leadership--serve to strengthen each member. Partnerships create, by their very structure, a network of communications and working relationships that can have far-reaching benefits for the local community.

In the partnership alliance, the nonprofit independent sector is granted the opportunity to work cooperatively with other members, while for-profit corporations have the chance to see their work and their role in the economic life of a community within the larger context of society as a whole.

In addition to the direct need for qualified, trainable potential hirees, companies also recognize that the quality of education will determine the economic vitality of the community. Thus, a company will be less prone to have its lobbyist work against reform initiatives in education because it will better understand the link between what it is trying to achieve in the partnership with actions taken on behalf of the company in other arenas.

By broadening community access, partnerships push government to be responsible and accountable for what it can do, while allowing others to realize that government cannot do everything.

These few pages present an overview of public-private partnerships and their strengths, weaknesses, and prospects for success. For African Americans, the partnership of the public and private sectors affords an important vehicle for change, but only if the members remain true to the basic principles of the partnership relationship.

But if a partnership is to prove a viable alternative for beleaguered African Americans, particularly within urban communities, it must be a partnership that stems from grassroots initiatives. Experience has indicated that partnerships work when those affected are intimately involved. Equal community involvement is mandatory, as well as is the recognition by all partners of the importance of the community sector within the infrastructure.

FACTORS FOR SUCCESS

A successful partnership of the public and private sectors must necessarily incorporate certain basic tenets. It is not the amount of capital invested nor the national presence of the contributors that makes for a successful venture. Rather, success is determined in large part by the following factors.

A Shared Interest and Atmosphere of Mutual Respect

As emphasized above, a public-private partnership is a cooperative undertaking, one that requires a meeting of the collaborators in an atmosphere of trust. The partners must recognize that understanding the perspectives of those contributing is critical to the overall success of the program that has been designed to address the problem. The process of building the partnership is as important as--or more important than--the outcome.

Appreciation of the complementary roles of the various partners within a given relationship is also important. Given the different structure and nature of public institutions versus those of private institutions, there needs to be a clear understanding of the various ways in which the partners contribute to and are involved in the partnership.

Each partner, be it government, nonprofit organization, or corporation, brings to the partnership relationship certain specific strengths. To be truly successful, a partnership relationship must blend and utilize these strengths to their fullest, thereby gaining a final product--a partnership--that is stronger and more effective than each of the separate parts.

A Membership-Driven Process and Agenda

To borrow from *The Community Collaboration Manual*, written by the National Assembly of National Voluntary Health and Social Welfare Organizations, a successful partnership, like a successful collaboration, requires that all participants acknowledge and clarify their needs and that the group as a whole work to meet those needs.[35]

Along with this, a public-private partnership must encourage, within each partner, a sense of ownership in the project. This ownership evolves naturally when, from the very beginning of the proposed joint venture, all interested parties are included to determine goals, to set objectives, and to devise procedures. Participation in the formulation of the plan provides an accurate reflection of the capabilities and aspirations of the members, while it gives each a personal stake in the success of the eventual partnership.[36]

Effective Leadership

Individuals with entrepreneurial ability make the best partners--and therefore, potentially the best leaders--within public-private partnerships. According to the CED, "An entrepreneur is someone with a vision of what can be achieved and the skill, energy, and determination to accomplish it. A civic entrepreneur is someone who applies that gift for his/her community."[37]

In a meeting before the 1986 Annual Conference of the Council on Foundations, Fletcher L. Byrom, Chairman of the Public Education Fund and retired Board Chairman of the Koppers Company, emphasized this point about effective leadership: "Leadership is not decision making. It's the enabling of other people to make better decisions than they would have made if you hadn't been around."[38]

It is imperative, however, in public-private partnerships, that potential leaders not be overlooked because members assume that only seasoned veterans can offer needed leadership skills. Leadership training is a vital component of the partnership process--especially in those partnerships involving grassroots organizations that must reach a measure of self-determination. The leader of the partnership must create a culture that enables and motivates the partnership to fulfill its mission. The leader, while traditionally a public or business official, can be and is being replaced by capable local nonprofit community executives. In contemporary partnerships, there is a much wider focus of interest and goals, requiring more people, especially those with a vested interest in the outcome, for implementation.

Flexibility and Accountability

Working together necessitates a high degree of adaptability on the part of the members, as each must give up some of his or her individual power to reach consensus and to create a viable entity from disparate groups. In order to approach realistically the process of consensus, the group should, first of all, agree upon a shared operating procedure. It must then work to devise tangible, short-term results that will demonstrate the success of the partnership venture. Finally, it should include mechanisms for conflict resolution and negotiation.

Partnerships exist to provide specific outcomes and results. By creating a method of accountability during the initial phases of policy determination, all involved parties will have a concrete base from which to assess success or failure. If the partners are to work in harmony, and if future partnerships are to be viable alternatives, it is imperative that success or failure be the shared responsibility of all involved.

244

To borrow once more from *The Community Collaboration Manual,* a public-private partnership, like a collaboration, benefits from the richness that comes from a group of racially and culturally diverse members. To be truly successful--especially because so many of these partnerships focus on urban areas where such diversity is a fact of life--a partnership of the public and private sectors must recognize the commonality and points of view of all racial and ethnic groups involved.[39]

Participants must discard preconceptions that will hinder the cooperative venture; to better understand the language, customs, and values of each member, they must open themselves. At the same time, they will often discover new arenas of creative ideas and strength in diversity.[40]

There appears to be consensus around the following factors needed to actualize an effective partnership: (1) a clearly articulated mission (jointly formulated and agreed to) that serves as the focal point of the commitment for the members of the partnership; (2) leadership that creates a culture enabling and motivating the partnership to fulfill its mission; (3) people at the table who can make decisions for multiple constituencies involved; (4) community leaders (in addition to decision makers for government/ corporation/nonprofit organizations involved); (5) a mechanism for communicating consistently; (6) a plan (process to achieve common vision that was jointly formulated and agreed to by members of the partnership); (7) staff; (8) broker/intermediary; (9) mechanism for conflict resolution; and (10) ongoing evaluation in order to make corrective actions as necessary.

POTENTIAL PROBLEMS

Problems can and do arise in the reality of public-private partnerships, combining as they do separate entities of divergent needs and history. Problems can and do arise when members of the partnership come to the table as unequals and when members assume relationships similar to those between parents and children. It may easily move from a partnership to an exercise in negotiation with individuals lining up on either side of the issues if care is not taken to ensure equality of participation and agreement on the goal.

Members of a partnership that aspires to be around for a while and have real viability must divorce themselves from the partisan interests of the public partners. At the same time, partnerships initiated by a national organization must be facilitated in such a way that its own parochial interests are not the dominating factor. A partnership must be based upon a set of interests that are local and genuine--not the institutional needs of an organization.

There are enormous gains being made by both nonprofits and for-profits. There is a serious need for monitoring and checking; oversight is important in order to prevent the partnership from being cheated out of the resources it has accrued.

While many applaud the self-reliance that the public-private partnership model fosters in grassroots organizations, others contend that the mechanism can be easily misused. The cooperative effort of a partnership can never supplant government responsibility. A public-private partnership is neither a complete substitute for government programs nor a complete answer to social needs.[41] It is important that partnership members--potential members--address the question: where does public responsibility end and private begin? Partnership--while a practical mechanism to enhance the limited power and resources of government--cannot, and should not, be called upon to do what government no longer feels it can do.

Internally, partnerships can encounter problems for a variety of reasons. Among those most detrimental to the successful partnership are:

- too broad an agenda;
- no clearly understood goals;
- an unbalanced relationship or weak partner;
- a lack of unifying leadership; and
- problems with resources (e.g., a project requires more funds than those available, partners disagree as to source and/or displacement of funds, public funding cuts).

The ultimate success or failure of a partnership relationship depends upon how committed each partner is to ironing out these or other potentially problematic situations that might arise within a given situation.

PROSPECTS FOR THE FUTURE

Historically, public-private partnerships have confirmed both their durability and their flexibility. New mechanisms, like the emergence of intermediaries, demonstrate the partnership's adaptability to the changing needs of society and its institutions.

"Public-private partnerships are a natural endeavor, one which flows very logically out of the needs of low- and moderate-income communities in cities," stated Talton Ray. "They are a natural growth of a policy which recognizes that cooperation is essential, and I don't see that recognition diminishing over time."[42]

Depending on public leadership, the growth of nonprofits, and the availability of public financial resources, we will see a shift in emphasis, not a decline in partnerships. The future mechanism for addressing community needs will be public-private partnerships because of their ability to adapt.

However, "before nonprofits, government, and corporations can truly collaborate, the nation will have to emerge from the 'political gridlock' and social 'paralysis' in which it finds itself," said Rockefeller's Peter Goldmark. He suggested that the nation was approaching a "renegotiation of its social contract, or its sense of shared values and common responsibilities."[43]

It is safe to assume that public-private partnerships, having survived infancy and matured into their adolescent years, will persist to reap the rewards of a ripe old age as long as organizations entering into partnership relationships are willing to work cooperatively to reach a consensus and to implement a common, shared goal. It may be that public-private partnerships at their best could be a form of that new social contract.

CONCLUSIONS

Public-private partnerships are still somewhat in their infancy when it comes to attacking social, economic, and political challenges of this society. The successes seem small when one looks at the magnitude of the problems. But, the only way to tackle them is one small success at a time until we embrace the whole nation. We must stay vigilant in our efforts until desired changes in the quality of life are made for every community, every state, and the nation.

Public-private partnerships offer opportunities for segments of our society for whom there has been little cause for hope. But if they are to fulfill their greater potential as builders of communities, individual members must meet around, not on opposite sides of, the partnership table. They must accept the mantle of responsibility for the partnership relationship, a mantle that presupposes their willingness to work jointly, to learn from their mistakes, and to strive toward the common good.

For the African American community, public-private partnerships are a means of empowerment where we live and work--a means of economic empowerment if the agendas also focus on the needs and concerns of African Americans in the local economy (e.g., entrepreneurs, employment, income, etc.).

We can no longer afford parent-child relationships to exist between governments/businesses and the African American communities. The challenges of businesses, governments, and communities are interdependent. All must share equally in the problems and their solutions in order to bring about desired changes.

Public-private partnerships are effective mechanisms for conducting community business across America. For African Americans, these partnerships provide the access for an equal role in building and saving our communities.

Interagency and Intergovernmental Coordination: New Demands for Domestic Policy Initiatives

Henry A. Coleman, Ph.D.

INTRODUCTION AND OVERVIEW

The National Urban League (NUL) has proposed a domestic Marshall Plan for America (MPA) to restore the international competitiveness of the U.S. economy and to improve the employment prospects for disadvantaged Americans, including many African Americans and other residents of the nation's urban areas. This MPA envisions ". . . a comprehensive, sustained, well-financed investment program in human resources and infrastructure development . . ."[1]

The MPA has several key components, including:

1. a set of human-resource initiatives designed to increase the employability and long-run productivity of the U.S. work force, especially potential new entrants;

2. a set of physical infrastructure initiatives designed to upgrade the nation's support system, to provide an employment stimulant, and to enable the United States to compete more effectively in international markets;

3. a price tag of $500 billion (allocated at $50 billion a year for ten years) above current levels of spending; and

4. a Cabinet-level administrator to facilitate coordination among federal agencies in the implementation of the MPA and to ensure efficient and accountable use of the additional resources used.

The MPA speaks primarily to the role of the federal government in pursuing the twin goals of greater international competitiveness and more efficient use of human and physical resources. The Plan stresses the need for more coordination and greater accountability among relevant federal agencies. Indeed, these are the primary objectives of the proposed Cabinet-level administrator. However, many of the activities anticipated under the MPA would complement programs and expenditures that are ongoing at the state and local government levels in America. For example, much of the human and physical capital investment that occurs in the United States takes place at the subnational levels of government. State and local governments are the leading actors, with the federal government resigned to a supporting role (or perhaps only a bit part). Therefore, in addition to the need to improve coordination and cooperation among federal agencies in addressing the goals outlined in the MPA, an equally pressing need exists to involve the state and local levels of government in the policy decision-making process and to coordinate their efforts with those of the federal government (and, presumably, the private sector).

State (and local) governments are often viewed as the "laboratories" for innovations and creative approaches to addressing policy problems within the federal system. Indeed, many national policies and programs were concepts that were originally introduced and subsequently refined through experimental or demonstration projects at the state level. Only after achieving a measure of success were these policies and programs emulated more broadly among states or adopted as national programs. However, this system is not without its drawbacks, as disparities in fiscal capacities and differences in perceptions about the role or scope of government among the states may retard introduction of new ideas or much-needed services in some areas. Moreover, much debate remains as to whether African Americans and other minorities have more leverage in dealing with the federal government or a myriad of subnational jurisdictions.

What is the current role of state and local governments in the provision of the human and physical capital investments so critical to the success of the MPA? If the state and local public sectors are to play an important (and perhaps increasing) role in the implementation of a domestic MPA, what obstacles must be overcome with respect to their differential fiscal abilities and (perhaps) political willingness to provide services that may disproportionately benefit poor, unemployed, and minority workers in particular and urban residents more generally? A more prominent role for state and local governments in the implementation of an MPA will add problems of intergovernmental coordination and accountability to those of interagency coordination among federal agencies already anticipated by the framers of the MPA. What type of coordination vehicles are available to the president and his Cabinet-level administrator to address these coordination concerns? These are among the issues to be explored in this essay.

U.S. STRUCTURE OF GOVERNMENT

Public services are provided in the United States through a system of over 83,000 independent units of government.[2] Two aspects of the structure of the federal system are worth noting. First, the mix of units of governments is changing as the overall number of units tends generally toward decline (see Table 1). The total number of units fell by more than 8,000 between 1962 and 1987. This decline primarily reflected the fact that the decrease in the number of independent school districts during this period (-19,937) more than offset the increase in the number of special-purpose districts (+11,164). These trends are particularly important, given the role of school districts in the delivery of educational services and the role of special districts in the delivery of various infrastructure services, including transportation, solid-waste disposal, and water supply.

Table 1

Structure of Government in the United States, Selected Years

Type of government	1962	1977	1987
Federal government	1	1	1
State governments	50	50	50
Local governments	91,186	79,862	83,166
Counties	3,043	3,042	3,042
Municipalities	18,000	18,862	19,205
Townships	17,142	16,822	16,691
School districts	4,678	15,174	14,741
Special districts	18,323	25,962	29,487
Total	91,237	79,913	83,217

Source: U.S. Department of Commerce Bureau of the Census, *1987 Census of Government: Preliminary Report*, November 1987.

The second noteworthy aspect is the large variation among individual states in terms of their number of units of government. For example, four states (Hawaii, Rhode Island, Alaska, and Nevada) have fewer than 200 units each, while four other states (Illinois, Pennsylvania, Texas, and California) have over 4,000 units each.

The change in the number and mix of governments may indicate efforts to respond to changes in economic conditions, demographic patterns, and voter/taxpayer preferences for public services. To that extent, these changes are a measure of responsiveness and a desirable feature of the federal system. However, the structural dynamics and the tremendous state-by-state variations in service-delivery systems may also signal the nature of the coordination problem that will likely confront the proposed Cabinet-level coordinator for the MPA.

MARSHALL PLAN SPENDING

This section will provide a brief review of public expenditures on services critical to the implementation of a domestic Marshall Plan. In particular, the focus is on the provision of educational services and on selected infrastructure expenditures. The concern is with the aggregate level of spending, the distribution by level of government, and the variations among states. This analysis will highlight the importance of the state and local sectors in the provision of these important services and will provide the first indication of how any additional resources (such as the $50 billion per year in additional spending called for by the MPA) might be best allocated.

Total direct expenditures by all governments in 1988-89 were $2,030.7 billion (see Table 2).[3] Of this total, the federal government spent $1,142.8 billion, and the remaining $887.9 billion were expended by state and local governments. However, if attention is focused on the services that are most central to the MPA, the relative importance of the federal and state-local sectors is reversed. For example, of the $185.2 billion spent on elementary and secondary education in 1988-89, 99 percent was spent by local governments, mostly by school districts. The federal government share of elementary and secondary education direct expenditures was negligible.

As shown in Table 2, a similar pattern of direct expenditures by level of government is evident for selected infrastructure services, including transportation (i.e., highways and airports), solid-waste management, and water supply. A federal presence is significant only in the provision of airport services, where the state-local sector still accounts for over 55 percent of total spending. For all the remaining services considered, including highways, water supply, and solid-waste management, the federal share of all government spending is less than 1.5 percent.

The federal government's role in financing these services may be more significant than its role in making direct expenditures. This is because of grants in aid to states and localities that better enable these recipient jurisdictions to provide services or to provide services at a higher level. In addition, federal mandates, which may be imposed as a condition for receiving federal assistance, may also influence the availability and level of each of the services considered. Still, whether states and localities pursue their own agendas or operate as partners or agents of the federal government in providing these services, their importance is undeniable.

Table 2

Government Spending by Function, 1988-89
(in $ millions)

	All Governments	Federal Government	State Governments	Total Local Governments
Total direct expenditure	$2,030,704	1,142,821	359,661	528,222
Elementary and secondary education	185,171	--	1,417	183,754
Highways	58,869	776	35,318	22,775
Airports	10,180	4,428	507	5,245
Solid-waste management	8,734	--	621	8,113
Water supply	20,524	--	128	20,396

Source: U.S. Bureau of the Census, *Government Finances in 1988-89.*

VARIATIONS AMONG STATES

There is considerable variation in the level of state-local spending on MPA-critical services among the states (see Table 3). In terms of total direct general expenditures, the highest spending state (Alaska) spent more than three times the national average, while the lowest spending state (Arizona) spent only two-thirds of the national average. The variations for individual functions are often much greater. Alaska spends nearly eight times the per capita level of expenditures than does California for highways. Several factors influence these sizable state-by-state variations in overall and selected expenditures by the state-local sector, including (1) differences in preferences and attitudes about the size and scope of the public sector, (2) needs, and (3) resources available to finance spending. An interesting policy issue raised in light of this information is that the overall level of resources devoted to these critical areas may be adequate but poorly allocated among spending jurisdictions, and, by inference, among households.

Table 3

Variations in Selected State-Local Expenditures
Per Capita FY 1989 Function

	U.S. Average	High	Low
Total direct general expenditures	$ 3,059	$9,843 (AK)	$2,047 (AR)
Direct elementary and secondary	746	1700 (AK)	502 (TN)
Direct highway	234	1107 (AK)	141 (CA)
Direct sewerage and sanitation	104	211 (CT)	36 (SD)

Source: ACIR, *Significant Features of Fiscal Federalism: 1991, Volume Two.*

VARIATIONS IN FISCAL CAPACITY AMONG STATES

The line of reasoning being developed in this article may warrant review at this point. First, the MPA is an ambitious, coherent, well-intended plan for revitalizing the United States. The success of the MPA is a function of improving the delivery of a set of services that are more the responsibility of state and local governments than that of the federal government. (Note that this "conclusion" is more a statement of fact as shown by the above data than a philosophical preference about where these responsibilities should reside within the federal system.) Next, there is considerable variation among the states with respect to the level of these MPA-critical services provided. This section briefly reviews the role of a state's fiscal capacity in accounting for these variations. Subsequent sections will examine the implications of these variations in fiscal capacity and level of spending among states for the role of the federal and state governments in an MPA-type effort.

Fiscal capacity has two components. The first is the ability of the state-local sector in one state to generate revenues relative to similar abilities on the part of the average state within the union. The second component of fiscal capacity focuses on the service needs in a state relative to the average for other states. Generally, differences in per capita income (i.e., the arithmetic ratio of personal income to population) among states are used to measure differences in fiscal capacity. This measure has been used primarily because all taxes are ultimately paid by individuals out of their income (no matter if the legal incidence of the tax falls on corporations or specific products) and because service needs tend to vary in proportion to population, although demographic and socioeconomic characteristics of the population (age, extent of poverty, and unemployment, etc.) are of considerable significance.

Numerous alternatives and refinements to the per capita income concept of fiscal capacity have been developed.[4] Table 4 presents information comparing the per capita income measure with an alternative measure developed by the U.S. Advisory Commission on Intergovernmental Relations (ACIR). In the ACIR measure, the Representative Tax System (RTS) estimates the revenue-raising ability of a state-local system within a state if the uniform set of taxes were imposed at the average rate structure.

Table 4

Variations in Fiscal Capacity Among States

Fiscal Capacity Measure	U.S. Average	High	Low
Per Capita Income	100	140 (CT)	67 (MS)
ACIR (RTS/RES)	100	156 (CT)	57 (MS)

Sources: ACIR, *State Fiscal Capacity and Effort* and *Representative Expenditures: Addressing the Neglected Dimension of Fiscal Capacity.*

This procedure circumvents the difficulties encountered in measuring fiscal capacity among states caused by the fact that states employ different taxes and, for any given tax, use different rate structures. The Representative Expenditure System (RES) shows relative expenditure needs if the same factors (so-called workload measures) influenced spending within each state.

In Table 4, both fiscal capacity measures are shown as indices based on the national average. Fiscal capacity according to the per capita income measure ranges from a low of two-thirds of the national average in Mississippi to 40 percent above the national average in Connecticut. The refined measure developed by ACIR shows a much larger disparity among states, from 43 percent below the national average in Mississippi to 56 percent above in Connecticut. Thus, disparities in fiscal capacity are considerable under either measure, with the more refined concept indicating greater disparities among states.

POLICY ISSUES

Several policy issues emerge from the analysis thus far. First, the problem of coordination is significantly more involved than that suggested by the MPA. In addition to the several federal agencies identified in the MPA, the actions of policymakers (i.e., governors and legislatures) in each of the 50 states, plus many of the 83,000 local units of governments, must be considered and coordinated for best results. The conceptual strength of the federal system, represented by significant choice and diversity among governments, is also a potential difficulty in achieving coordination objectives.[5]

Next, when viewed in the context of the total amount of money spent by government, the amount spent on MPA-critical services (i.e., education and infrastructure), and the total number of governments that ideally must be involved (a minimum of five federal agencies and the 50 state governments), the additional $50 billion per year called for by the MPA seems meager and unlikely to cause much of a ripple. However, if strategically targeted--perhaps inversely proportional to state fiscal capacity--$50 billion per year could prove to be decisive. Note that, even if federal direct expenditures increased by $10 billion for each of the five key services designated by the MPA (see Table 2), federal spending would exceed state and local spending only for airports and solid-waste management. State and local spending would continue to dominate the other areas.

Finally, the MPA recommends specific actions with respect to human initiatives (e.g., make the Head Start program an entitlement and increase the Job Corps program enrollments) and physical infrastructure initiatives (e.g., develop a world-class transportation system and system of telecommunications).[6] Each of these actions appropriately builds upon proven successes regarding extant programs or appeals to the long-held American tradition of expanding the frontier through research and other creative efforts. However, for many problems, including relieving drug dependency, combating teenage pregnancies, and educating a pluralistic society to confront the requirements of a technologically oriented workplace, the optimal policies have not yet been identified (or at least not implemented on a broad scale). Experimenting with national solutions has often been expensive, time-consuming, and ineffective. A decentralized system where states and localities serve as policy laboratories may prove to be the best device for determining which policies work best under varying conditions.

THE FEDERAL ROLE

In terms of direct expenditures, the federal government is not a major factor in the delivery of services critical to the implementation of the MPA. What then should be the role of the federal government? Should it merely use its superior (relative to states and localities) revenue-raising capabilities to generate resources to be scattered broadly or uniformly among the states and localities (as with the old General Revenue Sharing program) and hope for a desirable outcome? Such a role is consistent with the results of a recent poll by the ACIR on public attitudes about government.[7] Individuals polled felt that their state and (especially) their local governments exhibited more wisdom in spending decisions. However, such a passive and aimless role will likely not result in desirable outcomes and efficient uses of resources from society's perspective.

The federal role in the development and implementation of the MPA has several components. First, the federal government should work to ensure competitive domestic and international markets, free of the obstacles posed by domestic market domination and collusion and foreign trade restrictions. A moderate monetary policy, to ensure low interest rates and encourage investment, and incentives for basic research will help to keep overall aggregate demand, and therefore the demand for workers, strong. These general macromanagement efforts are essential. In the absence of these macroeconomic efforts, an improved quality of the work force and basic support structure will simply increase domestic competition among workers and communities; some will gain, but only at the expense of others. The proposed MPA is an investment strategy for the United States where all stand to benefit through improved productivity and better use of existing resources.

Second, where one resides should not be a major determinant of the availability or level of assistance for basic subsistence, including health care. The federal government should assume a larger role in the provision of core support for the major public assistance programs, including Aid to Families with Dependent Children (AFDC) and Medicaid. States would then be able to supplement federal support where special circumstances unique to an area exist or where preferences for greater support levels, beyond the basic subsistence, were evident. This is essentially the manner in which the Supplemental Security Income (SSI) program operates.

This wealth-redistributive role for the federal government should also extend to concerns about fiscal disparities among states. The happenstance of political boundaries and the types of resources valued in the marketplace mean that all states are not equally endowed with wealth (see the above discussion of state-by-state variations in fiscal capacity). If the states (and, by inference, their localities) are to play a more meaningful role in America's return to prominence as a leader in the international marketplace, then states (like households) must have resources that are adequate to provide the basic levels of human and physical capital investment.[8]

The roles outlined above for the federal government are not new and have been eloquently described elsewhere.[9] These are necessary but not sufficient actions to restore the international competitiveness of the United States and to improve the efficiency in its use of resources. Other steps, more specific to the MPA, are also required. First, specific, quantifiable (where possible) goals must be established and a timeframe for realizing these goals must be implemented. These goals and timeframes should be developed in cooperation with state and local officials as well as with leaders from other elements of American society, such as business and labor. However, the leadership must come from policymakers at the national level. Goals and timeframes could, for example, indicate the amount of the disparity in unemployment rates between African Americans and the general population to be reduced each year until parity is achieved. Alternatively, it could aim to raise the educational performance levels of urban students relative to nonurban students (or perhaps all U.S. students relative to their counterparts in other countries) within the ten-year span of the proposed MPA and note some quantifiable measure of success to be achieved each year.

These goals and timeframes are imperative. Otherwise, the effort is an endless one with no way of evaluating success or failure. Even if such goals and timeframes must be periodically revised to reflect emerging realities and changing circumstances, they still serve very useful purposes. Once these overall goals and timeframes are agreed upon, states can be left to develop programs unique to their specific circumstances. The federal government would establish minimum compliance standards and a system of penalties (for poor state performance in realizing established goals within given timeframes) and rewards (for innovative approaches and realizing goals ahead of schedule).

Finally, the federal government would have a role as the overall coordinator of the MPA-related activities of both federal and state-local government activities. Coordination includes a clearinghouse component so that information about successes and failures in one state is readily made available to other states. In addition, technical assistance (including basic research) would need to be coordinated and cooperative among the states and between the state and federal levels of governments.

The proposed MPA also calls for a federal Interagency Council to coordinate the efforts of the five federal agencies (the departments of Education, Health and Human Services, Housing and Urban Development, Labor, and Transportation) viewed as playing a special role in implementing the Plan. The arguments made earlier in this paper suggest that other federal agencies, such as the departments of Commerce and Treasury, may also play critical roles. Moreover, actions by other federal agencies must be monitored to guard against inadvertent inconsistencies or offsetting effects. For example, few would deny that the federal Interstate Highway System begun in the late fifties contributed to the decline of urban areas in America. The highway system was an initiative of the Department of Defense and originally designed to facilitate movement of people in the event of military aggression by foreign powers. Will the spate of military base closings currently underway produce similar deleterious effects on urban areas that offset revitalization efforts of the MPA? More generally, what is the best vehicle to achieve the desired coordination and accountability within the federal government and between the federal and state governments in an effort to implement the MPA?

COORDINATION MODELS

The proposed MPA calls for a Cabinet-level administrator and Interagency Council to achieve the coordination objectives of the plan. The proposed vehicle may be appropriate for coordinating activities within the executive branch of the federal government, even under the expanded scope of involved federal agencies suggested above. However, the federal government includes policymakers beyond the executive branch (i.e., the 535 members of Congress). Furthermore, the information provided above indicates that state (and local) policymakers currently play a significant role in providing services central to the MPA, and these individuals will likely be critical to future revitalization efforts as well. What mechanism is appropriate and workable for coordinating the activities of all these policymakers? The mechanism needed ideally should (1) involve all of the relevant policymakers (or their representatives), (2) have the authority to implement agreed-upon decisions, and, yet, (3) not be so large as to be unwieldy and unworkable.

The U.S. Advisory Commission on Intergovernmental Relations (ACIR) provides a useful prototype of the mechanism required.

> ... The ACIR was created by the Congress in 1959 to monitor the operation of the American federal system and to recommend improvements. The ACIR is an independent, bipartisan commission composed of 26 members--nine representing the federal government, 14 representing state and local governments, and three representing the general public.

> The president appoints 20 members--three private citizens and three federal executive officials directly, and four governors, three state legislators, four mayors, and three elected county officials from slates nominated by the National Governors' Association, the National Conference of State Legislatures, the Na-

tional League of Cities, the U.S. Conference of Mayors, and the National Association of Counties. The three Senators are chosen by the President of the Senate and the three Representatives by the Speaker of the House of Representatives.[10]

There are several aspects of the ACIR that make it an attractive model for MPA coordination. First, it has representatives from all three levels of government, each serving as a member of equal status. Second, from each level of government, there are representatives from both the legislative and executive branches. Finally, the ACIR is bipartisan, with a mix of Republicans and Democrats (for all but the federal executive branch representatives) required by statute. In light of these features, any consensus for policy actions or program structure that emerged from such an organization should at least be seriously considered by all of the relevant policymakers involved in the implementation of the MPA.

The ACIR is advisory, and therefore has no enforcement power or implementation authority. In addition, representatives of state and local governments are appointed to serve indirectly, through the president, rather than directly through the actions of their respective interests groups. Also, the absence of direct representation by certain types of local government (school districts in particular) could prove troublesome given the emphasis on educational services in the MPA.[11] Finally, the limited participation of minorities as ACIR members may be viewed as a problem in using a similar vehicle to implement the MPA. Overall, given the large number of units of government and the considerable diversity characterizing these units, a 26-member panel may not be viewed as representing sufficient depth and breadth of perspectives to develop and facilitate the MPA. A cross-acceptance process (CAP) may also be required.

THE CROSS-ACCEPTANCE PROCESS[12]

Cross acceptance is a component of the New Jersey growth-management system, where it is described as

> . . . a process of comparison of planning policies among governmental levels with the purpose of attaining compatibility between local, county, and state plans.[13]

The process itself has three phases. First, there is the "comparison" phase, where localities (1) compare their master development plan to guidelines developed by the state, (2) identify inconsistencies, inaccuracies, and incompatibilities between the state and local plans, and (3) make recommendations to resolve differences. The second phase is "negotiation," where appropriate parties meet to consider the recommendations offered by the localities and negotiate to resolve or reconcile differences. Finally, during the "issue resolution" phase, outstanding issues are either resolved by the New Jersey State Planning Commission or it is agreed that the differences are not significant enough to impede movement to the next stage of the planning process. A series of public hearings is also held during this phase.

Given the need for coordination of activities and resource use that characterize the implementation of the MPA, this type of CAP could prove very useful. Once MPA goals and timetables were established, each state could begin to work with its localities to develop plans to achieve those goals within the designated timeframe. State and local plans for complying with the MPA would first go through a comparison phase to identify (and quantify, where possible) differences between the national goals and local perceptions of conditions. State and local recommendations would be considered during a second phase, and, finally, an ACIR-type MPA coordinating panel could determine solutions to differences not reconciled through negotiations.

POLICY LEVERAGE FOR AFRICAN AMERICANS

How will the influence of African Americans and other minorities on public policy decisions regarding the development and implementation of the MPA be affected under the more decentralized system suggested here? While no definitive response to this inquiry is possible, several pieces of information may be indicative of what could be expected. First, over 80 percent of all African American elected officials represent local government, including city and county governments and education.[14] These are individuals that would have no role under an MPA that was solely a federal program. Alternatively, they would formally become a part of the process under a more decentralized approach involving an ACIR-type organization and a cross-acceptance process.

African Americans comprised 12.1 percent of the U.S. population in 1990[15] and about 10.4 percent of the voting-age population.[16] However, African Americans as a percent of the total population were 16 percent or more in ten states, including Mississippi (35.6 percent), Louisiana (30.8 percent), South Carolina (29.8 percent), Georgia (27 percent), Alabama (25.3 percent), Maryland (24.9 percent), North Carolina (22 percent), Virginia (18.8 percent), Delaware (16.9 percent), and Tennessee (16 percent).[17] To the extent that these population proportions represent potential political power, the opportunities for more policy influence would appear to be greater in some individual states than at the national level. However, once again, considerable state-by-state variations are evident.[18]

Finally, a look at the extent of participation by African Americans in the New Jersey growth-management CAP may be illuminating. The evidence there indicates that, although the concerns of African Americans parallel those of the general population with respect to various growth-related issues,[19] African American participation in the CAP appeared to be minimal at best.[20] This situation apparently reflects both a lack of outreach efforts by state policymakers and apathy by leaders and members of the African American community.

CONCLUSIONS

The public service delivery system in the United States is a network with a large and diverse group of governmental units, each operating with a degree of independence. Within this system, state and local governments are relatively more important than the federal government in terms of direct expenditures for services critical to the implementation of a domestic Marshall Plan, including educational and infrastructure services. However, considerable variations in actual expenditures and fiscal capacities are evident among the states. The additional resources called for by the NUL Marshall Plan will likely prove to be inadequate and ineffective unless somehow targeted to areas and individuals of greatest need. Two major roles for the federal government should be to reduce fiscal disparities among states and to ensure that a minimal level of resources is available for each state to meet its service needs.

Given the diversity of needs, resources, and preferences among states, a uniform program applied nationwide may not produce the best use of scarce resources. Moreover, although some successful programs have been implemented, the best policy approach to many of the ills targeted by the Marshall Plan have not yet been identified. "Testing" policies at the national level may prove expensive and time consuming. States (and localities) have served as policy laboratories in developing public policy solutions to many problems.

The problem of coordinating activities within the federal government, between the federal and state-local sectors, and across states may prove to be difficult and beyond the scope of the Interagency Council advocated by the Marshall Plan. However, a Cabinet-level coordinator working through an intergovernmental coordinating panel patterned after the ACIR may be an alternative worth considering. This intergovernmental panel, coupled with a cross-acceptance process to ensure coordination and consistency throughout the network of governmental units, may offer the best prospects for success.

A domestic revitalization program is needed to restore America to her place of prominence in the international marketplace and to improve the productivity and use of resources. Such a plan would require the commitment and coordination of policymakers throughout the federal system.

* * * * *

The views expressed in this article are the sole responsibility of the author and should not be attributed to the U.S. Advisory Commission on Intergovernmental Relations nor to the New Jersey Public Policy Research Institute.

Power and Progress: African American Politics In the New Era of Diversity

Dianne M. Pinderhughes, Ph.D.

INTRODUCTION

With the passage and implementation of significant civil rights legislation at the national level and the gradual increase of black elected officials, the black community operated with heightened political effectiveness in the 1960s and 1970s. However, the 1980s brought important institutional changes that have made it more difficult for blacks and the broader civil rights coalition to influence public policy. These institutional developments have been accompanied by changes in party politics and by significant demographic changes, which could also shape black political progress and the viability of the civil rights coalition in the years ahead.

It is imperative that blacks and their supporters understand and respond to the new conditions and challenges. Accordingly, this paper examines recent issues and events that bear upon the exercise of political influence by black Americans and the civil rights establishment in the 1990s. In the face of restructured institutions, possible shifts in partisan politics, and changing demographics, it may be necessary to reassess the conventional political strategies that have been used for almost 40 years.

INSTITUTIONAL CHANGES

Beginning with the 1957 Civil Rights Act, the civil rights interest group coalition created a network of relationships described by the author in 1983 as an "iron triangle" (Pinderhughes, 1983: 17). This network symbolized the close relationships among the Congress, administrative agencies, and the interest groups that seemed to dominate the policy process in the first legislative battle of the decade, the 1982 Extension of the 1965 Voting Rights Act (Davidson, 1984; Foster, 1985). The Reagan Administration lost this first round with the civil rights lobby, but it was the last round it lost.

The Reagan Administration increased its ability to control civil rights policy over the decade of the 1980s, and the Bush Administration, in turn, has increased its ability to define the terms of civil rights conflict and debate. In each instance, the Administration aggressively used federalism and the national system of shared powers to attack long-established civil rights policies and to undermine the institutions responsible for implementing or enforcing civil rights laws. The president is constitutionally empowered to reorganize these agencies, even though such actions might be broadly opposed by public interest groups. The president co-manages the executive branch with the Congress and, therefore, exercises authority over the agencies responsible for administering civil rights laws and equal opportunity policies.

The separation of powers clause of the Constitution and the shared governance of administrative agencies by the legislative and executive branches suggest that the president's control of civil rights policy is balanced by the functions and prerogatives of the legislative branch. Yet, because the president controls personnel appointments and the overall policy direction of these agencies through the enhanced authority of the Office of Management and Budget (OMB), both Presidents Reagan and Bush have had a dramatic effect on both the development and implementation of civil rights policy.[1] Policy changes, personnel changes, staff reductions, organizational restructuring, and the politicizing of agency activities are prominent among the actions that have been taken.

The next section examines major instances in which presidents exercised power to limit or weaken advances in civil rights. In particular, the review focuses on efforts to control the U.S. Commission on Civil Rights, the Civil Rights Division of the Department of Justice, and the federal courts.

The U.S. Commission on Civil Rights

From 1957 through the early 1980s, the U.S. Commission on Civil Rights served as a powerful institution for the civil rights interest group coalition, but by the mid-1980s, President Reagan had successfully eliminated the Commission as a resource for the civil rights coalition and for civil rights oversight. "The [Reagan] administration recognized that in order to redefine the federal interpretation of the meaning of civil rights, it also had to transform the institutional symbol of the old interpretation" (Thompson, 1985: 180-81).

The Civil Rights Commission was created by the Civil Rights Act of 1957 as a nonpartisan body whose members were nominated by the president to terms of no specific length. The agency's main responsibility was to gather information in a number of policy areas, including voting and political participation, in order to evaluate the current status of the black population and to recommend regulations or legislation (Walton, 1988: 11-14). The Commission's reports have often served as the basis from which interest groups and Congress garnered support to reform voting rights legislation. This was the cape with the Commission's 1981 report on the status of the 1965 Voting Rights Act, *The Voting Rights Act: Unfulfilled Goals.*

The nonpartisan commission reflected the bipartisan support that characterized the development of civil and voting rights policy from the passage of the 1957 Civil Rights Act until the beginning of the Reagan Administration. President Reagan took advantage of ambiguities in this legislation to remake the commission from the ground up. Two issues surfaced in this process--(1) the right of the president to remove commissioners and (2) the independence of the Commission from the president on issues of policy (Thompson, 1985).

The original legislation had not created specific terms for the commissioners, and previous presidents nominated new commissioners only when a vacancy occurred. Typically, they replaced a Democrat with another Democrat, and a Republican with another Republican. But President Reagan argued that the commissioners served at his pleasure and that he had the right to appoint his own choices at the outset of his Administration.

Previous chairmen of the Commission--Father Theodore Hesburgh, former President of Notre Dame, and Arthur Flemming, a Republican--had served comfortably under Democratic and Republican administrations. However, the bipartisan civil rights policy formulated over the previous quarter century was far too liberal for the Reagan Administration. President Reagan nominated a conservative, Clarence Pendleton, to chair the Commission. A black Republican, Pendleton was confirmed by the Senate in March 1982.[2]

Pendleton was, to put it mildly, controversial. He was sharply critical of black interest groups, affirmative action, and President Lyndon Johnson's Great Society programs. He was also widely quoted as having called the concept of comparable worth "a looney tunes" idea. Arthur Fletcher, another black Republican, replaced Pendleton after the latter's death in June 1988.

By late 1984, President Reagan had succeeded in renegotiating the terms of appointments and had created a new Commission that was sharply distinguished from its predecessor in its partisan loyalty to a specific administration. Even Republican commissioners who had been appointed by the president in 1982 at the same time as Chairman Pendleton were terminated because they had not supported the Administration's position on several issues (Thompson, 1985: 199).

The second issue, whether the Commission was independent of the executive branch in the formulation of policy, surfaced in different ways. Early in his chairmanship, Pendleton spoke about having followed the Administration's direction, and later "corrected" his misstatement after public controversy about this. Meanwhile, the OMB issued a directive that the Commission clear all reports and congressional testimony with it to assure "consistency with administration policies" (Thompson, 1985: 196). The successful reconstruction of the Commission, however, made this requirement moot.

The Reagan Administration changed the leadership personnel of this agency, revised its policies, and downsized and reorganized its operations in order to detach the agency from its long-term relationship with the civil rights coalition. Also created by the 1957 Civil Rights Act, the Department of Justice's Civil Rights Division had specific, legislatively mandated law enforcement responsibilities. The Civil Rights Division (CRD) acted to control violations of civil rights in voting, housing, education, and other areas. President Reagan appointed William Bradford Reynolds, who had no experience in civil rights law and who had no ties to the civil rights constituency, as Assistant Attorney General to head the division.

Howard Ball and Kathanne Greene (1985: 13) reported that the Reagan appointees reorganized the division to exercise much greater control over civil rights policy. Thereafter, the division was much less aggressive in the initiation of civil rights cases. For example, in 1981, it filed 80 percent fewer suits concerning prison inmates, school desegregation, and housing discrimination than were filed in 1980. Also, under the Reagan and Bush Administrations, the CRD has been more reserved in monitoring enforcement of the 1965 Voting Rights Act. Although the number of voting law changes has increased by 100 percent, the CRD has not objected to (i.e., blocked) implementation of new laws as frequently as it did under previous administrations. The doubling of the volume of voting law changes, without a comparable increase in the number of objections, arouses concern that some voting laws that have a discriminatory impact may have gone into effect (see Table 1). Assistant Attorney General Reynolds had responsibility for this policy area.[3]

Table 1
Voting Law Changes and Objections Offered by the U.S.
Department of Justice Civil Rights Division, 1975–1990.

	Number of Notifications/Objections	Ratio Objections/Changes
1975	2078/138	15.05
1976	7472/151	49.48
1977	4007/104	38.52
1978	4675/49	59.17
1979	4750/45	105.55
1980	7340/51	143.92
1981	7132/33	216.12
1982	14287/112	127.56
1983	12416/71	174.87
1984	16488/109	151.27
1985	14418/172	83.82
1986	21898/639	34.26
1987	15321/85	180.24
1988	18957/135	140.42
1989	12499/168	74.39
1990	16787/99	169.56

Source: Civil Rights Division, U.S. Department of Justice, April 1, 1991.

Reynolds' role in redirecting voting rights policy came to light after several years in office. During confirmation hearings for Reynolds for promotion to Associate Attorney General, Senate Judiciary Committee members "confronted him [Reynolds] with an internal Justice Department memo, with his signature, showing that he had actually supported all white county governments in their attempts to restrict black voting rights in Mississippi and Georgia, . . . and with other evidence revealing that he had ignored court approved desegregation orders and AA programs" (Smith, 1990: 108). He was not confirmed, but continued in his position as Assistant Attorney General.

Changes in top leadership and policy met strong opposition from and precipitated internal conflicts with long-term civil service employees and middle-level staff in the CRD. For example, the CRD staff clashed with Attorney General Edwin Meese and Assistant Attorney General Reynolds over their decision to grant tax-exempt status to segregated schools. Their opposition helped to overturn that decision. However, the conflicts within the CRD further hampered its ability to carry out its legislative mandates.

Finally, the size of agencies such as the Civil Rights Commission, the Justice Department Civil Rights Division, and the Equal Employment Opportunity Commission (EEOC) peaked in the late 1970s, but their employee base has been on the decline since 1980. The downsizing has diminished their institutional capacity to monitor and to enforce compliance with civil rights legislation (Shull, 1989: 214; Walton, 1988: 50-55).

The Federal Courts

The federal courts, including the U.S. Supreme Court and the lower courts, have been substantially influenced by presidential appointments over the past decade. Because the federal courts hear and decide civil rights cases, they are critical to the implementation of legislation and to the development of law. The Reagan and Bush Administrations' appointees have primarily been white, male, and conservative, that is, resistant to the laws enforced since 1964.

1. **The Supreme Court.** An unusually large number of vacancies--one third of the bench--occurred during the Reagan presidency. They were filled by conservative appointees Sandra Day O'Connor, Antonin Scalia, and Anthony Kennedy (after the Robert Bork nomination was defeated). Moreover, Chief Justice William Rehnquist, a conservative, replaced retiring Chief Justice Warren Burger. President Bush has already nominated and had confirmed Associate Justices Thomas Souter and Clarence Thomas. These appointments have successfully shifted the court's philosophical balance considerably to the right, with justices who were seen as conservative during the Nixon Administration now constituting the moderate to liberal

wing of the court. Thomas's appointment solidified a six-vote conservative majority.

2. **The Federal District Courts and the United States Courts of Appeal.** In 1965, there were 307 federal judgeships, 400 in 1975, 575 in 1985, and 837 in 1990 (Strumpf, 1988: 119). "As of March 6, 1988, President Reagan had appointed 367 federal judges. Only six, or 1.6 percent, of those were black; President Carter, by contrast, appointed 258 judges and 37 were black, an average of 14.7 percent" (Smith, 1990: 112). The overwhelming majority of the Reagan appointees to the federal courts were white conservative males. By 1990, Presidents Reagan and Bush had appointed a combined total of 504 or 52 percent of the federal judges with lifetime tenure (Alliance for Justice, 1991: 1).

Thus, the lower federal courts and the U.S. Supreme Court have been greatly reshaped during the Reagan and Bush presidencies. The number of judgeships has been expanded and appointments have been made based on the nominees' adherence to philosophical positions consistent with those of the presidents. President Carter, also, expanded the federal court system, but, as Table 2 indicates, 14.7 percent of his appointees were black judges and 15.5 percent were female. More than one-fourth of Bush's federal judicial appointees are also millionaires (Alliance for Justice, 1991: 5).

Table 2
Gender, Race, and Ethnicity Breakdown
of Judicial Appointments by President

	Women	African American	Hispanic Americans	Asian Americans	Disabled
Bush 1989–91	18	6	4	0	2
126	14.3%	4.8%	3.2%		1.5%
Reagan 1981–88	31	8	13	2	N/A
378	8.2	2.1%	3.4%	0.5%	
Carter 1977–80	40	37	16	2	N/A
258	15.5%	14.3%	6.2%	0.8%	
Ford 1974–76	1	3	1	2	N/A
65	1.5%	4.6%	1.5%	3.1%	
Nixon 1969–74	1	6	2	1	N/A
227	0.4%	2.7%	0.9%	0.4%	

Source: Alliance for Justice, *Judicial Selection Project, Year End Report*, December 1991, Washington, DC.

Overall, then, the Reagan and Bush Administrations have successfully altered the balance of power in the executive and judicial branches with regard to civil rights policy, in an effort to bring this policy area more firmly under their control. With radical philosophical differences from the civil rights coalition, they have altered policy, changed personnel, and downsized and reconstructed agencies responsible for the implementation of civil rights policy; they have also modified the institutional relationships between government agencies and interest groups. These changes have made it increasingly difficult for civil rights groups to have their interests addressed or even to introduce new issues to the public policy agenda.

New policy is formulated with information gathered by an administrative agency with the legal responsibility and the capacity to observe events routinely across large geographical areas and a variety of political settings. With centralized and specialized knowledge about political behavior, an agency such as the U.S. Civil Rights Commission could make policy recommendations for reform as needed. With a sharply reduced administrative staff and a chair who serves at the pleasure of the president and follows the directives of the OMB, policy changes are unlikely to reflect the concerns or recommendations of the civil rights coalition. Similarly, the Civil Rights Division has been largely detached from its connection to the civil rights coalition that evolved over the first two decades of the agency's existence. Finally, if the civil rights coalition seeks redress for violations in the federal courts, a significant proportion of the federal judges they encounter is likely to be of the same philosophical bent as that of the Reagan or Bush Administration.

In any event, the civil rights coalition now faces a significantly different balance of power at the national level than that in existence prior to 1980. The separation of powers in the federal branch of government will naturally lead to shifts in the political relationships that arise from or are associated with this branch. The interconnected institutions involve separately elected or appointed officials and, therefore, they will not be sustained by the same electoral coalitions over a long period of time. The changes are not obvious because they occur slowly, over a decade or more; the gradual accumulation of changes in these interconnected institutions exerts enormous influence on the power and influence of specific interest and population groups. Thus, institutional arrangements developed when Democrats and Republicans supported civil rights reforms in 1957, 1964, 1965, and 1968 may not survive when conservative Republicans dominate national institutions and policy. Thus, civil rights groups must always take the existing partisan balance and institutional arrangements into account in designing their strategies and tactics. They must also prepare alternative strategies, recognizing that the existing institutional arrangements will shift when new electoral coalitions come into power.

PARTISAN CHANGES

For over ten years, Republican administrations have attacked civil rights policies; they have also challenged the political and philosophical presumptions on which national civil rights policy stands. The Thomas nomination hearings suggest these administrations have had a profound impact on political values--and therefore on partisanship--in the black community. Judge Thomas's nomination and the debate about it within the African American community highlighted divisions that the Republican Party might seek to transform into pragmatic and/or ideological shifts in partisanship among blacks.

The decade-long attack on affirmative action and civil rights by two presidents, the titular leaders of the Republican Party, have brought about important substantive divisions and debates over policy among black voters. With careful nurturing and detailed attention to issues, the GOP and its leaders may be able to transform these substantive disagreements into important partisan divisions, so as to garner more African American support. New Jersey's state politics has already proved the success of such a strategy. Former Republican Governor Thomas Kean won election to office with the support of a bipartisan coalition which included a significant portion of the black voters in the state.

From 1952 through 1988, the Democratic Party secured no less than 64 percent of the black vote, while the Republican Party won its highest percentage, 36 percent of the black vote, in the second Eisenhower election in 1956. The Republican Party has virtually dominated the presidency since 1968 by winning large proportions of the white vote. Thus, 59.1 percent of whites voted for Richard Nixon in 1968, and 69.7 percent in 1972; 53.4 percent voted for Gerald Ford, in a losing year; 64 percent voted for Ronald Reagan in 1980, and 63 percent in 1984; 59 percent of whites voted for George Bush in 1988 (Pinderhughes, 1984: 92; *Statistical Abstract of the United States 1991*, 253). A slight fluctuation downward in white support for Republican Gerald Ford helped elect Jimmy Carter, the only Democratic president between 1968 and the present. The Carter victory demonstrates that as long as Democrats hold the loyalty of African American voters, a shift in the partisanship of European Americans could result in the election of a Democratic president. Republicans remain vulnerable with a black electorate loyal to the Democratic Party. The return of the "Reagan Democrats" to the Democratic mainstream, for example, would be a serious threat to Republican control of the presidency (Pinderhughes, 1986).

On the other hand, a shift in the partisan preference of African Americans, without significant changes in white voting behavior, could strengthen and stabilize the Republican hold on the presidency for some time to come. African Americans cast 3.4 percent of their vote for Nixon in 1968 and 13 percent in 1972; 10 percent voted for Ford in 1976; 18 percent voted for Reagan in 1980 and 9 percent in 1984; 8 percent voted for Bush in 1988.

In this connection, it is important to realize that there has been a shift in the posture of the African American community since the beginning of the Civil Rights era, when people could agree on a few basic goals, led by the eradication of legal discrimination, even though they might disagree on the means by which to attain them. The strength of the African American community and of the civil rights coalition was that their basic goals and the combination of litigation and protest strategies drew a broad cross-section of the African American population and its leadership--from ministers to political activists--under one banner. There was, in short, a unified coalition of leaders who were unwilling to compromise on the goal of integration. Most importantly, the civil rights coalition set the pace for political events.

In recent years, the coalition has eroded, and agreement on new goals and strategies has become difficult to achieve. The coalition has found the introduction of new issues to the political agenda to which the national administration must respond more difficult to accomplish. It is split and in disarray on the policy front, as its campaigns over the Civil Rights Acts of 1990 and 1991 and other legislation have shown. Instead, the Administration has defined the terms of civil rights debate and structured the agenda to conform to its preferences for civil rights policy. The nomination of Clarence Thomas to the U.S. Supreme Court is a compelling case in point.

The head of the NAACP, Benjamin Hooks, and others called for the nomination of a black person to replace retiring Associate Justice Thurgood Marshall. Such a request carried with it the assumption that the nomination of an African American to the Court would adequately represent the interests of the civil rights community and African Americans. President Bush obliged the coalition and also satisfied his own preference for a Republican conservative with the nomination of Clarence Thomas, which forced the policy debate back into the civil rights community. The debate revolved around the following choices:

1. Support a black person who was Republican and conservative, and who disagreed with many of the goals of the coalition.
2. Reject the black conservative and risk a second nomination of a white conservative.
3. Reject the black conservative and press for a liberal nominee, whether white or black.

Because President Bush has a reputation for making and keeping commitments, a significant proportion of the general public and interest group representatives felt they would risk more by rejecting Thomas than they would gain by defeating him.

Thus, the black community and the larger civil rights community were deeply split over the issue. Even organizations that typically speak with one voice were divided. The national NAACP opposed the nomination, but it allowed its local branches to support the nomination if they so chose, a very unusual policy. Wade Henderson, director of the NAACP's Washington office, speaking on behalf of the national organization, explained the position. He argued that, as head of the EEOC, Judge Thomas had not supported the enforcement of affirmative action laws; Judge Thomas's legal posture while with the EEOC reflected his own ideological perspective rather than the intent of the civil rights legislation he was obligated to enforce (Henderson, NCBL Panel on the Clarence Thomas Nomination, C-SPAN broadcast, August 22, 1991). By contrast, the Compton, California, branch of the NAACP sent a representative to Capitol Hill to testify on behalf of Judge Thomas.

Other organizations experienced a split within their membership. For example, the National Bar Association (NBA) narrowly opposed the nomination. Sharon McPhail of the NBA reported that 45 percent of its members opposed Judge Thomas, 44 percent supported him, and 11 percent were neutral. Otherwise, the National Council of Black Lawyers opposed the nomination, as did some black religious leaders, such as Reverend Archie LeMone of the Progressive National Baptist Convention. On the other hand, Reverend Joseph Lowery and the Southern Christian Leadership Conference (SCLC) supported the nomination. Likewise, the National Black Nurses Organization and Zeta Phi Beta Sorority supported the nomination of Judge Thomas. The presidents of Lincoln University and Prairie View A&M University also affirmed their support. The National Urban League decided to remain neutral on the nomination.

With respect to the broader African American population, opinion polls found a similar divergence of opinion on the Thomas nomination. In early July 1991, 57 percent of blacks were in favor of the nomination, 18 percent were opposed, and 25 percent had no opinion (Gallup, July 1991: 18). By early August, African American support for Thomas had dropped to about 46 percent, and opposition had risen to 37 percent. However, by October, after Attorney Anita Hill's sexual harassment charges before the Senate Judiciary Committee became public, support for Judge Thomas had reached 67 percent, while the level of opposition dipped to just 24 percent (Gallup, August 14, 1991; September 18, 1991; October 14, 1991). It should be pointed out that these widely cited survey findings are based on samples that include only a very small number of African American respondents, which entails a large margin of error (Gurin, Hatchett, and Jackson, 1989).[4] Hence, these surveys did not measure with great reliability the obvious divergence of opinion in the black population because of sampling limitations.

There was no organizational or popular consensus with respect to the Thomas nomination within the African American community. Rather, the nomination brought to the surface ideological divisions that had been controlled in recent decades. The intensity and depth of the disagreement over the nomination, the issues it raised, and the appropriate response to these issues were virtually unparalleled in decades. Whether or not these disagreements will affect the political behavior of African Americans remains to be seen. Those who supported the Thomas nomination may see reflected in the Republican Party some of the concerns of the African American community and, therefore, those voters may be attracted into affiliation with the party on a long-term basis. A small shift of 10 to 15 percent of black political support to the Republican Party could have a major impact on the Republicans' ability to dominate the presidency. The return of the "Reagan Democrats" to support Democratic presidential nominees, in the absence of any change in black voting behavior, would threaten the Republican Party's control of the presidency.

DEMOGRAPHIC CHANGES

For most of American history, the population has been dominated by blacks and whites.[5] However, the results of the 1990 census confirm that the United States faces fundamental changes in the racial and ethnic composition of the population. These changes present special challenges to the exercise of black political influence in the 1990s, and will require reassessment of political assumptions, reflections about political alliance, and a reformulation of political goals.

From 1980 to 1990, the U.S. population grew from 226.5 million to 248.7 million. The African American population increased from 26.4 million to 29.9 million, or from 11.8 to 12.1 percent of the total. While the black population expanded both in absolute numbers and as a percentage of the whole, the Hispanic and Asian populations grew much more rapidly. Hispanics (including Mexican Americans, Puerto Ricans, Cubans, and South Americans, among others) grew from 14.6 million, or 6.4 percent of the U.S. population, to 22.3 million, or 9 percent of the total (U.S. Bureau of the Census, *CenData*, June 18, 1991). The Asian and Pacific Islander population more than doubled from 3.5 million, or 1.5 percent of the total, in 1980 to 7.2 million, or 2.9 percent, in 1990 (U.S. Bureau of the Census, 1983, Table 77: 1-15; Table 75: 1-13). The rapid increase in the growth of the Hispanic and Asian populations resulted from a combination of natural increase and immigration. Immigration laws have only recently been liberalized.

The population changes that have occurred over the past decade suggest that, if the observed growth rates continue, the Hispanic population will surpass the size of the African American population, while Asians will approximate half its size by the year 2000. As recently as 1980, Hispanics and Asians were 55 percent and 12.5 percent of the African American total, respectively. This change will shift the political balance in racial/ethnic group interests from the long-standing situation in which African Americans were the dominant minority group. African Americans and European Americans will confront a national political environment that has a multiracial rather than a biracial character.

As Table 3 shows, the various racial and ethnic groups are distributed unevenly as a proportion of the population of each geographic region. Of course, whites are the largest group in all four regions, but they are most dominant in the Northeast and Midwest. The African American proportion is highest in the South, followed by the Northeast. The Asian-Pacific Islander group is most populous in the West, the region that also contains the largest proportion of Hispanics.

Table 3
U.S. Population By Race and Hispanic Origin, 1990

Race and Hispanic Origin	U.S.	Regions			
		Northeast	Midwest	South	West
Race					
All persons	248,709,843	50,809,229	59,668,632	85,445,930	52,786,082
All Persons	100.0%	100.0%	100.0%	100.0%	100.0%
White	80.3%	82.8%	87.2%	76.8%	75.8%
Black	12.1"%	11.0%	9.6%	18.5%	5.4%
American Indian, Eskimo, or Aleut	0.8%	0.2%	0.6%	0.7%	1.8%
Asian or Pacific Islander	2.9%	2.6%	1.3%	1.3%	7.1%
Other Race	3.9%	3.3%	1.4%	2.8%	9.4%
Hispanic Origin					
All persons	248,709,843	50,809,229	59,668,632	85,445,930	52,786,082
All Persons	100.0%	100.0%	100.0%	100.0%	100.0%
Hispanic origin (of any race)	9.0%	7.4%	2.9%	7.9%	19.1%
Mexican	5.4%	0.3%	1.9%	5.1%	14.8%
Puerto Rican	1.1%	3.7%	0.4%	0.5%	0.4%
Cuban	0.4%	0.4%	0.1%	0.9%	0.2%
Other Hispanic	2.0%	3.0%	0.5%	1.5%	3.8%
Not of Hispanic origin	91.0%	92.6%	97.1%	92.1%	80.9%

Source: U.S. Bureau of the Census, *Cendata*, Summary Tape File 1A, Table 3, "Race and Hispanic Origins for the United States and Regions: 1990," Washington, D.C. June 18, 1991.

Table 4 presents the population by race, Hispanic origin, and region as the groups are distributed across the regions. The region with the largest population is the South at 34.4 percent, followed by the Midwest at 24 percent, the West at 21.2 percent, and the Northeast at 20.4 percent. Whites are distributed in similar rank and proportions. The African American population is quite distinct from the national pattern with 52.8 percent being in the South. Asian-Pacific Islanders are as concentrated as a group as blacks, but 55.7 percent live in the West. About 45 percent of the population of Hispanic origin is located in the West, and 30.3 percent is in the South. Each of the groups which comprise "Hispanics" has different patterns of geographic concentration: 58 percent of the Mexican population is in the West; 68.6 percent of Puerto Ricans live in the Northeast; and 70.5 percent of Cubans are in the South.

With different proportions of these groups in each region, national

Table 4
U.S. Population by Race, Hispanic Origin, and Region, 1990

1990 Race and Hispanic Origin	U.S.	Total	Regions			
			Northeast	Midwest	South	West
Race						
All persons	248,709,873	100.0%	20.4%	24.0%	34.4%	21.2%
White	199,686,070	100.0%	21.1%	26.0%	32.8%	20.0%
Black	29,986,060	100.0%	18.7%	19.1%	52.8%	9.4%
American Indian, Eskimo, or Aleut	1,959,234	100.0%	6.4%	17.2%	28.7%	47.6%
Asian or Pacific Islander	7,273,662	100.0%	18.4%	10.6%	15.4%	55.7%
Other Race	9,804,847	100.0%	17.0%	8.5%	24.0%	50.6%
Hispanic Origin						
All persons	248,709,873	100.0%	20.4%	24.0%	34.4%	21.2%
Hispanic origin (of any race)	22,354,059	100.0%	16.8%	7.7%	30.3%	45.2%
Mexican	13,495,938	100.0%	1.3%	8.5%	32.2%	58.0%
Puerto Rican	2,727,754	100.0%	68.6%	9.4%	14.9%	7.0%
Cuban	1,043,435	100.0%	17.6%	3.5%	70.5%	8.5%
Other Hispanic	5,086,435	100.0%	30.0%	5.5%	25.2%	39.4%
Not of Hispanic Origin	226,355,814	100.0%	20.8%	25.6%	34.8%	18.9%

Source: U.S. Bureau of the Census, *Cendata*, Summary Tape File 1A, Table 3A, "Race and Hispanic Origins for the United States and Regions: 1990; Table 3B, "Race and Hispanic Origins for the United States and Regions: 1990 [Percentages], Washington, DC: June 18, 1991.

politics will take on one type of racial and ethnic dynamic, while the regions have their own peculiar character, depending upon the racial and ethnic mix. Thus, the South and northern and midwestern cities are likely to be strongholds for black politics, while Hispanic and Asian Americans will be particularly strong in western cities. Some mix of all of these groups will occur in all regions and political interactions will take on an increasingly complex dynamic throughout the nation. However, it is important to observe that Hispanics and Asians are composed of a number of different nationalities and have a much more varied history of experiences within the country after their arrival than African Americans (Thung, 1991; *Civil Rights Issues of Asians*, 1979). This heterogeneous past means their rapid population growth will not automatically lead to a common Asian American or Hispanic political identity.

On the other hand, rapid growth in the election of political officials by African Americans will be affected by the group's slowed population growth rate (Farley and Allen, 1987). Unless immigration policies admit more blacks from the African continent, South America, and the Caribbean, one cannot expect continued rapid expansion of the African American population across electoral districts to occur. The political strategies of the Civil Rights Movement and the more recent civil rights coalition have been developed and carried out based on this numerical and geographical expansion. The slowing of the black population's growth rate will influence the types of political strategies African Americans use in the coming decades.

Indeed, the demographic trends suggest that African Americans have come close to the upper limits of growth in their independent political influence based on their group alone. Therefore, they have to identify similarities in political interests across racial and ethnic lines. Coalition politics and strategies should be chosen to promote intergroup cooperation rather than conflict, given these demographic trends. Political experience has discouraged black interest in political coalitions or cooperative political structures, but that must be reevaluated and perhaps set aside.

The demographic data, showing the rapid expansion of racial and ethnic minorities in this country, also raise the prospect that whites may vote for racial conservatives if they perceive a threat to their political power. The popularity of David Duke might be viewed from this perspective. It could be a precursor to a more broad-based political movement generated, in part, by the demographic changes described above.

In his campaign for governor of Louisiana, David Duke used more than a century-old racist and "nativist"[6] tradition born out of the intersection of the Ku Klux Klan and southern populism. Duke, however, has tried to modernize the message to make it less repugnant and to give it broader appeal. Duke has experimented with a variety of racist constructions, having been a member of the Nazi party, the Grand Wizard of the Knights of the

Ku Klux Klan (1975-1980), and having founded the National Association for the Advancement of White People in 1980.

Duke deemphasizes direct racial attacks, neutralizes his language (that is, he does not say "nigger"), but attacks affirmative action, welfare, and welfare recipients. He is also quite explicit about the impact of increasing demographic change: "The time has come in America to limit and stop the illegal immigration into our society. . . . What's happening is, we are unraveling. We're losing our way. This country is overwhelmingly (sic) European descent. It's overwhelmingly Christian. And if we lose our underpinning, I think we're going to lose the foundations of America" (*New York Times*, December 5, 1991).

While he was defeated decisively in the Louisiana gubernatorial election, Duke has already announced that he is running for president. Moreover, the voting patterns in his failed race for governor deserve detailed examination. Duke received 39 percent of the total vote. However, he won 55 percent of the white vote, compared to just 4 percent of the black vote. The interaction of race and economic status was particularly prominent among whites, as Duke won comfortable majorities of 56 to 63 percent among whites with incomes under $50,000. He split the vote among whites in the $50,000 to $74,999 category, and won only 34 percent of the vote among those with an income of $75,000 or more. Duke also won majorities among whites who indicated that their family financial situation was about the same or worse than four years ago. Otherwise, Duke lost decisively among Democrats, but he split the independent vote and garnered 56 percent of the Republican ballots. Duke may show surprising strength in areas where blacks are not as large a portion of the population as they are in Louisiana. He could pose a serious problem to President Bush by splitting the conservative wing of the Republican Party, as white voters react to the economic downturn and the growing presence of racial and ethnic minorities whom they perceive to be competitors for scarce opportunities.

Hence, Duke's show of strength among white voters, among poor and middle-income voters, and among Republicans and independents is a potentially dangerous sign that African Americans, Asian Americans, Hispanic Americans, as well as other progressive-minded groups cannot afford to ignore. Ironically, the Republican Duke, a traditional representative of white supremacy, also represents a threat to the Republican Party, as his extremist views will limit the party's efforts to cultivate more black support. These conservative forces will be blunted if African Americans cultivate political alliances with other racial and ethnic groups.

CONCLUSION

This paper has examined some institutional, partisan, and demographic developments that have occurred over the past decade in terms of their consequences and implications for the political positioning of African Americans. The Reagan and Bush Administrations implemented comprehensive institutional changes in the area of civil rights. The nomination of Clarence Thomas to the U.S. Supreme Court highlighted partisan divisions within the African American community that the Republican Party might exploit to increase its control over the presidency. Finally, fundamental demographic changes in the racial and ethnic composition of the U.S. population are underway that will significantly affect political life. Indeed, in the long term, the demographic changes could well be the most consequential of all. They deserve further comment.

The increases in the Hispanic and Asian populations will present difficult choices to the African American political leadership. Blacks often view their historical experiences with slavery and segregation and the successes of the Civil Rights Movement as evidence that they should have a preeminent leadership position among the nation's racial and ethnic minorities. Although these groups have different areas of geographic concentration, and increasing populations, African Americans are more established in the political sector at present--based on their almost universal citizenship and historically similar socialization--than either Latinos or Asians. Given the population growth trends, however, this attitude will limit opportunities for political influence. While relations between blacks and these groups may involve conflict or cooperation, African Americans will better serve their own interests by pursuing shared, cooperative leadership and political activity with other key minority groups (Gomes and Williams, 1991; Jackson and Preston, 1991; McClain and Karnig, 1991).

The next decade will force black organizations and the black community generally to reevaluate their institutional connections, philosophical beliefs, and partisan ties. African Americans will also have to reassess their political strategies and choose carefully their friends and allies. How much power and progress the group enjoys in the future is heavily dependent upon how effectively these tasks are accomplished.

The Parity Imperative:
Civil Rights, Economic Justice, and the New American Dilemma

Julianne M. Malveaux, Ph.D.

> In this deceitful American game of power politics,
> the Negroes (i.e., the race problem, the integration
> and civil rights issues) are nothing but tools, used
> by one group of whites, called Liberals, against
> another group of whites, called Conservatives,
> either to get into power or to remain in power.
>
> *Malcolm X*
> *December 4, 1963[1]*

What happened to the parity imperative? Less than a year before the 1992 presidential election, and less than a decade before the turn of the century, issues of African American parity have receded to the policy sidelines. The race debate has been reconfigured, with buzzwords used to elicit responses from whites. According to pollster Stanley Greenberg, many whites had a negative reaction to the word "fair," seeing it as a proxy for programs designed to favor blacks.[2] As we move toward the 1992 election, it is clear that President George Bush, he of the "Willie Horton ad" and the "quota bill" description of the Civil Rights Act of 1992, will continue using racial rhetoric to score political points. His competitors for the Republican presidential nomination, columnist Patrick Buchanan and former Klansman David Duke, are likely to lack the finesse to send subtle racial messages, bluntly focusing on "affirmative action" and "welfare" as programs that exclusively favor African Americans and disadvantage whites.[3]

While the parity imperative is not likely to be revived by the Republicans, Democrats have hardly been enthusiastic proponents of parity in recent years. True, there was strong Democratic support for the Civil Rights Act of 1990 and the Civil Rights Act of 1991. But as white working-class Democratic constituencies have deserted that party over issues of race and taxes, Democratic candidates have learned to tiptoe around those issues. Without Rev. Jesse Jackson's presence in a 1992 campaign to articulate issues of parity, it is not likely that any of the Democratic contenders will make civil rights and parity a central part of their 1992 agenda. Indeed, some of the candidates are U.S. Senators who may have voted the right way on key issues but have no African Americans among their senior staff, few African Americans among their constituencies, and no history of dialogue with African American leadership.

Issues of race can generate headlines, interest, and heated discussions; issues of parity, civil rights, and economic justice are at the policy periphery today. The very validity of these concepts is under attack. Even among African Americans, there is little agreement, although much of the current dissent is angst-ridden, churlish whining by privileged middle-class academics, the beneficiaries of the programs they now question.[4] Dissent is not limited to that group, however. Depending on the source, there have been surveys that show that only a slim majority of African Americans support affirmative action programs, and that a growing number of African Americans are critical of public assistance recipients.[5]

The media have played a major role in shaping perceptions of welfare, affirmative action, black economic status, and the role of blacks in society on the part of both black and white Americans. For a very brief and shining moment, we were portrayed as moral giants, we of "turn the other cheek" and "We Shall Overcome." Now we are depicted as moral midgets, rapists, murderers, and welfare cheats. And many African Americans buy into those depictions with the same fervor that whites do. At the same time, because the media glorify athletes and entertainers, many of whom are African American, there is a public perception of African American privilege, not disparity.[6]

The reconceptualization of the race debate is, in many ways, a discussion about the efficacy of the system of resource allocation in the United States. Who gets jobs, income, housing? Why do not African Americans get their fair share? Though there are shades of gray, the two polar positions are that either (a) the system is flawed, burdened with barriers that prevent full African American participation or (b) some African Americans are so flawed that it is not possible for them to participate in the system. The scholarly designation of some of us as "underclass," that is, beneath class, lower than lower class, unresponsive to policy initiatives and to governments' assistance, serves the notion that there are some people so flawed that they cannot be helped. If this "underclass" is removed from consideration, some would argue that the system works for those who do "hard work," and there are scores of black success stories to prove it.[7] The problem is that these success stories offer little inspiration to the one-third of black families that live in poverty, many despite full-time, low-wage employment.

But what more can we do, policymakers ask? The signs do not say "white" or "colored" anymore, and every vestige of *de jure* segregation has disappeared. Many think the "statute of limitation" on past discrimination has run out.[8] But the gaps remain. In general, black people have less income and wealth, live in more dilapidated housing, and have access to a lower quality of social and public services than do whites. African Americans have less education, more infant mortality, a lower employment rate, and a higher rate of imprisonment than do whites. The signs do not say "white" or "colored," but one might argue that signs are no longer needed. Despite the unmistakable progress since the passage of the Civil Rights Act of 1964, a tenacious racial prejudice plagues this country and has an impact on virtually every aspect of African American life.[9] Black people earn less than whites, and while the earnings gap narrows with education, a gap remains despite education. Black people are often treated differently from whites in public accommodations, although the strict *de jure* exclusion of a generation past has been replaced by a more subtle form of differential treatment.[10]

The gaps remain, and so does the evidence of discrimination. And the outcome of this treatment is highlighted in an Urban Institute study, **Opportunities Denied, Opportunities Diminished: Discrimination in Hiring,**[11] which used the technique of a hiring audit to show that when black and white testers applied for entry-level jobs, blacks were unable to advance as far in the hiring process as often as whites 20 percent of the time, and were denied jobs offered to equally qualified whites 15 percent of the time. In other words, *even when white and black qualifications were identical, black job applicants experienced differential treatment, or discrimination.* These findings were not startling for African Americans, but they generated no comment from a president determined to cast legislation designed to remedy situations like this as "a quota bill."

Explorations of racist minutiae, of the day-to-day incidents experienced by African Americans are so frequently greeted with disbelief by whites that an ABC News Special Report used the technique of matched testers to illustrate differential treatment in housing and job searches, and in their treatment by automobile dealers and department store sales personnel.[12] This focus, however riveting, ignores the institutional and systemic differences in black-white economic status, as well as the staggering poverty experienced by one-third of all black families. Our nation once embraced the moral imperative to eliminate poverty, but now the poor have been recast as the "underclass" and distant from the rest of us. Like the race debate, the poverty debate has been reconceptualized as a discussion about values and behavior.[13] Implicit in President Reagan's assertion that there were no hungry people in 1984, implicit in President Bush's persistent denial of economic hard times in late 1991, has been the notion that poor people have personal problems that they ought to solve by getting more education, working at a job, no matter how poorly paid, and "getting off welfare" (even though more than 23 million Americans, the largest number of whom are white, received food stamps in October 1991).[14]

On one hand, the interest in dissecting racist minutiae, especially that experienced on the part of the black middle class, is the result of that group's frustration at having followed all the rules and still experiencing differential treatment. On the other hand, viewing minutiae reduces a structural and institutional problem to a personal and dramatic one and is consistent with the current policy focus on individual, not group, rights and responsibility, with prejudice, in the "bootstraps" sense representing merely another hurdle to be cleared.[15] That the underclass cannot clear hurdles, then, is considered more a function of "character" and "values" than of race. But how do we explain the hurdles that black jobseekers failed to clear in the Urban Institute study?

When the issue of racial economic gaps is recast in terms of "character" and "values," it is possible, plausible, and in a larger context acceptable for white politicians to engage in the subtle symbolism of racism, the "covert language and coded signals"[16] that produced Willie Horton as a Bush campaign signal, and made the racist rhetoric of his ideological descendent, David Duke, politically acceptable. This reconceptualization suggests that the system works, but that African Americans have deficiencies that result in gaps between black and white unemployment rates (in November 1991, 12.1 and 6.1 percent, respectively),[17] differences in pay (the median full-time earnings of white men who dropped out of high school are greater than the median earnings of black women who completed some college),[18] and differences in occupational status (while African Americans were 10.1 percent of those employed in 1990, they were fewer than 4 percent of all engineers, lawyers, or natural scientists, and underrepresented in most of the other professions, management, and skilled crafts positions.[19] Conveniently, studies like the Urban Institute study are ignored in the reconceptualization.

By implicitly blaming black people for racial economic gaps, political leaders in the past decade have challenged the efficacy of using any public policy approaches to close these gaps, although it is clear from the Urban Institute study that the enforcement of civil rights laws might improve the chances of black jobseekers. By ignoring or trivializing proven discrimination and asserting that the system works, this reconceptualization of the race debate may be partly responsible for whites' opposition to affirmative action as a policy goal. It may also explain the glee that greeted a late 1990 ruling (that was later "rescinded" for further study) that scholarships set aside for black students violated civil rights laws.[20] Many others, themselves the recipients of forms of public assistance (like Social Security or Medicare), oppose "welfare" spending because they perceive such programs as serving African Americans exclusively.[21] These attitudes weaken any parity imperative that might have existed and place those who are interested in closing gaps in a position of being forced to argue that there are compelling institutional reasons why gaps exist and that all of society gains when gaps are closed.

However, while whites have limited commitment to a parity imperative, most African Americans feel it is important to close racial economic gaps and remain concerned with unemployment differentials, educational and occupational representation, gaps in wealth and entrepreneurship, and other issues. African Americans and whites also seem to differ regarding the role government must play in closing gaps, providing employment, and moving toward equity. Many whites feel the government has done enough and that further intervention is undesirable,[22] while many feel that government intervention, however flawed, is important in guaranteeing that African Americans get fair opportunities in the economic system.

Given a bleak economic climate and the challenge of demographic change, this is a charged time to reexamine the issue of parity, but that is the purpose of this essay. Parity is a concept that implies that all economic participants have equitable shares in the economy, while economic justice implies that all have the opportunity to participate, and that no one's participation is exploited. Economic justice would suggest that full-time workers earn living wages, that high school graduates have access to employment, that the rich pay proportionally as much tax as the poor. This essay will first revisit the concept, place it in the context of economic and demographic trends, explore the strategies African Americans have pursued, then, finally suggest new strategies for parity and economic justice.

PARITY AND ECONOMIC JUSTICE: SUBJECTIVE CONCEPTS, ELUSIVE GOALS?

Parity is most simply defined as the "quality or state of being equal." But what kind of equality are we seeking? Equal access? Equal processes? Equal chances? Equal outcomes? Each of these implies something different, as well as a different type of policy, and has a different historical context. At the extreme, we can measure how close we are to parity by looking at the equality of outcomes. Then, parity is achieved when:

- per capita black income and wealth are approximately the same as white income and wealth;
- black labor force participation and unemployment rates are at approximately the same level as white rates; and
- black representation in all occupations is at approximately the same level as black representation in the population. In other words, if African Americans are 12 percent of the population, there is parity in occupational representation when blacks are also approximately 12 percent of all managers.

The parity imperative does not suggest that economic resources be allocated "by the numbers"; even the suggestion of such a method of allocation generates the kind of hysteria about "quotas" that hampered passage of the Civil Rights Act of 1991 for two years. But the Act was needed to combat erosions in civil rights law. In the *Wards Cove v. Atonio* case (1989), for example, the U.S. Supreme Court argued that there might be some "business necessity" to justify imposing certain workplace "qualifications," even though the result of these qualifications might be to concentrate minority workers in unskilled jobs at the bottom of the occupational spectrum.

Parity does not imply allocation by the numbers, but clearly numbers are useful in measuring how quickly we are moving toward parity and motivate us to both explain gaps and to develop policy to close them. The usefulness of a more precise statistical approach to resource allocation can be seen in studies of mortgage turndowns by race that were released in the fall of 1991. At the time, the Federal Reserve Bank issued a report showing "dramatic disparities in loan rejection rates" by race. New York's Manufacturer's Hanover Trust, for example, rejected 18 percent of the loan applications that came from high-income whites, but more than twice as many—43 and 45 percent respectively—from high-income African Americans and Hispanics.[23] In Boston, a black person with income more than 120 percent of the median income was more likely to be denied a loan (33.3 percent) than a white person with income less than 80 percent of the median.[24]

Bankers responded to the Federal Reserve Bank report by noting that it excluded many factors in analyzing loan denials. One banker indicated that minority rejection rates were higher because of unacceptable answers on standard loan applications. Unacceptable credit histories, insufficient income, and inconsistent employment histories were mentioned as partly responsible for loan denials.[25] While these factors may explain loan denials for low- and moderate-income people, they do not explain why blacks with higher incomes are more frequently denied loans than whites, in many cases with lower incomes. Moreover, the recursiveness of discrimination of economic markets is clear when gaps in loan success rates are explored. Given income and employment gaps, blacks may be less likely than whites to qualify for mortgages. But, in the absence of mortgage availability, blacks have a lesser opportunity than whites to accumulate wealth or to take advantage of tax credits that are related to holding a mortgage. A lack of access to capital, then, has long-run deleterious effects on the disposable income of African Americans.

The questions raised around mortgage denials are similar to questions raised about employment. If black and white loan applications are treated identically, and black loan applicants still experience greater rates of turn-down, is there a problem with the process of granting loans, with those applying for loans, or with some other set of factors? Is it possible to treat loan applications "identically," or do subjective attitudes influence the way some loans are handled? Is it clear that the criteria used are connected to a lender's ability to repay a loan, or have banking methods become stagnant over time? (Indeed, given the abuse of billions of dollars in the savings-and-loan debacle, with funds being lent without collateral, it is appropriate to consider whether the notion of loan "standards" is a selective one.)

Issues of lending do not pack the emotional wallop that issues of college admissions and hiring do, but the questions raised are quite similar. How are scarce resources allocated? Is the goal in allocation a "fair" process or a "fair" and "representative" outcome? How do we define "fair," and is subjectivity involved? Certainly, for African Americans, the persistence of significant gaps, even among those 14 percent with family incomes in excess of $50,000, belies any notion of fairness and suggests that there is still a need for activist public policy to close racial economic gaps.

Some have argued that parity is attainable, but only between those blacks and whites who are "similarly situated." Thus, Richard Freeman compared black college graduates with white college graduates in 1974, and found "rough parity" between their wages.[26] Others have compared the incomes of black and white women and, finding them comparable, indicated that sexism is more powerful than racism for explaining the labor market treatment of black women.[27] In arguing against affirmative action in college admissions, it has become popular to raise issues of class and suggest that poor whites, too, could benefit from preferential college admissions. And while the issue of "similar situation" is certainly one to consider, the fact is that discrimination has made "similar situation" impossible and untenable for many African Americans. Those similarly situated jobseeking youth in the Urban Institute study were not similarly situated for long. The whites found it easier to obtain employment offers than the blacks did.

Would the parity imperative be satisfied if there were proportional representation in every aspect of economic life? As current economic policy pressures the middle class and ignores the poor, it is appropriate to raise the question of economic justice *as quite distinct from parity.* Dr. Martin Luther King, Jr., perhaps best articulated the meaning of economic justice in his Nobel Peace Prize acceptance speech when he said, "I have the audacity to believe that peoples everywhere can have three meals a day for their bodies, education, and culture for their minds, and dignity, equality, and freedom for their spirits."[28] King referred to an economic system that generated opportunity and *provided for each person's basic needs*, a system that might well be sharply different from our current form of economic organization. At the very minimum, the economic vision that Dr. King articulated clearly allowed for income maintenance programs, government assistance, and perhaps both the right to employment and to health care. As defined here, parity speaks to none of that, but instead to the proportional representation of African Americans in every facet of economic life.

Consider, for example, some of the "parity gaps" that were calculated by authors in this volume last year. David Swinton calculated a gap based on differences in black/white per capita income that has been growing, not shrinking, since 1970[29]; similarly, measuring what black income would have been under parity, Billy Tidwell noted that racism reduced the gross national product by 1.8 percent.[30] Both these comparisons deal with the concept of an African American "share" of the economy, but they do not address ways this share is distributed. Further, issues of income distribution cannot be resolved among African Americans without dealing with the broader income inequality that exists in this society.

Still, it is important to note that goals of parity and economic justice are not necessarily compatible. It is possible to have parity, with the economy generating parallel outcomes for blacks and whites that include continuing high rates of poverty, low levels of health insurance coverage, and high unemployment. With black poverty at 33 percent and white poverty at 12 percent, a "parity outcome" might reduce black poverty to 20 percent and raise white poverty to that level. Current economic trends suggest that we revisit notions of both parity and economic justice with a view toward making both concepts part of the African American economic mission. Rev. Jesse Jackson's Rainbow Coalition has made every attempt to address these dual goals, calling for health insurance, guaranteed college admission, job creation, community reinvestment, greater federal subsidies to cities and states, and other measures. But issues of "fiscal responsibility," especially given the $3.5 trillion deficit, have made such programs easy to talk about but difficult to pass legislatively.

In any case, the push for parity without economic justice makes it easy for those who perceive the economic system as flawed in its treatment of them (unemployed manufacturing workers, for example) to oppose parity, in many instances on racial grounds.

PARITY AND ECONOMIC JUSTICE IN A CHANGING ECONOMY

Though the parity agenda is of primary importance to African Americans, it was the economy that dominated the headlines in 1991 and will likely determine the outcome of the presidential election in 1992. The U.S. economy entered a recession in the second quarter of 1990, but government economists did not acknowledge the existence of this recession until mid-January 1991. Even then, the president minimized the existence of the recession, describing it as a "temporary pause in economic growth." By

July 1991, President Bush had declared that the recession was "over," but the economy continues to languish, failing to respond to third quarter 1991 interest rate cuts, primarily because consumer and business confidence has been so low that borrowing is unattractive, even at a lower cost. With nearly 10 million officially unemployed Americans, only a third of whom were eligible for unemployment insurance in the fall of 1991, the president and Congress turned the unemployed into a political football, finally passing legislation to extend unemployment insurance benefits in November after failing to override two presidential vetoes.

When the U.S. economy gets a cold, Black America gets pneumonia, and so this recession threatened the oscillating economic gains that African Americans have made since the middle-1970s, when two decades of economic expansion began to falter. The 1990-91 recession affected blue-collar workers and their professional and managerial brethren; government workers, disproportionately African American, also felt the pinch as states and cities got fewer funds from the federal government. But Black America is used to pneumonia; the problem with the economy's stagnancy in the 1990-91 recession is that much of White America is only getting used to the idea that they will experience more than a three-day cold when Black America has pneumonia.

In other words, the 1990-91 recession exacerbates long-term structural shifts in the economy that have affected most workers, especially white manufacturing and other blue-collar workers, in the 1980-89 decade. In that decade, family income grew more slowly than that in the 1970s, with youngest families hardest hit. In contrast to previous generations, those entering the labor market in the 1980s could expect to fare economically better than their parents did. Income inequality increased in the decade, with the top fifth of American families receiving 44.6 percent of all income in 1989, a greater share of total income than they have received since 1947; in contrast, the bottom fifth received just 4.6 percent of all income, a smaller share than they received since 1947.[31] By any measure, the rich have gotten richer, the poor poorer, and the middle class more vulnerable to employment cuts, tax increases, and problems of poor service delivery that are a function of the reduced level and changed composition of intergovernmental grants that flow from the federal government to cities and states.[32]

In the waning months of 1991, the evening news could have easily been renamed the "layoff" litany. The African American adage that "you can always find work at the post office" became an anachronism when the U.S. Postal Service announced it would lay off 45,000 workers between 1991 and 1993. No industry or occupation was immune to layoffs, with employment reductions especially pronounced among sales workers, crafts workers, and laborers.

This economic uncertainty has had two impacts on African Americans. Those who are employed are keenly aware that they may have little job security. More importantly, as whites have also experienced economic uncertainty, some of these whites have expressed anger at African American people, not at the economy. Black people are an easy target. We are visible as anchors on the television news in each city, touted as "firsts" whenever another hurdle is cleared. The astronomical salaries received by sports personalities, many of whom are black, have generated an envious grousing of white male sportswriters that reflects the *vox populi* about black employment. "How do they have jobs when we don't," some whites wonder, and it is easier to blame reverse discrimination than the labor market and the economy.

But most Americans, black or white, depend on far less glamorous employment for their survival. One of the most drastic aspects of the 1980s has been the change in the way the labor market is organized, structural shifts that were exacerbated by the 1990-91 recession. Aspects of the market once taken for granted, like job security and guaranteed benefits, have been savaged. As the population ages, fewer employers are covered by pensions, forcing individuals to find economic security by combining full-time and part-time work, planning serial jobs and careers, and making other arrangements. With economic security more the exception than the rule, much of the resentment focused on African American people may actually represent misguided thinking against the vagaries of economic change, and in light of the nature of market changes, it is easy to see why so many are apprehensive about their economic futures and eager to scapegoat others for their plight. Among the most pronounced changes:

- The core work force is shrinking, while the peripheral, or contingent, work force is growing. While some contingent work is well paid, little of it offers health insurance, pensions, and other benefits. Even as total employment dropped by about 750,000 between October 1990 and October 1991, self-employment grew by about 120,000.[33] But the growth in self-employment is part of the growth in the peripheral sector, where workers are disconnected from health insurance and retirement benefits. Part-time employment, which is growing more quickly than full-time employment, is another example of contingent employment. About seven million workers moonlighted in 1991.

- Employment in small businesses has grown more rapidly than employment in large ones. Smaller businesses are less likely to offer benefits than their larger counterparts, and, when they have fewer than 15 employees, are exempt from discrimination laws and other forms of regulation.

- Unionization levels continue to drop, meaning that fewer employees have protection from collective bargaining. Because unionized black workers earn between 30 and 50 percent more than black workers who are not union members, declining unionization has been a special hardship to semiskilled and blue-collar African American men.

- The structural shift from manufacturing to service employment has increased the number of low-wage jobs in the economy. Much of the growth in family income in recent years has been longer hours of work for less pay.[34]

- The labor market has bifurcated, so that there is more distance between high-wage and low-wage workers. The highest fifth of all families saw their incomes rise by 28.9 percent in the 1980s, while the lowest fifth saw their income decline by 4.4 percent. The bifurcation is so severe that economist Robert Reich[35] said just 20 percent of the labor market have stable economic futures, while the remaining four-fifths face precarious futures.

- Though much has been written about the number of unskilled workers in the labor market, some economists argue that black labor market *entrants* (i.e., as opposed to those who do not participate in the labor market) are more skilled than they have been in the past. "We have never had better educated black work-force entrants; years of schooling have risen, high school and college completion rates are significantly higher, and test scores—at the bottom as well as at the top—have dramatically improved, especially relative to whites. The wage problem facing noncollege educated black and white workers lies in access to high-paying or skilled jobs, not in their academic credentials.[36]

- Despite the way the job market has been weakened, there has been a total absence of federal employment policy in the 1980s and certainly during the current recession. Until Congress recessed in November, there had been no countercyclical employment program proposed, partly because of the deficit. The passage of a six-year, $151 billion highway and mass transit bill in November 1991[37] will generate some jobs in 1992, but it represents a slow response to a recession that began in mid-1990.

Beyond that, the pressure for deregulation has meant that many of the labor regulatory agencies have been weakened, and workers are lacking occupational health and safety, and wage and hour legislation is going unenforced. As a consequence of deregulation, 25 workers perished in a fire at a poultry processing plant in Hamlet, North Carolina, because the firedoor had been locked to prevent theft. Workers at Imperial Foods earned about $4.50 an hour; 18 of them were women, and a disproportionate number were African American. The factory had not been inspected in a decade.[38] Similarly, in the Mississippi Delta, catfish processors, mostly black women workers, struck for months to get their wages raised to about $5 an hour. In the absence of a federal employment policy, there has been no oversight in exploitative employment situations and little encouragement for employers to develop the higher wage jobs that are missing in the economy.

The government's disengagement in service provision and emphasis on market provision of things like education, health care, and even corrections has led to the economic alienation of many workers, some of whom hold full-time employment and have no health insurance. About 37 million Americans have no health insurance, and a disproportionate number, about seven million, are African American. Some are self-employed or part-time workers who cannot afford insurance, while others are full-time employees who must either wait before their employer-provided insurance becomes effective or cannot afford the copayments that employers increasingly require. The lack of health insurance is a direct cause of the fiscal instability that many workers experience.

Economic alienation is further exacerbated by the condition of financial institutions. It is estimated that the collapse of the savings-and-loan industry will cost about a trillion dollars, with every American family paying about $2,500 in increased taxes to cover this obligation. Ironically, some of the very African American families who will pay this assessment are denied equal treatment from the savings-and-loan industry, failing to secure mortgages and other loans with the same frequency that whites do. Further, the Federal Deposit Insurance Corporation has a skewed sense of equity, allowing the failure of the black-owned Freedom Bank of Harlem while bailing out the larger (and more debt-ridden) Bank of New England. Besides weakness in the savings-and-loan industry, there have been questions raised about the stability of the commercial banking industry as well as the life insurance industry, all of which undermine people's confidence in these institutions and send people looking for scapegoats.

Another feature of our changed economy is a shift in the tax burden away from the wealthy and toward the poor. At the federal level, tax changes have favored the very rich, increasing the top income quintile's share of after-tax income, while decreasing the income of the poor. Rates dropped for the top 5 percent of the population between 1977 and 1990, while they increased for everyone else. Further, more and more corporate income went untaxed in 1990 than in 1977. Finally, because the Social Security contribution is capped, the lowest fifth of the population pays proportionately more Social Security tax than the top 10 percent of the income distribution. State and local taxes compound the federal effect of favoring the rich. On average, the richest 1 percent of the population pays 7.6 percent of its income in state taxes, while the poorest 20 percent pays 13.8 percent of its income in taxes.[39]

Finally, world economic changes have raised questions about the role the United States will play in the "new world order." With the fall of the

Soviet Union and the economic unification of Europe, the United States must move from its role of world leader to a more equitable role as one of three or four world powers who are roughly equals. To be sure, we continue to dominate the world militarily, at great cost to our domestic economy. But our per capita gross national product trails that of Japan and of Germany, and we have maintained a trade imbalance with Japan. Insecurity about our world position has raised questions about foreign investment in the United States and caused us to take protectionist positions in a world economic context.

These economic changes all combine to create a climate of economic insecurity and alienation and make it easy to seek out targets for blame, and politicians have risen to the bait, using words like "welfare" and "affirmative action" to separate the black economic condition from that of others. The result has been that workers, who feel attacked, have failed to organize around an agenda of economic justice, choosing, instead, the easy division that comes with race rhetoric. The further result is that issues of African American parity have receded in importance as legislators and policy analysts attempt to grapple with the economic dilemmas that face our nation. Implicitly, the presumption is that of "rising tides"—if the macroeconomy does better, so will African Americans, it is argued. The "rising tides" argument has not been proven, though. Certainly, the "recovery" of 1983-88 did little to improve the relative economic position of African Americans.

PARITY AND ECONOMIC JUSTICE IN A MULTICULTURAL CONTEXT

Economic conditions are one barrier to achieving parity in this country, but the extent to which several racial and ethnic minorities compete for access is another. The Civil Rights Movement is the model that most underrepresented groups have used to address issues of fairness—mirroring the African American model of agitation and street protests, drafting of legislation, formation of legal defense and education funds to wangle limited concessions for representation in politics, economic development, higher education, employment representation, and other areas. But those who mirror the civil rights model are often insensitive or oblivious to civil rights issues as they affect African Americans. Black people are often used as a "litmus test" or "bottom line" of methods of political discourse,[40] but the limited efficacy of our model, especially as it relates to closing racial economic gaps, is infrequently mentioned.

Thus, it was amusing and ironic to read that a Korean American writer fervently wished for a Korean "Al Sharpton" to silence rapper Ice Cube and to stop boycotts against shops owned by Korean Americans.[41] The irony was compounded because only weeks before, a Korean American woman was sentenced to a mere *400 hours of community service and a $500 fine for shooting a young black girl in the back over an altercation about a bottle of orange juice*,[42] so that the writer who wished for a Korean Al Sharpton was wishing that African American tools be used to mute justifiable African American rage over the callous death of a black youngster and the persistent cash register conflict between blacks and Koreans that have partial roots in racism.

Of course, there is a bigger picture—neither blacks nor Koreans are fully empowered, and conflict between these two minority groups does little to reduce the stranglehold of economic power that a small group of capitalists have maintained. Writer Itabari Njeri describes this as "capitalism and white tribalism fueling black-Korean tensions,"[43] and while her portrayal is accurate, it does not speak to the way black life has been so thoroughly devalued that recent immigrants, in behavior that is clearly imitative of that of whites and reflective of media messages, feel free to physically assault, maim, and kill African Americans over pennies. In San Francisco, the conflict was not black-Korean as it has been in New York and Los Angeles, but black-Arab. Again the dispute was over a beverage that cost less than two dollars. In this case, there was no trial, no probation, just a police report.

Cash register conflict is not the only inter-ethnic conflict that takes place. In Washington, DC, tensions between black police officers and Latinos in the Adams Morgan community erupted into two days of looting. When the dust cleared, the very legitimate question was raised—why were Latinos so underrepresented on the DC police force? Does their share of city employment, program funding, and representation on boards and commissions reflect their population in the District?

When these questions are raised, it is easy for African Americans to become defensive. Having not yet attained parity ourselves, it is difficult to accept a challenge that comes from other minority groups who have experienced both disadvantage and discrimination. In many ways, the competition among minority groups has only one possible outcome—while minorities fight for scraps, white power is consolidated.

Thus, the efficacy of coalitions is an issue that African Americans must continually confront. Are black issues and needs submerged in coalitions that argue for "multiculturalism" and "diversity"? Are these goals (multiculturalism, diversity) desirable purely on grounds of inclusion, or because there has been some prior, institutional reason for the exclusion of a certain racial or ethnic group? How can African Americans justify the push for parity for ourselves without being open to the parity demands of others? On the other hand, is self-interest not in order when an outcome of our "diversity" agitation is that the black agenda is ignored?

The historical reasons for exclusion and the various remedies each ethnic group may seek in order to reach parity must be addressed. Public assistance systems, for example, have treated some Asian immigrants differently from African Americans, providing them with assistance unavailable to others. Is it sensible, then, to compare the business success of Asians with the relative failure of African Americans in entrepreneurship? With vastly different wealth profiles and differences in access to capital, are minorities competing on a "level playing field," and should public policy treat them in the same manner? As nonblack minority legislators are elected and deal with these matters from a policy perspective, it is incumbent upon African Americans to develop a strategy for reaching parity that answers some of these questions.

It is also important to recognize the competing needs of minority groups around issues like reapportionment. In San Francisco, a city that is "majority" minority, lines have been drawn for assembly districts that essentially (1) keep much of the black population in one district; (2) keep much of the gay community in the same district; but (3) divide the Chinese American community between two districts. With the black community a scant 10 percent of the San Francisco population, pundits suggest that the new district lines make the election of a gay representative likely, but of an Asian representative difficult. These types of competition are likely to occur more and more frequently as the demographic profile of our nation changes.

According to the 1990 census, 80 percent of the national population is white, 12.1 percent is black, 9 percent is of Hispanic origin and 2.9 percent is Asian-Pacific Islanders. Few states have the population mix of California, where 69 percent of the population is white, 26 percent is Hispanic, 9.6 percent is Asian, 7.4 percent is African American, and nearly 1 percent is American Indian. When whites are less than 70 percent of the population in any state, the more common pattern is that of Mississippi, where the majority of the population is either black or white. But the increased diversity of the population and increased agitation for access force African Americans to justify the continuing quest for parity and force us to compare our situation with that of other groups.[44]

Demographic and population trends make it difficult for African Americans to claim the sole benefit legislation and programs designed to close racial (or gender based) economic gaps. Indeed, white women, gays, lesbians, and others who can claim "disadvantage" or "discrimination" have had their competing claims recognized by legislation at either the national or local level. There is a distinction between disadvantage and discrimination, the distinction between those prepared to compete but prevented from so doing, and those who are both unprepared and also barred from the competition. The "pity party"[45] approach to set-asides often pits those prepared to compete against the unprepared (i.e., white middle-class women competing for small business funds against working-class blacks), and it raises the question of who is "qualified" to compete.

The question of gender is important in this context, especially among African Americans who justifiably feel that the women's movement has often ignored their needs or used its struggle to advance the cause of white women to the exclusion of black men. Certainly, white women have experienced less disadvantage than discrimination, and some have argued that they have been the primary beneficiary of affirmative action programs when they are classified as "minorities."[46] Public reaction to the Senate Judiciary Committee hearings on Professor Anita Hill's accusations against Judge Clarence Thomas indicated the extent to which African American women feel varying degrees of discrimination and disadvantage because of both race and gender.[47] From the perspective of closing racial economic gaps, the issue of gender and entitlement to parity-oriented programs is one that must be further examined.

If those who were underrepresented in their access to economic opportunities were to form a coalition that included minorities and some women, this coalition might well represent a majority. Within this majority, though, African Americans would represent the minority that has defined some of the tactics and strategies of a parity imperative but that has been granted little deference (and often the contempt or the position as "litmus test") in the community of minorities struggling for parity. As the community of minorities grows (which it is projected to do through the early 21st century), this dynamic will pose a challenge for African Americans.

PARITY, CIVIL RIGHTS LAW, AND STRATEGIES FOR BLACK ECONOMIC ADVANCEMENT

In the years since the passage of the Civil Rights Act of 1964, the racial economic gap first narrowed, then widened. In the early years, strategies, remedies, and programs were discussed and initiated, but the "chilling effect" of both the *Bakke* and *Weber* cases brought public support for the parity imperative to a near-screeching halt. There are few tools available to those who would attempt to close the racial economic gap, and the tools have been so battered by the current conservative environment that attempts to close the gap can be likened to attempts to put out a raging fire with a small bucket that has been riddled with buckshot.

Civil Rights Law and Affirmative Action

Between 1989 and 19991, a series of U.S. Supreme Court decisions had made it difficult for employees to bring action against their employers for discrimination. In a stunning reversal of *Griggs v. Duke Power* (1971), the Court made it an employee's responsibility to show that an employer used practices that adversely affected women and minorities in *Wards Cove Packing Co. v. Atonio* (1989). In *Martin v. Wilks* (1989), the Court allowed workers to challenge consent decrees, even if they failed to challenge the decree at the time it was imposed. In *Price Waterhouse v. Hopkins* (1989), the Court allowed employers to escape liability when there was intentional discrimination if there was another motive for the discrimination. In *Lorance v. AT&T Technologies, Inc.* (1989), the Court said those laid off because of discriminatory seniority rules could only object when rules were passed, not later, when they were affected. In *Patterson v. McLean Credit Union* (1989), the Court ruled that while race discrimination was illegal in hiring and promotion, the law did not prevent harassment, discriminatory firing, or other job bias. The Court's ruling in *Patterson* led to the dismissal of more than 200 claims of race-based harassment on the job. In *EEOC v. Aramco* (1991), the Court determined that discrimination law did not apply to U.S. citizens who worked for American companies abroad. Finally, in *West Virginia University Hospitals v. Casey* (1991), the Court made it more difficult for plaintiffs to bring lawsuits by indicating that provisions allowing successful plaintiffs to recover legal fees did not include the cost of hiring expert witnesses.[48]

When the effect of these cases was combined with the relative inaction of the Equal Employment Opportunity Commission (EEOC)--which had been restructured with reduced funding in the Reagan years and had shifted focus from bringing class action suits and seeking consent decrees to simply monitoring the law,[49]--there was concern that the U.S. Supreme Court was sending a signal that racially motivated workplace behavior was acceptable. It took almost two years (a version of the bill was vetoed by President Bush in October 1990), several drafts of legislation, and hundreds of hours of negotiation to secure the passage of a bill to reverse the effects of these Court rulings in 1991. The Civil Rights Act of 1991, although ambiguous on issues of "business necessity," restored workers' rights under the law and provided limited money remedies to women (unlimited remedies were already available to minorities) who experienced sex discrimination.

It would be a mistake to say that passage of the Civil Rights Act of 1991 makes it "easy" for plaintiffs to find a remedy in the courts. Indeed, the case of Brenda Patterson is interesting because of the amount of time this case had taken to prepare and to bring it to courts at every level. Patterson had worked for the McLean Credit Union for about a decade before she sued it. She was subject to racist comments from the start—when she was hired as an accounting clerk, her white supervisor told her that her coworkers would dislike her because she was black. The only African American employee at her bank, Patterson was the brunt of an endless stream of racial remarks and workplace hazing. Her supervisors and coworkers told her that black people were, by nature, slower than whites, then they piled extra work on her to see if she could do it. She was ordered to dust and sweep the office, something no other accounting clerk had to do.

Patterson was laid off in 1982, even though people who were on the job less time than she were retained. She brought a lawsuit against her employers for denying her a promotion, for an unjustified layoff, and for racial discrimination on the job. She and her attorneys fought through the district court, to the court of appeals, and to the U.S. Supreme Court which found, in 1989, that discrimination is not allowed at the point of hire, but that it is acceptable after hiring. This woman's case of a decade of harassment and hazing has still not been resolved. Indeed, among all the courts, claims of racial harassment and discrimination have been dismissed, and the only pending action she has against the McLean Credit Union is based on whether she was unjustifiably denied a promotion.[50]

Brenda Patterson could not have brought her case before the U.S. Supreme Court were it not for the assistance of the NAACP Legal Defense and Educational Fund. How many plaintiffs are able to secure such legal assistance and have the patience to stick with a case for nearly a decade? The *Patterson* case raises questions about the efficacy of the legal system with regard to civil rights law, and it suggests that these laws and the affirmative action programs that were a product of these laws are presently, at best, a limited tool for black economic advancement.

Affirmative action was not always such a limited tool. During the 1972-1980 period, affirmative action and government consent decrees could be credited with changing the black occupational distribution in this country and with increasing the black employment share in several industries. Though many believe these programs were mostly effective in the professions and among academics, in the *AT&T* case, writer Phyllis Wallace credited a consent decree with increasing the number of black women in skilled clerical positions by some 65 percent in the 1978-79 period, when overall black women's employment increased by just 11 percent. Similar shifts in the occupational distribution of black men also took place during this time period.[51]

While affirmative action generates much heat in the political arena, Wallace noted that the majority of corporations remain fully committed to affirmative action *as a human resource strategy*. Referring to a 1989 survey of 202 CEOs, Wallace noted that 42 percent described themselves as "fully committed" to affirmative action policies despite court decisions. Two-thirds characterized the effect of affirmative action programs on U.S. business as good, very good, or outstanding. Wrote Wallace: "Thus, where moral suasion, threats of litigation, and back-pay or front-pay adjustments may have yielded limited benefits, the new demographic dynamics in labor markets and the widespread use of computers in human resource management systems may assist in the institutionalization of affirmative action programs in a representative segment of corporate America. One of the beneficial byproducts of affirmative action has been its effect on human resource procedures. Without affirmative action, U.S. industry would not have set up human resource planning tools and procedures."[52] Wallace noted, however, that many corporations have shifted the focus from affirmative action as a remedial tool (i.e., recompense for past discrimination) to a prospective tool (i.e., as an important way to meet corporate human resource goals). Indeed, the corporate focus on "managing diversity" and "achieving multiculturalism" is consistent with the notion that organizations benefit from including those who have been previously excluded *whether or not the motivation for inclusion is past discrimination.*[53]

But this means that an increased black presence, at the top or at the bottom, is not guaranteed by law but is a function of the goodwill of corporate leadership, and the extent to which this leadership perceives that affirmative action works to its advantage. The weakening of the EEOC means there will be little enforcement of civil rights laws at the federal level, and the fact that some 30 states face fiscal crises in the coming year means that little relief will be available at that level. The passage of the Civil Rights Act of 1991 suggests that plaintiffs will get a better hearing from the courts, but only if they are prepared to endure a multiyear legal ordeal. The current climate has significantly weakened civil rights law and created disincentives to filing lawsuits under these laws.

What about affirmative action? Wallace and others have made the case that these policies have benefited an occupational cross-section of African Americans, and that they are more helpful than harmful because they make it possible for more people, and a more diverse group of people, to participate in the economy. Yet Wallace made it clear that the recasting of affirmative action as a human resource strategy, not a race-based remedy, makes it more acceptable, given the current political climate. Recent administrative decisions to stop "race norming" employment tests suggest this is the case. Political energy might be better spent developing better testing instruments than arguing that blacks and Hispanics should get extra points on biased tests.

Small Business Development and Minority Set-Asides

Another of the 1989 cases that attacked the parity imperative was the *Richmond v. Croson* case, where the majority opinion was ironically written by Justice Sandra Day O'Connor, herself the beneficiary of affirmative action. Justice O'Connor essentially reversed several provisions of the *Fullilove v. Klutznick* case of 1980, which allowed the practice of setting aside portions of public works funds for minority contractors. O'Connor argued that past discrimination, which may have contributed to a lack of opportunities for black entrepreneurs in the past, could not justify "rigid racial quotas in the awarding of public contracts in Richmond," a misstatement since rigid quotas were never imposed.

Absent opportunities for upward mobility in the private sector, many African Americans have turned to self-employment and entrepreneurship as ways of participating in the economy, and an indirect goal of set-aside legislation is to close the racial economic gap by creating more black-owned businesses. Between 1982 and 1987, the number of black-owned businesses grew by 35 percent, or more than 7 percent a year, and although these businesses were smaller, less likely to have employees, and more undercapitalized than in the past, growth was seen as a positive.

Some municipalities have continued to use set-asides to assist in the development of minority businesses, sometimes doing studies to establish a record of past discrimination. In Atlanta, Brimmer and Associates studied the history of exclusion of black businesses from the contracting process prior to 1972, and in San Francisco, the city's Human Rights Commission has conducted similar studies.

Given the economic changes outlined in an earlier section of this essay, black business development may be of critical importance in closing the racial economic gap. The trend is toward more jobs being generated by small, not large, employers, and the availability of set-aside business may encourage the growth of some of these smaller businesses.

The courts have effectively made it difficult for municipalities to offer set-asides. Black politicians, with growing power, may be able to influence the awarding of contracts at the state and local levels, but this policy, like affirmative action, now depends on goodwill (or political largesse) and not on the law for enforcement.

Leveling the Playing Field: Education and Racial Economic Gaps

While traditional human capital theory does not work and racial gaps persist even between highly educated blacks and whites, those blacks with educations will clearly fare better than those who are not educated. Thus, the issue of "qualifications" is inevitably mentioned when the racial economic gap is discussed. If black people were only "prepared" for the labor market, they might be better able to compete, it is asserted. Yet, the gap between black and white levels of education is smaller now than it has ever been historically.

Still, the condition of the urban public schools that enroll the majority of black youngsters and the extent to which these schools are capable of preparing black youth to enroll in college suggest the need for public policy interventions in education.

The Bush Administration's sole educational innovation has been its support for the school choice movement. According to proposals, parents would be given vouchers and allowed to take them to the schools of their choice. The thought behind this program is that the market would work and that good schools would attract students with vouchers to support them, while poor schools would fail because they could not attract enough students.

What is wrong with this picture? It seems likely to the author that some of the best schools will price themselves out of heavily black urban areas. It is also possible that schools may develop admissions criteria that discriminate. A more significant educational reform might be the shift away from the property-tax basis of school funding, which seems to guarantee educational inequities (and later labor market inequities) to a different basis for funding education.[54]

It seems possible to prepare youngsters to compete in the labor market of the future, but is such preparation in the interest of capitalists who have not yet decided to develop a high-wage economy? If we accept the notion that there are limited "good jobs" available, issues of urban education may become more understandable. In other words, do we still need a "reserve army" of unemployed people to exert downward pressure on wages, or are wage levels so low that it is imperative that the educational system improve? Further, to what extent can civil rights law secure a better funding basis for urban public schools?

What Tools Can We Use to Close the Racial Economic Gap?

The traditional tools that have been used to move toward parity have been hampered by the law, the current political climate, and the economy. The challenge for African Americans is the development of a new set of tools. In developing these tools, it seems important to raise a number of questions:

- Have existing laws been fully exploited, or can civil rights laws be used in different ways to secure black economic rights? Are we monitoring law enforcement as closely as we might? In other words, are existing tools being used to capacity?
- To the extent that black taxpayers subsidize institutions that exclude them in employment or contracting (i.e., universities, pension funds, etc.), is there a basis for lawsuits?
- Can the law be used to further the cause of economic justice, to secure the right to food, housing, medical care? To the extent that we address the purely poverty-rooted problems of those on the bottom, we may take steps toward narrowing racial economic gaps.

301

PARITY AND THE "NEW" AMERICAN DILEMMA: WHERE DO WE GO FROM HERE?

> The gold of her promise
>   has never been mined
>
> Her borders of justice
>   not clearly defined
>
> Her crops of abundance
>   the fruit and the grain
>
> Have not fed the hungry
>   nor eased that deep pain
>
> Her proud declarations
>   are leaves on the wind
>
> Her southern exposure
>   black death did befriend
>
> Discover this country
>   dead centuries cry
>
> Erect noble tablets
>   where none can decry
>
> "She kills her bright future
>   and rapes for a sou
>
> Then entraps her children
>   with legends untrue"
>
> I beg you
>
> Discover this country.
>
> *Maya Angelou*[55]

When Gunnar Myrdal wrote *An American Dilemma* in 1948, he challenged this country to make its racial practices consistent with its ideals. That challenge might well be reissued today, especially when the world's enthusiasm for participatory democracy is contrasted with the increasing alienation that Americans, black and white, experience--an alienation that is best illustrated by the large number of us who do not participate politically and the growing number who find their opportunities for economic participation limited.

Much of our problem is rooted in our economic system, not simply because it is capitalist, but because unchecked and unregulated capitalism leads to the kind of economic exploitation and wage deterioration that we experienced in the 1980s. We have failed to examine fully our economic problems because our political leadership has shifted the focus from the economy to race.

It may well be that 1992 will represent a turning point. If Democratic candidates are able to articulate solutions to long-term economic problems and avoid the race-baiting that has been a product of political discourse in the past, then perhaps we can begin to develop those labor market policies that are an essential component of the economic justice so many are seeking. African Americans must evaluate candidates on the basis of both their commitment to economic justice and their commitment to parity.

The author would suggest that economic justice is a necessary condition for the attainment of racial economic parity, but that parity without justice is attainable, but not sustainable. The fragile nature of black economic gains in the years since the passage of the Civil Rights Act of 1964 would only serve to underscore this point.

Recommendations

MARSHALL PLAN FOR AMERICA

The National Urban League has taken the concrete step of developing a bold new initiative for investing in this nation's human and physical infrastructure through a set of specific proposals, *Playing to Win: A Marshall Plan for America*. Implementing this Plan would move our nation forward towards meeting the challenges of global competitiveness, would strengthen our security, and would improve our quality of life.

The Urban League, therefore, calls upon the Congress and the Administration to enact legislation that implements the major human resource and physical infrastructure proposals in its Marshall Plan for America:

- That all disadvantaged children be provided quality preschool learning opportunities.
- That all disadvantaged elementary and secondary students be provided the support they need to ensure the acquisition of a sound basic education in public schools.
- That the nation's employment and training system be expanded and restructured to deliver more relevant and viable job skills to today's youth.
- That the nation invest in the development of a world-class transportation system.
- That major investments be made to improve the nation's water supply and treatment facilities as well as to relieve the crisis in solid-waste disposal.
- That the nation pursue more aggressively the development and application of advanced telecommunications technology.

FEDERAL BUDGET

To invest in the Urban League's Marshall Plan for America, the Congress and the Administration must join together in modifying the Budget Enforcement Act (BEA) of 1990. The BEA is now obsolete in light of the changes in the Soviet Union, the end of the Cold War, and the devastation of our communities. To guide the reordering of our national priorities, the following key principles should be adopted, which are supported by a number of organizations, including the National Urban League:

1. Defense expenditures should be reduced in FY1993 significantly below the levels projected in the president's FY1992 five-year plan.
2. Congress and the Administration should allow for the transfer of funds from defense to domestic discretionary spending programs in FY1993,

while maintaining the overall deficit reduction goals set forth in the budget agreement.

3. Defense savings or other discretionary funds should not be used for cutting taxes. Instead, any personal income tax relief package should be financed by shifting the tax burden to upper-income taxpayers.

EDUCATION

During 1991, President Bush announced two proposals for a new generation of American schools. The proposal, "America 2000," established six goals for reforming education in the United States. Education Secretary Lamar Alexander's Commission for Achieving Necessary Skills (SCANS) proposal identified broad areas that schools must address in order to prepare adequately Americans to meet the nation's labor force needs. SCANS, like America 2000, must be based on a solid commitment to provide the means to ensure that every student, whether attending school in a wealthy suburban district or in an impoverished urban district, will benefit from the reform activity.

While each is equally important, neither proposal addresses the structural inequities that currently plague urban public education. Education reform without the long-term commitment and appropriate funding to rectify current inequities can only further marginalize students who are underserved by public education. The Administration must create a system of education capable of overcoming gross inequities in funding, staffing, facilities, and curriculum.

We were disturbed by the Department of Education's recent proposed policy on racially based minority scholarships. The Department's proposed rules send the wrong message about a legitimate and necessary minority scholarship program. Race-based scholarships are few in number, do not result in deprivation to nonminority students, and are targeted to fulfill important educational goals. Our experience with targeted race-based scholarships demonstrate that they are not only good for African American students, but also that they are good for America because they increase the pool of skilled, educated people that our economy needs.

We call upon the Bush Administration and the Department of Education to keep these vital scholarships that have proven successful in expanding educational opportunities. There is no reason to issue new rules restricting racially based minority scholarships!

EMPLOYMENT

The current recessionary times have dramatized the devastating impact that the lack of, or loss of, jobs can have on individuals and families throughout America. Out-of-work and underemployed Americans need jobs, need training and retraining, and want to work. The cumulative impact of persistent double-digit unemployment rates on African Americans, even in nonrecessionary times, has taken its toll on the economic and social well-being of African American individuals and families. The National Urban League calls upon the Congress and the Administration to place employment and training of America's work force at the top of their economic growth agenda.

As an immediate step, the National Urban League urges the Congress and the Administration to enact, in 1992, the long overdue amendments to the Job Training Partnership Act (JTPA). In doing so, the League urges that any amendments to the JTPA ensure that, in actuality, the law reaches those most in need. To achieve this result, we urge that two very important principles be kept in mind when amending the Act: (1) that community-based organizations (CBOs) serve as primary vehicles for reaching those most in need and (2) that there is a critical connection between JTPA programmatic procedures and their impact on the capacity of CBOs to meet the needs of the least skilled, particularly in the JTPA contracting process.

CIVIL RIGHTS

The next critical civil rights issue that must be addressed is the need for legislation to reverse the 1989 U.S. Supreme Court decision of *Richmond v. Croson*, which is having a significant impact on the growth of African American-owned businesses. The *Croson* decision declared the Richmond, Virginia, set-aside program unconstitutional and brought into question similar state and local programs across the nation. As a result, several jurisdictions have voluntarily abandoned their set-aside programs. The National Urban League views the minority business set-aside issue just as critical to African American economic self-sufficiency as employment discrimination. We urge the Congress and the president to work together and expedite action to remedy this flawed public policy.

Civil rights issues are the cornerstone of the National Urban League and its mission to ensure parity for all African American citizens. In this upcoming election year, we urge all candidates for political office to view civil rights in a positive mode. This nation must bring a halt to over a decade of regression and divisiveness in civil rights matters. Our country must move forward as our future wears heavily on the shoulders of civil rights causes. The National Urban League remains firmly committed to keeping civil rights at the forefront of its legislative agenda.

HEALTH

Good health is essential to our nation's productivity, yet 38 million Americans are totally without health insurance. Twenty-five percent of African Americans have no form of health insurance. Until a few months ago, the issue of national health insurance seemed to have a low priority in the Bush Administration. However, as more people find themselves out of work, their cries, coupled with those who have been without coverage for a long time, have forced the Congress and the Administration to focus on this problem.

The National Urban League feels strongly that there should be a uniform health program in the United States which provides health care coverage for all Americans. The 102nd Congress needs to come together and adopt a comprehensive bill that provides equitable health care for all Americans.

CRIME AND CRIMINAL JUSTICE

During his 1988 election campaign, President Bush pledged that he would be "tough on crime." Yet, violent crime has gone unabated. The problem will not disappear by itself. The public is frustrated by our national leadership's inability to bring this social problem under control. The National Urban League urges Congress and the Administration to put an end to partisan bickering over the fight against crime and pledge themselves to end the killing in our streets *now*. We urge that both bodies come together and formulate constructive solutions in the areas of crime prevention, criminal justice system reform, and the transformation of our incarceration system from a training ground for hardened criminals to true rehabilitation.

The availability of drugs, guns, and assault weapons continues to serve as the key instruments of bloodshed in communities throughout America and to pose major obstacles to law enforcement agencies in their efforts to make our streets safer. The National Urban League reiterates its call upon the Congress and the president to get all guns, particularly military assault weapons, out of the hands of criminals. These instruments of death and human devastation must not be readily accessible to anyone involved in illegal activity and must be banned--period--from the public. We, therefore, urge that, in addition to gun-control measures, a ban on all types of assault weapons be included in the omnibus crime bill under reconsideration by Congress.

APPENDIX

African Americans in Profile: Selected Demographic, Social, and Economic Data

National Urban League Research Staff

The overriding purpose of *The State of Black America* is to provide instructive information and analyses on the contemporary condition of the African American population and related issues. The separate papers in the current volume fulfill this purpose from a number of different vantage points. As a supplement, the following set of statistical tables and charts is intended as a ready reference source of data on some of the salient dimensions of the African American condition in the 1990s.

The material was compiled as a collective effort by staff members of the National Urban League Research Department--Dr. Billy Tidwell, Director; Dr. Dionne Jones, Senior Research Associate; Dr. Betty Watson, Senior Research Associate; Monica Jackson, Research Associate; and Syrianna Maesela, Research Intern. Deborah Searcy, Administrative Secretary, also contributed to the effort. Marcus Gordon, MIS consultant, assisted with the graphic displays.

Although the presentation covers just a partial list of the extensive array of characteristics that might be of interest, the selected data provide key summary information that is useful for general profiling purposes. In most instances, African Americans are compared to the majority white population.

Table 1
U.S. Population by Race, 1980 and 1990
(numbers in thousands)

Race	Resident population		Percent of total population		Percent change 1980-90
	1980	1990	1980	1990	
Total population[1]	226,546	248,710	N/A	N/A	9.8
African American	26,495	29,986	11.7	12.1	13.2
White	188,372	199,686	83.2	80.3	6.0

Source: Bureau of the Census, *Summary Population and Housing Characteristics*, 1990.
[1] Includes others not shown separately

Figure 1

U.S. Population by Race
1980 and 1990

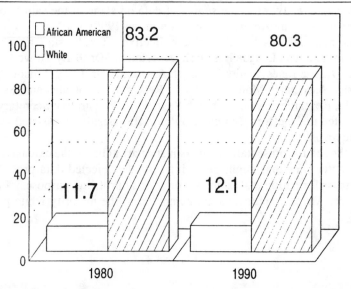

Source: Bureau of the Census, Summary Population and Housing Characteristics, 1990

Table 2
African American Population by Region, 1980 and 1990
(numbers in thousands)

Year and region	Number	Percent distribution
1980		
Total	26,033	100.0
Northeast	4,839	18.6
Midwest	5,349	20.5
South	13,599	52.2
West	2,246	8.6
1990		
Total	29,986	100.0
Northeast	5,613	18.7
Midwest	5,716	19.1
South	15,829	52.8
West	2,828	9.4

Source: Bureau of the Census, *Summary Population and Housing Characteristics*, 1990.

Figure 2.
African American Population
by Region, 1980 and 1990

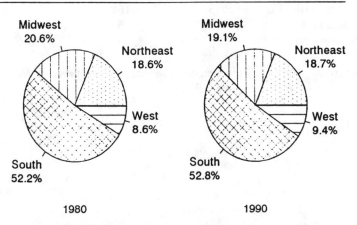

1980   1990

Source: Bureau of the Census, *Summary Population and Housing Characteristics*, 1990.

Table 3
Cities with African American Populations
of 150,000 or More, 1990

City, state	Total population	African American population	Percent African American
		(in thousands)	
New York, NY	7,326	2,102	28.7
Chicago, IL	2,784	1,088	39.1
Detroit, MI	1,028	778	75.7
Philadelphia, PA	1,586	632	39.9
Los Angeles, CA	3,485	488	14.0
Houston, TX	1,631	458	28.1
Baltimore, MD	736	436	59.4
Washington, DC	607	400	65.9
Memphis, TN	610	335	54.9
New Orleans, LA	497	308	62.0
Dallas, TX	1,007	297	29.5
Atlanta, GA	394	264	67.0
Cleveland, OH	506	235	46.4
Milwaukee, WI	628	191	30.4
St. Louis, MO	397	188	47.4
Birmingham, AL	266	168	63.2
Indianapolis, IN	742	166	22.4
Jacksonville, FL	673	164	24.4
Oakland, CA	372	163	43.8
Newark, NJ	275	161	58.6

Source: Bureau of the Census, *Summary Population and Housing Characteristics*, 1990.

Table 4
States with African American Populations
of 1 Million or More, 1990

State	Total population	African American population	Percent African American
		(in thousands)	
New York	17,990	2,859	15.9
California	29,760	2,209	7.4
Texas	16,986	2,022	11.9
Florida	12,938	1,760	13.6
Georgia	6,478	1,747	27.0
Illinois	11,431	1,694	14.8
North Carolina	6,629	1,456	22.0
Louisiana	4,220	1,299	30.8
Michigan	9,295	1,292	13.9
Maryland	4,781	1,190	24.9
Virginia	6,187	1,163	18.8
Ohio	10,847	1,155	10.6
Pennsylvania	11,882	1,090	9.2
South Carolina	3,487	1,040	29.8
New Jersey	7,730	1,037	13.4
Alabama	4,041	1,021	25.3

Source: Bureau of the Census, *Summary Population and Housing Characteristics*, 1990.

Table 5
Ten States with the Largest Percentage
of African Americans, 1990

State	Total African American population	Percent of state population
Mississippi	915,057	35.6
Louisiana	1,299,281	30.8
South Carolina	1,039,884	29.8
Georgia	1,746,565	27.0
Alabama	1,020,705	25.3
Maryland	1,189,899	24.9
North Carolina	1,456,323	22.0
Virginia	1,162,994	18.8
Delaware	112,460	16.9
Tennessee	778,035	16.0

Source: Bureau of the Census, *Summary Population and Housing Characteristics*, 1990.

Table 6
Ten States with the Largest Increase in
African American Population, 1980-1990

State	Amount of increase (in thousands)	Percent change
New York	457	19.0
Florida	417	31.0
California	390	21.4
Texas	311	31.0
Georgia	281	19.2
Maryland	232	24.2
Virginia	154	15.3
No. Carolina	137	10.4
New Jersey	112	12.1
Michigan	93	7.7

Source: Bureau of the Census, *Summary Population and Housing Characteristics*, 1990.

Table 7
Percent Distribution of the Total U.S. Population, African Americans and Whites by Residence, 1990

Residence	Total U.S.	African American	White
Metropolitan areas	77.7	83.8	76.4
Central cities	30.5	56.8	26.2
Suburbs	47.2	27.0	50.2
Nonmetropolitan areas	23.3	16.2	23.6

Source: Bureau of the Census, *Summary Population and Housing Characteristics*, 1990.

Table 8
Age Distribution of Total, African American, and White Populations, 1990

Age group	Total population	African American	White
Total (thousands)	246,191	30,392	206,983
Percent	100.0	100.0	100.0
Under 5 years	7.7	9.6	7.7
5-9 years	7.4	9.3	7.1
10-14 years	7.0	8.9	6.6
15-19 years	7.0	8.8	6.7
20-24 years	7.3	8.2	7.2
25-29 years	8.6	8.9	8.5
30-34 years	9.0	8.9	8.9
35-44 years	15.1	13.4	15.3
45-54 years	10.3	8.8	10.5
55-64 years	8.6	6.9	9.0
65-74 years	7.3	5.0	7.8
75 years & older	4.7	3.2	5.0
Median age (years)	32.8	27.9	33.7

Source: Bureau of the Census, *Current Population Survey*, March 1990.

Table 9
Marital Status by Race and Sex, 1990

Marital status	Both sexes	African American Male	African American Female	Both sexes	White Male	White Female
Total, 15 and older	21,914	9,948	11,966	163,417	78,908	84,508
Percent	100.0	100.0	100.0	100.0	100.0	100.0
Never married	39.9	43.4	36.9	24.2	28.0	20.6
Married, spouse present	34.8	38.8	31.4	58.3	60.4	56.4
Married, spouse absent	7.7	6.3	8.8	2.6	2.3	2.8
Widowed	7.9	3.4	11.6	7.2	2.4	11.6
Divorced	9.8	8.1	11.2	7.7	6.8	8.6

Source: Bureau of the Census, *Current Population Survey*, March 1990.

Table 10
Type of Family by Race, 1990
(numbers in thousands)

Type of family	African American	White
All families	7,470	56,590
Percent	100.0	100.0
Married-couple families	50.2	83.0
Female householder, no husband present	43.8	12.9
Male householder, no wife present	6.0	4.1

Source: Bureau of the Census, *Current Population Survey*, March 1990.

Table 11
Living Arrangements of Children Under 18
by Race, 1990

Living arrangement	African American	White
Both parents	37.7%	79.0%
Mother only	51.2	16.2
Father only	3.5	3.0
Neither parent	7.5	1.8
	100.0%	100.0%

Source: Bureau of the Census, *Current Population Survey*,
           March 1990.

Figure 4.
Living Arrangements of Children
Under 18 by Race, 1990

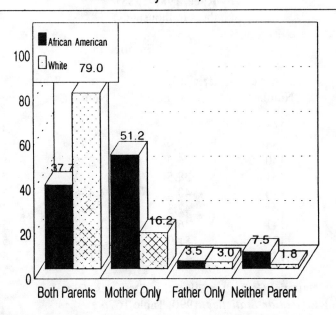

Source: Bureau of the Census, Current Population Survey, March 1990.

Table 12
Percentage of High School Dropouts
among 16-to-24-Year Olds by Race and Sex, 1989

	African American	White
Both sexes	13.8	12.4
Male	14.9	13.4
Female	12.9	11.4

Source: National Center for Education Statistics, *Digest of Education Statistics*, 1990, Table 97.

Table 13
College Enrollment Rates of High School Graduates
by Race, 1980-1988
(numbers in thousands)

	Enrolled in college			
	African American		White	
Year	Number	Percent	Number	Percent
1980	151	41.8	1,339	49.9
1981	154	42.9	1,434	54.6
1982	140	36.5	1,376	52.0
1983	151	38.5	1,372	55.0
1984	176	40.2	1,455	57.9
1985	141	42.3	1,332	59.4
1986	141	36.5	1,292	56.0
1987	175	51.9	1,249	56.6
1988	172	45.0	1,328	60.7

Source: National Center for Education Statistics, *Digest of Education Statistics*, 1990, Table 167.

Table 14
Median Income of Families
by Race and Family Type, 1990

Type of family	African American	White	Ratio: African American/- White
All families	$21,423	$36,915	58.0
Married-couple families	33,784	40,331	83.8
Male householder, no wife present	21,848	30,570	71.5
Female householder, no husband present	12,125	19,528	62.1

Source: Bureau of the Census, *Current Population Survey*, March 1990.

Table 15
Families Below Poverty Level
by Race and Type of Family, 1990
(numbers in thousands)

.Race and family type	Number of families	Number below poverty level	Percent below poverty level
.All families	66,322	7,098	10.7
.African American	7,471	2,193	29.3
Married-couple families	3,569	448	12.6
Male householder, no wife present	472	97	20.6
Female householder, no husband present	3,430	1,648	48.1
White	56,803	4,622	8.1
Married-couple families	47,014	2,386	5.1
Male householder, no wife present	2,277	226	9.9
Female householder, no husband present	7,512	2,010	26.8

Source: Bureau of the Census, *Current Population Survey*, March 1990.

Table 16
Persons Below Poverty Level by Race, 1990
(numbers in thousands)

Race	Total persons	Number below poverty level	Percent below poverty level
Total	248,644	33,585	13.5
African American	30,806	9,837	31.9
White	208,611	22,326	10.7
Other races	9,227	1,422	15.4

Source: Bureau of the Census, *Current Population Survey*, March 1990.

Table 17
Official and Hidden Unemployment by Race, Third Quarter 1991
(numbers in thousands)

Measure and race	Number unemployed	Percent unemployed
Official unemployment		
African American	1,666	12.1
White	6,327	5.8
Hidden unemployment*		
African American	3,330	22.2
White	12,673	11.3

* The hidden unemployment measure includes discouraged and involuntary part-time workers.

Source: Bureau of Labor Statistics, unpublished data.

Table 18
Official Unemployment Rates
by Age, Race, and Sex, 1990 and 1989
(numbers in thousands)

	All Races	African American	White
		1990	
Total population	5.5	11.3	4.8
Males	5.6	11.8	4.8
Females	5.4	11.3	4.6
Teenagers	15.5	31.1	13.1
Males	16.3	32.1	14.2
Females	14.7	30.0	12.6
		1989	
Total population	5.3	11.4	4.5
Males	5.2	11.5	4.5
Females	5.4	11.4	4.5
Teenagers	15.0	32.4	12.7
Males	15.9	31.9	13.7
Females	14.0	33.0	11.5

Source: Prepared by the National Urban League from unpublished Bureau of Labor Statistics data.

Table 19
Hidden Unemployment Rates by Age, Race, and Sex, 1990 and 1989*

	All Races	African American	White
		1990	
Total	11.3	21.5	9.9
Males	10.0	19.8	8.6
Females	13.0	17.9	13.1
Teenagers	30.1	53.1	25.0
Males	54.1	60.9	26.5
Females	30.0	53.7	39.4
		1989	
Total	11.5	24.5	9.9
Males	9.3	19.8	8.1
Females	12.9	24.1	11.2
Teenagers	28.6	52.9	24.5
Males	29.2	52.8	25.3
Females	27.9	52.9	23.7

*: The Hidden Unemployment Rate includes discouraged and involuntary part-time workers among the unemployed.

Source: Prepared by the National Urban League from unpublished Bureau of Labor Statistics data.

Table 20
Labor Force Participation Rates by Race, 1990

	Total	African American	White
Total	66.4%	63.3%	66.8%
Male	76.1	70.1	76.9
Female	57.5	57.8	57.5
Teenagers	53.7	38.6	57.5
Male	55.7	40.6	59.4
Female	51.8	36.7	55.4

Source: Department of Labor, Bureau of Labor Statistics, *Employment and Earnings* (January 1991), Table 2, pp. 163-65.

Figure 5.
Labor Force Participation Rates
by Race, 1990

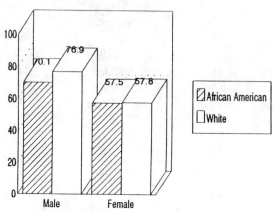

Source: Department of Labor, Bureau of Labor Statistics,
Employment and Earnings, (January 1991), Table 2, pp. 163-65.

Table 21
Median Weekly Earnings by Race and Sex, 1990 and 1989

	African American	White	AA/Wh Ratio
		1990	
Total	$329	$427	.77
Male	360	497	.72
Female	308	355	.87
		1989	
Total	$319	$409	.78
Male	348	482	.72
Female	301	334	.90

..Source: Data from Bureau of Labor Statistics, *Employment
and Earnings*, Vol. 36, No. 6 (June 1989), Table
54, p. 219; *Employment and Earnings*, Vol. 38, No. 1
(January 1991), Table 54, p. 221.

Table 22

Occupational Distribution by Race and Sex, 1990

(numbers in thousands)

Occupation	African American			Total	White	
	Total	Male	Female		Male	Female
Total 16 years and over	11,966	5,915	6,051	102,087	56,432	45,654
Percent	100.0	100.0	100.0	100.0	100.0	100.0
Managerial and professional	16.0	13.3	18.6	27.1	26.9	27.2
Technical, sales, and administrative support	28.2	17.1	39.1	31.5	20.3	45.3
Service	22.8	18.2	27.3	12.2	8.7	16.4
Precision production, craft, and repair	8.9	15.6	2.3	12.0	20.0	2.1
Operators, fabricators, and laborers	22.4	32.7	12.2	14.3	19.4	7.8
Farming, forestry, and fishing	1.7	3.2	.3	3.1	4.6	1.1

Source: Bureau of Labor Statistics, *Employment and Earnings*, January 1991, Table 21, p. 184

NOTES AND REFERENCES

Black America, 1991: An Overview, *John E. Jacob*

FOOTNOTES

[1] Center on Budget and Policy Priorities, "Drifting Apart: New Findings on Growing Income Disparities Between the Rich, the Poor, and the Middle Class" (Washington, DC: Center on Budget and Policy Priorities, 1990).

[2] George Will, "Who's Better Off These Days?", *The Washington Post*, October 31, 1991.

[3] Jason DeParle, "Poverty Rate Rose Sharply Last Year as Incomes Slipped," *The New York Times*, September 27, 1991.

[4] National Center for Children in Poverty, *News and Issues*, Fall 1991, Columbia University School of Public Health.

[5] David Whitman, "The Rise of the Hyper-Poor," *U.S. News & World Report*, October 15, 1990.

[6] National Urban League Research Department, *Quarterly Economic Report on the African American Worker*, Report No. 30, Third Quarter 1991 (forthcoming).

[7] Brent Mitchell, "States Burdened by Surge in Welfare Caseloads," *The Washington Post*, July 28, 1991.

[8] This quotation is taken from the review of *The Years of Lyndon Johnson: Volume 1, Means of Ascent* by Robert A. Caro in the July 21, 1991, *Washington Post Book World*.

[9] Economic Policy Institute, "Increasing Public Investment" Briefing Paper, Washington, DC, 1991.

[10] Robert Heilbroner, "Lifting the Silent Depression," *The New York Review of Books*, October 24, 1991.

[11] The *New York Times*/CBS News national poll was conducted during the week of October 22, 1991.

[12] Billy J. Tidwell, *Playing to Win: A Marshall Plan for America* (New York: National Urban League, Inc., 1991).

Serving the National Interest: A Marshall Plan for America, *Billy J. Tidwell, Ph.D.*

FOOTNOTES

[1] For a more detailed presentation of the Marshall Plan, see Billy J. Tidwell, *Playing to Win: A Marshall Plan for America* (New York: National Urban League, Inc., 1991).

[2] Data from *International Financial Statistics*, March 1991, for first three quarters of 1990.

[3] Lawrence Mishel and David M. Frankel, *The State of Working America* (Washington, DC: Economic Policy Institute, 1991).

[4] *Ibid.*

[5] Anthony Patrick Carnevale, *America and the New Economy* (Alexandria, VA: American

329

Society for Training and Development, 1991), p. 17.

[6]Samuel Bowles, David M. Gordon, and Thomas E. Weisskopf, *After the Wasteland: A Democratic Economics for the Year 2000* (Armonk, NY: M.E. Sharpe, Inc., 1991), p. 45.

[7]Carnevale, *op. cit.*

[8]*Ibid.*, pp. 24-25.

[9]Mishel and Frankel, *op. cit.*

[10]Carnevale, *op. cit.*, p. 17.

[11]Isaac Shapiro and Robert Greenstein, *Selective Prosperity: Increasing Income Disparities Since 1977* (Washington, DC: Center on Budget and Policy Priorities, 1991).

[12]U.S. Department of Labor, Bureau of Labor Statistics, "Outlook 2000," *Monthly Labor Review*, Vol. 112, No. 11 (November 1989).

[13]The work of Johnston and Packer on this subject is widely credited with having galvanized public attention to the issue. See William B. Johnston and Arnold H. Packer, *Workforce 2000: Work and Workers for the 21st Century* (Indianapolis, IN: The Hudson Institute, 1987).

[14]For a recent attempt at defining the basic proficiencies workers will need, see *What Work Requires of Schools: A SCANS Report for America 2000*, U.S. Department of Labor, The Secretary's Commission on Achieving Necessary Skills, June 1991.

[15]For example, *The Forgotten Half: Non-College Youth in America* and *The Forgotten Half: Pathways to Success for America's Youth and Young Families*, William T. Grant Foundation, 1988. Also, Gordon Berlin and Andrew Sum, *Toward a More Perfect Union: Basic Skills, Poor Families, and Our Economic Future* (New York: Ford Foundation, 1988).

[16]Berlin and Sum, *op. cit.*

[17]National Council on Public Works Improvement, *Fragile Foundations: A Report on America's Public Works* (Washington, DC: Government Printing Office, 1988).

[18]U.S. Department of Transportation, *Moving America: New Directions, New Opportunities* (Washington, DC: Government Printing Office, 1990); *The 1991 Status of the Nation's Highways and Bridges: Conditions, Performance, and Capital Investment Requirements* (Washington, DC: Government Printing Office, 1991).

[19]For a good summary, see Merrill Lynch, *Weekly Economic and Financial Commentary*, "Our Neglected Infrastructure" (New York: Merrill Lynch, Pierce, Fenner & Smith, 1989).

[20]*Ibid.*

[21]Robert B. Reich, "The Real Economy," *The Atlantic* (February 1991), pp. 35-52.

[22]Democratic Study Group, "Decade of Disinvestment," paper no. 101-26, January 1990, Washington, DC.

[23]U.S. General Accounting Office, *Training Strategies: Preparing Noncollege Youth for Employment in the U.S. and Foreign Countries*, GAO/HRD-90-88, 1990, Washington, DC.

[24]David Alan Aschauer, *Public Investment and Private Sector Growth: The Economic Benefits of Reducing "America's Third Deficit"* (Washington, DC: Economic Policy Institute, 1991).

[25]Democratic Study Group, *op. cit.*

[26]Aschauer, *op. cit.*

[27]Reich, *op. cit.*

²⁸Aschauer, *op. cit.* Also, Congressional Budget Office, *How Federal Spending for Infrastructure and Other Public Investments Affects the Economy* (Washington, DC: Government Printing Office, 1991). Apogee Research, *Enhancing U.S. Competitiveness Through Highway Investment: A Strategy for Economic Growth* (Bethesda, MD: Apogee Research, Inc., 1990).

²⁹U.S. General Accounting Office, *op. cit.*

³⁰Commission on Skills of the American Workforce, *America's Choice: High Skills or Low Wages* (Rochester, NY: National Center on Education and the Economy, 1990).

³¹AFL-CIO, AFL-CIO Reviews the Issues, "Creating Jobs in the Recession: Public Works," Report No. 51 (May 1991). Also, Apogee Research, *The Jobs Impact of an Expanded Federal Highway Program* (Bethesda, MD: Apogee Research, Inc., 1991).

The Demographic Revolution: Diversity in 21st Century America, *Bernard C. Watson, Ph.D.*

FOOTNOTES

¹Merrill Simon, *God, Allah, and the Great Land Grab* (New York: Jonathan David Publishers, Inc., 1989).

²William A. Henry, III, "Beyond the Melting Pot," *Time*, April 9, 1990.

³Carolyn Pesce, "NJ Town's Changing Face Typifies Trend," *USA Today*, April 11, 1991.

⁴The events and dates cited in this section and the next are from several sources. Among those sources: Stephanie Bernardo, *Ethnic Almanac* (Garden City, NY: Doubleday, 1981); Irving J. Sloan, *Our Violent Past: An American Chronicle* (New York: Random House, 1970); and Richard B. Morris, *Encyclopedia of American History* (New York: Harper & Row, 1961).

⁵Ronald Takaki, *Strangers from a Different Shore: A History of Asian Americans* (Boston: Little, Brown and Company, 1989).

⁶Sergio R. Bustos and Gary Cohn, "Misunderstood in Mushroom Country," *The Philadelphia Inquirer*, May 19, 1991.

⁷David Shribman, "Republicans, Often Hoping for More than Good Government, Help Minority Redistricting Efforts," *The Wall Street Journal*, April 2, 1991.

⁸*Newsweek*, January 14, 1991.

⁹R.W. Apple, Jr., "In Clashes: A Hispanic Agenda Enters," *The New York Times*, May 8, 1991.

¹⁰Howard J. Ehrlich (of the National Institute Against Prejudice and Violence), quoted in "New Racial Diversity Fuels Hate-Crime Wave," *The Philadelphia Inquirer*, September 10, 1991.

¹¹"New Racial Diversity," *op. cit.*, quoting Lynn Duvall (of Klanwatch).

¹²California Tomorrow, Fort Mason Center, Building B, San Francisco, California 94123.

¹³Max DePree, quoted in "Today's Leaders Look to Tomorrow," *Fortune*, March 26, 1990.

¹⁴"Today's Leaders," *op. cit.*, quoting James R. Houghton.

¹⁵Peter T. Kilborn, "When Equal Rights Is A Goal, Workers' Response Is Mixed," *The New York Times*, May 12, 1991.

[16]*Workforce 2000: Work and Workers for the Twenty-first Century* (Indianapolis, IN: Hudson Institute, 1987); *Opportunity 2000: Creative Affirmative Action Strategies for a Changing Workforce* (Washington, DC: Government Printing Office, 1988).

[17]*Opportunity 2000* . . ., p. 1.

[18]Towers Perrin and the Hudson Institute, *Workforce 2000: Competing in a Seller's Market: Is Corporate America Prepared?* (August 1990).

[19]Jerry Gray, "Panel Says Courts Are 'Invested with Racism,'" *The New York Times*, June 5, 1991.

[20]Bob H. Suzuki, "Unity with Diversity: Easier Said than Done," *Liberal Education* 77 (January-February 1991): 33, 34.

[21]David Halberstam, *The Next Century* (New York: William Morrow and Company, Inc., 1991), pp. 122, 124. See also, for instance: Robert B. Reich, *The Work of Nations: Preparing Ourselves for 21st-Century Capitalism* (New York: Alfred A. Knopf, 1991).

[22]For excerpts from and discussion of the major studies, see Beatrice and Ronald Gross (eds.), *The Great School Debate: Which Way for American Education?* (New York: Simon & Schuster, 1985).

[23]See, for instance, Lisbeth B. Schorr, *Within Our Reach: Breaking the Cycle of Disadvantage* (New York: Doubleday, 1988).

[24]The William T. Grant Foundation Commission on Work, Family and Citizenship, *The Forgotten Half: Non-College Youth in America* (Washington, DC: The William T. Grant Foundation, 1988).

[25]Arthur M. Schlesinger, Jr., *The Disuniting of America: Reflections on a Multicultural Society* (Knoxville, TN: Whittle Books, 1991), p. 2.

[26]Joyce Carol Oates, "Unless We Share, We Are Not Fully Human," in "Rediscover America," a special advertising section presented by Chrysler Corporation and included in *Time*, March 18, 1991.

[27]Alex Kotlowitz, *There Are No Children Here* (New York: Doubleday, 1991).

[28]Nicholas Lemann, *The Promised Land: The Great Black Migration and How It Changed America* (New York: Alfred A. Knopf, 1991).

[29]Emma Lazarus, "The New Colossus" (poem written for the 1886 dedication of the Statue of Liberty and engraved on its base).

The Economic Status of African Americans: Limited Ownership and Persistent Inequality, *David H. Swinton, Ph.D.*

REFERENCES

Swinton, David H. 1990. "The Economic Status of Blacks 1990," *The State of Black America 1990*, ed. Janet Dewart. New York: National Urban League, Inc.

_____. 1988. "The Economic Status of Blacks 1988," *The State of Black America 1988*, ed. Janet Dewart. New York: National Urban League, Inc.

_____. 1987. "The Economic Status of Blacks 1987," *The State of Black America 1987*, ed. Janet Dewart. New York: National Urban League, Inc.

_____. 1986. "The Economic Status of the Black Population 1986," *The State of Black America 1986*, ed. James D. Williams. New York: National Urban League, Inc.

U.S. Department of Commerce Bureau of the Census. 1991. *Money Income of Households, Families, and Persons in the United States: 1990*. Washington, DC: Government Printing Office.

_____. 1991. *Money Income of Households, Families, and Persons in the United States: 1988 and 1989*. Washington, DC: Government Printing Office.

_____. 1991. *Poverty in the United States: 1990*. Washington, DC: Government Printing Office.

_____. 1991. *The Black Population in the United States: March 1990 and 1989*. Washington, DC: Government Printing Office.

_____. 1990. *Money Income and Poverty Status of Families and Persons in the United States: 1989* (advance data from the March 1990 *Current Population Survey*). Washington, DC: Government Printing Office.

_____. 1990. *Money Income and Poverty Status in the United States: 1989*. Washington, DC: Government Printing Office. (Data from this annual report are cited in this essay for the years covering 1987-1990; the facts of publication are unchanged except for the year of publication.)

_____. 1990. *Survey of Minority-Owned Businesses: Black, 1987*. Washington, DC: Government Printing Office.

_____. 1990. *Household Wealth and Asset Ownership: 1988*. Washington, DC: Government Printing Office.

_____. 1986. *Household Wealth and Asset Ownership: 1984*. Washington, DC: Government Printing Office.

_____. 1986. *Statistical Abstract of the United States: 1986*. Washington, DC: Government Printing Office.

U.S. Department of Labor Bureau of Labor Statistics. 1991. *Employment and Earnings, January, June, and August 1991*. Washington, DC: Government Printing Office.

_____. 1990. *Employment and Earnings, January and October 1990*. Washington, DC: Government Printing Office. (Data from this annual report are cited throughout this essay for the years 1986-1989; the facts of publication are unchanged except for the year of publishing.)

_____. 1990. *Employment Situation: November 1990*. News release, December 1990, Table A-3.

_____. 1990. *Geographic Profile of Employment and Unemployment, 1989*. Washington, DC: Government Printing Office.

_____. 1990. *Geographic Profile of Employment and Unemployment, 1987*. Washington, DC: Government Printing Office.

_____. 1985. *Handbook of Labor Statistics, June 1985*. Washington, DC: Government Printing Office.

Racial Earnings Inequality into the 21st Century, *William A. Darity, Jr., Ph.D., and Samuel L. Myers, Jr., Ph.D.*

FOOTNOTES

[1]Hoffman and Link (1984) attempt to estimate population earnings equations from *Current Population Survey* (CPS) data and to "correct" for selection bias by using a procedure suggested by Heckman (1979). Large standard errors are reported for the selection effect for young blacks and whites, suggesting to Hoffman and Link that the role of labor force withdrawal in driving up the relative wage ratios may be negligible. Charles Brown also has examined the effect of zero earners on the racial earnings gap. Using aggregate data and correcting the median earnings for truncation, most of the earnings gained by blacks remained after "correction" for zero earners was made. He concludes that sample selection may be a much less important contributor to the observed increases in black earnings than the Heckman school would have one believe. Wayne Vroman (1986) combines the CPS tapes on current earnings with the earnings histories from the Social Security Administration's Earning Record data. Vroman discovers that the effect of removing people from the sample who subsequently become transfer recipients decreases their median earnings and does not increase them. According to Vroman's estimates, it is not the lowest productivity people who withdraw from the labor market in favor of the receipt of transfers; rather, it is the higher wage earners who withdraw. Smith and Welch also examine the Heckman argument. Their technique is to link adjacent years of the CPS where the same individuals can be found due to the sample rotation method used by census enumerators. Smith and Welch conclude that more than half of the racial earnings improvement from 1970 to 1980 among 25-to-30-year-old males can be accounted for by labor force withdrawal. Among older age groups, however, less than 10 percent of the wage gains by blacks can be so accounted.

Moreover, in their optimistic assessment, Smith and Welch conclude that overall sample selection has played a minor and insignificant role in raising the measure of black economic well-being. In an earlier paper (Darity-Myers, 1980), we also found mixed support for a Heckman-type withdrawal process. Our results confirmed that there is a sample selection process that reduced the black-white earnings ratios among those with positive earnings. But this reduction is not the result of low productivity blacks withdrawing from the labor market. Instead, it is attributable to the reduction in labor force participation of higher productivity whites. Indeed, this proposition gains added support in light of data that show young whites with higher levels of education experiencing reduced weeks worked from 1968 to 1978, along with higher levels of unemployment. Intriguingly then, the Heckman argument is turned on its head to suggest that it is the voluntary withdrawal of more productive whites and not less productive blacks that has contributed to the observed declines in racial earnings.

[2]William A. Darity, Jr., and Samuel L. Myers, Jr., "Public Policy Trends and the Fate of the Black Family," *Humboldt Journal of Social Relations*, Vol. 14:1 & 2 (Fall/Winter & Spring/Summer 1986-87) 134-164.

[3]We have estimated four versions of our econometric model: (1) single equation estimates using ordinary least squares; (2) single equation estimates obtained by maximum likelihood methods and with correction for selection bias using the Heckman procedure; (3) a full model version of the ordinary least squares estimates; and (4) a full model version of the Heckman procedure. The full model estimates consider a recursive structure whereby earnings depend on labor force participation, which depends on family structure, which depends on welfare and mate availability. In principle, each step along the way of this causal chain depends on educational outcomes. Therefore, the total impact of education on earnings inequality should account for intermediate as well as direct effects.

[4]William D. Bradford, "Wealth, Assets, and Income in Black Households," *AASP Working*

Paper Series: Policy Research, Analysis and Minority Communities, University of Maryland at College Park, February 1990; Faith Ando, *An Analysis of Access to Bank Credit* (Los Angeles: UCLA Center for Afro-American Studies, 1988); Timothy Bates, "Discrimination and the Capacity of New Jersey Area Minority- and Women-Owned Businesses," Graduate School of Management and Urban Policy, New School of Social Research, August 1991.

[5]The percent of increase or decrease in inequality, *I*, is given by:

$$\ln(I) = \ln(Y^B)_t - \ln(Y^W)_t - \ln(Y^B)_{t+1} + \ln(Y^W)_{t+1}.$$

To determine the effect of a uniform increase in one year of education, x, on earnings inequality, one computes:

$$\partial \ln(I)/\partial x = \partial \ln(Y^B)_t/\partial x - \partial \ln(Y^W)_t/\partial x - \partial \ln(Y^B)_{t+1}/\partial x + \partial \ln(Y^W)_{t+1}/\partial x.$$

A resulting positive value means that education increases inequality. A resulting negative value means that education reduces inequality.

[6]U.S. Department of Commerce, *The Black Population in the United States* (Washington, DC: Government Printing Office, 1991).

[7]See Robert Johnson, "Black Underrepresentation in Science and Technology," *Trotter Institute Review*, Winter/Spring 1991, pp. 13-18.

[8]William A. Darity, Jr., "The Political Economy of Uneven Development from the Slave(ry) Times to the Managerial Age," paper presented at the 1991 Conference on Africology, June 1991, University of Wisconsin at Milwaukee.

[9]Specifically, we estimate a polynomial distributed lag model.

REFERENCES

Bianchi, Suzanne M. *Household Composition and Racial Inequality*. New Brunswick: Rutgers University Press, 1981.

_____. "Racial Differences in Per Capita Income, 1960-76: The Importance of Household Size, Headship, and Labor Force Participation," *Demography*, 17, No. 2, May 1980: 129-43.

Brown, Charles. "Black-White Earnings Ratios Since Civil Rights Act of 1964: The Importance of Labor Market Dropouts," *Quarterly Journal of Economics*, February 1984: 31-44.

Butler, Richard and James Heckman. "The Government's Impact on the Labor Market Status of Black Americans: A Critical Review," *Equal Rights and Industrial Relations*, eds. Leonard Hausman et al. Madison, WI: Industrial Relations Research Association, 1977: 235-281.

_____. "A New Look at the Empirical Evidence on the Assertion That Government Policy Has Shifted the Aggregate Relative Demand Function in Favor of Blacks." Chicago: The University of Chicago Department of Economics, 1978.

Darity, Jr., William and Samuel Myers, Jr. "Changes in Black-White Income Inequality, 1968-78: A Decade of Progress?", *Review of Black Political Economy* 10 (Summer 1980): 365-379.

_____. "Changes in Black Family Structure: Implication for Welfare Dependency," *American Economic Review*, 73 (May 1983): 59-64.

_____. "Does Welfare Dependency Cause Female Headship? The Case of the Black Family," *Journal of Marriage and the Family*, 46 (November 1984): 765-780.

_____. "Public Policy and the Conditions of the Black Family Life," *Review of the Black Political Economy*, 1 & 2 (1984): 165-187.

_____. "Public Policy Trends and the Fate of the Black Family," *Humboldt Journal of Social Relations*, 14 (1 & 2), 1986-87: 134-164.

_____. "Black-White Earnings Gaps Have Widened: The Problem of Family Structure, Earnings Inequality, and the Marginalization of Black Men," *AASP Working Paper Series: Policy Research, Analysis, and Minority Communities*, 1 (5), August 1991, University of Maryland at College Park.

Darity, Jr., William A. "The Political Economy of Uneven Development from the Slave(ry) Times to the Managerial Age." Paper presented at the 1991 Conference on Africology, June 1991, University of Wisconsin at Milwaukee.

Farley, Reynolds. *Blacks and Whites: Narrowing the Gap?* Cambridge: Harvard University Press, 1984.

_____. "Three Steps Forward and Two Back? Recent Changes in the Social and Economic Status of Blacks," *Ethnic and Racial Studies*, 9:1 (January 1985): 4-28.

Freedman, Richard B. "Changes in the Labor Market for Black Americans, 1948-1972," *Brookings Papers on Economics Activity*, 1, 1973.

_____. "Decline of Labor Market Discrimination and Economic Analysis," *American Economic Review: AEA Papers and Proceedings*, May 1973.

_____. "The New Job Market for Black Academicians," *Industrial and Labor Relations Review*, January 1977.

_____. "Black Economic Progress after 1964: Who Gained and Why," *NBER Working Paper*, 282, Cambridge, MA, October 1978.

Heckman, James J. "Sample Selection bias as a Specification Error," *Econometrica*, January 1979.

Johnson, Robert. "Black Underrepresentation in Science and Technology," *Trotter Institute Review*, Winter/Spring 1991, 13-18.

Link, Charles. "Black Education, Earnings, and Interregional Migration: A Comment and Some New Evidence," *American Economic Review*, 65 (March 1975): 236-40.

McLanahan, Sara. "Family Structure and Reproduction of Poverty," *American Journal of Sociology*, 9 (1985): 873-901.

Smith, James P. "Race and Human Capital," *American Economic Review*, September 1984: 685-698.

_____. and Finis Welch, "Inequality: Race Differences in the Distribution of Earnings," *International Economic Review*, June 1979: 515-526.

_____. "Black-White Male Wage Ratios: 1960-1970," *American Economic Review*, June 1977.

Taylor, Patricia A., Patricia Gwartney-Gibbs, and Reynolds Farley. "Changes in the Structure of Earnings Inequality by Race, Sex, and Industrial Sector, 1960-1980." *Research in Social Stratification and Mobility*, ed. Robert V. Robinson, 5 (1986): 105-138.

U.S. Department of Commerce Bureau of the Census. *The Black Population in the United States*. Washington, DC: Government Printing Office, 1991.

_____. *Current Population Survey*. Washington, DC: Government Printing Office, various years.

Vroman, Wayne. "Changes in Black Workers' Relative Earnings: Evidence from the 1960s." *Patterns of Racial Discrimination*, Vol. 2, eds. George von Furstenberg et al. Lexington, MA: Lexington Books, 1974.

336

Welch, Finis. "Black-White Differences in Returns to Schooling,"*American Economic Review*, December 1973: 893-907.

Wilson, William J. *The Declining Significance of Race*. Chicago: University of Chicago Press, 1982, 2nd edition.

_____. *The Truly Disadvantaged: The Inner City, The Underclass, and Public Policy*. Chicago: University of Chicago Press, 1987.

_____. and Robert Aponte. "Urban Poverty," *Annual Review of Sociology*, Vol. II, 1985: 231-258.

Wilson, William J. and Katherine Neckerman. "Poverty and Family Structure: The Widening Gap between Evidence and Public Policy Issues." *Fighting Poverty: What Works and What Doesn't*, eds. S. Danziger and D. Weinberg. Cambridge, MA: Harvard University Press, 1986.

===

The Condition of African American Education: Changes and Challenges, *Shirley McBay, Ph.D.*

FOOTNOTES

[1]The Quality Education for Minorities Project, *Education That Works: An Action Plan for the Education of Minorities* (Cambridge: Massachusetts Institute of Technology, 1990), p. 18.

[2]*The Black Population in the United States: March 1990 and 1989* (Washington, DC: U.S. Government Printing Office, August 1991), p. 6.

[3]*Ibid.*

[4]*Ibid.*

[5]National Center for Children in Poverty, *Five Million Children: A Statistical Profile of Our Poorest Young Children* (New York: National Center for Children in Poverty, 1990), p. 20.

[6]Western Interstate Commission for Higher Education and The College Board, *The Road to College Educational Progress by Race and Ethnicity* (Boulder, CO: Western Interstate Commission for Higher Education, July 1991), p. 11.

[7]*Education That Works, op. cit.*

[8]*Education Daily*, Vol. 24, No. 180, September 17, 1991, p. 1.

[9]Commission on Professionals in Science and Technology, *Professional Women and Minorities* (Washington, DC: Commission on Professionals in Science and Technology, March 1991), p. 17.

[10]*The Road to College, op. cit.*

[11]*Professional Women and Minorities, op. cit.*

[12]*Education That Works, op. cit.*

[13]Kenneth J. Cooper, "Middle-Class Blacks Fear Schools Fail Their Children," *The Washington Post*, November 4, 1991, p. A13.

[14]Margaret L. Usdansky, "USA at Home: Streets Still Isolate Racists," *USA Today*, November 11, 1991, p. 2.

[15]*Black Issues in Higher Education*, Vol. 8, No. 17, October 24, 1991, p. 1.

[16]Higher Education Extension Service *Review*, Vol. 3, No. 1, Fall 1991, p. 3.

[17]U.S. Department of Education, *America 2000: An Education Strategy* (Washington, DC: Government Printing Office, 1991).

[18]*Education That Works, op. cit.*

Science, Technology, and Human Resources: Preparing for the 21st Century, *Walter E. Massey, Ph.D.*

FOOTNOTES

[1]Robert B. Reich, "The REAL Economy," *The Atlantic Monthly*, February 1991, p. 40.

[2]*Ibid.*

[3]*Ibid.*, p. 36.

[4]Commission on the Skills of the American Workforce, *America's Choice: High Skills or Low Wages* (Rochester, NY: National Center for Education and the Economy, 1990), pp. 31-36.

[5]National Science Foundation (NSF), Division of Science Resources Studies, *Women and Minorities in Science and Engineering, 1992 Edition* (Washington, DC: National Science Foundation, forthcoming), Table 28.

[6]*Ibid.*, Table 31.

[7]National Science Foundation, Division of Science Resources Studies, *Blacks in Undergraduate Science and Engineering Education* (Washington, DC: National Science Foundation, forthcoming), p. 1.

[8]NSF, *Women and Minorities*, Tables 28 and 31.

[9]NSF, *Blacks in Undergraduate Science*, p. 2.

[10]*Ibid.*

[11]*Ibid.*, Chart 4.

[12]Eugene Cota-Robles, paper presented at the National Science Foundation, September 24, 1991, Washington, DC.

[13]National Science Foundation, Division of Science Resources Studies, *Science and Engineering Doctorates: 1960-90* (Washington, DC: National Science Foundation, 1991), p. 88.

[14]National Science Board, *Educating Americans for the 21st Century* (Washington, DC: National Science Board, 1983), p. 3.

[15]Alliance for Undergraduate Education, *The Freshman Year in Science and Engineering: Old Problems, New Perspectives for Research Universities* (Washington, DC: Alliance for Undergraduate Education, 1990), p. 7.

[16]Sheila Tobias, *They're Not Dumb, They're Different: Stalking the Second Tier* (Tucson, AZ: Research Corporation, 1990), p. 86.

[17]Project Kaleidoscope, *What Works: Building Natural Science Communities* (Washington, DC: Project Kaleidoscope, 1991), p. 59.

Clear and Present Danger: The Decay of America's Physical Infrastructure, *Sylvester Murray*

FOOTNOTES

[1]For more discussion on this productivity link, see Claire Felbinger, "Rethinking the Infrastructure-Economic Development Linkage," unpublished paper, Cleveland State University, Ohio, 1991.

[2]David A. Aschauer, "Infrastructure: America's Third Deficit," *Challenge*, March-April 1991.

[3]Pat Choate and Susan Walter, *America in Ruins: The Decaying Infrastructure* (Durham, NC: Duke Press Paperbacks, 1983), pp. 4-7.

[4]Ken Anderberg (ed.), *American City and County*, "What Are the Issues for 1985?", Washington, DC: International Management Association, February 1985, pp. 12-15.

[5]National League of Cities, *The State of the Small City: A Survey of American Cities of Less Than 50,000 Population*, Washington, DC, 1987, p. vii.

[6]U.S. Congress Office of Technology Assessment, *Delivering the Goods: Public Works Technology, Management, and Financing* (Washington, DC: Government Printing Office, 1991), p. 3.

[7]National Council on Public Works Improvement, *Fragile Foundations, A Report on America's Public Works* (Washington, DC, 1988), pp. 33-36.

[8]Ralph Gakenheimer, "Infrastructure Shortfall: The Institutional Problems," *American Planning Association Journal*, Winter 1989, pp. 14-23. **"Full constrained needs"** are defined as the least tolerable conditions that would allow highway authorities to ensure safety and to improve long-term solutions to capital needs.

[9]"Are Cities Obsolete." *Newsweek*, September 9, 1991, pp. 42-44.

[10]Jason DeParle, "Number of People in Poverty Shows Sharp Rise in U.S.," *The New York Times National Edition*, Sepetember 27, 1991, p. A1.

[11]Discussed in Roger J. Vaughan, *Rebuilding America: Financing Public Works in the 1980s* (Washington, DC: The Council of State Planning Agencies, 1983).

[12]U.S. Department of Labor, *Workforce 2000 Report and 1990 Outlook 2000* (Washington, DC: Government Printing Office, 1988 and 1990).

[13]A detailed discussion on public jobs can be found in Gerald D. Jaynes and Robin M. Williams, Jr. (eds.), *A Common Destiny: Blacks and American Society* (Washington, DC: National Academy Press, 1989), and Billy J. Tidwell, *Playing to Win: A Marshall Plan for America* (New York: National Urban League, Inc., 1991).

[14]Leonard Silk, "Bleak Job Picture Darkens the Mood," *The New York Times*, November 1, 1991, p. C2. Silk also argued that a public jobs program is the best approach out of the current recession.

REFERENCES

American Public Works Association, Michigan Chapter. *1991 Infrastructure Survey.* 1991.

Brain, Sally. "America's Infrastructure: The Key to Our Quality Life," *Constructor.* November 1989, pp. 25-40.

City of Cincinnati. *Infrastructure Commission Report, 1987.* Cincinnati, Ohio. December 1987, pp. 7-8.

Commission on Budget and Financial Priorities of the District of Columbia. 1990. *Financing the Nation's Capital.* Washington, DC. November 1989, pp. viii, 4-4.

Kaplan, Marshall. "Infrastructure Policy: Repetitive Studies, Uneven Responses, Next Steps," *Urban Affairs Quarterly.* Vol. 25, 1990, pp. 371-388.

U.S. Department of Commerce Bureau of the Census. *Selected Population and Housing Characteristics.* Washington, DC: Government Printing Office, 1990.

U.S. Department of Labor Bureau of Labor Statistics. *Geographic Profile of Employment and Unemployment: 1990.* Washington, DC: Government Printing Office, 1990.

Urban Infrastructure: Social, Environmental, and Health Risks to African Americans, *Robert D. Bullard, Ph.D.*

FOOTNOTES

[1]Walter L. Updegrade, "Race and Money," *Money* 18 (1989): 152-172.

[2]Franklin J. James, B.I. McCummings, and E.A. Tynan, *Minorities in the Sunbelt* (New Brunswick, NJ: Rutgers University Center for Urban Policy Research, 1984), p. 138.

[3]See Joe T. Darden, "The Status of Urban Blacks 25 Years after the Civil Rights Act of 1964," *Sociology and Social Research* 73 (1989): 160-173; and Robert D. Bullard, "Blacks and the American Dream of Housing," in Jamshid A. Momeni (ed.), *Race, Ethnicity, and Housing in the United States* (Westport, CT: Greenwood Press, 1986), pp. 53-68.

[4]Judith Feins and R.G. Bratt, "Barred in Boston: Racial Discrimination in Housing," *Journal of the American Planning Association* 49 (1983): 344-355; Katherine L. Bradbury, Karl E. Case, and Constance R. Dunham, "Geographic Patterns of Mortgage Lending in Boston, 1982-1987," *New England Economic Review* (September/October 1989): 3-30; Joe R. Feagin, *Building American Cities: The Urban Real Estate Game* (Englewood Cliffs, NJ: Prentice-Hall, 1990), chapter 1; Gerald D. Jaynes and Robin M. Williams, Jr., *A Common Destiny: Blacks and American Society* (Washington, DC: National Academy Press, 1989), pp. 55-112; Bill Dedman, "The Color of Money," *The Atlanta Journal/Constitution*, May 16, 1988; Bill Dedman, "Blacks Turned Down for Home Loans from S&Ls Twice as Often as Whites," *The Atlanta Journal/Constitution*, January 22, 1989.

[5]Federal Financial Institutions Examination Council, "Home Mortgage Disclosure Act: Expanded Data on Residential Lending," *Federal Reserve Bulletin* (November 1991): 859-881; also see Robert A. Rosenblatt and James Bates, "High Minority Mortgage Denial Rates Found," *The Los Angeles Times*, October 22, 1991, pp. A1, A25.

[6]Robert D. Bullard and Joe R. Feagin, "Racism and the City," in Mark Gottdiener and C.V. Pickvance (eds.), *Urban Life in Transition* (Newbury Park, CA: Sage, 1991).

[7]Nancy A. Denton and Douglas S. Massey, "Residential Segregation of Blacks, Hispanics, and Asians by Socioeconomic Status and Generation," *Social Science Quarterly* 69 (1988): 797-817.

[8]Denton and Massey, p. 814; Robert D. Bullard, "Endangered Environs: The Price of Unplanned Growth in Boomtown Houston," *The California Sociologist* 7 (Summer 1984): 84-102; Robert D. Bullard and Beverly H. Wright, "The Politics of Pollution: Implications for the

Black Community," *Phylon* 47 (March 1986): 71-78; Robert D. Bullard and Beverly H. Wright, "Blacks and the Environment," *Humboldt Journal of Social Relations* 14 (Summer 1986): 165-184; Robert D. Bullard, *Dumping in Dixie: Race, Class, and Environmental Quality* (Boulder, CO: Westview Press, 1990), chapter 1.

[9]See Paul Ong and Evelyn Blumenberg, "Race and Environmentalism," Graduate School of Architecture and Urban Planning, UCLA (March 14, 1990): p. 9; Eric Mann, *L.A.'s Lethal Air: New Strategies for Policy, Organizing, and Action* (Los Angeles: Labor/Community Strategy Center, 1991), p. 31.

[10]Sue Pollack and JoAnn Grozuczak, *Reagan, Toxics, and Minorities* (Washington, DC: Urban Environment Conference, 1984), p. 20; John R. Logan and Harvey L. Molotch, *Urban Fortunes: The Political Economy of Place* (Berkeley: University of California Press, 1987), p. 158; Robert D. Bullard, *Invisible Houston: The Black Experience in Boom and Bust* (College Station, TX: Texas A&M University Press, 1987), chapter 6; Robert D. Bullard, "Ecological Inequities and the New South: Black Communities under Siege," *Journal of Ethnic Studies* 17 (Winter 1990): 101-115; Robert D. Bullard and Beverly H. Wright, "Toxic Waste and the African American Community," *The Urban League Review* 13 (Spring 1990): 67-75.

[11]Darden, "The Status of Urban Blacks," pp. 160-173; Robert D. Bullard, "Solid Waste Sites and the Black Houston Community," *Sociological Inquiry* 53 (Spring 1983): 273-288; Joe R. Feagin, *Free Enterprise City: Houston in Political and Economic Perspective* (New Brunswick, NJ: Rutgers University Press, 1987); Robert D. Bullard (ed.), *In Search of the New South: The Black Urban Experience in the 1970s and 1980s* (Tuscaloosa, AL: University of Alabama Press, 1989).

[12]Robert D. Bullard and Beverly H. Wright, "Environmentalism and the Politics of Equity: Emergent Trends in the Black Community," *Mid-America Review of Sociology* 12 (Winter 1987): 21-38; Robert D. Bullard, "Environmentalism, Economic Blackmail, and Civil Rights," in John Gaventa and Alex Willingham (eds.), *Communities in Economic Crisis* (Philadelphia: Temple University Press, 1989), pp. 190-199.

[13]Denton and Massey, "Residential Segregation of Blacks," p. 814.

[14]Bullard, *Dumping in Dixie*, p. 7; Jaynes and Williams, *A Common Destiny*, pp. 144-145.

[15]Richard Kazis and Richard Grossman, *Fear at Work: Job Blackmail, Labor, and the Environment* (New York: The Pilgrim Press, 1983), chapters 1 and 2.

[16]Jim Ritter, "Robbins to Get Incinerator," *Chicago Sun-Times*, January 31, 1990, p. 3.

[17]*Ibid.*

[18]Sentiment expressed by Reverend Adolph Coleman--a resident of Robbins and associate pastor of the West Pullman Church of God, personal interview, November 17, 1991.

[19]See Bunyan Bryant and Paul Mohai, *Race and the Incidence of Environmental Hazards* (Boulder, CO: Westview Press, forthcoming); Logan and Molotch, *Urban Fortunes*, pp. 95-96; Bullard, *Dumping in Dixie*, p. 33.

[20]Mark Gottdiener, *The Social Production of Urban Space* (Austin, TX: University of Texas Press, 1988), p. 172.

[21]E.D. Kelly, "Zoning," in F.S. So and J. Getzels (eds.), *The Practice of Local Government Planning*, 2nd ed. (Washington, DC: International City Management Association, 1988), pp. 251-284; S. Plotkin, *Keep Out: The Struggle for Land Use Control* (Berkeley: University of California Press, 1987), pp. 75-110.

[22]P.G. Marshall, "Not in My Back Yard," *Editorial Research Reports* 1 (June 1989) 312.

[23]*Ibid.*, p. 313.

[24]Logan and Molotch, *Urban Fortunes*, p. 158.

[25]Bullard, "Solid Waste Sites and the Black Houston Community," pp. 273-288.

[26]Bullard, *Invisible Houston*, pp. 62-63.

[27]Pat Costner and Joe Thornton, *Playing with Fire* (Washington, DC: Greenpeace Report, 1990), pp. 48-49; Greenpeace, "Home Street, USA," *Greenpeace Magazine* (October/November/December 1991): 8-13.

[28]Bullard and Wright, "Environmentalism and the Politics of Equity," pp. 22-24.

[29]Samuel S. Epstein, Lester O. Brown, and Carl Pope, *Hazardous Waste in America* (San Francisco: Sierra Club Books, 1983), pp. 33-39.

[30]Michael R. Greenberg and Richard F. Anderson, *Hazardous Waste Sites: The Credibility Gap* (New Brunswick, NJ: Rutgers University Center for Urban Policy Research, 1984), pp. 158-159; Bullard, *Dumping in Dixie*, pp. 4-5.

[31]Cerrell Associates, *Political Difficulties Facing Waste-to-Energy Conversion Plant Siting*, Report prepared for the California Waste Management Board (1984), p. 65.

[32]Commission for Racial Justice, *Toxic Wastes and Race in the United States* (New York: United Church of Christ Commission for Racial Justice, 1987), pp. xiii-xiv.

[33]*Ibid.*, pp. 18-19.

[34]K. Taeuber, "Racial Residential Segregation, 28 Cities, 1970-1980," Center for Demography and Ecology, Working Paper 83-12 (University of Wisconsin, Madison, 1983), p. 3.

[35]Statement by Hazel Johnson--resident of Chicago's Altgeld Gardens and Executive Director of People for Community Recovery, personal interview, November 17, 1991.

[36]Greenpeace, "Home Street, USA," p. 13.

[37]Jane Kay, "Fighting Toxic Racism: L.A.'s Minority Neighborhood is the 'Dirtiest' in the State," *San Francisco Examiner*, April 7, 1991, p. A1.

[38]For detailed discussions of the LANCER project, see Louis Blumberg and Robert Gottlieb, *War on Waste: Can America Win Its Battle with Garbage?* (Washington, DC: Island Press, 1989), pp. 155-188; and Dick Russell, "Environmental Racism," *The Amicus Journal* (Spring 1989): 22-32.

[39]Citizens for a Better Environment, *Richmond at Risk: Community Demographics and Toxic Hazards from Industrial Polluters* (San Francisco: CBE Report, 1989), p. 1.

[40]*Ibid.*, p. 121.

Urban Redevelopment: Developing Effective Targeting Strategies, *Robert B. Hill, Ph.D.*

FOOTNOTES

[1]Wilhelmina A. Leigh (ed.), "Special Issue on Housing," *The Review of Black Political Economy*, Vol. 19, Nos. 3-4 (Winter/Spring 1991).

[2]Davis McEntire, *Residence and Race* (Berkeley: University of California Press, 1960).

[3]Dorothy K. Newman et al., *Protest, Politics, and Prosperity* (New York: Pantheon Books, 1978).

[4]Leigh, *op. cit.*

[5]*Ibid.*

[6]Sar Levitan et al., *Still A Dream* (Cambridge, MA: Harvard University Press, 1975).

[7]William Mirengoff and Lester Rindler, *CETA:L Manpower Programs under Local Control* (Washington, DC: National Academy of Sciences, 1978).

[8]Stokely Carmichael and Charles Hamilton, *Black Power* (New York: Vintage Books, 1967).

[9]Louis L. Knowles and Kenneth Prewitt (eds.), *Institutional Racism in America* (Englewood Cliffs, NJ: Prentice-Hall, 1969).

[10]Veronica M. Reed, "Civil Rights Legislation and Housing Status of Black Americans: Evidence from Fair Housing Audits and Segregation Indices," *The Review of Black Political Economy*, Vol. 19, Nos. 3-4 (Winter/Spring 1991), pp. 29-42.

[11]Robert K. Merton, "Discrimination and the American Creed," in R.M. MacIver (ed.), *Discrimination and the National Welfare* (New York: Harper, 1948), pp. 99-126.

[12]Harold M. Baron, "The Web of Urban Racism," in Knowles and Prewitt, *op. cit.*, pp. 142-143.

[13]John O. Calmore, "To Make Wrong Right: The Necessary and Proper Aspirations of Fair Housing," in Janet Dewart (ed.), *The State of Black America 1989* (New York: National Urban League, 1989), pp. 88-89.

[14]Robert B. Hill, "Economic Forces, Structural Discrimination, and Black Family Instability," *The Review of Black Political Economy*, Vol. 17, No. 3 (Winter 1989), pp. 1-23.

[15]Robert B. Hill, *Economic Policies and Black Progress* (Washington, DC: National Urban League Research Department, 1981).

[16]Newman, *op. cit.*

[17]Phillip L. Clay, "Housing Opportunities: A Dream Deferred," in Janet Dewart (ed.), *The State of Black America 1990* (New York: National Urban League, 1990), pp. 73-84.

[18]*Ibid.*

[19]Robert B. Hill, "Financial Impact of the 1990 Census Undercount on Selected States and Cities," Institute for Urban Research, Morgan State University, July 1991.

[20]Carla J. Robinson, "Racial Disparity in the Atlanta Housing Market," *The Review of Black Political Economy*, Vol. 19, Nos. 3-4 (Winter/Spring 1991), pp. 85-109.

[21]*Ibid.*

[22]Anne B. Shlay, "Maintaining the Divided City: Residential Lending Patterns in the Baltimore SMSA," Institute for Policy Studies, The Johns Hopkins University, March 1987.

[23]Robinson, *op. cit.*

[24]Testimony of Jack Kemp, Secretary of the Department of Housing and Urban Development, on enterprise zone legislation before the U.S. Congress House Ways and Means Committee, October 17, 1989.

[25]Edward G. Goetz, "Promoting Low Income Housing through Innovations in Land Use Regulations," *Journal of Urban Affairs*, Vol. 13, No. 3, 1991, pp. 337-351.

²⁶Bill Alexander, "The Black Church and Community Empowerment," in Robert L. Woodson (ed.), *On the Road to Economic Freedom* (Washington, DC: Regnery Gateway, 1987), pp. 45-69.

²⁷*Griggs v. Duke Power Co.*, 401 U.S. 424 (1971).

²⁸*Wards Cove Packing Co. v. Atonio*, 104 L.Ed.2d 733; 109 S.Ct. 2115 (1989).

Public Investment for Public Good: Needs, Benefits, and Financing Options, *Lenneal J. Henderson, Ph.D.*

FOOTNOTES

¹See William P. O'Hare et al., *African Americans in the 1990s*, Washington, DC: Population Reference Bureau, Vol. 46, No. 1, July 1991.

²See The Hudson Institute, *Workforce 2000* (Washington, DC: Government Printing Office, 1987).

³Penelope Lemov, "Local Government and the Budget Axe," *Governing*, Vol. 4, No. 11, August 1991, pp. 26-30.

⁴Congressional Budget Office, *Reducing the Deficit: Spending and Revenue Options* 1989 Annual Report (Washington, DC: Government Printing Office, February 1989).

⁵Billy J. Tidwell, *Playing to Win: A Marshall Plan for America* (New York: National Urban League, 1991).

⁶B.J. Reed and John W. Swain, *Public Finance Administration* (Englewood Cliffs, NJ: Prentice-Hall, 1990), p. 8.

⁷*Ibid.*, pp. 8-9.

⁸Nancy Smith Barrett, *The Theory of Microeconomic Policy* (Lexington, MA: D.C. Heath Company, 1974), p. 50.

⁹Paul A. Samuelson, "Diagrammatic Exposition of a Theory of Public Expenditures," *Review of Economic Statistics*, Volume 37, November 1955, pp. 350-356.

¹⁰Barrett, *op. cit.*, p. 51.

¹¹Thomas Dye, *Understanding Public Policy* (Englewood Cliffs, NJ: Prentice-Hall, 6th edition, 1987).

¹²O'Hare et al., *op. cit.*, pp. 7-8.

¹³*Op. cit.*, p. 9.

¹⁴*Op. cit.*, pp. 9-10.

¹⁵William Julius Wilson, *The Truly Disadvantaged: The Inner City, The Underclass, and Public Policy* (Chicago: University of Chicago Press, 1987).

¹⁶Population Reference Bureau, "Human Resource Development," *America in the 21st Century* (Washington, DC: 1990), and David Swinton, "The Economic Status of African Americans: 'Permanent' Poverty and Inequality," in Janet Dewart (ed.), *The State of Black America 1991* (New York: National Urban League, 1991), pp. 25-75.

¹⁷Household infrastructure is defined as housing, appliances, personal transportation, and other material amenities of homes.

[18]"A Shift in Military Spending to America's Cities: What It Means to Four Cities and the Nation" (Washington, DC: U.S. Conference of Mayors, 1988), p. 1.

[19]*Ibid.*, pp. 1-2.

[20]U.S. Congress Joint Economic Committee, *Hard Choices: A Report on the Increasing Gap between America's Infrastructure Needs and Our Ability to Pay for Them* (Washington, DC: Government Printing Office, 1984), p. 119.

[21]Elaine S. Sharp, *Urban Politics and Administration* (New York: Longman Publishing Company, 1990), pp. 195-196.

[22]On the concept of political incorporation, see Rufus Browning, Dale Rogers Marshall, and David H. Tabb, *Protest Is Not Enough: The Struggle of Blacks and Hispanics for Equality in Urban Politics* (Berkeley and Los Angeles: University of California Press, 1984).

[23]See Dye, *op. cit.*, pp. 12-45.

[24]Sharp, *op. cit.*, p. 160.

[25]Terry Nichols Clark and Lorna Crowley Ferguson, *City Money* (New York: Columbia University Press, 1983), and Sharp, *op. cit.*, pp. 149-167.

[26]See Lenneal J. Henderson, *Proposition 13: Measuring the Income Security Impacts* (Washington, DC: The National Institute for Public Management, 1981).

[27]See Lenneal J. Henderson, "The Impact of Military Base Shutdowns," *The Black Scholar*, March 1973.

Public-Private Partnerships: Prospects for America ... Promise for African Americans, *Sandra T. Gray*

FOOTNOTES

[1]"Columbia Commons Provides Affordable Units," *Baltimore Business Journal*, September 27-October 3, 1991, p. 2.

[2]"Corporate Public/Private Partnerships: Is It a New Time?", Council on Foundations Occasional Paper No. 1, August 1986, p. 4.

[3]*Ibid.*, p. 5.

[4]Neal R. Peirce and Carol F. Steinbach, *Enterprising Communities: Community-Based Development in America* (Washington, DC: Council for Community-Based Development, 1990), p. 25.

[5]"Public-Private Partnerships: an Opportunity for Urban Communities," a Statement by the Research and Policy Committee of the Committee for Economic Development (CED), February 1982, p. 2.

[6]*Ibid.*

[7]Brian O'Connell, "What Voluntary Activity Can and Cannot Do for America," *Public Administration Review*, Vol. 49, No. 5 (September/October 1989), p. 487.

[8]Peirce, p. 4.

[9]"Public-Private Partnerships," p. 5.

[10]"Against All Odds," a March 1989 study cited in Peirce, *op. cit.*, pp. 7-8.

[11]O'Connell, p. 486.

[12]*Ibid.*, p. 491.

[13]Peirce, pp. 49-50.

[14]"Corporate Public/Private Partnerships," p. v.

[15]Peirce, p. 50.

[16]*Ibid.*, p. 52.

[17]"Public-Private Partnerships," p. 4.

[18]"Comprehensive Services for the Most in Need," Center for Employment Training annual report, 1989, p. 27.

[19]*Ibid.*

[20]*Ibid.*, p. 37.

[21]*Ibid.*, p. 43.

[22]*Ibid.*, p. 45.

[23]Lisa Lapin, "Jobs Center Shows a Quick Way Off Welfare," *San Jose Mercury News*, October 26, 1990, p. 1B.

[24]*Ibid.*, p. 2B.

[25]"Comprehensive Services for the Most in Need," Center for Employment Training annual report, 1989, p. 18.

[26]*Ibid.*, p. 23.

[27]*Ibid.*, p. 5.

[28]Baltimore Housing Partnership, *Annual Report, 1991*, inside front cover.

[29]*Ibid.*, p. 1.

[30]*Ibid.*, p. 6.

[31]"Public-Private Partnerships," p. 61.

[32]*Ibid.*, p. 64.

[33]*Ibid.*

[34]*Ibid.*, p. 75.

[35]"Understanding Successful Collaborations," from "Collaboration and Conflict," Report of INDEPENDENT SECTOR's 1991 Annual Membership Meeting, October 13-16, 1991, p. 7.

[36]"Public-Private Partnerships," p. 13.

[37]*Ibid.*, p. 24.

[38]"Corporate Public/Private Partnerships," p. 11.

[39]"Understanding Successful Collaborations," p. 7.

[40]*Ibid.*

[41]"Corporate Public/Private Partnerships," p. i.

[42]Peirce, p. 4.

[43]"Charities See Collaboration on Social Problems as Essential--But Full of Pitfalls," *The Chronicle of Philanthropy*, October 22, 1991, p. 12.

TELEPHONE INTERVIEWS*

David Bergholz, Executive Director, George Gund Foundation, Cleveland, OH: November 5, 1991.

Ada Cole, Executive Director, Marcus Foster Educational Institute, Oakland, CA: November 7, 1991.

Pablo Eisenberg, President, Center for Community Change, Washington, DC: October 22, 1991.

Columbia Hartwell, Manager--Job Training and Disability Assistance Programs, IBM Corporation, Atlanta, GA: October 22, 1991.

Robert Hollister, Director, Lincoln Filene Center, Tufts University, Medford, MA: October 24, 1991.

Vivian Kidd, Executive Director, West Virginia Educational Fund, Charleston, WV: November 6, 1991.

Wendy Puriefoy, President, Public Education Fund Network, Washington, DC: October 29, 1991.

Talton Ray, President, The Council for Community Based Development, Washington, DC: October 16, 1991.

Mary Sarris, Foundation Administrator, Lynn/Business Education Foundation, Lynn, MA: November 6, 1991.

Kathleen Tullberg, Vice President of Community Relations, Shawmut Bank, NW, Boston, MA: October 22, 1991.

*The following is a list of contacts made by the author in preparing her chapter for inclusion in this publication.

Interagency and Intergovernmental Coordination: New Demands for Domestic Policy Initiatives, *Henry A. Coleman, Ph.D.*

FOOTNOTES

[1]See B.J. Tidwell, *Playing to Win: A Marshall Plan for America* (New York: National Urban League, Inc., 1991), p. vii.

[2]The U.S. Constitution guarantees sovereignty for only the federal government and the 50 state governments. All local governments are creatures of their parent states. This feature of the Constitution has raised some interesting policy issues in the past, such as whether the federal government or the parent state government should be responsible for improving the fiscal conditions of poor local governments.

[3]Direct expenditures are all payments to employees, suppliers, contractors, beneficiaries, and other final recipients of government payments. The concept includes all expenditures other than intergovernmental expenditures. See U.S. Advisory Commission on Intergovernmental Relations (ACIR), *Significant Features of Fiscal Federalism: Revenues and Expenditures*, Volume Two (Washington, DC: Government Printing Office, 1991), p. 315.

[4]Differences in preferences and attitudes regarding public services may imply that these figures provide a distorted picture in that low levels of public expenditures may be augmented in some states by more spending by private and/or nonprofit entities. See W.E. Oates, *Fiscal Federalism* (New York: Harcourt Brace Jovanovich, 1972), for a general discussion.

[5]This may actually overstate the problem somewhat. Presumably, once agreement is reached between the federal and state governments, and among state governments where appropriate, coordination of activities among local governments within a state becomes the state's responsibility. See the later discussion on the cross-acceptance process.

[6]See Tidwell, *Playing to Win*, chapter 4.

[7]See ACIR, *Changing Public Attitudes on Governments and Taxes* (Washington, DC: Government Printing Office, 1991).

[8]Of course, the potential for perverse redistribution (i.e., from poor to rich) exists because rich (poor) municipalities and households are found within poor (rich) states. Such outcomes are impossible to avoid where redistribution occurs among aggregations of municipalities or households, rather than individual units.

[9]See R. Musgrave, *The Theory of Public Finance* (New York: McGraw-Hill, 1959).

[10]See any ACIR report, such as *Significant Features of Fiscal Federalism* (footnote 3, above).

[11]John Shannon, former executive director of the ACIR, first brought these concerns to my attention, although he bears no responsibility for the context in which they are raised here.

[12]See C. Ashmun, *The Cross-Acceptance Game: Planning in Common for the Common Good* (Trenton, NJ: New Jersey Conservation Foundation, 1989), and New Jersey State Planning Commission, *Communities of Place: A Legacy for the Next Generation*, Volume One (Trenton, NJ: State of New Jersey, 1988).

[13]New Jersey State Planning Act, P.L. 1985, c. 398 (New Jersey Statutes Annotated 52: 18A-196 et alia), p. 8.

[14]U.S. Department of Commerce, Bureau of the Census, *Statistical Abstract of the United States: 1990* (Washington, DC: Government Printing Office, 1990).

[15]U.S. Department of Commerce, Bureau of the Census, *Race and Hispanic Origin: 1990 Census Profile* (Washington, DC: Government Printing Office, 1991).

[16]M. Barone and G. Ujifusa, *The Almanac of American Politics 1986* (Washington, DC: The National Journal, 1985), p. 24.

[17]*Race and Hispanic Origin, op. cit.*

[18]For example, there were no African American elected officials in three states (Idaho, Montana, and North Dakota) as of January 1989. See *Statistical Abstracts 1990*, p. 260.

[19]See R. Anglin, "African Americans and Their Support for Growth Management," in H. Coleman and R. Anglin (eds.), *Planning for a Better New Jersey: Managing Growth and the Implications for the African American Community* (Trenton, NJ: New Jersey Public Policy Research Institute, 1990), pp. 9-22.

[20]See articles by Vereen, Epps and Moody-Lane, Yeldell, Moseley, and Eanes in *Planning for a Better New Jersey*.

REFERENCES

Ashmun, C.M. 1989. *The Cross-Acceptance Game: Planning in Common for the Common Good.* Trenton, NJ: New Jersey Conservation Foundation.

Barone, M. and G. Ujifusa. 1985. *The Almanac of American Politics 1986.* Washington, DC: The National Journal.

Coleman, H. and R. Anglin, eds. 1990. *Planning for a Better New Jersey: Managing Growth and the Implications for the African American Community.* Trenton, NJ: New Jersey Public Policy Research Institute.

Musgrave, R. 1959. *The Theory of Public Finance.* New York: McGraw-Hill.

New Jersey. 1985. State Planning Act, P.L. 1985, c. 398. New Jersey Statutes Annotated 52:18A-196 et alia.

New Jersey State Planning Commission. 1988. *Communities of Place: A Legacy for the Next Generation.* Volume One, The Preliminary State Development and Redevelopment Plan. Trenton, NJ: State of New Jersey.

Tidwell, B.J. 1991. *Playing to Win: A Marshall Plan for America.* New York: National Urban League, Inc.

U.S. Advisory Commission on Intergovernmental Relations. 1991. *Changing Public Attitudes on Governments and Taxes.* Washington, DC: Government Printing Office.

_____. 1990. *1988 Fiscal Capacity and Effort.* Washington, DC: Government Printing Office.

_____. 1990. *Representative Expenditures: Addressing the Neglected Dimension of Fiscal Capacity.* Washington, DC: Government Printing Office.

_____. 1991. *Significant Features of Fiscal Federalism: Revenues and Expenditures.* Volume Two. Washington, DC: Government Printing Office.

U.S. Department of Commerce Bureau of the Census. 1991. *Race and Hispanic Origin: 1990 Census Profile.* Washington, DC: Government Printing Office.

_____. 1991. *Government Finances 1989-90.* Washington, DC: Government Printing Office.

_____. 1990. *Statistical Abstract of the United States: 1990.* Washington, DC: Government Printing Office.

==

Power and Progress: African American Politics in the New Era of Diversity, *Dianne M. Pinderhughes, Ph.D.*

FOOTNOTES

[1]In 1985, the Office of Management and Budget (OMB) "agreed with the Supreme Court ruling in *Firefighters v. Stotts* and *Palmore v. Sidoti* that affirmative action goals and quotas were 'dead' programs and that the government and the OMB would no longer move to enforce these civil rights concepts or the programs designed to enforce them" (Walton, 1988: 160). Hanes Walton's "Realistic Model of the Federal Enforcement Process" more accurately suggests the complexity of the relationships between those interests involved in civil rights policy (Walton, 128). Although Walton does not explicitly incorporate interest groups into his model, it shows the main points at which interest groups have access to influence policy.

[2]Among the candidates that President Reagan considered was the "Reverend Edward Hill, a black fundamentalist Baptist minister from Los Angeles," who refused the nomination to chair the Commission because of his concern about the reactions to his "status as a conservative black Republican, . . . his connections to Jerry Falwell's Moral Majority, and his antihomosexual and anti-ERA views" (Thompson, 1985: 187).

[3]Bullock and Butler (1985: 33) reported no significant difference in voting law changes submitted to the division, but over the past decade, the numbers have risen by more than 100 percent, although the number of objections has not risen proportionately.

[4]However, these findings, which were widely cited, contain a large margin of error because the overall sample size was smaller than is appropriate for a high accuracy rate. The largest sample of blacks was of 101 persons, which would produce a large margin of error; the sample is too small to be used as an accurate representation of black opinion on a national basis. There may have been, for example, an even split within the black population, but there is no way to know without developing a more representative survey. The author thanks Linda F. Williams for her helpful comments on this matter.

[5]Native Americans of varying kinds were also present, but they were not part of the "political" population and were not counted in the decennial censuses that began in 1790 (*Statistical Abstract* 1991: 17). The population of African descent--as large as 20 percent of the nation's population in 1790--has fallen as a proportion of the whole until recent decades.

[6]Nativist is a word used in historical studies to refer to the white Anglo Saxon Protestant sectors, which looked to the native born (hence "nativist") as a reflection of true American values. This emphasis on nativism grew strong by the late nineteenth century as non-English speaking Catholic peasants flooded American cities and precipitated resistance to their arrival.

REFERENCES

Alliance for Justice. 1991. *Year End Report: Judicial Selection Project*. Washington, DC.

Ball, Howard and Kathanne Greene. 1985. "The Reagan Justice Department," *The Reagan Administration and Human Rights*, ed. Tinsley E. Yarbrough. New York: Praeger. Pages 1-28.

Bullock, Charles and Katharine Inglis Butler. 1985. "Voting Rights," *The Reagan Administration and Human Rights*, ed. Tinsley E. Yarbrough. New York: Praeger. Pages 29-54.

Davidson, Chandler, ed. 1984. *Minority Vote Dilution*. Washington, DC: Howard University.

Farley, Reynolds and Walter R. Allen. 1987. *The Color Line and the Quality of Life in America*. New York: Russell Sage Foundation.

Foster, Lorn S., ed. 1985. *The Voting Rights Act: Consequences and Implications*. New York: Praeger.

Gallup Poll Monthly, "Public Supports Thomas for Supreme Court." July 1991.

Gallup Poll News Service, Vol. 56, No. 15A, August 14, 1991; Vol.56, No. 19, September 18, 1991; Vol.56, No. 22e, October 14, 1991; Volume 56, No. 22f, October 15, 1991.

Gomes, Ralph C. and Linda Faye Williams. 1992. *From Exclusion to Inclusion: The Long Struggle for African American Political Power*. New York: Greenwood Press.

Gurin, Patricia, Shirley Hatchett, and James S. Jackson. 1989. *Hope and Independence: Blacks' Response to Electoral and Party Politics*. New York: Russell Sage Foundation.

Hawk, Beverly. 1987. "Keeping the Africans Out: Immigration Law as Cultural Engineering." Paper presented at the American Political Science Association, Chicago, Illinois.

Henderson, Wade. 1991. National Conference of Black Lawyers Annual Meeting, Panel on the Clarence Thomas Nomination, C-SPAN Broadcast. August 22, 1991.

Jackson, Bryan O. and Michael B. Preston, eds. 1991. *Racial and Ethnic Politics in California*. Berkeley, CA: Institute of Governmental Studies.

McClain, Paula D. and Albert K. Karnig. 1990. "Black and Hispanic Socioeconomic and Political Competition, *American Political Science Review* 84, No. 2. Pages 535-545.

New York Times National Edition. 1991. "Fearing Duke, Voters in Louisiana Hand Democrat Fourth Term." November 18, 1991.

_____. 1991. "Duke Takes His Anger into 1992 Race." December 5, 1991.

Pinderhughes, Dianne M. 1990. "Governing Governing: Voting Rights in the Twenty-Fifth Anniversary of the Voting Rights Act in 1965." Presented at the annual meeting of the American Political Science Association. San Francisco, CA.

_____. 1986. "Strategic Choices: A Realignment in Partisanship among Black Voters?", *The State of Black America 1986*, ed. James D. Williams. New York: National Urban League, Inc.

_____. 1984. "The Black Vote: The Sleeping Giant," *The State of Black America 1984*, ed. James D. Williams. New York: National Urban League, Inc.

_____. 1983. "Interest Groups and the Passage of the Voting Rights Act in 1982." Paper presented at the annual meeting of the National Conference of Black Political Scientists. Houston, TX.

Senate Confirmation Hearings for Judge Clarence Thomas. 1991. C-SPAN Broadcast, September 19, 1991.

Shull, Steven. 1989. *The President and Civil Rights Policy.* New York.

Smith, Calvin C. 1990. "The Civil Rights Legacy of Ronald Reagan," *Western Journal of Black Studies* 14 (102-114), No. 2.

Strumpf, Harry P. 1988. *American Judicial Politics.* San Diego: Harcourt Brace Jovanovich.

Thompson, Robert J. 1985. "The Commission on Civil Rights," *The Reagan Administration and Human Rights*, ed. Tinsley E. Yarbrough. New York: Praeger.

Thung, Andrew. 1991. "Asian Americans and Politics." Seminar paper presented at the University of Illinois. Urbana-Champaign, IL.

U.S. Commission on Civil Rights. 1981. *The Voting Rights Act: Unfulfilled Goals.* Washington, DC: U.S. Commission on Civil Rights.

U.S. Department of Commerce Bureau of the Census. 1991. *CenData*, Summary Tape File 1A.

_____. 1991. *Statistical Abstract of the United States 1991.* Washington, DC: Government Printing Office.

_____. 1983. *Characteristics of the Population, Volume 1, General Social and Economic Characteristics*, Chapter C, U.S. Summary. Washington, DC: Government Printing Office.

_____. 1979. *The Social and Economic Status of the Black Population in the United States: An Historical View, 1790-1978, Current Population Reports*, Series P-23, No. 80. Washington, DC: Government Printing Office.

U.S. Department of Justice Civil Rights Division. Section 5 Reports. April 4, 1991.

Walton, Jr., Hanes. 1988. *When the Marching Stopped: The Politics of Civil Rights Regulatory Agencies.* New York: State University of New York Press.

The Parity Imperative: Civil Rights, Economic Justice, and the New American Dilemma,
Julianne M. Malveaux, Ph.D.

FOOTNOTES

[1]Imam Benjamin Karim (ed.), *The End of White Supremacy: Four Speeches by Malcolm X* (New York: Arcade Publishing, 1971).

[2]Stanley Greenberg, private conversation with the author, August 1991; see also Greenberg, "From Crisis to Working Majority," *The American Prospect*, Fall 1991, pp. 104-117.

[3]California governor Pete Wilson has proposed a ballot initiative to reduce Aid to Families with Dependent Children (AFDC) payments by 10 percent, to reduce them further by 15 percent if families receive assistance for more than six months, to pay those who have lived in the state of California for less than a year only at the level of benefits they would have received in their home state, and to pay no additional monies if women give birth to additional children while they receive assistance. Further provisions of this ballot initiative would restrict minors with children as well as those who are high school dropouts. Though some 600,000 signatures are necessary to put this measure on a June 1992 ballot, Wilson is expected to spend more than one million dollars to reach this goal. In proposing the initiative, the California governor sought to distance himself from David Duke, but his proposal is more punitive than are Duke's proposals. See Steven A. Capps, "Wilson Reaches for Welfare Reins," *San Francisco Examiner*, December 10, 1991.

[4]See, for example, Shelby Steele, *The Content of Our Character* (New York: St. Martin's Press, 1990). A more recent contribution to this genre comes from Stephen L. Carter in his *Reflections of An Affirmative Action Baby* (New York: Basic Books, 1991). Carter might be described as a "kinder, gentler" Shelby Steele; he equivocates before noting his opposition to affirmative action and the "by the numbers" approach. However, much of Carter's volume is in defense of dissent, a defense that seems especially narrow in that the only dissent that he acknowledges is that of black conservatives and in that he fails to mention the pecuniary rewards of conservative (as opposed to liberal, radical, Marxist, Communist, etc.) dissent.

[5]For example, a "Bay Area Attitudes Survey" conducted for KPIX-TV in October 1991 showed that 48 percent of the black respondents opposed "quotas," while blacks (41 percent) were more likely than any other racial/ethnic group to disagree with the statement, "Fairness in education, hiring, and promotion can be accomplished without quotas." Though the survey in question was methodologically flawed, it illustrated significant dissent around affirmative action and quotas among African Americans.

[6]At a University of Michigan conference on political correctness, conservative critic Nate Horowitz defended his "right" to be racist, based on the fact that he felt "Americans have no royalty, only entertainers and athletes, and in these groups, blacks are the highest paid." The flaw in his argument, of course, is the fact that few of these athletes/entertainers own means of production or generate significant employment. This is changing with the establishment of Harpo Productions (Oprah Winfrey) and of other similar groups.

[7]Dennis Kimbro and Napoleon Hill, *Think and Grow Rich: A Black Choice* (New York: Fawcett Columbine, 1991).

[8]Greenberg, *op. cit.*, p. 106.

[9]This prejudice was so persistent that a 1990 National Opinion Research Center poll indicated that the majority of whites believed that black people do not want to work, are violent, and prefer public assistance to employment. See Tom Smith, *Ethnic Images*, National Opinion Research Center, University of Chicago, GSS Topical Report No. 19, December 1990.

[10]See, for example, Joseph Feagin, "Responding to Racial Discrimination: The Black Middle Class in Public Places," *American Sociological Review*, February 1991; and Julianne Malveaux, "Economic Racism," *Essence Magazine*, September 1989.

[11]Margery Austin Turner, Michael Fix, and Raymond Struyk, "Opportunities Denied, Opportunities Diminished: Discrimination in Hiring," Washington, DC: Urban Institute Report 91-9.

[12]"Prime Time Live," ABC News, September 26, 1991.

[13]See Julianne Malveaux, "Race, Class, and Urban Poverty," *The Black Scholar*, Vol. 19, No. 3, May/June 1988.

[14]U.S. Department of Agriculture Food and Nutrition Section, *Characteristics of Food Stamp Households* (Washington, DC: Government Printing Office, 1989). According to this publication, 46 percent of the households receiving food stamps were headed by whites, 37 percent were headed by African Americans, and 13 percent were headed by Hispanics. As of September 1991, 23.76 million Americans received food stamps, 3.6 percent more than the year before.

[15]The "up from poverty" testimony that dominated the first half of the Judge Clarence Thomas confirmation hearings, the extent to which President Bush felt compelled to mention the judge's family background in his introduction of him, and the extent to which Thomas himself mentioned his grandfather in his ostensibly *legal testimony* before the Senate Judiciary Committee are all consistent with the notion of prejudice as a challenge that successful individuals simply "overcome." See, especially, Neil A. Lewis, "From Poverty to the Bench," *The New York Times*, July 2, 1991, and Neil A. Lewis, "Thomas Subjected to Toughest Day by Senate Critics," *The New York Times*, September 13, 1991.

[16]Thomas Byrne Edsal and Mary D. Edsal, *Chain Reaction: The Impact of Race, Rights, and Taxes on American Politics* (New York: W.W. Norton, 1991).

[17]U.S. Department of Labor, Bureau of labor Statistics, *The Employment Situation* (Washington, DC: Government Printing Office, November 1991).

[18]U.S. Department of Commerce, *Money Income of Households, Families, and Persons in the United States: 1990*, P-60, No. 174, August 1991. According to Table 29, a white male high school dropout who worked full-time, full-year earned $21,048, while a similarly situated black woman with some college earned $19,922. Even among the most educated full-time workers, there are significant gaps--white men with more than five years of college earned a median of $47,787, compared to $36,802 for black men, $31,991 for white women, and $31,119 for black women.

[19]Bureau of Labor Statistics, *Employment and Earnings*, January 1991, Table 22.

[20]Andrew Rosenthal, "White House in Disarray: Mishandling of Scholarships for Minorities Reflects Struggle for a Civil Rights Agenda," *The New York Times*, December 20, 1991.

[21]Edsal and Edsal, *op. cit.*, p. 283.

[22]*Op. cit.*, p. 279.

[23]Michael Quint, "Mortgage Race Data Show Gap," *The New York Times*, October 14, 1991.

[24]Charles Stein, "A Problem That Won't Go Away," *Boston Globe*, October 22, 1991.

[25]Quint, October 14, 1991.

[26]Richard Freeman, *Black Elite: The New Market for Highly Educated Black Americans* (New York: McGraw-Hill, 1976).

[27]Indeed, among full-time women workers in 1990, black women had median incomes of $18,838, compared to $20,759 for white women--a pay gap of 10 percent, compared to the male

pay gap of 28 percent. For women with more than four years of college, earnings were virtually identical. But this does not necessarily mean that racism is a weaker influence on women's earnings than sexism; see Julianne Malveaux, "Gender Difference and Beyond," in Deborah Rhode (ed.), *Theoretical Perspectives on Sexual Difference* (New Haven: Yale University Press, 1990), for a discussion of the many differences in the labor market status of black and white women that are masked by "near parity" wages.

[28]James M. Washington (ed.), *A Testament of Hope: The Essential Writings and Speeches of Martin Luther King, Jr.* (San Francisco: Harper San Francisco, 1986).

[29]David H. Swinton, "The Economic Status of African Americans: 'Permanent' Poverty and Inequality," in Janet Dewart (ed.), *The State of Black America 1991* (New York: National Urban League, 1991).

[30]Billy J. Tidwell, "Economic Costs of American Racism," in Janet Dewart (ed.), *The State of Black America 1991* (New York: National Urban League, 1991).

[31]Lawrence Mishel and David M. Frankel, *The State of Working America* (New York: M.E. Sharpe, 1991), pp. 12-47.

[32]Intergovernmental grants grew by 9.8 percent between 1985-86, fell in 1986-87, and grew more slowly during 1987-89. Since some cities and states counted on these grants to provide essential services, their unavailability both put a tax squeeze on the residents of some states and helped to cause a service squeeze as well, especially in urban areas where service needs are highest.

[33]Bureau of Labor Statistics, *The Employment Situation*, October 1991.

[34]Mishel and Frankel, *op. cit.*, p. 69.

[35]Robert Reich, *The Work of Nations: Preparing Ourselves for 21st Century Capitalism* (New York: Alfred A. Knopf, 1991).

[36]Lawrence Mishel and Ruy A. Teixeira, "The Myth of the Coming Labor Shortage," *The American Prospect*, Fall 1991, pp. 98-103.

[37]Passed on November 27, 1991, the highway and mass transit bill was perceived as a way of pumping dollars into the economy and creating jobs, especially in the construction industry. See wire services, November 27-28, 1991, or Helen Dewar, "Huge Transportation Bill Passed," *San Francisco Chronicle*, November 28, 1991.

[38]Mark Shields, "Hamlet 1991," *The Washington Post*, October 1, 1991.

[39]"Soaking the Poor," *Dollars and Sense*, July/August 1991, pp. 9-11.

[40]See Julianne Malveaux, "Blacks Are Everyone's Worse Case," *The Los Angeles Times*, October 13, 1991.

[41]Marie Lee, "We Koreans Need An Al Sharpton," *The New York Times*, December 12, 1991.

[42]A probation report recommended that Son Ja Du be sentenced to a 16-year prison term for shooting to death 15-year-old Latasha Harlins after she accused her of shoplifting a $1.79 bottle of orange juice, but Judge Joyce Karlin opted instead to sentence Du to probation and community service. See "NAACP Angered by Slaying Sentence," *San Francisco Chronicle*, November 25, 1991; see also "No Reassignment from Judge in L.A. Grocery Slaying Case," *San Francisco Chronicle*, November 28, 1991.

[43]Itabari Njeri, "Power Elite Turns Out a Bitter Brew," *The Los Angeles Times*, November 29, 1991.

[44]U.S. Department of Commerce, Bureau of the Census, *The Census and You* (Washington, DC: Government Printing Office, April 1991), Volume 26, No. 4, April 1991.

[45]The "pity party" approach is one that encourages people to compare oppressions and to justify access to parity-producing programs on the basis of greater oppression.

[46]Jonathan Leonard, "Affirmative Action," *American Economic Review*, May 1986.

[47]See Rosemary Bray, "Taking Sides against Ourselves," *The New York Times Magazine*, November 17, 1991; see also Julianne Malveaux, "Black Women Caught between Race and Gender," *Baltimore Sun*, October 22, 1991.

[48]Phyllis A. Wallace, "Affirmative Action from a Labor Market Perspective," Alfred P. Sloan School of Management (Massachusetts Institute of Technology [MIT]), Working Paper 3124-90-BPS, April 1990.

[49]See Manning Marable, *Race, Reform, and Rebellion* (Jackson, MS: University of Mississippi Press, 1991), pp. 197-198, for a discussion of this.

[50]Penda Hair, NAACP Legal Defense and Educational Fund, personal conversation with the author, October 17, 1991.

[51]Phyllis A. Wallace, "Title VII and the Economic Status of Blacks," Alfred P. Sloan School of Management (MIT), Working Paper 1578-84, July 1984.

[52]It is important to note how sharply these views differ from those of Shelby Steele and Stephen Carter (see footnote 4) underlying the point that many who have opposed affirmative action have written from the narrow perspective of the academy, instead of from the broader perspective of the overall labor market.

[53]Phyllis A. Wallace, "Affirmative Action . . .," pp. 11, 19-20.

[54]See Jonathan Kozol, *Savage Inequalities* (New York: Crown Publishers, 1991).

[55]Maya Angelou, *Maya Angelou: Poems* (New York: Bantam Books, 1986).

Chronology of Events
1991[1]

Jan. 1: **Margaret Santiago** retires from the Smithsonian's National Museum of Natural History. She is the nation's first black registrar of a major scientific museum. Appointed to her position in 1977, Santiago was the record-keeper of the museum's accession, donation, loan, and collection transactions dating to 1834.

Jan. 2: **Sharon Pratt Dixon** is sworn in as Mayor of the District of Columbia, becoming the first female--black or otherwise--to be chief executive. She promises to "clean house." **Marion Barry** turns over the reins of government and, for the first time in more than a decade, is out of a political leadership role in the District.

Jan. 2: **Jean Camper Cahn**, a lawyer who helped establish federal financing of legal services to the poor and who was a cofounder of the now-defunct Antioch School of Law in Washington, DC, dies of breast cancer in Miami Beach, FL; she was 55. She served as associate general counsel for the New Haven (CT) Redevelopment Agency, the nation's first neighborhood legal services program. She was also the first director of the National Legal Services Program in the Office of Equal Opportunity; she founded the Urban Law Institute at George Washington University.

Jan. 3: House Speaker **Tom Foley** (D-WA) designates the civil rights legislation that lost a Senate override of President **Bush's** veto by a single vote as HR 1--a symbol of importance. Opening the 102nd Congress, the Speaker picked the civil rights legislation from more than 300 bills submitted on the first day for the crucial number-one designation.

Jan. 3: Legislation to deny federal tax write-offs to major Madison Avenue advertising firms that ignore black-owned communications--both print and broadcast--is introduced by Rep. **Cardiss Collins** (D-IL). Her first act in the new session, Collins

---

[1]*This chronology is based on news reports. In some instances, the event may have occurred a day before the news item was reported.*

tells reporters the Non-Discrimination in Advertising Act is "designed to correct a serious injustice against black and other minority-owned media."

Jan. 4: **Agnes Coates Kendrick,** cofounder of the *Capital Spotlight* newspaper and a civic activist, dies of head injuries she received from a fall in her Washington, DC, home; she was 79. Kendrick was the first black ever to receive the Navy's Merit Award for distinctive service.

Jan. 5: *The Washington Post* reports the National Society of Film Critics has awarded the Best Screenplay for 1990 to **Charles Burnett,** for "To Sleep With Anger." Burnett is the first African American to win in this category in the group's 25-year history.

Jan. 5: A group of black Maryland state troopers has agreed to a $1 million settlement of a discrimination suit filed last spring. *The Washington Post* reports the settlement between the state and the **Coalition of Black Maryland State Troopers Inc.** contains a five-year timetable for increasing black representation in the ranks through first sergeant to 22 percent.

Jan. 5: **Giselaine Felissaint,** the woman who touched off the black boycott of two Korean-owned grocery stores in Brooklyn (NY), testifies in criminal court that she was slapped, punched, and kicked when she tried to leave one of the stores on January 19, 1990. The boycott embroiled the city in a long, bitter controversy, reports *The New York Times*.

Jan. 7: Civil rights leaders join with families of crime victims in Atlanta to launch a nationwide campaign to end black-on-black violence. Southern Christian Leadership Conference president **Joseph Lowery** calls for a street "revival," noting, according to *USA Today*, that the hardest part of solving black-on-black crime is working within the black community--where poverty, poor education, broken homes, and a lack of male role models erode self-esteem and respect for others.

Jan. 7 The investigation of former HUD Secretary **Samuel Pierce** is expanding, with special prosecutor **Arlin Adams** getting approval to probe whether Pierce lied to Congress and whether he showed favoritism toward his old law firm in awarding a contract to sell HUD mortgages. Pierce is already under investigation for lying to a congressional panel probing charges he favored politically connected developers who sought three lucrative HUD programs.

Jan. 7   The United States--with the world's highest incarceration rate--tops South Africa in black imprisonment. A new study by the nonprofit **Sentencing Project** published in *USA Today* finds that the United States has 426 prisoners per 100,000 population, followed by 333 in South Africa, and 268 in the Soviet Union. Further, the incarceration rate for black males in America is four times South Africa's--3,109 per 100,000 population, compared with 729 in South Africa. "We can build all the jails we think we need and slam the doors down on thousands of people, but we won't make a bit of difference until we address the fundamental cause of crime," responds Rep. **John Conyers** (D-MI), senior member of the Congressional Black Caucus.

In a related study, for the first time, more than half of all murder victims in America in 1990 were black. Authorities tell *USA Today* that the problem of rising homicide rates in poor, black communities is born of poverty and naturally progresses to violence.

Jan. 8:   The nation's deepening recession and the impact of the Persian Gulf crisis will cause greater hardship for blacks than whites, assesses **John E. Jacob**, President and Chief Executive Officer of the National Urban League. In releasing the 16th annual *The State of Black America* in Washington, Jacob said, "It is immoral to ask [the blacks, Hispanics, and women who make up almost half the nation's armed forces] to put their lives on the line for the rest of us, while, at the same time, refusing to support a civil rights act that protects their rights when they reenter civilian life."

Jan. 8:   Three out of four whites believe blacks and Hispanics are more likely than whites to prefer living on welfare, and the majority of whites also believe blacks and Hispanics are more likely than whites to be lazy, violence-prone, less intelligent, and less patriotic. These are the primary findings of a new survey conducted by the University of Chicago's **National Opinion Research Center**.

Responding to the report, Chicago NAACP representative **Syd**

Finley described racism "as American as apple pie and mother, . . . [i]t's a lack of awareness of what an ethnic group is about."

Jan. 8: Seven-time American League batting champion **Rod Carew** becomes the 22nd player elected to the Baseball Hall of Fame in his first year of eligibility. He is joined by pitchers **Ferguson Jenkins** and **Gaylord Perry**, who barely won enshrinement on their third attempts. The trio will be inducted at Cooperstown (NY) on July 21.

Jan. 8: **Althea Gibson** becomes the first woman recipient of the Theodore Roosevelt Award, the NCAA's highest honor. Gibson was the first black to win Wimbledon and U.S. tennis titles, and the first black to play on the women's pro golf tour.

Jan. 9: Black and white children attend class and play together at some previously all-white public schools for the first time in Johannesburg, South Africa. A government plan permitting schools to determine their own admissions policies was passed last September.

Jan. 10: White households on average are ten times wealthier than black households and have eight times the wealth of Hispanics. A new U.S. Census Bureau report, based on a 1988 survey, finds that households headed by whites had a median net worth of $43,280 in that year; for Hispanics, it was $5,520; and for blacks, it was $4,170.

John E. Jacob, President and Chief Executive Officer of the National Urban League, said, "It really means the poverty we see demonstrated in the African American community is likely to continue for some time . . . without doing something about unemployment . . . business ownership" and similar problems.

Jan. 12: Civil rights activist Rev. **Al Sharpton** is stabbed in the chest as he prepares to lead a protest in New York's racially tense community of Bensonhurst, where black youth **Yusuf Hawkins** was killed by a white mob in 1989. **Michael Riccardi**, a white man with an assault record, is charged with attempted murder and criminal possession of a weapon; he is ordered held without bail.

Jan. 14: **Roland W. Burris** is sworn in as the first black Attorney General for the state of Illinois in Springfield. The former state comptroller is the first black Democratic attorney general in the nation and only the second black attorney general ever. The first, **Edward Brooke** of Massachusetts, was a Republican.

Jan. 15: The **U.S. Supreme Court** allows school systems that once discriminated on the basis of race to be freed from court-ordered busing plans if they have done their best to eliminate the effects of their segregated systems. More than 500 school systems are operating under such court orders. Writing for the 5-to-3 majority, Chief Justice **William Rehnquist** says federal court supervision of local school systems was "intended as a temporary measure to remedy past discrimination" and was not meant "to operate in perpetuity." **Julius Chambers**, director-counsel of the NAACP Legal Defense and Educational Fund, which brought the case on behalf of black schoolchildren in Oklahoma City, says it is "good news" that the court rejected the argument that a school board should be allowed to abandon a desegregation plan "simply because it's complied with the order for a brief period of time." But Chambers says the Court's application of that test "did raise some serious concerns . . . because it's clear that this school board hasn't eliminated the vestiges of discrimination 'to the extent practicable.'"

Jan. 16: Veteran black journalist **Bernard Shaw** is one of the first to report that the United States and the allied coalition have begun to bomb Iraq because of its invasion of Kuwait. Shaw--CNN's principal anchor--reports live via a four-wire from the Al-Rasheed Hotel in Baghdad, describing "Operation Desert Storm" to millions of viewers: "It feels like we're in the center of hell."

Jan. 19: The **United Church of Christ**, with its 1.6 million members, calls for an end to racism with a pastoral letter urging reform of racist attitudes and institutions across the country. *Jet* magazine reports the letter, the first on racism by a major denomination in America, is read in more than 6,000 churches during observances of the Martin Luther King, Jr., holiday.

Jan. 21: Former Atlanta mayor **Andrew Young** says "Now is not the time to lay blame" for the war in the Persian Gulf. Speaking at an observance of the sixth federal holiday honoring the late Dr. **Martin Luther King, Jr.,** Young told his audience that "now is the time to seek a solution." **Coretta Scott King** adds, "I believe with militant commitment to love and nonviolence, the forces of peace will overcome this violence."

Jan. 22: The black out-of-wedlock rate has more than doubled in the last 25 years, to 63.5 percent, according to the National Center for Health Statistics. *The Washington Post* reports the agency found what it regarded as a startling statistic: More than one-quarter of *all* children born in America are born out of wedlock. The white rate has more than quadrupled from 1965 to 1988 (the last year for which figures are available), from just over 4 percent to 17.8 percent. "Illegitimacy levels that were viewed as an aberration of a particular subculture 25 years ago have become the norm for the entire culture," observes Sen. **Daniel Patrick Moynihan** (D-NY), who sparked a nationwide controversy when he disclosed--as Assistant Labor Secretary--that one-quarter of all black children were born out of wedlock a generation ago.

Jan. 24: The **U.S. Civil Rights Commission** is urging President **Bush** to support college scholarships reserved for minorities and to clarify government policy on such race-specific grants. *The Washington Post* reports the action was prompted by an Education Department official's decision last December that such grants are in most cases permissible only if funded by earmarked private gifts. The Commission advised the president that "this area of vital national concern" should not "be relegated to sub-Cabinet level pronouncements."

Jan. 25: **Ellis B. Haizlip**, a New York stage and television producer and mentor of black performing artists, dies in Washington, DC, of lung cancer at the age of 61. Haizlip was an executive producer at public station WNET in New York from 1967 to 1981. Starting in 1986, he was director of special programs at the Schomburg Center for Research in Black Culture. He helped further the careers of such artists as **Roberta Flack, Nicholas Ashford** and **Valerie Simpson,** and actress **Anna Horsford.**

Jan. 26: The Episcopal Church consecrates its first black bishop in the western United States in an elaborate ceremony. The Rev. **Chester Lovelle Talton**, 49, becomes the suffragan bishop of the Diocese of Los Angeles, which is the fourth largest in the nation and encompasses parts of six southern California counties.

362

Jan. 26: Former Houston Oilers running back **Earl Campbell** is elected to the Pro Football Hall of Fame in his first year of eligibility. The Heisman Trophy winner is the NFL's 10th-leading rusher with 9,407 yards, even though he played in just eight NFL seasons. He will be inducted into the Hall of Fame in Canton, Ohio, on July 27.

Jan. 28: The **Bush** administration is asking the U.S. Supreme Court to decide that the state of Mississippi continues to operate a racially segregated system of state colleges and universities, thereby overturning a finding by a lower court. *The Washington Post* reports the Justice Department wants to know how far states that once operated separate white and black colleges must go to desegregate their higher education systems. NAACP Legal Defense and Educational Fund attorney **Janell Byrd** welcomes the department's action, saying, "With this administration, it's been particularly difficult to tell what's happening on civil rights."

Jan. 28: Chinese and black Canadians in Montreal recently joined forces to combat racism in their country. *Jet* magazine reports the newly formed group, known as the **Montreal Head Tax Redress Committee**, is demanding that the country acknowledge past wrongs, such as laws sanctioning slavery, the $500 "head tax" on Chinese immigrants, and the 24-year ban on Chinese immigrants.

Jan. 28: Despite the increasing use of the term "African American," 72 percent of 769 blacks throughout the country prefer to be called "black," according to a survey conducted by the **Joint Center for Political and Economic Studies** in Washington, DC.

Jan. 28: While public funds are being used to shore up the Bank of New England, the U.S. Treasury Department sharply cuts back similar deposits at the **Freedom National Bank**, thus hastening the collapse of the small, minority-owned Manhattan institution.

Jan. 29: President **Bush** asserts in his second State of the Union message that "Civil rights are also crucial to protecting equal opportunity. Every one of us has a responsibility to speak out against racism, bigotry, and hate. We will continue our vigorous enforcement of existing statutes, and I will once again press the Congress to strengthen the laws against employment discrimination without resorting to the use of unfair preferences."

Jan. 29: African National Congress leader **Nelson Mandela** and Zulu Chief **Mangosuthu Buthelezi** meet in Durban, South Africa, for the first time in more than 30 years. *The Washington Post* reports the pair issued a dramatic joint appeal for an immediate end to the bloody rivalry among their followers that has taken more than 5,000 lives in the past five years.

Jan. 30: North Carolina's General Assembly elects its first black speaker since Reconstruction. Rep. **Daniel T. Blue** says, "It is a change of leadership with a new generation of ideas and goals, but it is a renewal of our uncompromising commitment to provide opportunities--economic, educational, political, and cultural--and fair treatment to all the citizens of this state," quotes *The Washington Times*.

Jan. 30: A Montana House committee approves legislation that would create a state holiday honoring Dr. **Martin Luther King, Jr.**, setting the stage for House debate. The state Senate has already approved the measure, which designates the third Monday in January as the holiday. Montana is one of only three states without a holiday recognizing the slain civil rights leader; the others are Arizona and New Hampshire.

Jan. 30: A New York jury acquits Korean grocer **Pong Ok Jang** of attacking a black customer in an incident that led to a year-long black boycott. *USA Today* reports Pong's lawyer said **Giselaine Felissaint** started the disturbance by throwing hot peppers at a cashier, but was not assaulted.

Jan. 31: Blacks are at least three times more likely to suffer serious kidney failure than whites, but do not get as many transplants or donate as many kidneys, according to a new study published in the *New England Journal of Medicine*. Conducted by the American Society of Transplant Physicians, the study also finds that transplants are 10 percent less likely to be successful for blacks. The report concludes that a combination of social, biological, and economic factors accounts for the racial disparity--particularly a shortage of black organ donors. Secretary of Health and Human Services **Louis Sullivan** orders a contract with the Rand Corporation to study what he calls the "unexplained discrepancies" in organ transplantation between blacks and whites, according to *The Washington Post*.

Jan. 31: Former Gary, IN, Mayor **Richard Hatcher** announces he is running for his old post because the city has been in "reverse gear" since he left office three years ago. *The Washington Post* quotes Hatcher as saying, "Not a house has been built, not a brick has been laid since we left office. . . . The present leadership has sold out and hocked out. Now it's time for them to get out." Hatcher was elected mayor of Gary for two decades, beginning in 1967; he was one of the first blacks to head a major U.S. city.

Feb. 1: South African President **Frederik de Klerk** announces he will seek repeal of laws key to maintaining the system of racial discrimination. *USA Today* reports de Klerk will move by June to repeal laws that reserve much of South Africa's land for whites; that segregate living areas; and that place all South Africans into four racial groups. Sen. **Paul Simon** (D-IL), who chairs a Senate subcommittee on South Africa, says, "South Africa is closer to meeting the terms for lifting sanctions." Still missing: Full political participation for blacks.

Feb. 2: **Albert C. Johnson,** a member of the world-famous **Harlem Globetrotters** basketball team in the 1930s and '40s, dies of a heart attack in Chicago; he was 77.

Feb. 4: A defiant **Winnie Mandela** appears in court on kidnap and assault charges as her lawyers demand the state drop its case, claiming South African prosecutors failed to present adequate evidence. In the Johannesburg courtroom, Mandela denies she took part in the December 1988 kidnapping and assault of four youths who allegedly were beaten at her Soweto home; one subsequently died. Published reports claim the trial poses a threat to the credibility of her husband, ANC leader **Nelson Mandela**, who is talking with government and black leaders on ending white-minority rule in South Africa.

Feb. 4: The **European Community** promises to lift its remaining sanctions against South Africa once proposals to scrap apartheid laws have been formally offered to Parliament.

Feb. 4: Dr. **Pearl Verna Williams-Jones**, a concert musician and singer, teacher, and gospel music expert, dies of breast cancer in Washington, DC. The 59-year-old artist made her debut in 1966 at Town Hall in New York; she later toured in America and Europe, accompanied usually by the Pearl Williams-Jones Trio.

Feb. 5: The Heritage Foundation has established a minority journalism fellowship in honor of the late **Lawrence Wade**, who left *The Washington Times* in 1987 to syndicate his column nationally. The newspaper quotes Foundation president Edwin Feulner as saying the $1,000 scholarship and 10-week-paid internship will go to the minority student journalist who "best exemplifies Wade's high ideals and professional standards."

Feb. 5: A judge refuses to dismiss kidnapping charges against **Winnie Mandela**, overruling defense claims that prosecutors failed to provide enough evidence to proceed with the trial [see Feb. 4]. *The Washington Times* reports the judge ruled Mandela should be given more details about the state's charges on her alleged role in the kidnapping of four youths in December 1988.

Feb. 6: The higher rates of high blood pressure found in African Americans may be due more to living with racial discrimination than to genes, according to a new study published in the current *Journal of the American Medical Association*. The study, done by Johns Hopkins University and published in *USA Today*, also finds that people with darker skin had higher blood pressure--only if they also were poor and less educated. Higher blood pressures were not found in dark-skinned blacks with higher socioeconomic status.

Feb. 6: President **Bush**'s choice for Secretary of Education promises at his confirmation hearing that he would discard new federal restrictions on race-specific minority scholarships and "start over" by ordering a broad review of the department's policy on such scholarships. *The Washington Post* quotes former Tennessee Governor **Lamar Alexander** as saying, "[The new policy announced last December] sent out exactly the wrong signal. Our signal . . . to minorities is 'we want you in,' not that 'we want you out.'"

Feb. 6: Rep. **Louis Stokes** (D-OH) is appointed chairman of the House Ethics Committee by Speaker **Thomas Foley** (D-WA). Stokes chaired the panel for three years in the 1980s.

Feb. 7: The Rev. **Jean-Bertrant Aristide**, Haiti's first democratically elected president, is sworn into office without incident.

Feb. 7: The Bush Administration's top civil rights official says he could not support a new civil rights bill similar to one vetoed by the president last year. *The Washington Times* quotes **John Dunne** as telling a House Judiciary subcommittee that the proposed 1991 civil rights bill is one that the Administration "will not accept" . . . because it is "a bill that results in quotas or other unfair preferences." Supporters deny the measure is aimed at setting up quotas and frequently point to language specifically denying such an intention.

Feb. 7: Two white men are acquitted of the 1989 racial slaying of black teenager **Yusuf Hawkins** that followed a confrontation with a bat-wielding mob in Bensonhurst, a mostly white section of Brooklyn, New York. The trials of **Charles Stressler** and **Steven Curreri** are the seventh and eighth in a case that has polarized the city and led to bitter protests and violence [see Jan. 12].

Feb. 8: **Montana** adds a holiday honoring the Rev. **Martin Luther King, Jr.**, to its calendar on the third Monday in January. The action leaves only New Hampshire and Arizona without some form of paid state holiday honoring the slain civil rights leader.

Feb. 8: Dr. **Aris Allen**, a pioneer in politics who was the only black Republican in the Maryland General Assembly, dies of what police say was a self-inflicted gunshot wound. The 80-year-old legislator was recently diagnosed as having inoperable cancer; his friends told *The Washington Times* they believed Allen committed suicide because he did not want to be a burden to others. Allen was the first black to seek statewide office in Maryland, running for lieutenant governor in 1978; before that, he had been the first black chairman of the state Republican Party.

Feb. 9: The Rev. **James Cleveland**, revered by the music world as the "King of Gospel," dies of heart failure in Los Angeles at age 59. The three-time Grammy winner and holder of 16 gold albums, was a pianist, singer, composer, arranger, and producer. He was the first gospel artist to receive a star on Hollywood's Walk of Fame. He had worked with such performers as **Aretha Franklin, Quincy Jones,** and **Edwin Hawkins.**

Feb. 10: The Rev. **Bernard Lee**, a civil rights worker who was a close aide to Dr. **Martin Luther King, Jr.**, dies of a heart attack at his home in Washington, DC, at the age of 55. He was a founding member of the Student Nonviolent Coordinating Committee (SNCC) and an organizer of Freedom Rides in the South and civil rights protests in Albany, GA, and elsewhere.

Feb. 11:   *Jet* magazine reports law professor **Derrick Bell** is named one of the recipients of the First Annual Feminists of the Year Awards by the Feminist Majority Foundation, a nonprofit women's rights organization in Arlington, VA. Bell, the first black professor at Harvard Law School, left his position last April to protest the absence of a woman of color who is tenured on the faculty--vowing he would not return until one was hired and tenured. Also honored: ABC News anchor and correspondent **Carole Simpson**, for speaking out for better opportunities for women and minorities in the media.

Feb. 11:   Several civil rights groups say they will support a lawsuit by Harvard Law school students who claim the school discriminates against women and minorities when hiring faculty. *The Washington Times* reports the law school's hiring practices gained attention last year when **Derrick Bell**, Harvard's first tenured black law professor, said he was taking an unpaid leave of absence until a woman of color receives tenure [see previous item, above].

Feb. 11:   **Darwin Turner**, an authority on African American literature who taught at the University of Iowa for two decades, dies in Iowa City at the age of 59. Dr. Turner taught at Clark, Morgan State, and Florida A&M universities and chaired the English Department at A&T State University in Greensboro, NC, before joining the Iowa faculty in 1972.

Feb. 13:   Two crucial state witnesses in the trial of **Winnie Mandela** say they are too scared for their lives to testify against her. *The Washington Post* reports the pair's refusing to testify leaves the judge and the prosecution in a quandary over whether to continue the proceedings [see Feb. 4]. Another key witness was allegedly kidnapped on February 10.

Feb. 14:   The kidnap and assault trial of **Winnie Mandela** is postponed in Johannesburg, South Africa, until March 6. Published reports indicate prosecutors need the time to search for a witness whose disappearance put their case in jeopardy [see previous item, above].

Feb. 15:   The Justice Department files suit against the city of Memphis (TN), charging its system for electing the City Council and school board discriminates against blacks. The suit contends that the city adopted several measures that dilute minority voting strength in violation of the Voting Rights Act of 1965, including the election of some council and school board members from at-large, citywide districts rather than from separate districts, and an aggressive pattern of annexing suburban white areas into the city.

Feb. 16: Conservative **Shelby Steele** wins one of the National Book Critics Circle Awards for *The Content of Our Character: A New Vision of Race in America.* The controversial collection of essays challenge generally accepted wisdom about the value of affirmative action and other racial policies and trends of the last several decades.

Feb. 21: **Quincy Jones**'s "Back on the Block" is named Album of the Year during the 33rd Grammy Awards. Jones is also named nonclassical producer of the year. With 19 previous awards and six for "Back on the Block," Jones becomes the musician with the second-highest number of Grammys, behind Sir Georg Solti, who has won 28.

Feb. 23: Members of the **Harlem Hell Fighters**, one of the country's oldest and most renowned black National Guard units, reports it has been broken up, stripped of much of its equipment, and moved into front-line positions without proper preparation or training in the Persian Gulf War. Many of the Guardsmen from the 369th Transport Battalion who had served in Vietnam and were over age 40 tell *The New York Times* that they were appendaged to regular Army combat battalions that failed to respect their experience, age, or professional status.

Feb. 25: Responding to complaints that there is a disproportionate number of blacks in the Persian Gulf forces, President **Bush** calls the American military the "greatest equal opportunity employer around" and praises black military heroes--living and dead. At a White House ceremony marking Black History Month, Bush is quoted by *The Washington Post* as saying, "Black soldiers have established a record of pride in the face of incredible obstacles."

Feb. 26: A bronze sculpture of civil rights activist **Rosa Parks** by **Artis Lane** goes on display at the National Portrait Gallery in Washington, DC, joining the gallery's collection of images of Americans of historical interest. Parks's refusal to move from a whites-only section of a bus in Montgomery, AL, in 1955 helped to ignite the Civil Rights Movement.

Feb. 28: Gen. **Colin Powell**, Chairman of the Joint Chiefs of Staff, promises to investigate allegations by members of the **Harlem Hell Fighters** National Guard unit that they were placed into a combat situation in the Persian Gulf without proper training [see Feb. 23]. His promise is announced by Rep. **Charles Rangel** (D-NY) and reported in *The New York Times*.

March 1: Blacks and Hispanics in Chicago wield more clout when it comes to policy-making decisions in its public school systems than in any other school system in the country, according to a new study published by Designs for Change, a school reform group. *Jet* magazine reports about 4,500 blacks serve in school board positions across the country, while about 3,200 blacks hold positions on Chicago's school councils.

March 1: The **Bush** Administration's proposed civil rights legislation maintains its past positions on job discrimination, going against the stand voted in 1990 by Congress. The Administration also renews its insistence on what kind of business reasons could be used in court to justify employment practices that discriminated against women and minorities, reports *The Washington Post*.

March 5: **E.K. Hardaway** is sworn in as the first black elected mayor of Enfield, NC--his hometown--after a two-year struggle, reports *Jet* magazine. After Hardaway's narrowly winning in 1989 and facing election officials who refused to confirm his victory, the matter was referred to the U.S. Justice Department. In a special election last year, Hardaway won again by more than 200 votes.

March 6: Less than one year after being appointed president of Howard University, Dr. **Franklyn Jenifer** steers through a set of sweeping changes intended to alter the shape and strengthen the tradition of Howard University, reports *The Washington Post*.

March 6: **Lemuel Tucker**, a radio and television reporter and correspondent who served with ABC, CBS, and NBC News networks, dies of liver failure in Washington, DC, at the age of 52. He won two Emmy Awards for excellence in television reporting during his 10-year tenure at CBS.

March 7: A two-minute amateur videotape of the beating of a black unarmed motorist, **Rodney King**, by a group of Los Angeles police officers horrifies the city, reviving charges that the police department has failed to confront an alleged pattern of police brutality and official abuse of minorities among its officers. *The*

New York Times quotes Police Chief Daryl Gates as saying he will seek felony criminal charges against the officers.

March 7: **James "Cool Papa" Bell**, the sharp-eyed batter and blazing base runner who was widely regarded as the fastest man ever to play baseball, dies at age 87 in St. Louis (MO) after suffering a heart attack. A prominent player for several Negro League teams--including the St. Louis Stars and Kansas City Monarchs, Bell never played in the major leagues because of baseball's ban on black players.He was inducted into the Baseball Hall of Fame in 1974.

March 9: A Los Angeles grand jury announces an investigation of all 15 police officers who were present when black motorist **Rodney King** was clubbed, kicked, and stomped by three officers who did not realize they were being videotaped [see March 7].

March 10: The racial and ethnic complexion of the United States changed more dramatically in the past decade than at any other time in the 20th century, with nearly one in every four Americans claiming African, Asian, Hispanic, or Native American ancestry. The 1990 census found that one in five Americans had a minority background. *The New York Times* reports that much of the surge was among those of Hispanic ancestry--an increase of 7.7 million people, or 53 percent over 1980.

March 11: The conspiracy and tax-evasion trial of Rep. **Floyd Flake** (D-NY) and his wife, **Margaret Elaine**, opens in federal district court in New York. The Flakes are charged with underreporting income from Allen African Methodist Episcopal Church, where Flake is the pastor, and embezzling federal money for a housing program that the church runs, reports *The New York Times*.

March 12: After 19 months of legal proceedings, the Bensonhurst case--which once transfixed New Yorkers--ends, leaving many of those who cared about it most dissatisfied with its results and leaving unanswered questions about race in New York City. *The New York Times* reports the clearing of murder charges against **Pasquale Raucci** was the last of the proceedings against eight Bensonhurst defendants charged with murdering black teenager **Yusuf Hawkins**, who was shot to death while looking for a used car in the predominantly white neighborhood.

March 12: Outraged over the videotaped beating of **Rodney King**, a black unarmed motorist, by three Los Angeles police officers, the

Congressional Black Caucus asks the Justice Department to conduct a wide-ranging inquiry into police brutality in the city [see March 7 and 9].

March 13: A pair of U.S. House of Representatives panels approves Democratic versions of a new civil rights bill, rejecting President **Bush**'s less sweeping alternative. Reflecting its sponsors' new emphasis on extending job protections to women, the House Education and Labor Committee also votes to change the bill's title from the Civil Rights Act of 1991 to the Civil Rights and Women's Equity in Employment Act of 1991.

March 14: Secretary of Health and Human Services **Louis Sullivan** says more teenage boys die from gunshot wounds than from all other natural causes combined. Speaking at Hampton University, Sullivan is quoted by *The (Newark) Star Ledger* as saying that a black teenager is 11 times more likely to be murdered with a gun than a white male. In a related development, the National Center for Health Statistics finds that nearly half of all black male Americans ages 15 to 19 years old who died in 1988 were killed by guns.

April 1: The minimum wage increases by 45 cents an hour to $4.25, but labor advocates press for more, saying that three million Americans earn minimum wage, not enough to lift low-wage earners out of poverty.

April 17: Georgetown University law student **Timothy Maguire** apologizes for the uproar caused by a commentary he wrote contending that black students at the law school are less qualified than whites. Maguire had written in the *Georgetown Law Weekly* that "the academic credentials of white and black students accepted at the law school were dramatically unequal," reports *The New York Times*.

April 19: A Louisiana high school golf team withdraws from matches against two other high schools at the Caldwell Parish Country Club in Columbia, LA, when its black player, **Dondre Green**, is not allowed on the course. Club president **Iley Evan** confirms that the policy has been in effect since the club opened in 1971.

April 25: *The New York Times* reports that **Andino Ward** and his son, **Michael**--the only child to survive a Philadelphia fire that killed 11 members of the radical group MOVE--will receive $840,000, and monthly payments that could total $9 million in a settlement reached with the city. Michael, age 13 when the May 1985 incident occurred, was disfigured by second- and third-degree burns over 20 percent of his body. His mother was killed in the fire.

April 29: Eleven months after issuing orders that were to have ended a federal district court's role in Boston's school desegregation case, the judge who closed the case reopens it, ruling that Boston's schools failed to meet goals for hiring minority teachers, reports *The New York Times*.

April 30: **Floyd B. McKissick**, an early leader of the Civil Rights Movement who became a state district judge in North Carolina in June 1990, dies at age 69 in Durham. McKissick, regarded as a maverick among civil rights leaders, served as director of the Congress of Racial Equality in 1966-67. He also was a prominent backer of President **Richard M. Nixon** and spent several years in the late 1970s in a vain attempt to build a North Carolina town, Soul City, run by blacks.

May 8: **Richard G. Hatcher**, former mayor of Gary, IN, fails in his bid to regain the job he held for 20 years, while a former prosecutor and a state senator win Indianapolis's mayoral primaries, reports *The (Newark) Star-Ledger*.

May 8: *The New York Times* reports that the nation's largest black-owned companies, despite weakness in the economy, increase their sales by 5.2 percent last year over the previous year, according to an annual survey released by *Black Enterprise* magazine. By contrast, the top 500 companies listed by *Fortune* magazine show a 1990 sales increase of 6.4 percent.

May 9: San Francisco's Pacific Gas and Electric Co., International Business Machines Corp., and Digital Equipment Corp. win praise from the Labor Department for pushing civil rights in the workplace. In the past decade, PG&E, for example, put hundreds of female, black, Hispanic, and Asian workers into jobs that were once the exclusive domain of white men, reports *The New York Times*.

May 10: National drug control director **Bob Martinez** fires former DC Superior Court Judge **Reggie B. Walton** as one of his top deputies after complaining that Walton mishandled his post and repeatedly missed office staff meetings for out-of-town speaking trips. Walton said he was unaware of Martinez's dissatisfaction with his work performance, reports *The Washington Post*.

May 15:   After sending carefully selected pairs of young black and white men to apply for 476 entry-level jobs, researchers at the **Urban Institute** find that blacks were three times as likely as whites to face discrimination. The findings demonstrate that racial discrimination in employment is still widespread in the United States 27 years after it was outlawed, reports *The Wall Street Journal*.

June 1:   Approximately 200 researchers, ethnicists, doctors, and other health care professionals gather in Minneapolis at a meeting organized by the U.S. Public Health Service to discuss the notorious experiment of 412 black men suffering from syphilis who were led to Alabama without any knowledge of their disease. The meeting examined the long-term effect on the relationship between blacks and the medical establishment and how it has failed low-income blacks, a group that provides most of the patients in many prestigious urban teaching hospitals, reports *The New York Times*.

June 1:   Temptations singer **David Ruffin**, whose distinctive voice was featured in such hits as "My Girl" and "Ain't Too Proud To Beg," dies of an apparent drug overdose in Philadelphia at age 50. Ruffin joined the Temptations in the early 1960s, bringing a gospel style that blended well with the group's harmonies.

June 3:   The Associated Press reports that Democratic congressional leaders accuse President **Bush** of playing politics with civil rights, as the war of words continues over a bill scheduled to be taken up in the House. The Bush Administration contends that the Democratic bill would force employers to be guided by quotas in their minority hiring practices; the Democrats deny that assertion.

June 3:   In a significant expansion of earlier decisions, the U.S. Supreme Court rules that jurors may not be excluded from civil cases on account of race. The 6-to-3 ruling extended into the civil area a landmark 1986 decision that barred prosecutors in criminal trials from using peremptory challenges to exclude potential jurors on the basis of race.

June 4:   **John E. Jacob**, President and Chief Executive Officer of the National Urban League, charges that President **Bush** is using "smear tactics" to defeat a Democratic-backed civil rights bill. At issue are efforts to reverse U.S. Supreme Court rulings that made it more difficult to sue for job discrimination, reports the *New York Post*.

374

June 5: While the percentage of white or Hispanic students who finish high school or pass an equivalency exam has shown little improvement for two decades, the percentage of blacks who do so has continued to rise. The general broadening of the black middle class and blacks' historic emphasis on education, Head Start programs, and changes in the economy that necessitate a high school diploma attributed to the increases, reports *The New York Times*.

June 8: Virginia Gov. **L. Douglas Wilder** and Sen. **Charles S. Robb** (D-VA), the state's two preeminent Democrats--both possible presidential candidates in 1992--are pummeling each other with such verbal ferocity that some analysts and party leaders say they are endangering not only their political futures but also their party's dominance in Virginia.

In a related development, Sen. Robb confirms that his office once had in its possession a secretly recorded telephone conversation of Gov. Wilder, but that it shredded the tape in recent weeks. The tape was "received anonymously" in a brown envelope in 1988 when Robb was campaigning for the U.S. Senate and Wilder was a lieutenant governor, reports *The Washington Post*.

June 18: Denver auditor **Wellington Webb**, 50, erases a 28-point deficit in opinion polls to win election as Denver's first black mayor. Webb, who won by 57 to 43 percent, with nearly 116,000 votes cast, waged his campaign by walking the streets and meeting the voters, reports *The New York Times*.

June 18: In the black neighborhoods of Houston, only six of 18 black voters interviewed are familiar with the 1991 civil rights bill recently passed by Congress. But the issue of job discrimination and quotas evokes impassioned and sometimes painful accounts of the struggle for equality, reports *The Washington Post*.

June 20: House Majority Whip **William H. Gray, III** (D-PA), announces that he will leave Congress in September to become president of the United Negro College Fund, reports *The Washington Post*. The decision by Gray, 49, to cut short a congressional career that seemed destined to make him the first black speaker in U.S. history baffles many House members and leaves them speculating about other motives for his resignation. Gray's concern about his family's financial security is cited as the reason for his decision.

June 26: **Herbert O. Reid, Sr.**, a prominent civil rights lawyer and long-time advisor to former Washington, DC, Mayor **Marion Barry**, dies at the age 75 of prostate cancer in the District. Reid, who served on the faculty of the Howard University School of Law for 41 years, also taught many of today's black leaders, including Virginia Governor **L. Douglas Wilder** and Washington Mayor **Sharon Pratt Dixon**.

June 26: **Josephine Davis**, 48, becomes the first black woman to head a City University of New York senior college. Davis, a vice president at St. Cloud State University in Minnesota, succeeds Milton Bassin. She was selected for the $116,000 a year job after a yearlong search, reports the *New York Daily News*.

June 27: In a legislature that just a generation ago was entirely white and Democratic, Reps. **Edward G. Blackmon**, Jr., a black Democrat, and **Edward G. Buelow**, a white Republican, have emerged as warring generals in a battle where the outcome will have widespread ramifications for Mississippi's political future, reports *The Washington Post*.

A plan supported by an alliance of blacks and whites and organized by Blackmon would redraw districts to guarantee virtually the defeat of the House leadership which has maintained its influence on state politics since the 1960s.

June 28: After interviews with Sen. **Charles S. Robb** (D-VA), federal agents serve his office with a subpoena in connection with their investigation of secretly taped telephone conversations involving Virginia Gov. **L. Douglas Wilder**, a longtime rival of Robb's in the Virginia Democratic Party.

June 28: The racially troubled city of Miami is uneasy after police shoot a black man that set off a night of violence. A Miami police officer, responding to reports of a gunfight in Overtown, shot and wounded one of the suspects involved, **Charles Brown**. Observers say the city's hostile race relations stem from disenfranchised blacks and the more affluent Cuban American population that dominates Miami's politics and economics, reports *The Washington Post*.

June 28: U.S. Supreme Court Justice **Thurgood Marshall** announces he is retiring on the advice of his wife and doctor. He blasts as "a double-barreled lie" suggestions that he was depressed and frustrated about the future of the conservative-dominated Court. "I looked at the facts and the law and put them together and came out with an opinion and then went to work on the next one," **Marshall** told a packed news conference in the Court's ornate East Conference room in Washington. He said he had been contemplating retirement for six months, reports *The Washington Post.*

Marshall adds that the most important factor in choosing his successor should be "picking the best person for the job, not on the basis of race one way or another." While race would inevitably be a factor in choosing someone for the Court, "it should not be used as an excuse for picking the wrong Negro and saying, 'I'm picking him because he's a Negro,'" *The New York Times* quotes Marshall as saying.

June 29: President **Bush** says he expects to move quickly on a "fairly short" list of candidates to fill the newly created vacancy on the Supreme Court, adding that he does not believe in a "quota system" for replacing the country's only black justice. Three of the eight members on the president's list are minorities: **Clarence Thomas**, a black federal appeals court judge in the District; Hispanic **Emilio Garza**, elevated in May to the 5th U.S. Circuit Court of Appeals; and **Richard H. Hinojosa**, a Hispanic federal district judge in Texas.

June 30: Bishop **Smallwood E. Williams**, 83, a former street preacher who founded the Bible Way Churches Worldwide and used a message of faith, self-confidence, and salvation to become one of the most influential ministers in Washington, DC, dies in a local hospital after undergoing heart surgery. His ministry claims 100,000 members and has about 330 congregations in the United States, the United Kingdom, Africa, Latin America, and the Caribbean, reports *The Washington Post.*

June 30: Philadelphia Mayor **W. Wilson Goode** announces he will complete his term in office and will not enter the race for the House seat soon to be vacated by Rep. **William Gray, III** (D-PA) [see June 20]. Goode, Philadelphia's first black mayor who cannot run for a third consecutive term, says he owes the city "continuity of leadership during its current financial crisis," reports *The Washington Post.*

June 30: **Wellington E. Webb**, formerly Denver's auditor, takes office as the city's first black mayor after waging a successful campaign on issues rather than on color, reports *The Washington Post* [see June 18].

July 1: President **Bush** nominates federal appeals court judge **Clarence Thomas**, a conservative Republican with a scanty judicial record on civil rights and abortion, to replace retiring Associate Justice **Thurgood Marshall** on the U.S. Supreme Court. *The New York Times* reports that, if Judge Thomas is confirmed, he would be only the second black to sit on the nation's highest court. Thomas, the product of poverty and segregation from Pin Point, GA, said after the Bush announcement: "As a child, I could not dare dream that I would ever see the Supreme Court, not to mention be nominated for it. In my view, only in America could this have been possible."

Responding to the Thomas nomination, National Urban League President and Chief Executive Officer **John E. Jacob** says, "We welcome the appointment of an African American jurist to fill [Justice Marshall's] seat. . . . Obviously, Judge Thomas is no Justice Marshall. But if he were, this Administration would not have appointed him. We are hopeful that Judge Thomas's background of poverty and minority status will lead him to greater identification with those in America who today are victimized by poverty and discrimination."

July 3: On the street where Dr. **Martin Luther King, Jr.**, was slain in Memphis, TN, stand two competing yet related symbols, reports *The Washington Post*. One is a rough concrete wall in the 400 block of Mulberry Street that bears blood-red graffiti that reads, "Save the Black Man!" On the other side is a $9.7 million National Civil Rights Museum documenting the blood, sweat, and pain of the Civil Rights Movement, which had as its goal to create a society in which no one would need to spray-paint a plea for racial salvation.

July 8: Football great **Alan Page**, a former defensive lineman for the Minnesota Vikings, is awarded the National Education Association's highest honor--the Friend of Education Award-- during the NEA's annual convention in Miami Beach, FL, for his encouraging minority students to stick with their education.

July 8: Leaders of the NAACP meet privately during their convention in Houston, TX, to decide how to respond to the nomination of conservative jurist **Clarence Thomas** to the Supreme Court. *The Washington Post* reports the Thomas nomination poses a problem for the group because it wants a black justice to replace

Thurgood Marshall, who is retiring after a quarter century on the bench, but it also wants a justice whose views mirror Marshall's.

July 10:   New York Mayor **David Dinkins** announces plans to visit South Africa in late September or early October, returning the visit of African National Congress president **Nelson Mandela** to New York last year. *The New York Times* reports that Dinkins' trip, to include a delegation of labor, business, and government leaders, is to be financed with private funds.

July 10:   **Betty Shabazz** sues a New York publisher on the grounds of copyright infringement, charging improper use of the writings of her late husband, **Malcolm X**. *The New York Times* reports the suit names Writers & Readers, Inc., and Abdul Alkalimat, author of *Malcolm X for Beginners*.

July 10:   In a statement on sanctions against South Africa, **John E. Jacob**, President and Chief Executive Officer of the National Urban League, says, "We know that sanctions worked to move South Africa away from its apartheid system. And we know that the conditions sanctions tried to eradicate have not been fully eradicated. Until change in South Africa is firmly established and irreversible, the United States should maintain maximum diplomatic, economic, and legal pressure on the government of South Africa."

July 11:   The **Congressional Black Caucus** votes 19 to 1 to oppose the nomination of Judge **Clarence Thomas** to succeed retiring Associate Justice **Thurgood Marshall** on the U.S. Supreme Court [see July 1].

July 12:   President **Bush**'s nomination of Judge **Clarence Thomas** to the nation's highest court brings attention to a small group of critics of the traditional civil rights agenda who are identified as black conservatives, reports *The New York Times*. But rather than a cohesive movement, those who--like Judge Thomas--are called black conservatives, are a diverse group that share frustration with the idea that black people have one agenda defined by the Civil Rights Movement.

July 13:   Although Supreme Court nominee **Clarence Thomas** praised Nation of Islam leader **Louis Farrakhan** in a 1983 speech as "a man I have admired for more than a decade," *The Washington Post* reports Thomas is now moving swiftly to "repudiate the antisemitism of Louis Farrakhan or anyone else."

July 13:   A three-judge federal appeals court panel unanimously upholds the drug conviction of former Washington, DC, mayor **Marion Barry** and sends his case back to the trial judge for resentencing. *The Washington Post* reports the panel has ordered the judge to explain fully his reasons for giving Barry a six-month prison sentence.

July 13:   Gunfire and pandemonium break out at movie theaters around the nation at the opening of an urban drama with an anti-gang message. Much of the violence appears to have been staged by rival gangs in Los Angeles where the film "Boyz N the Hood" is set, reports *The New York Times*.

July 14:   The National Women's Political Caucus votes to oppose the nomination of Judge **Clarence Thomas**. *The Washington Post* reports the group as saying that the judge's nomination presents a "clear and present danger to women's rights" because of his opposition to affirmative action and his 1987 endorsement of a magazine that recognized the right to life of a fetus.

July 14:   A House proposal is made to void an inmate's death sentence if he can show that the race of a defendant or victim influenced decisions by prosecutors, juries, or judges in the jurisdiction where the case was tried, reports *The Washington Post*. The House plan reflects the difficulties in deciding what statistics show and how much they should be trusted. Supporters of such a measure see it as a way to solve an injustice; opponents view it as a "back-door attempt to abolish the death penalty."

July 18:   **Harold Perry**, the first black American consecrated as a Roman Catholic bishop in the 20th century, dies of complications associated with Alzheimer's disease at the age of 74 in New Orleans.

July 18:   The discord among black groups over Judge **Clarence Thomas's** nomination to the Supreme Court escalates, as black conservatives accuse his opponents of holding him to an unfair political standard because of his race, reports *The New York Times*.

July 24:   **John E. Jacob**, President and Chief Executive Officer of the National Urban League, declares the League's four-day annual conference in Atlanta a "record-breaking success" with some 4,200 registered participants. "By any barometer you can use, we have accomplished all our goals. . . . We have created a platform for all of us to engage in analyses and to develop appropriate solutions." Jacob renews his call for an urban

Marshall Plan: "There have been proposals for a Marshall Plan for eastern Europe and the gulf, . . . there's only one place where a Marshall Plan makes sense, and that's right here at home."

July 26: The life expectancy for blacks in the United States dropped for the third straight year, while the life expectancy for whites reached a new record, according to federal officials quoted in *The New York Times*. Black life expectancy is 69.2 years, while it is 75.6 years for whites, according to the national Centers for Disease Control.

July 27: **Betty Allen**, executive director of the Harlem School of the Arts, is named president of the school founded in 1964. *The New York Times* reports the school is the nation's first to offer comprehensive preprofessional arts training primarily to black and Hispanic children.

July 27: **Arthur Fletcher**, appointed by President **Bush** to head the U.S. Commission on Civil Rights, says he supports the nomination of **Clarence Thomas** and predicts the black conservative jurist will be easily confirmed, according to *The Washington Post*.

July 28: The **NAACP Legal Defense and Educational Fund** releases a study it says bolsters its position in a dispute with the White House over employment discrimination provisions of the pending civil rights bill. *The Washington Post* reports the pro bono study by the law firm of Fried, Frank, Harris, Shriver, and Jacobsen found that the courts almost uniformly forced employees to show that hiring practices were related to ability to do the job and not to some broader criteria giving the employer more leeway.

July 30: The **Alliance for Justice**, a liberal group that helped to spearhead the defeats of Supreme Court nominee **Robert Bork** and appeals court nominee **Kenneth Ryskamp**, announces its opposition to Judge **Clarence Thomas**. *The Washington Post* quotes the group's executive director as saying that Thomas has "a radical philosophy that exalts his own views over the Constitution," and that during his tenure as chairman of the Equal Employment Opportunities Commission, Thomas transformed it into a "nickel and dime claims adjustment agency" rather than as an aggressive force for fighting employment discrimination.

Sept. 7: **Francis Turner**, an educator who, in the 1950s, became the first black assistant superintendent in the New York City public school system, dies of a heart attack at age 95 in Martha's Vineyard (MA).

Sept. 7: Nearly half a century and at least 1,000 executions after it last happened in the United States, a white person is executed for killing a black, according to *The New York Times*. **David (Peewee) Gaskins** is electrocuted in Columbia, SC, for the 1982 hired killing of **Rudolph Tyner**, a fellow inmate and black man who had himself been convicted of murder.

Sept. 13: Gov. **L. Douglas Wilder** of Virginia announces he will seek the Democratic nomination for president in 1992. The *Richmond News Leader* quotes Wilder as saying that Virginians have always taken the lead when the nation is in trouble. Wilder, the first elected black governor, chastises President **Bush** for allowing race relations to drift in America as well as lambasts him for not doing something to reduce the widening budget deficit.

Sept. 17: The governing regents of the Smithsonian Institution give the go-ahead for the creation of a new **National African American Museum** on the Mall in Washington, DC. *The (Newark) Star-Ledger* reports the recession leaves unanswered the question of when the museum might open.

Sept. 17: Nearing the end of his Senate confirmation hearing, Supreme Court nominee **Clarence Thomas** endorses capital punishment, saying, "philosophically, there is nothing that would bother me personally about upholding it [the death penalty] in appropriate cases." His confirmation would give the Court--for the first time in decades--nine justices with no absolute objection to capital punishment.

Sept. 20: Sen. **John Danforth** (R-MO) announces he will try to resolve the **Bush** Administration's objections to civil rights legislation by using antidiscrimination standards accepted by the president in 1990 in the Americans with Disabilities Act, according to *The New York Times*.

Sept. 20: College-educated white men earn nearly one-third more than black men with similar backgrounds, according to a Census Bureau study. The survey, conducted in 1989 and 1990, showed blacks lagging economically behind whites by almost every measure.

Sept. 25: Scholars and civil rights supporters call for the federal government to expand the use of undercover testers to root out discrimination in employment, housing, and business, reports *The New York Times*. **Michael Fix**, a senior researcher at the Urban Institute--a nonprofit research institute in Washington, DC, describes such usage as "cheap, doable, and able to provide conclusive evidence of discrimination."

Sept. 28: Jazz legend **Miles Davis** dies after a stroke in Santa Monica, CA, at the age of 65. The trumpeter was considered an original, an innovator, and a trendsetter among jazz musicians. Davis first gained prominence in 1949 as a 22-year-old veteran of the **Charlie Parker** quintet, which turned bebop on its head with the sessions that became known as "the birth of cool." He repeated that success a decade later, with the modal improvisations of "Kind of Blue," and again, several times in the '60s, as he incorporated electronic instruments and rock rhythms on "In a Silent Way" and the best-selling "Bitches Brew."

Sept. 28: Virginia Gov. **L. Douglas Wilder**, who is a Democratic contender for president, and the Rev. **Jesse Jackson**, who has yet to announce his intentions for the 1992 presidential campaign, hold a summit at the Executive Mansion in Richmond, VA. *The New York Times* quotes Wilder as saying, "The leadership of the '80s cannot be the leadership of the '90s." Jackson observed that "My support base today is broader than it was three years ago."

Sept. 28: In a rebuke to the White House, the Senate Judiciary Committee splits 7 to 7 on the confirmation of Judge **Clarence Thomas** to the Supreme Court, throwing the question of confirmation to the full Senate. *The New York Times* reports that all the majority Democrats on the panel--except for Sen. Dennis DeConcini (D-AZ)--voted against Thomas; all the minority Republicans voted for him.

Sept. 30: The **Justice Department** reports that blacks still make up a much larger share (40 percent) of death-row inmates than of the nation's population, reports *The Washington Post*. The 1990 census found the U.S. population is 12.1 percent black.

Oct. 3: The Senate begins debate on the nomination of **Clarence Thomas** to be an Associate Justice of the Supreme Court; a 12th Democrat announces support for Thomas while a leading Thomas critic said there is only a "slim chance" that the nomination will be rejected, reports *The Washington Post*.

Oct. 4: **Willie W. Herenton**, who rose from poverty in Memphis (TN) housing projects to become the city's first black school superintendent, is elected the first black ever elected mayor of Memphis. He defeats incumbent **Richard Hackett** by just 172 of the 270,000 votes cast, reports *The New York Times*. Herenton won the election despite the division among black voters and a lack of visible white support. Herenton is a former member of the National Urban League Board of Trustees.

Oct. 4: **Byron de la Beckwith** is extradited to Mississippi to stand trial a third time for the 1963 slaying of civil rights leader **Medgar Evers**, reports *The Washington Post*. Two all-white juries were unable to reach verdicts, resulting in mistrials in 1964.

Oct. 6: Five veterans of the Urban League Movement are presented the prestigious **Whitney M. Young, Jr.** Medallion at the National Urban League headquarters. Receiving the award in honor of **Whitney M. Young, Jr.**, the fourth executive director of the National Urban League, are: **Raymond R. Brown**, former director of the League's mid-eastern regional office; **Lucille Chapelle**, former deputy director of the National Urban League's Program Evaluation Department: **E. Shelton Hill**, former director of the League's Economic Development, Employment, and Training program; and **Clarence N. Wood**, former vice president for the National Urban League's External Affairs department.

Oct. 9: The Senate ends a frantic, dramatic day of uncertainty about the fate of Supreme Court nominee **Clarence Thomas** by delaying by a week a vote on his confirmation and authorizing a full investigation of sexual harassment charges leveled by former aide **Anita F. Hill**, reports *The Washington Post*. Thomas, whose confirmation is in clear danger, asked the Senate for a chance to "clear my name" and released a sworn statement categorically denying he ever displayed improper behavior toward Anita Hill, now a University of Oklahoma law professor.

Oct. 9: **John E. Jacob**, President and Chief Executive Officer of the National Urban League, repeats his call for a 10-year, $500 billion Marshall Plan for America as an investment in the nation's productivity. "The Urban League's Marshall Plan is an annual $50 billion of investments in the nation's physical and human infrastructure, targeted to the areas of greatest need," said Jacob to participants at the 1991 American Magazine Conference at the Ritz-Carlton Hotel in New York.

Oct. 11: With their reputations on the line, **Anita Hill** and **Clarence Thomas** retreat from public view, and their supporters worked at a fever pitch, reports the *New York Daily News*. "Neither of them is going to walk out of this a whole person," says Sen. **Orrin Hatch** (R-UT).

Oct. 11: **Redd Foxx**, 68, the ribald and cantankerous comic who played nightclubs for decades before becoming an "overnight" national star as a harried junk dealer on NBC-TV's "Sanford and Son," dies in a Los Angeles hospital after a heart attack.

Oct. 12: **Bobby Seale**, cofounder of the Black Panther Party during the 1960s, announces he will run for Congress to capture the seat vacated by Rep. **William Gray** (D-PA), who until recently was the highest ranking black on Capitol Hill. Gray resigned last month to become head of the United Negro College Fund.

Oct. 13: During testimony in congressional hearings to clear his name of the sexual harassment charges leveled by a former aide, **Clarence Thomas** hits a nerve among black Americans by angrily portraying himself as a victim of historical racial stereotypes about the alleged sexual prowess of black men, reports *The Washington Post*. Thomas also says he would "rather die than withdraw" his nomination. His increasingly bitter confirmation battle escalated into a no-holds-barred attack on his accuser, law professor **Anita Hill**, and open warfare broke out among Senate Judiciary Committee members.

Oct. 14: Four witnesses testify that law professor **Anita Hill** told them years ago that she was sexually harassed by Supreme Court nominee **Clarence Thomas**; meanwhile, Hill's lawyers release results of a polygraph test that they say demonstrated her truthfulness, reports *The Washington Post*.

Oct. 14: About 300 people march against bigotry in North Attleboro, MA, after reports that white supremacists were active in the area, reports *The New York Times*. The march was organized by Neighbors Against Bigotry, a group that was formed during the summer of 1991.

Oct. 14: The high rate of hypertension among blacks may be linked to elevated levels of norepinephrine--a blood-vessel-constricting chemical that is produced during stress and is also associated with melanin, the skin pigment, reports *The Washington Post*. Recent experiments by **Roger Allen** of the University of Maryland show that high blood pressure after stress lasts at least 10 times as long in blacks as in whites.

Oct. 15:	After three days of televised inquiry into an accusation that **Clarence Thomas** had sexually harassed his former aide, **Anita Hill**, Americans still favor the judge's confirmation to be Associate Justice of the Supreme Court by a ratio of 2 to 1, reports *The New York Times*.
Oct. 15:	The **Congressional Black Caucus** announces the establishment of a national commission to study federal education policies, to propose alternatives, and to stimulate efforts in black communities to promote learning, reports *The Washington Post*. The **National Citizens Commission for African American Education**, which will have 100 members, immediately issues a broadside that criticizes President **Bush** for his education plan and congressional Democrats for not offering a comprehensive alternative.
Oct. 15:	Virginia Gov. **L. Douglas Wilder**, who has been in the Far East for half of the time since he formally announced his candidacy for president in September, learns that his campaign raised only $100,889 in the last three months, and is just halfway to qualifying for federal matching funds, reports *The Washington Post*.
Oct. 15:	A defunct Rockville (MD) employment agency admits that it turned away scores of black applicants in the 1980s and agrees in federal court to pay $50,000 to settle a discrimination lawsuit in Baltimore, reports *The Washington Post*.
Oct. 15:	After a long, bitter, and explosive debate over his sexual conduct, the Senate votes 52 to 48 to confirm **Clarence Thomas** as Associate Justice of the Supreme Court. Forty-one Republicans and 11 Democrats decided **Anita Hill's** sexual harassment charges--that Thomas hounded her with lurid talk while she was his aide--were not enough to reject his nomination. Thomas, 43, will succeed retired Associate Justice **Thurgood Marshall** and become the second black, after Marshall, to sit on the nation's highest court.
Oct. 16:	"We congratulate **Clarence Thomas** on his confirmation as an Associate Justice to the U.S. Supreme Court," says **John E. Jacob**, President and Chief Executive Officer of the National Urban League. "We neither supported nor opposed his nomination, believing that his public positions on issues of concern to us were questionable, but also believing that as an African American who has suffered from poverty and from America's racial inequities, he might bring a fresh viewpoint to this Court."

Oct. 18: **Clarence Thomas** swears to protect the Constitution as the nation's 106th Supreme Court Justice during a joyous celebration that belied the brutal route the 43-year-old judge had traveled to reach the Court, reports *The Washington Post*. Thomas recalled the "many difficult days" of his confirmation battle and in reference to the 30th Psalm, said: "But on this sunny day in October at the White House, there is joy in the morning."

Oct. 19: **Sylvia Hughes** of Hackensack, NJ, is installed as president of the National Urban League Guild at the League's headquarters in New York. Hughes succeeds the late **Mollie Moon** who was founder and longtime president of the organization.

Oct. 19: **Reggie Waller** is named director of scouting for the San Diego Padres, becoming the team's first black executive.

Oct. 19: White students at the University of Alabama, once a bastion of segregation, painted themselves black for an Oct. 3 pledge party that mocked poor blacks, reports *The Washington Post*. The account shocked the university administration, which has been trying to attract more black students, and outraged the school's black minority. The school immediately cancels parties between fraternities and sororities.

Oct. 19: Former Ku Klux Klansman **David Duke**'s candidacy for governor fails to stir up anything other than resentment and disinterest among residents of New Orleans's Tupelo Street, reports *The Washington Post*. Says Loyola University political scientist **Ed Renwick**, "Many blacks say Duke is not their problem, he's the white man's problem."

Oct. 19: **William Harvey Dinkins, Jr.**, the father of New York's mayor, **David N. Dinkins** and a retired real estate broker in Trenton, NJ, dies at age 85 at the Delaware Valley Medical Center in Langhorne, PA.

Oct. 20: After watching **Harlem Hospital** undergo weeks of intense public scrutiny and criticism, more than 200 Harlem residents go to the hospital to express support for it, reports *The New York Times*.

Oct. 22: The Senate clears the way for consideration of long-delayed civil rights legislation that has been cast in a new light by the public furor over the Senate's handling of sexual harassment charges against Supreme Court nominee **Clarence Thomas**, reports *The Washington Post*. Voting 93 to 4, the Senate agrees to limit delaying tactics and begin debate immediately on the measure that is aimed at making it easier for workers to win suits against all forms of job discrimination, including sexual harassment.

Oct. 24: The White House, Senator **John C. Danforth** (R-MO), other Senate Republicans, and Sen. **Edward M. Kennedy** (D-MA) reach agreement on the shape of a compromise for a civil rights bill, reports *The New York Times*. **John H. Sununu**, President Bush's chief of staff, said bipartisan efforts had produced a bill that Bush would sign. "It is a no-quota bill," he said, removing the "quota" label that the Administration had recently placed on Danforth's own measure.

Oct. 24: Asserting that minorities suffer the most damage from industrial pollution yet attract the least attention from the Environmental Protection Agency, community groups open a national conference in Washington intended to prevent their neighborhoods from being the targets of toxic contamination. Top issues include cleaning up lead contamination in soil and homes, battling aggressive moves by waste service industries to establish new plants in minority areas, and compelling local factories to improve safety for workers and reduce air and water contamination, and not to try to escape regulations by moving away.

Oct. 24: Prosecutors seeking to block the release on bond of **Byron de la Beckwith**, the man accused of assassinating civil rights leader **Medgar Evers**, have linked the white supremacist to a little-known racist group whose members are said to consider themselves "God's executioners," reports *The New York Times*. The group, identified as the Phineas Priesthood, holds "that integration and race mixing is strictly forbidden by the Bible and that it is their ordained duty to strike down those who are viewed as enemies of the pure white race," according to documents filed in preparation for Beckwith's third trial [see Oct. 4].

Oct. 30: Seeking to still two years of bitter debate over discrimination and quotas, the Senate passes 95 to 5 a civil rights bill intended to make it easier to sue in job bias cases. The House is expected to move quickly to adopt the compromise bill, which was worked out by Senators **John C. Danforth** (R-MO) and **Edward M. Kennedy** (D-MA) and the **Bush** Administration. President Bush is expected to sign it immediately.

Oct. 31: **Anita F. Hill**, the law professor who accused Judge **Clarence Thomas** of sexual harassment, has been edited out of a promotional videotape of the University of Oklahoma, reports *The New York Times*. The brief session on Hill was shot in August and included about two seconds on Hill and four seconds of her voice. "Her national and international exposure" at the Senate Judiciary Committee's hearings into Thomas's fitness to serve on the Supreme Court "changed the whole concept of the spot," said **David Smeal**, head of electronic media for the university.

Nov. 7: Los Angeles Laker's basketball staff **Earvin "Magic" Johnson** shocks the world with his announcement that he is retiring from basketball because he has tested HIV positive, the virus that causes AIDS. Though Johnson's fans are devastated, the stellar player delivers his announcement with the same grace and aplomb demonstrated throughout his 12-year career with the Lakers.

Nov. 8: Basketball star **Earvin "Magic" Johnson** contracted the potentially deadly AIDS virus from a "heterosexual transmission," says a Los Angeles Lakers official quoted in *The Washington Post*. The official, however, could not pinpoint either a specific event or specific partner responsible for the transmission of the virus.

Nov. 17: The **Rev. Jesse Jackson** has written the foreword for a new book in which **James Earl Ray** asserts that he was an unwitting scapegoat in the assassination of the Dr. **Martin Luther King, Jr.**, reports *The New York Times*. Jackson who was at the motel in Memphis were Dr. King was slain on April 4, 1968, has said before that he thinks Ray could not have acted alone and that the federal government participated in a conspiracy to kill the civil rights leader.

Nov. 18: **John E. Jacob**, President and Chief Executive Officer of the National Urban League, says the defeat of **David Duke** in Louisiana's gubernatorial election is a victory for the forces of decency, but he warns that Duke's electoral strength signals a dangerous resurgence of racism.

Nov. 18: Black churches and mosques across the nation are beginning to turn their influence to the fight against AIDS, reports *The New York Times*. Forced to confront the overwhelming reality of the epidemic today--that AIDS, in fact, is their disease, that blacks along with Hispanic people account for an alarming proportion of the new cases being diagnosed--a cadre of black clergymen and women are speaking out in sermons, starting counseling and support groups, even sponsoring housing for homeless people with AIDS, the newspaper reports.

Nov. 20: President **George Bush** is expected to direct all federal agencies to phase out regulations authorizing the use of racial preferences and quotas in hiring and promotions when he signs the civil rights bill recently passed by Congress. The regulations affect all companies as well as federal agencies, reports *The New York Times*.

Nov. 21: Lawyers for the state of Connecticut argue that a lawsuit attacking the de facto segregation that divides Hartford from its suburbs raises questions of social policy far too sweeping and complex for any single judge to decide, reports *The New York Times*. Assistant Attorney General **John R. Whelan** also said the state should not be held responsible for segregation that arose out of residential patterns, rather than from intentional government policies such as the Jim Crow practices of the South before the 1960s.

Nov. 22: President **Bush** signs the Civil Rights Act of 1991 in a Rose Garden ceremony that was overshadowed by the hasty withdrawal of a proposed presidential order that would have ended government affirmative action and hiring guidelines that benefit women and minorities, reports *The Washington Post*.

Nov. 23: A secret weapon helping Virginia Gov. **L. Douglas Wilder's** campaign for president is his association with a handful of organizations, little known beyond middle-class Black America, reports *The Washington Post*. They include the Guardsmen, an exclusive social club to which no more than 30 black men can be admitted in any city; the Boule, officially Sigma Phi Pi, the oldest of the black Greek-letter organizations whose members must be college graduates of distinction, and Omega Psi Phi, one of the eight historically black undergraduate fraternities.

Nov. 24: Virginia Gov. **L. Douglas Wilder**, campaigning for president in Dubuque, Iowa, where eight cross-burnings have occurred in recent months, warns of "a rising tension of racism" spreading across the country. Wilder, speaking at St. Mark's Community Center for the Ministry, also said that "**David Duke** may have lost an election in Louisiana, but the message was not killed."

Dec. 2: The National Urban League announces a new program to involve young people throughout the country. The program, the

National Urban League's Incentive to Excel and Succeed (NULTIES), is designed to enhance their personal development and to develop leadership potential. "It is the most exciting program that the National Urban League has developed relative to young people," says **William Haskins**, vice president, programs, for the NUL. "It is a hands-on approach to the massive problems involving young African American children."

Dec. 3: Education Secretary **Lamar Alexander** is expected to propose a new policy that would prohibit colleges from issuing scholarships based solely on race, but would allow them to consider race as a factor in making awards, reports *The Washington Post*. The new policy, to be published as regulations in the *Federal Register*, would allow colleges to issue scholarships to achieve "diversity" as long as both white and minority students can compete for them, officials said.

Dec. 6: **William D. Alexander**, a pioneer in black film making, dies at age 75 at Calgary Hospital in the Bronx. In 1947, after a year of producing short films, Alexander produced the film "The Fight Never Ends" featuring boxer **Joe Louis**.

Dec. 7: The Beverly Hills home of the late **Sammy Davis, Jr.,** sells for $2.7 million, far below the $4.2 million asking price. Davis's widow, **Altovise,** and teenage son **Manny**, were living at the house at the time of the sale. Davis left his wife with a $5 million debt to the Internal Revenue Service.

Dec. 9: Washington, DC, mayor **Sharon Pratt Dixon** takes a new husband and a new name as she marries banker-turned-entrepreneur **James R. Kelly III**, in a private ceremony at her sister's house in Brookline, MA.

Dec. 12: **Buck Clayton**, a jazz trumpeter who was a star of Count Basie's orchestra in the late 1930s and early '40s, dies at age 89 at his home in Washington.

Dec. 16: *The New York Times* quotes the **U.S. Conference of Mayors** as saying America's cities have more hungry and homeless people than they can feed and house, and the situation is getting worse. In a report on a survey of 28 cities, the Conference also says that officials in nearly half of those cities reported evidence of a public backlash against homeless people.

Dec. 18: **J. Max Bond**, a retired American educator who was president of the University of Liberia in the early 1950s, dies at age 89 at his home in Washington.

Dec. 20: *The New York Times* reports that, although critics contend Virginia Governor **L. Douglas Wilder's** first year in office is one of few accomplishments and that he is spending too much time out of the state running for president, Wilder contends he is running on his record of huge achievement.

Dec. 20: **J. Morris Anderson**, the founder of the Miss Black America Pageant, announces that he has reached a settlement with Mike Tyson and the Rev. Charles Williams of the Indiana Black Expo and that he has dropped his $21 million suit against them, reports *The New York Times*. In the suit, Anderson accused Tyson of fondling at least 10 of the contestants in the Miss Black America Pageant, which was part of the Indiana Black Expo last July in Indianapolis.

Dec. 20: North Carolina's new congressional redistricting plan, which creates one new district in which a black candidate could win election, violates the Voting Rights Act by failing to create a second such district, according to the Justice Department in an article in *The Washington Post*. The department's ruling indirectly calls for creation of a district in which blacks and Lumbee Indians would be the majority.

Dec. 20: The "Godfather of Soul," **James Brown,** is scheduled to receive the Award of Merit for his lifetime contributions to music at the American Music Awards next month. Past recipients include **Bing Crosby, Irving Berlin, Ella Fitzgerald, Stevie Wonder, Paul McCartney,** and **Elvis Presley.**

Dec. 20: The six-member school board in Jefferson County, KY, passes a new school desegregation plan that will allow a substantial reduction in the busing of school children for integration, prompting angry reactions from some civil rights leaders, reports *The New York Times*.

Dec. 21: Civil rights leaders in Louisville, KY, react angrily to a newly approved plan that they said could resegregate public schools and reverse benefits of 15 years of court-ordered busing.

Dec. 21: The Justice Department will not seek indictments following its 2-1/2 year investigation of alleged insider tradings and political corruption by Los Angeles Mayor **Tom Bradley**, reports *The Washington Post*. The decision increases chances that the 74-year-old major will run for a sixth term and become the longest serving black mayor in U.S. history. "This decision is the greatest Christmas present I'm going to receive this year or any other year," said a jubilant Bradley.

Dec. 21: The Justice Department closes its book on the 1989 racial killing of **Yusuf K. Hawkins** in Brooklyn, saying it had concluded an extensive investigation and would file no federal civil rights charges in a case that came to symbolize the conflict of blacks and whites in America, reports *The New York Times*. Officials said that federal charges in the Bensonhurst killing were unwarranted because New York State had "vigorously pursued" criminal prosecutions that had led to the convictions of the gunman, **Joseph Fama**, and three other defendants on felony charges, as well as another young man on a misdemeanor violation.

Dec. 22: **Harlem Hospital Center** in New York regains full accreditation after it was put on probation for eight months for poor record-keeping and safety violations.

Dec. 22: After being nurtured for a decade by state and local government that set aside a portion of their contracts for minority businesses, thousands of such companies have closed or are floundering in the aftermath of court rulings that the racial preferences are unconstitutional, reports *The New York Times*.

Dec. 26: *The Washington Post* reports that during the current fiscal year, federal agencies are expected to provide about $100 million in race-specific scholarships under a dozen programs earmarked to help more minorities finish college and to enter professions where they are underrepresented.

Dec. 26: **Walter Hudson**, once listed in *The Guinness Book of Records* as the heaviest man on earth, dies at age 46 in his Hempstead, Long Island (NY) home. He weighed 1,125 pounds at the time of his death.

Dec. 28: Dr. **Lenora Fulani**, a presidential candidate on the New Alliance ticket, receives $624,497 in federal matching funds for her campaign. The amount is determined based on Fulani's fund-raising efforts; the allocation ranks her third behind President **Bush** and Sen. **Tom Harkin** (D-IA).

Dec. 30: The **Equal Employment Opportunities Commission** declares that the new civil rights law does not apply to the thousands of cases filed by people who stated that they suffered job discrimination prior to November 21, when the measure was signed into law by President **Bush**.

Acknowledgments

The National Urban League acknowledges with sincere appreciation the authors who contributed articles to this publication.

Also, special thanks are owed, again, to associate editor Paulette J. Robinson, whose expertise, conscientiousness, and commitment were vital to the successful production of the volume. We also acknowledge the fine work of Johnnie Griffin, proofreader; Michele Long Pittman, project assistant; and Bonnie Stanley, support writer.

The National Urban League staff performed in exemplary fashion. In particular, we acknowledge Leslye L. Cheek; Ernie Johnston, Jr.; B. Maxwell Stamper; Farida Syed; Faith Williams; and Denise Wright of the Public Relations and Communications Department; Daniel S. Davis and Betty Ford in the Office of the President; and members of the various program departments in New York.

Staff in the Washington Operations office made important contributions. Acknowledgment is owed to Robert McAlpine, Suzanne Bergeron, Ron Jackson, and Lisa Bland-Malone of the Policy and Government Relations Department. From the Research Department, we acknowledge Dr. Dionne Jones, Dr. Betty Watson, and Monica Jackson. Deborah Searcy is due special recognition for her assistance in all stages of production. Finally, Marcia Taylor, MIS specialist, and Marcus Gordon, MIS consultant, are acknowledged for their technical support.

Order Blank

National Urban League Publications
500 East 62nd Street
New York, NY 10021

	Per Copy	# of Copies	Total
The State of Black America 1992	$24.95	_____	_____
Recent Volumes in series:			
The State of Black America 1991	$19.95	_____	_____
The State of Black America 1990	$19.00	_____	_____
The State of Black America 1989	$19.00	_____	_____
The State of Black America 1988	$18.00	_____	_____
Postage and handling:			
Individual volumes--	$2.00 each Book Rate	_____	_____
	$3.00 each First Class	_____	_____
	Amount enclosed		_____

"No Place Like Home" Lithograph

The limited edition, numbered lithograph of "No Place Like Home" is signed by the artist, Louis Delsarte. "No Place Like Home" is the sixth in the "Great Artists" series commissioned by the National Urban League through a generous donation from the House of Seagram. Proceeds benefit the National Urban League.

Unframed lithograph 26-3/4"x36". Full color. $1,000 each, which includes postage and handling.

For information and to order, contact:

National Urban League, Inc.
Office of Development
500 East 62nd Street
New York, New York 10021

Please make check or money order payable to:
National Urban League, Inc.